House of Cards

The Legalization and Control of Casino Gambling

JEROME H. SKOLNICK

Little, Brown and Company   Boston Toronto

FIRST EDITION

T11/78

LIBRARY OF CONGRESS CATALOGING IN PUBLICATION DATA
Skolnick, Jerome H
  House of cards.

  Includes bibliographical references and index.
  1. Gambling—Nevada. 2. Gamblers—Psychology
3. Gambling systems. I. Title.
HV6721.N45S5   364.1'72'09798   78-16991
ISBN 0-316-79699-9

Designed by Susan Windheim
Published simultaneously in Canada
by Little, Brown & Company (Canada) Limited

PRINTED IN THE UNITED STATES OF AMERICA

A000003886566

Acknowledgments

There are many people to thank with whom I, or my associates John Dombrink and Tom Gray, had formal interviews or numerous briefer conversations. Some people spent long, long hours, often arguing, cajoling, disagreeing, pointing out misconceptions, and permitting me to observe. Several became close friends.

On the nature of gambling and its control, I want to thank Shannon Bybee, Phil Hannifin, Jeff Silver, and Jack Stratton.

Leo Lewis, Morris Shenker, William Weinberger, and especially Steve Wynn gave me access to Nevada casinos and contributed much to my understanding of them. In England, Dave Kopkin was my chief guide and mentor, and I appreciated the hospitality of Cyril Levan, Bernard Coral and Philip Isaacs.

Robbins Cahill, Frank Johnson, Ed Olsen, Grant Sawyer, Earl Johnson and Gabe Vogliotti were knowledgeable commentators on events of earlier years; and Jim Drinkhall about those involving the Teamsters Central States Pension Fund.

Ron Tanner, Ernie Rivas, Ralph Quintel, Gary Aiazzi, Billy Suggs, Gene Close, and Butch Mills showed me the ins and outs of law enforcement in Nevada, as did Sir Stanley Raymond and Chief Inspector Reginald Doak in England.

Tom Carrigan and Garry Reese helped in teaching me about the limits of background investigations.

I probably learned more about the complexities of gaming control from Dennis Gomes than from anyone else. His associates Joe Zerga, John Corapi, Rich Iannone, and Dick Law also contributed greatly to that understanding.

Bud Hicks, Mike Sloan, Sam Belford, Frank Schreck, and Pete Echeverria taught me much about the possibilities and limitations of the administrative law of gaming. Whatever else might be said of the Nevada gaming industry, it certainly produces capable lawyers.

Finally, I want Jan Thomas, Margaret Brown, Lynne Carter, and Rosemary McIntyre to know how much I have appreciated their kindnesses and cooperation; and Gayle Evans to know how much I appreciated the original invitation to lecture at the University of Nevada, Las Vegas. The University of Nevada librarians, Susan Anderl at Las Vegas, and Mary Ellen Glass at Reno, were most helpful.

This study was supported by several institutions. The University of California provided the resources and colleagues of the Center for the Study of Law and Society, and a sabbatical leave. As usual, Sheldon Messinger proved to be a thoughtful and constructive critic of the development of the sociological inquiry. Jan Vetter shared legal and other observations over a series of delightful lunches. Neither they, nor other colleagues — Jesse Choper, Sanford Kadish, Phillip Selznick, Caleb Foote, Phillipe Nonet, Steve Sugarman, Bob Mnookin, Paul Mishkin, Jack Coons — who made various and useful suggestions, should be held responsible for the inadequacies of the book.

The National Science Foundation's Law and Social Science Division provided research funds (Grant #SOC74-13683), and the proper stance for a research donor: complete intellectual freedom, for which I am most appreciative. Thus, the NSF bears no responsibility for any views or errors found in this work.

The National Institute of Mental Health (Grant #TO1-

MH12765) gave funds under similar conditions to train students and research assistants. As I taught them, they taught me.

John Dombrink and Tom Gray were outstanding and thoroughly involved research associates and collaborators. John was particularly helpful in editing and putting the manuscript together in its final form.

Evelyn Bogen and Jim Heller provided able and cheerful research assistance.

Rod Watanabe administered the project with the poise and confidence of a samurai swordsman. Both Wendy Rakocy and Wendy Roy Lefler typed endless drafts, as did Tina Miller at the home stretch. I am grateful for their patience, as well as their skill.

My Little, Brown editors, Llewellyn Howland III and Richard McDonough, were thoroughly professional. I enjoyed working with them, as I did with Denis O. Sutro, of Cooper, White and Cooper, who advised me about revising those portions of the manuscript which might defame or invade privacy.

Arlene, as usual, made sensible suggestions about writing and organization. Better yet, she treated my frequent absences in just the right spirit: pleasantly, but not so cheerfully as to be offensive. Thank you, love, and Mike and Alex, too.

My parents, Gussie and William Skolnick, inadvertently trained me to write this book. My father was — is — a New York lawyer and a dedicated horse and card player. My mother gambles occasionally, but with no great enthusiasm. Still, when I was twelve or thirteen years old, my parents' idea of a family outing was an evening trip to Roosevelt Raceway. My father took his nine- or ten-year-old to Belmont or Aqueduct racetracks, and showed him how to read a racing form. Thus, gambling has never been exotic to me, but actually it hasn't proved enchanting either. As an adult, I can take it or leave it. This perspective, I believe, helped throughout the study and guaranteed a measure of what I hope was sympathetic objectivity. Anyhow, for my early immersion and understanding of the world of gambling, I want to dedicate this book to the first players I ever knew.

Contents

I

Gambling as a Social Problem

1

Introduction

IF I WISHED TO APPEAR RIGOROUSLY SCIENTIFIC, I MIGHT CLAIM THAT I began this study of legal casino gambling to test some formal hypotheses, deduced after a careful search and analysis of the relevant literature. The problem is, it didn't happen that way at all. The initiation of the research was largely fortuitous, although its subject matter related to issues in law, society, and social deviance that I had been considering for many years — as far back as 1957, when as a fledgling sociology Ph.D. I taught a seminar at Yale Law School with Harold Lasswell and Richard Donnelly called "Criminal Law and Public Order."

The research began quite unexpectedly when in April 1974, I was invited to give a lecture at the University of Nevada, Las Vegas, on "The Police and the Media." Among the discussants was a police captain serving for that one evening as acting sheriff of Clark County. After the talk and discussion, the captain invited me to join him on the remainder of his duties. We would, he said, see the gaming clubs, particularly their security measures and personnel, and the jail; and be available for any interesting calls on the police radio. I accepted, gladly.

The captain was true to his word. I learned that former deputy sheriffs were frequently selected to be security officers at the clubs, and that consequently there was a close relationship between the sheriff's department and club security. I learned how difficult it would be to hold up a casino, in contrast to a bank, because of the large number of casino personnel assigned to watch everything, particularly the cage. Even in the event that the robbers could escape from the casino, they could never make it very far by automobile, because Las Vegas is a solitary city, and the long roads to California and other points in Nevada would soon be blocked. Later on, at 4:00 A.M., I would sit next to the acting sheriff as he directed officers who were going after and capturing armed fugitives from the Dakota war taking place in the north between representatives of the United States government and contemporary descendants of the Native Americans.

I learned also from that captain about how ordinary "respectable" people related to the gambling industry in Nevada. The captain and his wife, he told me, were Mormons who did not drink and did not gamble. But she worked as a cocktail waitress in one of the major clubs and cleared around $100 a night in tips. His nephew, also a Mormon, parked cars at the Sands Hotel. Like others I was to interview later, the captain expressed nostalgia for the good old days before the big corporations and their accountants cold-bloodedly itemized the costs of rooms, food, and drinks. The old gamblers — many call them gangsters — were fondly remembered as vaguely generous to long-term local residents who could thus afford to enjoy the pleasures and rewards the rise of gambling had brought to their small town.

I found the evening fascinating and began to think how interesting it would be to study law enforcement here. What distinctive problems would arise in such a place? How did police agencies relate to the casinos? Were they corrupted and if so, how? How were associated "vices" — such as prostitution — handled? I began to think that if I could gain access to the Las Vegas County Sheriff's Department, especially to its vice squad, I might be able to write something interesting.

At the time, I was involved with anthropologist Laura Nader and law professor Jan Vetter in teaching graduate and law students how to undertake and write about field research in some area relevant to law and the social sciences. We were supposed — under our National Institute of Mental Health training grant — to concentrate on areas where "mental health" issues were involved. Gambling, particularly in the form of "compulsive" gambling, was just such an issue, and the observation of law enforcement in Las Vegas seemed a sensible way to begin to study it.

I offered one of the students, a former policeman and criminology graduate student, now Dr. Thomas Gray, the opportunity to join me for a few days of field work in Las Vegas with the vice squad of the sheriff's department, an arrangement I had made with my captain friend. Gray accepted.

We rode along with the vice squad and with patrol police for three days, taking notes on what they did, asking questions, and writing up our notes in our spare downtown hotel rooms after 10 to 12 hours in the field.

We learned much from the vice squad, but not as much as I had hoped. The squad was not directly concerned with the operation and control of the casinos and how they were regulated by state authorities. Casino regulation, I was told, was the job of the Gaming Control Board. The vice squad could arrange an introduction with the board member who headed the Las Vegas office, but there was doubt that I would be able to gain access to its inner sanctum. Anyhow, the board was located just down the block, and the man I was to see I shall call "Kimball Bixbe."

(After much consideration, I have decided to employ pseudonyms for gaming authorities or individuals in the industry, except where it would be absurd — as with someone like Howard Hughes — or inappropriate — as in a major legal case — to do so. Otherwise I have used pseudonyms whenever possible — even if thinly disguised — to underscore that I am trying to investigate types and events, structures and processes, not individuals. I have also used pseudonyms where I have had access to confidential data available only to state officials.)

After I met Bixbe, I began unexpectedly to perceive the advantages of middle age for the researcher. This sort of research, where an observer participates with his subjects in their work or in their lives, has usually been carried out by young men. Indeed, the first really major social science study employing this method, William

F. Whyte's *Street Corner Society*,[1] was carried out by a college senior at Harvard.

Mr. Bixbe was a genial man in his early 30s, who was, it turned out, happy to see me. He had read some of my work on criminal justice, particularly *Justice Without Trial*,[2] a study of police, while in law school. He said he would be pleased to cooperate and support a similar study of the gaming control authorities in Nevada. He introduced me to board personnel, and told his subordinates they could show me anything they wanted, although he would not require them to do so.

During the study, which was to last into 1977, some of the agents, board members, and I became very good friends. I would go to Nevada for three or four days at a time, subsidized in part by a grant from the Law and Social Science Division of the National Science Foundation, to which I applied for support after I had gained access. The NSF stressed that I might acknowledge its financial support, but that I must point out that I did not represent the National Science Foundation. I took pains to distinguish between *subsidy* and *agency*.

During the early part of the study, I would work about 14 to 16 hours a day, including time for field notes. During the morning and most of the afternoon I would generally hang around the Gaming Control Board, mostly in the offices of the board members, but also with agents and division heads on daytime duty to see what their workday and its problems were like. Late in the afternoon, I would go to my hotel room, take some exercise and a nap, and then meet someone for dinner; either an agent, with whom I would work until early morning, or a casino manager or executive. Later on, when I studied the casinos, I usually worked at night — after being at the Gaming Control Board offices during the day — although I once spent a four-day, round-the-clock session at one casino. The hours were long, but I was rarely bored.

2

In October 1975, I spent a month in London, following much the same pattern. I was introduced to the gaming board for Great

Britain by its Nevada counterpart. My introduction to the English casinos was through the good offices of the president of a leading Las Vegas casino. His introduction did more than open doors. As his "dear and personal friend" I was offered good food and drink, plus the expertise of several executives, one of whom, in particular, introduced me to the casino business as it is practiced in England.

3

Eventually, after about a year or so, and increasingly for the next couple of years, I became a bona fide consultant to the board — unpaid — and a confidant to some of the board members and the staff. In good part, I occupied the role of the "stranger" who, writes Simmel, is "not radically committed to the unique ingredients and peculiar tendencies of the group," and therefore approaches people in it with "objectivity . . . composed of distance and nearness, indifference and involvement."[3] Thus, I possessed no authority, and made no decisions, but could serve as a sounding board for people seeking to test their conceptions.

These were, on the whole, serious professional people, who cared about their work, wanted to be right, and to be thought right. An outsider, a professor who might eventually write about what they were saying — but unlike a newspaper reporter, not tomorrow — could be confided in. There were critical times when I was aware of different views held by different people in various segments of the Gaming Control Board who could not, or would not, communicate these to each other.

During all of this, issues occurred to me in discussions with casino personnel and control authorities and agents. Why is casino gambling so widely regarded as sinful or immoral? How does it relate to the "law and morals" issue historically? How does it relate to the notion of victimless crime? What kinds of models might be used to legalize an activity widely considered to be a "vice"? How does England's legalization of this "vice" compare with Nevada's?

4

Vice is a fascinating social phenomenon. Leading dictionaries define it as immoral or evil conduct. But the dictionary definition is incomplete. The term vice suggests pleasure — and popularity — as well as immorality. Murder, robbery, and theft are generally regarded as immoral, but not much fun. In contrast, gambling, illicit sex, and drug use are vices because they combine pleasure with "evil." The whole point about the phenomenon of vice is its duality: it is conduct that can be enjoyed and deplored at the same time, sometimes by the same people.

Vice tends, because of its dual character, to be among the most controversial of public topics. If it were merely immoral, like murder, theft, or robbery, it would pose no particular problem. Nobody has claimed to notice a sentiment among any segment of the public, favoring the legalization of murder. But people do enjoy gambling, marijuana, and illicit sex. Thus, even when such conduct is outlawed, the laws are widely violated.

When legalization occurs, the moral character of the activity becomes negotiable. It is still "evil" conduct? A variety of publics must reconsider, perhaps redefine, their interest in it. These include, in addition to potential consumers, governmental bodies ranging from legislatures to police agencies. Furthermore, such capital-generating institutions as stock exchanges, banks, insurance companies, and pension funds must also reconsider the activity; as well as such commercial interests as airlines and building contractors. Even religious organizations must consider such questions as whether worshippers should be permitted or even encouraged to work in the industry; and whether donations emanating from the legalized industry are to be considered acceptable.

There have been debates without number about vice, and various commissions have been appointed to consider public policy in relation to vice. But commissions suffer from built-in limitations. They are composed of people selected to represent different interest groups — religious, political, racial, or economic — and they rarely enjoy the capacity to probe deeply. For example, when a National Commission on Gambling was appointed, its membership included one of the United States senators from and the attorney general of Nevada. The chairman of the commission was an attorney for the Teamsters Union.

Thus, the regulation of legalized gambling remains, as Herbert Packer has pointed out, "an area totally untapped by serious students of social control."[4] If a carefully organized and well-financed campaign were mounted to legalize casino gambling, Packer suggested that a point of special interest would be: "which side [is] the underworld on?"

Economic

5

Packer shrewdly perceived that interest in vice is economic as well as moral. Indeed, to study legalized gambling seriously implies studying how legal controls operate, and how politics and economics affect these. To employ an old-fashioned terminology, the study of legal casino gambling is the study of the political economy of a vice. To employ a newer-fashioned terminology, such a study translates into what James O'Connor calls "fiscal politics . . . The sociological foundations of government or state finances,"[5] and of what Joseph Schumpeter called "fiscal sociology."[6]

O'Connor titles his book *The Fiscal Crisis of the State*, by which he means the "tendency for government expenditures to outrace revenues." He quotes a statement by Arthur G. Burns in the *Federal Reserve Bulletin* to explain the concept. "We stand at a crossroads in our fiscal arrangements," the quote goes. "Many of our citizens are alarmed by the increasing share of their incomes that is taken away by Federal, State, and local taxes. . . . The propensity to spend more than we are prepared to finance through taxes is becoming deep-seated and ominous."[7]

In the United States, the characteristic motive behind legalizing casino gambling, and other forms of gambling, is revenue production. For some states, legal gambling helps to resolve the fiscal crisis of the state. In Nevada, legal casino gambling does more than help — it is essential for economic survival. No politician could be elected to high office in the state of Nevada who ran on a platform of making casino gambling illegal. It is the single largest industry in the state, employing nearly a third of the work force. Roughly half of Nevada's 1978 budget of $221 million was derived from the casino-gambling and entertainment taxes. The Nevada gaming industry in 1977 counted $1.5 billion in gross gaming revenues. This was a 25 percent increase over 1976.[8] The remainder of the budget derived from numerous other taxes, principally the sales and use tax, which is only 3½ percent, as compared to California's 6 percent. This tax amounted in 1978 to nearly $83 million.[9]

Without legalized casino gambling, the sales tax figures would be reduced substantially. For example, the nongaming aspects of the casinos — room, food and beverage sales — accounted for more than another $1 billion in revenue, or about half the sales and use tax. Moreover, since most of the sales of other goods and services are related to the presence of legalized casino gambling, tax figures would be reduced still further by the absence of the gambling industry. Pull casino gambling out of Las Vegas and most of the filling stations and clothing stores go out of business.

6

Of course, the political economy of vice is scarcely of novel concern. From the middle of the 19th century to the present, scholars and officials have debated two persistent issues relating to vice: one is whether criminal law should be employed to enjoin conduct that some find pleasurable and some think repugnant. The other is what limits should be set on the government's authority to regulate various sorts of "enterprise."

When so-called vices are decriminalized and subjected to regulation by administrative agencies the two issues are joined. For example, when casino gambling, involving such games as roulette, blackjack, and craps, is legalized in Nevada or England, administrative agencies are created to regulate the state-approved industry. In England, the principal motive for legalizing casino gambling is to control it in the interests of a vision of a civilized society. In Nevada, where the motive is primarily economic, where legal casino gambling resolves the fiscal crisis of the state, the authorities must reconcile control with industrial expansion. The similarities, it turns out, are as suggestive as the differences.

Whatever the purpose, the transformation from the criminal to the legal is not lacking in paradox. Usually, legalization connotes a less moralistic and rigid attitude toward the activity in question. (Thus, proponents of marijuana legalization are generally regarded as liberals, their opponents as conservatives.) But if legalization of marijuana were to occur, the alcohol and casino gambling models would suggest that strong bureaucratic controls would be applied to dealing in marijuana; whereas the present illegal traffic in marijuana actually constitutes the freest of enterprise, entirely unconstrained by controls deplored by doctrinaire conservatives.

It could be argued perhaps that there is no inconsistency. Conservatives would like to see the activity outlawed — or, if that is not possible, then strongly regulated. But observation indicates that that is not how the process works. Once an activity has been made licit, those who pursue it come to regard themselves as legitimate businessmen, and both resent and resist the state's attempt to exercise control over them. This creates, especially in Nevada, a major dilemma: To be effective, the controlling agency must point out the precariousness of the activity — the possibility of infiltration by organized crime, the unusual possibilities of consumer fraud — suggesting willy-nilly that the now-legalized activity maintains features of its formerly opprobrious self. How is the controlling agency supposed to maintain the rationale for strict control while justifying legalization on grounds that the legalized activity isn't all that harmful? That dilemma, although never quite articulated, was to puzzle and frustrate me during the three years that I studied, consulted, and worked with the Nevada gaming authorities. It continues to do so.

Furthermore, the economic and cultural imperatives of capitalism begin to operate. An industry must be profitable; to be profitable it must grow; to grow it must accumulate capital; to accumulate capital it needs social legitimacy, at all levels of society, but perhaps especially at the level of high finance. Where legal casino gambling seeks to resolve fiscal problems the industry's dilemma is a variant of the fundamental problem of the capitalistic state: to provide the social legitimacy needed to acquire the economic capital for operation and expansion of the industry.

7

The thesis of *House of Cards* is reflected in the title: the control of legal casino gambling is an uncertain, even precarious, enterprise. The book is arranged to show why.

It begins with what might be considered a digression — a discussion of whether gambling is play or pathology. In part, that discussion proceeds because one writing a book about gambling inevitably becomes interested in why people do it; but more importantly, in why other — or even the same — people see it as an undesirable, even deplorable, activity. The point is not so much to decide whether it is or not, but to suggest how certain features of the activity — sometimes the same ones — render it both enjoyable and opprobrious: in sum, a "vice." Legal controllers must take account of that reality.

This is followed by a discussion of alternative legal models for social control of vice. As pressures mount to decriminalize or legalize traditional vices, policymakers and the public are becoming increasingly interested in such models.[10] But a model is necessarily abstract. The book tries to make the abstract come alive, by showing what can happen in practice when vice is made legal and is regulated. In this study, the reality is the world of the legal gambling casino, and the subject of the study is its control.

Just as one really could not understand and assess control over the coal or steel industries without an introduction to the mine or mill, so also must the casino be introduced; especially since, unlike the mine or mill, the gambling casino "sells" directly to the consumer. So, to begin the study, the reader is introduced to the gambling casino from the player's point of view — as a house of stimulation, action, excitement. Then the casino is considered from the manager's point of view — as a house of profit. It is hoped that the reader, after exposure to both these vantages, will have gained an understanding of the active and elusive industry gaming authorities seek both to protect and to control.

Of course, casino gambling in Nevada has a history — of mining and drinking, whoring and respectability-come-lately; then of depression and war, gangsters and lawmen, the threat of extinction and the rise of control. Thus, after considering the casino as a social organization, the book offers three chapters on the history of this pariah industry, its search for revenue and respectability, and the growth of its legal controls.

Most of the remainder of the book considers control from the perspective of the agency carrying out its regulatory mandate — how it is organized, how it goes about its business, and its major problems: employee movement back and forth from agency to industry; the limits of the investigative process; the challenge of due process in administrative law; the difficulty of enforcing rules against an incredibly inventive array of crooks and cheating schemes; the uncertainty of loyalties to casino or consumer; the undermining of tax collection through embezzlement and skimming; the ambiguities of organized crime infiltration and control; and finally, the major related problem, persuading legitimate sources of capital to lend substantial sums to a pariah industry.

In conclusion, the book returns to a discussion of models in detail and compares England's control system with Nevada's. The issues raised in this book persist. Nevertheless, like any study, *House of Cards* freezes time. When the field work ended in the summer of 1977, it was clear that a fairly discrete and identifiable era in the history of gaming control had been completed. The chairmen of both the board and commission resigned, and a new election for governor was slated for 1978. Still, new events will take place in the legalization of deviance, in Nevada and elsewhere, even as this book rolls off the presses. Atlantic City's first casino opened on Memorial Day weekend, 1978. The erosion of previously strict legal controls, leading to that opening, sustains the major conclusion of this book: the larger the economic interest of the state in legal casino gambling, the greater the outside pressure to soften the mechanisms of control. By joining concerns over the legalization of vice with those over the fiscal crisis of the state, this book touches a changing and problematic area of contemporary American life. It surely will not provide the last word on it.

2

Gambling: Play or Pathology?

"AS WE CONSIDER THE WHOLE RANGE OF MORAL ISSUES," LEGAL philosopher Lon Fuller has written, "we may conveniently imagine a kind of scale or yardstick which begins at the bottom with the most obvious demands of social living and extends upward to the highest reaches of human aspiration. Somewhere along this scale there is an individual pointer that marks the dividing line where the pressure of duty leaves off and the challenge of excellence begins. The whole field of moral argument is dominated by a great undeclared war over the location of this pointer."[1]

Gambling, particularly casino gambling, is one of the major territories of this undeclared war. When I began this book, only one state, Nevada, had legalized it. New Jersey legalized casino gambling in Atlantic City toward the conclusion of the study. New York City legalized it for charitable purposes.[2] At any moment, legalization may occur in other cities or states.

Obviously, casino gambling is a controversial social activity. In many places it is considered a crime; and other forms of gambling, although often tolerated, are nevertheless regarded as socially deplorable. It is not entirely clear why this should be so.

2

Unlike drugs, such as alcohol, heroin, tobacco, or cannabis, gambling cannot produce physiological effects in an individual. Even nonmarital sex can, however implausibly, be considered damaging to one's health: venereal disease being an obvious case in point. In contrast, gambling does not readily lend itself to analysis as a medical model of pathology. No one could possibly allege that it is linked with a high incidence of cancer, pulmonary disorder, or brain damage. Nor is gambling physiologically addicting. If a player suffers from withdrawal symptoms, these obviously must be entirely psychological. Still, a variety of apparently intelligent commentators persist in discussing gambling in terms of social and personal pathology.

It is fascinating to observe the commonalities of what might be called the "social pathology syndrome," irrespective of any claim to physiological consequences. The idea of social pathology has been around for a long time. It can be located in numerous textbooks and treatises on American social problems.[3]

Where the term originated is hard to say, but Jeremy Bentham claimed credit for introducing it into philosophical literature; and late 19th- and early 20th-century sociologists did not stray far from the Benthamite conception, which, for all its vaunted rationality, was rooted in a religious ethos. "Pathology," wrote Bentham, "is a term used in medicine. It has not been introduced into morals, where it is equally needed, though in a somewhat different sense. . . . Morality is the medicine of the soul; and legislation, which is the practical part of it, ought to have for its foundation, the axioms of mental pathology."[4]

Coincidentally, and interestingly, Bentham uses the example of gambling to illustrate social pathology, which he sought to record on a "moral thermometer" measuring degrees of happiness and misery. Bentham plainly understood that the metaphorical "moral thermometer" could never be achieved in reality. Nevertheless, his goal — like that of so many after him — was to be able to quantify social and personal phenomena, and to construct scientific laws from which to generate legislative enactments.

Gambling suited his purposes. Money is, after all, measurable;

and injury to the pocketbook can, at least arguably, be compared to injury to an organ. But Bentham had a larger and more analytical purpose: to transform objective quantity into subjective meaning by considering the marginal utility of gambling to the one who gambles. To reverse the metaphor, transform gold to flesh: an obese person who loses a pound of flesh is rewarded; a premature newborn who loses it may die. Amounts possess value — a pound of flesh, or money — only in context.

To illustrate, Bentham offers the example of "deep play."[5] A man worth a thousand pounds bets half his fortune on a roll of the dice or the toss of a coin. If he loses, his fortune is reduced by one-half; if he wins it rises only by one-third. If he were to bet his whole fortune, and lose, he would be utterly destroyed. But if he were to win the thousand-pound bet his happiness would not be doubled. All this is obviously true. Yet for some reason it apparently never occurred to Bentham to consider the utility of the small bet; what might be termed "shallow play." If a man with a thousand pounds bets one of them — one one-thousandth of the whole — his financial position is not substantially changed. He loses little "happiness." Moreover, if he bets long shots, the utility of what he could win — however unlikely the chance of winning — is considerably greater than his loss. Obviously the possibility of a big win based on a small bet is the foundation for the attractiveness of many gambling games, particularly of insurance games like lotteries and sweepstakes. And, in fact, earlier in his treatise, Bentham praised insurance as an extraordinarily rational social invention.

But Bentham never perceived that the lottery is a mirror image of insurance. The only difference is that, instead of a large group insuring against the risk of loss, a large group pools its resources and selects, through chance, a beneficiary. Provided that the play is "shallow" and not "deep," the logic of gambling and insurance are strikingly similar.

From an anthropological vantage, even "deep play" demonstrates a surprisingly respectable aspect. Bentham's concept recently generated an eloquent and subtle interpretation of the social functions of gambling in Balinese society. Clifford Geertz analyzed cockfighting among the Balinese, where individuals risk amounts on the outcome that are quite substantial in terms of their general financial situations — wagers representing days or even weeks of work. But as Geertz points out: "It is in large part *because* the marginal disutility of loss is so great at the higher levels of betting that to engage in such betting is to lay one's public self, allusively and metaphorically through the medium of one's cock, on the line. And though to a Benthamite," Geertz adds, "this might seem merely to increase the irrationality of the enterprise that much further, to the Balinese what it mainly increases is the meaningfulness of it all. And as (to follow Weber rather than Bentham) the imposition of meaning on life is the major end and primary condition of human existence that access of significance more than compensates for the economic costs involved."[6] Obviously a functional anthropologist does not so easily relegate gambling to the realm of pathology. Yet, it persistently is drawn there by the phenomenon of so-called pathological or addictive gambling.

Although the idea of social pathology has presumably been passé in sociology since the 1960s, as late as 1975 a review in *Society* magazine lambasted a National Science Foundation-sponsored study of the impact of legalized gambling for ignoring the consequences of legalized gambling on individuals and social institutions.[7] The authors of the review argue that the study fails to comprehend the insidiousness of "compulsive gambling." They claim that the phenomenon is widespread, although one finds in the review neither hard evidence for that assertion, nor thoughtful analysis. Whatever "compulsive gambling" may be, the authors are confident that it involves such social costs as "criminality, family disruptions, work effectiveness, impoverishment, incarceration, hospitalization and suicide." Moreover, in an adaptation of the stepping-stone argument about drugs — that marijuana use leads to heroin use — the *Society* review concludes that New York's legalized off-track betting is also a stepping stone to "harder" gambling forms. "Statistics on OTB," the review avows, "cannot indicate how many citizens, who are introduced into gambling through an OTB parlor, graduate into track and bookie-betting and undergo behavior changes."[8] True enough, the statistics do not reveal these things. But it is hard to believe that OTB is a major cause of track and bookie betting.

3

Actually, the most daring and provocative analysis of gambling as pathology is not sociological, but psychoanalytic: Freud's original essay on "Dostoevsky and Parricide."[9] Dostoevsky was, in Freud's words, a "rich personality": a creative artist, a neurotic, a moralist, and a sinner. It was not merely that he gambled, but that for him gambling was both a form of self-punishment and self-actualization. His literary production never went better than when he had lost everything, pawned his last possessions, and was forced to write. Freud observes that "when his sense of guilt was satisfied by the punishments he had inflicted upon himself, the inhibition upon his work became less severe and he allowed himself to take a few steps along the road to success."[10]

Such an outcome doesn't tell us whether to lament or to rejoice at Dostoevsky's gambling. If his gambling losses released in him the energy to write *The Brothers Karamazov* and to dictate, over a period of four months, in an astonishing burst of creativity, the final chapters of *Crime and Punishment* while completing the full novel *The Gambler*, it becomes difficult to label Dostoevsky's gambling as pathological, at least in outcome.[11]

Freud is aware of the difficulty. He begins his essay by asking how one is to find one's way in this bewildering complexity of a "rich personality." He acknowledges Dostoevsky's eminence as a creative artist, ranking him not far behind Shakespeare, but undertakes no examination of this aspect of Dostoevsky. "Before the problem of the creative artist," Freud writes, "analysis must, alas, lay down its arms."[12] Yet Freud's own interpretation does show a relationship between the sinner and the creative artist. It suggests that without Dostoevsky's compulsive gambling, either the creative artist would have been less productive, or would have required a functional substitute for the self-destructiveness provided by gambling losses.

Dostoevsky was not alone in employing casino gambling to harm himself. No doubt many use the instrument of gambling to make life more painful for themselves and those around them. Even so appreciative a social functionalist as Clifford Geertz never denies the possibilities of pathological attachment to deep play. The

Balinese are well aware of the phenomenon and even incorporate it into their folk tales, which portray such gamblers as madmen.[13]

A number of psychoanalytic writers have attempted to develop a theory of the compulsive gambler. A recent and ambitious example is that of Peter Fuller, who, following Freud, locates an individual's interest in gambling in unresolved oedipal conflicts.[14] Like Dostoevsky, Fuller's compulsive gambler is portrayed as a person who develops latent homosexual or bisexual tendencies to resolve such conflicts. The theme of sadomasochism is also introduced. Dostoevsky's father was harsh and severe. Presumably, gambling losses enabled the writer to punish himself out of oedipal guilt.

One encounters two other principal themes in Freud and later Freudian writers. These themes account both for the pleasure taken in gambling and society's resentment of it. According to these interpretations, gambling represents a substitute for genital masturbation and anal eroticism. The observation of gamblers in a casino supports such an interpretation. Gamblers play with chips, pull slot machine handles, shake dice. As Robert Lindner comments on the relationship between gambling and masturbation: "I believe the evidence speaks in favor of a number of common genetic factors in the morphology of gamblers. They seem all to be strongly aggressive persons with huge reservoirs of unconscious hostility and resentment upon which that neurosis feeds; and chronic masturbators to boot. Freud's remarkable discovery relating masturbation and gambling stands unimpeachable. The correspondence is so close that, as we have seen, the one can and does substitute for the other."[15]

The masturbatory suggestiveness of casino gambling helps explain public resentment toward it, as do the anal and scatological expressions surrounding gambling. In poker, for example, you "make a big pot." The slot machine victor "hits the jackpot." Or take the name of the dice game, "craps." One British official I interviewed was distressed by the increasing popularity of "craps" in England. He found the name so offensive, he said, that he could not pronounce it in mixed company.

There are other reasons, as well, for the perception of gambling as an immoral activity. Clearly, the fatalistic value system of gambling violates the puritan work ethic. Like masturbation, it is nonproductive or counterproductive. One is not supposed to be rewarded for masturbatory indulgences, but only for hard work, thrift, prudence, rationality, methodical adherence to routine. The British Gaming Board, for example, sets limits on the amount possible to be won at bingo games at around $1,000; not because players could not be persuaded to put more into the pool, with the same statistical chances and a higher payoff, but because the board feels that there is something indecent about a person gaining a large reward from chance alone. In this respect, gaming conflicts with the underpinnings of the ethic of capitalism.

Paradoxically, gambling also challenges a Marxist revolutionary ethic.[16] From this point of view, the possibility of accumulating a great deal of money through sheer luck might well be interpreted as a falsification of workers' consciousness, diverting attention from the realities of working-class oppression into the fantasy of the rapid accumulation of wealth. Whether or not such an analysis is true, even the most superficial observation makes clear that it would be difficult to persuade contemporary Western workers that they should avoid betting so as to foster their revolutionary consciousness.

There is moreover no doubt that large numbers all around the world participate in and enjoy gambling.[17] What proportion are so-called "compulsive" gamblers is difficult to estimate. Gamblers Anonymous puts the number in the United States at 6 million,[18] but the figure is hard to believe: the concept of compulsion as employed by that organization is so broad that it includes large numbers of persons with all kinds of troubles. Or perhaps Gamblers Anonymous, like other organizations, seeks to upgrade its importance by exaggerating the problem.

The idea of "compulsion" is, anyhow, very complicated, particularly when attached to a specific social action. We speak of someone as having an alcohol "problem" who has experienced social difficulties following drinking: one who doesn't show up for work, say, or misses an appointment. No doubt a problem exists for such a person, but similar difficulties might have arisen in connection with a variety of activities unrelated to drinking. Such interpretations of compulsion are woefully ambiguous for informing public policy.

For the sake of argument, though, let's assume the truth of the psychoanalytic interpretation: that the person who gambles heavily and self-destructively suffers from unresolved oedipal conflicts propelling him toward unrealistic assessments of risk that result in self injury. Should gambling therefore be outlawed? Regardless of other problems such outlawing might produce, and even assuming we could achieve it, the world is surely full of other opportunities for risk and self destruction. The entire consumer credit industry is based upon maximizing consumption. Should we outlaw the pathological purchasing of automobiles or color TVs or sailboats?

Vacation and leisure sport activities can also be awfully expensive and self-destructive. One can scarcely imagine an expert skier who did not sometimes miss a day of work because ski conditions were so terrific he couldn't leave the slopes, and made up some excuse to stay; or who sustained an injury serious enough to disable him in some way from normal work pursuits. But skiing does not violate the puritan work ethic. To ski well is an achievement, while, apparently, to gamble well is not.

But that is not true either. Although in the long run a gambler must lose because of the house edge, gambling *per se* does not need to be self-destructive. That is why such psychoanalysts as Peter Fuller, who insist upon perceiving gambling as a neurosis, are not persuasive. For example, Fuller criticizes psychological behavior theorists on the ground that gambling doesn't fit theories of reward and punishment. "Simple conditioning theories," he writes, "just will not work. When a man becomes a gambler, and persists in gambling despite repeated losses, he flies in the face of behavioural learning theory. He is like a rat who keeps returning to the pot for food, even after it has been conditioned long enough to learn that all it will get from that particular source is an electric shock. And, irritatingly for those who wish to equate human behavior precisely with that of rodents, no such rats exist."[19]

But the analogy is wrong. Those who gamble do not necessarily lose repeatedly. The pot is not all pain, all electric shock. Moreover, casino gambling may be attractive precisely because it is unpredictable. A partial and random reinforcement schedule, as Skinner and others have clearly shown, is the most powerful behavioral conditioner.[20] A typical casino-gambling game is exactly that — a partial- and random-reinforcement game where rewards occur with irregular frequency. Thus, gamblers talk about "streaks" of winning and losing — and laws of probability suggest the reality of these — and the "high" of a winning streak.

Even the repeated loser seems to get something out of gambling. As Jay Livingston, who studied members of Gamblers Anonymous, concluded: "The compulsive gambler continues to bet because the action has come to be a refuge from thoughts of the outside world. His anxieties associated with his wife, family, debts, or job disappear when he concentrates on money and action. . . ."[21]

If the "action" captures the compulsive it also attracts the so-called "normal" person. What accounts for "normal" gambling? Why the high volume of betting around the world? What brings tourists to Nevada? Nobody really knows. A perceptive student of human behavior, Erving Goffman, spent months observing casinos. "Fatefulness," he wrote later, "which many persons avoid, others for *some* reason approve, and there are those who even contract an environment in which they can indulge it. *Something* meaningful and peculiar seems to be involved in action."[22] (Italics added.)

Fatefulness can be found in a variety of settings. Human mortality renders life itself a game of chance, and perhaps creates a need to experience control over what Sumner and Keller called the "aleatory elements," the unpredictable and elemental features of human existence.[23] So widespread is the general phenomenon of risk-taking in America that the *New York Times* ran a front-page article on the subject. The article listed such activities as pleasure flying, hang-gliding, skiing, sailing, drag racing, go-karting, moped and moto-cross events, scuba diving, snowmobiling, and bicycling, which, among others, have prompted insurance actuaries "to worry about the number of Americans injuring, maiming, and even killing themselves in a list of activities that seems to grow longer each year."[24]

If gambling and hedonism, like formal religion, provide solace from the ultimate certainty of death, they are perhaps justifiably considered "universal neuroses." But perhaps, too, they should not be presumed "pathological," unless we regard as sickness any departure from the highest aspirations of human conduct. Nevertheless, the fact that gambling attracts a good deal of moral indignation is consequential for Bentham's policy question: What sort of legislation is appropriately directed toward a socially opprobrious activity? To move the discussion of this question forward, it is worth examining legal experience in the light of social and cultural change in the areas of drinking, drugs, and prostitution, with particular interest in the consequences of possible models of legislation.

3

The Legalization of Deviance

LOOKING BACKWARD, IT SEEMS REMARKABLE THAT IN 1919 THE cumbersome process of constitutional amendment could produce a national prohibition against the sale and distribution of alcoholic beverages, and that only 14 years later the same process could ratify an amendment to repeal prohibition.

Drinking was, in one sense, part of a countercultural movement; but in another it most emphatically was not. True, from the viewpoint of the prohibitionist advocate of the early 20th century, the issue of national prohibition was not merely a question of drinking: it involved a test of strength between different value systems and social orders. On one side was Bible Belt puritanism rooted in the American dream of farm and village, intertwined with fealty to sectarian and fundamentalist Christianity. On the other side was the threat posed by European immigration to the cities. By the end of the First World War, the United States population balance had shifted to the cities, which represented commerce, industry, technology, and either secular attachments or a Romanized or Anglicanized Christianity. In short, to the fundamentalist, rural Christian the city signified sin, and it ominously attracted the children of the farms. As Walter Lippmann wrote in 1927, when it was becoming increasingly evident that the dominion of rural America was waning in American life: "The defense of the Eighteenth Amendment has . . . become much more than a mere question of regulating the liquor traffic. It involves a test of strength between social orders, and when that test is concluded, and if, as seems probable, the Amendment breaks down, the fall will bring down with it the dominion of the older civilization."[1]

Yet Lippmann was only partly right. If drinking symbolized the ascendance of a new social order, the dominion of the older civilization fell as soon as it became clear that large numbers of Americans supported the illegal manufacture and sale of alcohol. In that sense, the 18th Amendment accelerated the decline of rural Protestantism, and did not, as its proponents believed, strengthen their hold on the country. A commission appointed by a dry — Republican President Hoover — and headed by a Wall Street lawyer, was to report that distilled liquor was being used widely and increasingly in places and connections where formerly it was banned. The commission was most distressed by the drinking practices of the "better" class of people, those who composed the constituency of the Republican Party, who may have voted dry, but were drinking wet and heavily. With sad resignation, the Wickersham Commission on Law Observance and Enforcement reported in 1931: "It is evident . . . taking the country as a whole, people of wealth, businessmen and professional men, and their families, are drinking in large numbers in quite frank disregard of the declared policy of the National Prohibition Act."[2]

Ironically, then, the great experiment in prohibition firmly established drinking as a customary activity across all social classes, and especially among the solid occupants of business and professional positions. The test of social order was won by the cities because human beings appear to be limited in their capacity to endure an inconsistency easily susceptible to the label of hypocrisy. When a majority of citizens engage in an activity, it seems difficult for a minority — at least in a democracy — to maintain that the activity in question is sinful. Personal participation seems something of an antidote to social opprobrium (but not entirely, as the families of alcoholics will testify).

2

If national prohibition was a test between rural and urban America, the counterculture of the 1960s was a generational and pluralistic phenomenon. Dissent assumed a bewildering variety of forms and postures and produced an assortment of experiments and changes in sensibility probably unparalleled in American history. Governmental authority was eroded by the failure of the political system to deal effectively with problems of race, poverty and urban decline, the conduct of the war in Vietnam, the government's evasions in response to criticism of war policies, and finally, with the government's incredibly uninformed yet highly influential views on the effects of marijuana, the use of which was in many respects a counterpart to the use of alcohol during the 1920s.

The official interpretation of marijuana and its effects permeated law enforcement at every level — state and local, as well as national. Even the supposedly most advanced sectors of the law enforcement community were affected. For example, as late as 1963, the Department of Police Science and Administration of Los Angeles State College could state that "Marijuana, unlike opium, is an excitant drug. It disrupts and destroys the brain and distorts the mind, resulting in crime and degeneracy. . . ."[3]

Of course such a description belied the personal experience of an entire generation of student users. The debate on the effects of marijuana was continued, and will continue, but no responsible researcher would subscribe to the extreme view of the effects of marijuana presented by law enforcement authorities for several decades; nor, indeed, would contemporary law enforcement officials. Whatever its harmful effects may be, marijuana is now recognized as less potentially harmful than cigarette smoking and alcohol. Even Mississippi, the last state to legalize alcohol, voted in 1977 to end criminal penalties for possession of small amounts of marijuana for personal use.[4]

Political issues are decided by the powerful. As those who were most directly influenced by the post-Vietnam morality become older and achieve power, society will probably grow more libertarian, not because libertarianism represents the unfolding of a preordained historical process, but because of the difficulty of sustaining parochial conceptions of sin in an increasingly differentiated and secular society.

For example, during the 1960s and 1970s when challenges to traditional family and sex role patterns emerged from women's liberationists, people living in nontraditional family arrangements, and an astonishing and well-publicized variety of outspoken homosexuals, those challenges involved fundamental changes in the concept of the "natural" and its parallel — sin.

It was pointed out that strong and independent women, the communal family or group marriage, and homosexual or bisexual inclinations are as "natural" as their traditional counterparts; it was demonstrated that traditional social patterns are taken for granted and perceived as "natural" so long as they are subject to only marginal challenges. When that happens, the challengers are easily and successfully labelled as deviant. But when the idea of the natural itself comes to be seen not as a matter of fact but of cultural definition, what is or is not natural, and therefore deviant and possibly immoral, becomes a political question in a contest among competing ideologies.

Already there are numerous legislators and governors who are part of the generation that used marijuana when pot smoking was criminal, a generation that has been directly associated with a more accepting sexual morality. For future generations and therefore for society, the problem increasingly will be to develop models for decriminalization to replace earlier models of morality enforcement. The trouble is that when we move from concepts like sin (and its legal counterpart, vice) to concepts like decriminalization and legalization we solve some problems, but create new ones. In fact, we find ourselves shifting from the relative conceptual simplicity of the criminal sanction to the subtlety and complexity of administrative regulation.

Consider the decriminalization of marijuana use. The most acceptable model for decriminalization has been to penalize heavily the sale and manufacture of marijuana products, while attaching no criminal penalties to use or possession of marijuana in small amounts. This model, which was recommended by the National Commission on Marijuana and Drug Abuse, is emerging as the most acceptable decriminalization model for marijuana.[5]

The model is obviously not rational. By allowing personal use while heavily prohibiting sale and manufacture it recapitulates all of the problems of the alcohol-prohibition model. Since the user is immune from arrest and conviction, the model creates a sizable market for marijuana use. Moreover, the prohibition on sale and exchange makes dealing in marijuana both dangerous and profitable for the high-risk taker in this illegal enterprise. Yet, in this as in many other areas of the law, change takes place not so much in terms of rational development as on the possibility of legislative innovation grafted to a history of legal rules and social symbols. Basically, the strategy of decriminalization has been to reduce penalties for the socially acceptable and powerful users.

Eventually, more rational and consistent models will need to be developed. Yet, for some years we can expect that the commission's recommendations, which have already been adopted by several states, will be the hallmark of the decriminalization model for marijuana. As the commission itself pointed out when making its recommendations in 1973, symbolic feelings regarding marijuana use were so strong that no rational policy could even be suggested. Thus, the commission was itself reluctantly forced into the position of recommending a fundamentally irrational model as a stopgap measure. As it wrote in its final report: "Lastly, it is painfully clear from the debate over our recommendation that the absence of a criminal penalty for private use is presently equated in too many minds with approval, regardless of a continued prohibition on availability. The commission regrets that marijuana's symbolism remains so powerful, obstructing the emergence of a rational policy."[6]

This is an important statement for our understanding of legalization of casino gambling, and other "vices," because it shows the powerful negative effect of public imagery on our capacity for rational thinking in these areas.

But even if a rational legislative policy were able to be put into effect, it's not clear what such a policy should be. One policy might be called *deregulation*. Under such a model marijuana would be treated like a plant or vegetable. Thus, one could buy seed packets at a neighborhood gardening store, plant them in the backyard, cure the leaves oneself, and use the resulting product freely. It could also be grown commercially in fields, and sold as a vegetable in vegetable stores.

Yet, two imperatives militate against the adoption of such a model. One derives from norms of consumer protection, the other from government's almost constant need for sources of taxable revenue. Puritanism aside, one is scarcely able to sustain an argument that an activity heretofore regarded as a vice deserves to escape the regulatory mechanisms of government. While a sense of justice may persuade that "vice" turned into "pleasure" should not be discriminated against by legal constraints, grounds for rewarding a former vice are not apparent.

Prostitution, the oldest vice of all, strikingly illustrates the problem. Because it usually involves sex between consenting adults, prostitution, as a result of the new morality, has been increasingly projected as a candidate for legalization.[7] But prostitution also implies consensual *payment*. It is a commercial as well as a sexual activity. Why should sex, as a commodity, be exempted from regulation when other commercial activities are regulated? For example, when one person invites another home for a meal, the state ordinarily evidences no interest in the activity. But when the meal is available to the general public provided they can pay, when a private kitchen is transformed into a public restaurant, other considerations emerge.

Those selling food are regulated in a variety of ways. A restaurant may not operate in an area zoned solely for residences. A street vendor must normally obtain a permit before being allowed to sell peanuts, pretzels, or hot dogs. In addition, those who sell food, in contrast to those who give it to friends, are normally regulated for cleanliness. The private kitchen can be unwashed. But when the public is charged a price for the privilege of eating, consumer-protection norms formalized into law propel the state into an obligation to inquire whether the kitchen is clean. Although it does not follow as day from night, ordinarily, legalization provokes regulation.

The idea of legalization implies other complexities as well. For example, legalization is frequently called for on grounds that so-called "victimless crimes" ought to be legalized, for a variety of reasons which many have enumerated and supported, including myself. But, as Herbert Packer foresaw, the variation and consequences of legalization have not begun to be studied and analyzed.

To make the simplest illustration, the concept of victimless crime first generated controversy in legal circles over the issue of whether consenting adult homosexuals, acting in private, should be charged with a crime. By now it seems scarcely credible that so much time and concern, countless hours of writing, debate, political argument, and rhetoric could have been generated by what turns out to have been a simple issue, really a nonissue from a practical rather than a symbolic perspective. After all, how could police ever discover that two men or women, living or visiting together in private, were engaging in illicit sexual acts? The criminal law was simply to affirm, formally, the deviance of the act: to confirm by statute its immorality.

If we move from a moralistic to an enforcement perspective, the idea of victimless crime means that citizen complaints are not forthcoming: "victims" of drug dealers, bookmakers, and prostitutes do not relate to their so-called victimizers as do the quarry of robbers, burglars, and rapists. That is because they are not prey, but customers.

Victimless crime means something else as well. It suggests that the act in question is *only* socially opprobrious rather than seriously harmful, either to an individual or the social system. For example, again from an enforcement perspective, the problems involved in apprehending those who sell counterfeit money are virtually identical to those involved in catching dealers of illegal drugs. Years ago, when I studied a vice squad intensively, the squad was asked to assist the United States Secret Service in apprehending a counterfeiting ring. They were asked because vice squads are specially experienced in law enforcement involving the use of informants, intrigue, the security of information, and the apprehension of offenders whose criminality is proved by the possession for sale of illegal materials. Yet, despite the similarity of counterfeiting and drug-enforcement patterns, counterfeiting is justifiably regarded as a serious crime. Ultimately, the phony money is intended to be used to defraud an unsuspecting victim. It could be argued of course that profits from such activities as illegal drugs, gambling, and prostitution are funneled into broad criminal conspiracies — organized crime — and thus are as socially destructive as the predations of the counterfeiter or the armed robber. True enough. But the more remote the harm is from the act to be outlawed, the more difficult it is convincingly to provide justification for outlawing it.

A final aspect of victimless crime is its commercial potential as a legitimate business enterprise. The classic victim crimes enjoy no such potential. Robbery, burglary, and murder cannot be legalized. It would be facile — even facetious — to argue that murder is legal in time of war, or in the name of national security. There is a simple distinction between murder and killing. The latter may be justified for a variety of reasons, ranging from medical necessity to self-defense. Murder is killing without any justification.

If victimless crimes are potentially commercial, since they usually involve the sale of a good or service, some enjoy more commercial potential than others. One can scarcely imagine how to commercialize homosexuality. Homosexual prostitution exists, of course, but so does heterosexual prostitution. It is the sale of the sex, regardless of the gender of the parties, that yields profit. Still, although prostitution enjoys a commercial potential, it does not lend itself easily to the sort of industry-wide organization as do the manufacture and sale of such drugs as beverage alcohol, tobacco, marijuana, and cocaine; and various forms of gambling.

Other questions follow. When a deviant social activity, formerly outlawed because it was regarded as immoral, becomes legal, however restricted, does it lose its stigma through legalization? Is the ill repute of the activity reduced by its association with legal authorities who have declared it to be within the realm of acceptable conduct? Or, does the moral obloquy attaching to the activity discredit the legalizers? The movement to decriminalize deviance thus carries in its weight two associated sets of problems: the problem of how to develop and organize legal institutions to assess, define, and manage the economics of an ill-reputed activity through the use of state power; and the problem of how to insulate the controllers from the stigma associated with the activity.

The legalization of vice is thus a problematic enterprise, particularly in a society guaranteeing due process of law to those deprived of legal rights. For example, what standards should be employed to decide who is to be allowed to practice the legalized activity? Should applicants be excluded because of a prior occupational history when it was illegal? Does it matter what sort of history they have? Is it relevant to ask whether they were part of organized crime? If so, how is organized crime to be defined?

Those who did hold positions in prior illegal enterprises were usually involved in corrupting government officials. That being so, how is it possible to maintain honesty in contemporary governmental control operations when an industry contains operators who have probably, if not demonstrably, corrupted public officials in the past? What standards should be employed for selecting controllers and for assessing their present work? What sort of relationship should obtain between them and contemporary political authorities? The study of the legal regulation of casino gambling illuminates these political, social, and economic issues. Since it is hard to understand a control system without some notion of the activity it seeks to control, the next chapters will review a fascinating social institution, the gambling casino. I shall try not only to suggest what is fascinating about the gambling casino, but how its very attractions engender problems of control both for management and the state.

II

The
Gambling Casino

4

The Player's Casino

NEVADA NOT ONLY HAS LEGALIZED CASINO GAMBLING, BUT ALSO HAS developed the industry to appeal to a broad variety of players, from different walks of society, with different interests in its delights. Las Vegas, in particular, has developed a casino gambling complex with a number and variety of casinos as in no other city in the world. Tourists come to Las Vegas not only to gamble, but also to immerse themselves in a culture of gambling, which means a culture of entertainment, swimming pools, golf courses, food, booze, hookers — hedonism 24 hours a day.[1] Las Vegas "Strip" casino-hotels — built after World War II in what was then the outskirts of Las Vegas — are adjoining recreational cities in relatively deserted country. There is lots of traveling between the cities as one moves from Caesars Palace to the Dunes to the Riviera. And there are restaurants and bars along the way. Still, the destination is invariably another casino-hotel complex. There is also "downtown," housing office buildings and some lively casinos. But the glamour remains on the Strip.

In the 1950s and 1960s, when former bootleggers openly ran

hotel-casinos, Las Vegas restaurants and hotels were not supposed to earn money. Primarily, they were intended to attract visitors who would play at the casinos. Increasingly, as the major corporations have moved into Nevada, this concept is changing and in some instances considerable profit is being derived from the hotels and restaurants. Major Strip casinos enjoy occupancy rates of better than 90 percent. Hotel rooms, though not inexpensive, are a good value compared to those in other resorts.[2]

One way to describe a major casino complex is as a shopping center with casino games. Each hotel-casino attempts to remain a self-contained unit, with a hotel housing up to several thousand persons, round-the-clock coffee shops or delicatessens, and a variety of restaurants and entertainments. In addition, the major casinos offer men's and women's clothing stores, children's wear, child care, sporting goods and equipment, hair salons, and the inevitable American drug store which carries everything from exercise equipment to Alka-Seltzer.

The idea, of course, is not only to render the casino area itself timeless (a casino never has a clock or alteration in lighting, which makes it socially comfortable for a gambler to risk money at any hour of the day or night), but also to allow a touring gambler to spend his entire bankroll within the confines of the given casino. A gambler located in one casino complex can purchase wardrobes several times over, pick up an elegantly designed fur coat, dine on escargot, gefilte fish, canneloni, sukiyaki, drink Chambertin '61 or 1966 Dom Perignon as well as assorted spirits, smoke Havana cigars, play tennis, swim, golf, sweat in dry or wet heat, be massaged and coiffured, be entertained by the likes of Frank Sinatra, Ann-Margret, and Sammy Davis, and never feel sexually deprived.

2

"Las Vegas," as Mario Puzo observes, "has more beautiful women than any town its size in the world. It may have as many beautiful women as any city in the world no matter what its size. The reason for this is quite simple and only superficially cynical:

MONEY and beautiful women zing together like two magnets. Especially in Vegas."[3]

The state of Nevada permits prostitution on local option.[4] Neither Las Vegas nor Reno legalizes prostitution — not because of moral reservations, but because legal prostitution would be against the casinos' interest and, it so happens, the hookers'. Casinos are opposed for several reasons: Las Vegas's image as "sin city" is well enough established so that publicized legal prostitution might reduce tourism, especially by conventions. Legal houses might drive customers out of the casinos, while illegality permits the casinos to control hookers' activities discreetly. Hookers earn more money working illegally in casinos than in legal whorehouses. Whatever the service offered, prices run several times more in casinos than outside.

Local police, it is frequently alleged, receive money and favors from prostitutes. Such allegations have never been proven in a courtroom. But even from a noncorrupt law enforcement perspective, illegality has advantages. Prostitutes provide information to police — who still maintain a vice squad.

And periodically, before election time, the sheriff can order visible roundups of prostitutes to inspire the confidence of local voters, as well as the assurance that prostitution is not out of control in Las Vegas. Perhaps the main beneficiaries of prostitute payoffs are casino security police, bellmen — particularly bell captains — taxi drivers, and bartenders. The latter are not pimps — who live with and from the earnings of the prostitute — but procurers, who bring her business.

There are, roughly speaking, five classes of prostitutes in Las Vegas, ranging from expensive call girls to streetwalkers. The call girls, available to the highest rollers, are sometimes starlets, sometimes showgirls. Neither the physical or the social distance between Las Vegas and Hollywood is consequential — particularly for those with private planes — and the sexual mores of the well-to-do in one place are scarcely distinguishable from those in the other. Gaming authorities frown upon casino employees using casino revenues to provide sex for players. It is done, but more rarely than a skeptic might imagine. The reason: a man betting

$50 or $100 on every throw of the dice doesn't require the casino's financial aid to pay for a high-priced hooker. What he might need — and can obtain from various casino employees — is an introduction to an especially attractive young woman.

Hookers are available in every casino, but — with some exceptions — the higher the status of the casino, the less likely will hookers be visible at the bar or lounge. The more marginal the business position of the casino, the more likely will it be to permit hookers to use the casino to entice customers. At least one Strip casino requires hookers to register with house security before they are permitted to ply their trade. They photograph the girls, take their addresses, verify their identifications, and check out their police records. Such precautions protect the customer, the casino, and the women. The casino and the customers are reasonably confident that the women are not thieves who roll their tricks. And if a hooker runs into difficulty with a trick, she can seek the aid of casino security.

By a hooker I mean a woman — male prostitutes may exist in Nevada but, if they do, they are scarcely visible — who earns her living at prostitution, having no other known means of income. She is, in the Las Vegas lexicon, a party girl who sets a price for sexual favors. She is also a woman known to, and acceptable to, casino personnel, who receive 10 to 40 percent of her fees for recommending customers to her. Thus, many casino functionaries benefit from the earnings of prostitutes.

To be acceptable to the casino a hooker must be cooperative. She must therefore understand that she is a "customer service," like food and beverages, and is not an individual entrepreneur. In these circumstances, a "deviant" prostitute is one who does not conform to the overriding goal of the casino, which is to keep the player gambling. The shorter the time the prostitute keeps the player away from the gaming tables, the more likely is she to be accepted. A cardinal sin, in these circumstances, would be to suggest to the player that they move on to another casino.

"Chip-hustling" is a comparable sin. An attractive young woman — often a prostitute, and known to be so by casino personnel — latches onto a winner on a streak. To curry her favor, or perhaps out of exuberant generosity, or perhaps because the gambler believes she has brought him luck, he gives her chips, which often seem unreal as money anyhow. Were she to use the chips to gamble, that would be acceptable. But if she pockets them, and cashes them in later, eliminating the casino's chance to win them back, she is looked upon with considerable disfavor.

Chip-hustlers may or may not be full-time prostitutes. Numerous women, either residents of Las Vegas or elsewhere — the outsider is, in Las Vegas terminology, "a Los Angeles secretary" — turn occasional weekend tricks in Las Vegas. Some clubs, when hiring cocktail waitresses or keno runners, will inquire of the applicant whether she is interested in turning tricks. Her job will ordinarily not depend upon such an interest, but some casinos prefer to employ a few women whom they can count on to fulfill the request of a high-rolling gambler.

One rarely encounters a black prostitute in Las Vegas Strip casinos — and prostitutes, regardless of color, are rarely to be seen in the downtown casinos, away from the high-roller action. Most black prostitutes, and some white ones, walk the street, usually the "Strip" or the area proximate to the downtown casinos. Streetwalkers engender the hostility of local police, who regard them as potential thieves and assaulters, associated with pimps and drug traffickers. Such attitudes derive partly from sheer racial bigotry and partly from the fact that, to the extent they detract from the attractiveness of Las Vegas as a gambling resort, these prostitutes are "deviant." Thus, although prostitutes are present in large numbers in Las Vegas, they are not as manifestly visible as prostitutes in Manhattan or San Francisco.

Las Vegas is a small town, so far as local residents are concerned, and the requirements of the gambling industry shape the policies and perceptions of law enforcement at every level, from the sheriff's department to the gaming control authorities. Increasingly, the industry has attempted to portray Las Vegas as a resort city with gambling facilities, rather than as a gambling town with some swimming pools. Open prostitution would undermine the former image, while discreet, controlled prostitution permits a visitor to project an image or act out a reality of Las Vegas either as a recreation center featuring entertainment, restaurants, golf, and tennis, with gambling on the side; or a city of sin where, as one enthusiastic interviewee put it, you can "gamble, drink, fuck, and eat steak all night long."

3

Still, the casino is the key social institution in Las Vegas. In this respect, and perhaps in this respect only, the casino is like the university. All universities perform similar functions — teach chemistry and biology and English and mathematics and law and anthropology — but if you've seen one you haven't seen them all. Just as alumni from Oxford and Cambridge, Harvard and Yale, Berkeley and Stanford, could point to characteristics distinguishing these most related of universities, so can the Roman architecture of Caesars Palace be set off from the elegance of the MGM Grand.

Depending upon the location and the expected clientele of the casino, its facade, amenities, and interior will vary considerably. The Golden Nugget, the largest casino in downtown Las Vegas, for years included neither a hotel nor a showroom, but commanded extraordinary profit, the goal of every casino management. The art of casino management is in generating a feeling that will prove attractive to an envisioned clientele. There is associated ballyhoo, the communication of that feeling through advertising, public relations, and other forms of promotion. But ballyhoo can sometimes be guided by carefully collected information, as when sophisticated managers commission consumer surveys to determine customer preferences.

As with almost any business, the first question the casino manager and designer must address is the nature of the anticipated clientele. The development of casino ambience thus implies an explicit application of social-class distinctions. Downtown casinos, some with hotels, some not, are called in the trade "grind joints," a term suggesting a larger number of less affluent bettors and smaller bets — $1 to $5 — and heavy slot machine action. By contrast, a "class joint" depends heavily upon fewer and more affluent bettors who will not uncommonly risk $5 to $25 and more per bet.

I have watched numerous games in class joints where the player bet $100 per hand; but I have also observed a downtown 21 game where a player risked $1,000 per wager. Still, the norm remains. Major downtown clubs cater mainly to working-class bettors or those who are thought to feel more comfortable in what has been planned carefully to represent working-class feeling: western-style paintings, wood paneling, country and western music. But of course a really well-conceived downtown casino achieves broader appeal. So, although they mainly compete with downtown neighbors — such as the Fremont and the Four Queens, as well as the newer Union Plaza and the older Golden Gate — clubs like the Golden Nugget and Binion's Horseshoe also compete to a certain extent with the classier joints on the Strip.

But an even closer look at the casino world reveals a social stratification system that renders inapplicable the simple "grind" vs. "Strip" distinction. Harrah's in Reno presents the outward appearance of a grind joint, with lots of slot machine action visible from the street; but combines that with the carefully managed interior of an elegant class joint to maintain one of the longest running successful operations in Nevada. Similarly, the Golden Nugget — presumably a grind joint — offers one of the most attractively designed and best general restaurants in Las Vegas, with probably the tastiest Cantonese cooking in the western United States. Again, this is all carefully managed. The Chinese cook is a western tradition. Besides, the Golden Nugget has had to compete with the almost legendary Mexican food at Binion's Horseshoe — and still maintain the western motif.

When we consider casinos as socially stratified phenomena, there are even finer distinctions to be drawn, largely between casinos on main thoroughfares — Casino Center and the Strip — and those on the periphery. Casino elegance is not so different from elegance in any other consumer activity. Elegant restaurants, shops, even garages, are notable in achieving an atmosphere of repose. The action in a high-stakes baccarat game at London's Curzon Club is marked by a prevailing hush. The event is ritualized, rather like a dance with commentary spoken in French, and highlighted by the dealer's exquisite skill in employing a palette to separate and disperse oversized chips.

By contrast, noise is the mark of the déclassé casino. If one casino extreme is the private room housing one baccarat table, the déclassé other is the casino dominated by slot machines that whirr, buzz, jingle, ring and whine, with revolving lights and crashing coins — the sound of the jackpot. Heavy slot action implies other features: floors dirtied by discarded papers that formerly cased rolls of nickels, dimes, and quarters, bodies jammed closely into frigid air-conditioned rooms, quantities of cigarette smoke that challenge even the most advanced filtration systems and tolerant lungs.

Cuisine is possibly the most explicit and visible indicator of the social-class aspirations of a casino. The casino that features a 49¢ breakfast 24 hours a day is aiming for slot action, while one featuring several restaurants — with purportedly haute cuisine of varied ethnicity — aspires to capture the more substantial bettor. But casinos will also offer a variety of restaurants, with scaled prices, to attract different levels of bettor. Harrah's in Reno perhaps best illustrates the multiclass-oriented casino. It has dining rooms and restaurants agreeable to bargain hunters and elegance seekers alike.

4

The casino's credit policy is less explicit, but more consequential. Compared to major Strip casinos like Caesars Palace or the Dunes, or the MGM Grand, Binion's Horseshoe or the Golden Nugget offer little by way of credit. A major Strip casino may hold IOUs for as much as $30 million in outstanding credit at any given time, while downtown casinos rarely reach $1 million. According to its annual report to the SEC, Caesars Palace extended more than $160 million in credit during 1977. A credit-oriented clientele and casino present a set of attractions and problems different than those that do not feature credit.

Casinos not attached to hotels operate at something of a disadvantage, since they cannot accommodate "high rollers," while those with hotels set aside from 5 to 50 percent of their rooms for favored players.

Who are the "high rollers" (a term that eludes definition but suggests someone who is willing to risk — and in fact lose with some frequency — upwards of several thousand dollars on a single visit to Las Vegas or Reno)? Obviously, a high roller is someone other than a nominally affluent person, such as a business executive who draws an annual salary of $50,000 to $150,000. That sort of person pays substantial federal, state, and local taxes and probably has incurred other obligations: a family, children, home, and so forth. He or she simply cannot afford to lose thousands of after-tax dollars. To be sure, there are people in this category who lose more than they can afford. But they cannot continue to lose it without a major impact on their lives — and sources of income. So they either stop rolling high or locate an alternative source of income.

As a class, players must lose. The individual gambler can win, particularly in certain games. It is possible, but hardly likely, that someone who wins $25,000 at keno has put anything like that amount into the purchase of tickets. Indeed, the Internal Revenue Service has taken this position, and requires keno winners of amounts over $600 to pay taxes on their winnings.[5] It is also possible for an individual to win heavily but not consistently in craps. Even the IRS is willing to concede that those who win big at the casino games also lose big.

Stories periodically appear of responsible executives, usually in banking or finance, who embezzle to maintain their tastes for gambling. One inference to be drawn from such stories is that gambling lures essentially respectable people into irrational, even compulsive, activity that destroys their lives. Doubtless that happens, but with an unknown frequency. Whatever the frequency, one must suspect that it varies, and would occur less in groups normally characterized by thrift, prudence, and other classic correlates of deferred gratification. However sensational the story of the wayward bank executive, an industry whose gross revenue in 1976 totaled $1.2 billion could scarcely depend upon the occasional embezzler for a substantial portion of its earnings.

There is no way to estimate how much the industry — particularly the major clubs — earns from high rollers, because no statistical breakdown is given for this mythical category in accounting procedures. Some estimate is possible by ascertaining how many hotel rooms are paid for by the casino, or how many players are brought to Nevada with air fare, room, food, and beverages paid for by the casinos. In effect, the casino offers such players $500 to $1,500 simply to obtain their gambling business, with no guarantee or requirement that they will gamble only in the club that pays for them. The only requirement is that they gamble adequate amounts to pay for their trip, an issue to be discussed in greater detail when we examine the casino from the management perspective. However inadequate the statistics on "high rollers" or "good players," there is no doubt that casino personnel cater to them and regard them as essential to the financial success of the major casino.

That still doesn't tell us who they are; and casinos — as well as the state — take care to protect their anonymity. Nevertheless, my interviews and observations suggest several characteristics of the high roller. First, a high roller lives in a social world of gamblers. He — usually but not invariably it is a he — is also a sizable bettor, who pays gambling debts. This sort of credit information isn't obtainable from Dun and Bradstreet, but it is available from other people who gamble and from bookmakers, who may themselves be junketeers.

Second, high rollers have sizable amounts of spare cash to lose. What is the source of such cash? One obvious source is personal wealth. Some high rollers are essentially rich people who have accumulated fortunes, whether through earnings or inheritance: oilmen, businessmen, entertainers, real estate developers, and so forth. Such people earn so much that a $20,000 or $30,000 loss is not significant. They are not merely affluent, they are rich.

Even if they should care about winning, losing at gambling can actually make sense for those in high tax brackets. Although losses are not legally deductible, neither in practice are winnings taxable. The IRS simply cannot keep track of who wins and loses at Nevada gaming tables. Let me elaborate by considering a group of 10 well-to-do gamblers. Altogether they start with and risk $20,000 apiece over a couple of days of gambling at a Nevada casino. Ordinarily, at the end of that time the losers in the group will have lost about $120,000 and the winners will have won $80,000 in the exchange. If the losers can afford to regard loss as primarily an entertainment expense, the winners can enjoy the benefits of tax-free income. As in other areas of the economy, a progressive system of taxation differentially benefits those who can shield income. Since gambling winnings are rarely reported, the "legitimately" rich high roller is offered an additional dividend.

But high rollers need not necessarily be rich. All depends upon the sources of their incomes. Las Vegas casinos pay little attention to this. The issue for the casino is not source of income, but probability of payment. Someone who promptly pays off credit advances with cash is not questioned about where the cash came from. The only issue is whether gambling debts are paid off in negotiable currency.

Suppose a gambler deals in illegal drugs and accumulates a substantial sum of money, say $100,000. If a drug dealer has no visible source of income, or a source of gainful employment that earns relatively little income — he is a bartender or a musician — investments or expenditures for consumer goods can become quite conspicuous and arouse the suspicions of various authorities. But he can take a trip to Las Vegas with no questions asked. Thus the world of gambling offers a portfolio of anonymous expenditure.

And Nevada offers a number of additional benefits. The gambler can enjoy a smashingly good time — free transportation, room, fine food, all he can drink, top-flight entertainment — provided only that he risks thousands of dollars at the gaming tables, an activity which he also enjoys, particularly since he can gamble freely without accountability to legal authorities.

He can be reasonably confident that he will not be cheated or otherwise abused. Erving Goffman makes a lovely observation on the prevailing norms regarding treatment of players. Goffman says: "A player can engage in all manner of calculation and divination. . . . But he also may, if he wants, merely push an uncounted pile of money or chips in the general direction of the commitment area and the dealer will scrupulously do the rest. (I have seen a dealer assist a blind man to play, and one too arthritic to handle his own cards.) A great range of player effort is thus managed neatly by the same organization of play."[6]

Like carnivals, gaming casinos are places of amusement. But

they are also serious businesses, where large quantities of money are exchanged rapidly under watchful eyes. Sometimes a player becomes falling-down drunk, but that is a rarity. Most, even those who drink, try to attend to their play. The player is offered a decorous environment. One vice squad detective offered an interesting observation on casino decorum. He explained it on the 24-hour-open-town principle: "This is a place where you can get a drink at any time. So nobody ever has to rush their drinking, getting it in before closing."

The player can enjoy rare deference. The gaming casino offers deference not on the basis of inherited or achieved distinction, but purely and simply on the basis of size of bet and frequency of betting — plus willingness and ability to pay off any gaming debt. In this sense, the Nevada casino is the most democratic, or perhaps simply undiscriminating, of social organizations. A player can enjoy a whole new world of social acceptance within its confines. Outside, he may be a bookmaker or a pimp, a banker or a physician. Inside, the only question is: "How's his action?"

A player who makes large and frequent bets may win even though he loses, a paradox that is explained when one considers the distinction between "clean" and "dirty" money.[7] The earnings of a steelworker or a business executive or a professor are outstandingly "clean." Not only are they automatically recorded as taxable income, but a portion — roughly the equivalent of actual future tax liability — is withdrawn in advance. Such monies as remain offer the advantages of obvious legitimacy. Gambling can legitimize "dirty" money by providing an easy and relatively uncheckable attribution of source of funds and consequent payment of taxes. To make this claim, the gambler need not have won. Just as it is extremely difficult to prove that an individual sustained a net gain while on a gambling trip, so it is difficult to prove somebody did *not* win, even when in fact he lost. For somebody holding dirty money, it may be advantageous even if he loses to claim he has won. The musician–drug dealer visits Las Vegas three times a year, loses $15,000, and claims winnings of $60,000, on which he pays taxes. Gambling provides a credible source for income otherwise derived. The "dirty" money is by such a process transformed into "clean" money. In the vernacular of Watergate, it is laundered.

5

Accordingly, gamblers — especially high rollers — are not necessarily dupes of the casino, compulsive personalities bucking the odds. Las Vegas casinos offer more than gaming opportunities, food, entertainment, and so forth: they provide certain tax advantages to the wealthy and are also a most accessible and enjoyable laundry for the vast quantities of dirty money that accumulate annually in the United States, through skimming, bribery, corruption, and crime.

This method of laundering requires no collusion or illegal activity between the player and the management of the casino. Casino management cannot be expected to investigate the character of every player who steps up to the gaming table and lays cash on the line. Even when a casino offers complimentary rooms, food, and beverages it could not, even if it wanted to — which it assuredly does not — investigate the true source of gambled funds. Not only does the illegal drug dealer, the illegal bookmaker, the professional arsonist, the burglar, or the loan shark normally occupy some other occupational category, but the possession of dirty money is scarcely limited to "illegitimate" occupations.

At least three major sources of dirty money are to be found among nominally legitimate business and professional people: the cash transaction, the skim, and corruption. The cash transaction is a classic method of avoiding taxes. The method is widespread and hard to measure. It works something like this: The reasonable price of a thing of value — ownership in a business, a packet of jewelry, a load of furniture, a professional fee — is $50,000. The parties agree upon a recorded price of $40,000, plus $5,000 in cash "under the table." Some transactions may be made entirely in cash. However the deal is put together, cash transactions produce unaccountable money, "shoebox" money. Possessors will characteristically wish to avoid attracting attention to the money. Thus, in addition to its sensuous delights, casino gambling offers an extraordinarily valuable service to a society with immeasurable but evidently institutionalized sources of dirty money: the legitimization of unlawful funds through functional unaccountability.

The "skim" is a second major source of funds. The word "skimming" is often associated with the gaming industry, and for good reason. Unless very strict controls exist — we shall later discuss contemporary Las Vegas controls — any high-cash-flow business produces an opportunity for skimming, which is simply the pocketing of a portion of the cash flow by ownership interests, without reporting it as taxable income. Every retail business that accepts cash, from a local delicatessen to a chain of department stores, is susceptible to skimming. When questioned, several gaming executives either pointed out or acknowledged that "good players" tend to be in high-cash-flow businesses.

Schoolteachers are generally regarded in Nevada as inactive gamblers. Thus, those casino hotel executives who seek out convention business discourage conventions composed mainly of schoolteachers. Even were the teachers inclined to gamble large sums of money — which they aren't — they don't have it; and what they do have is in post-tax dollars. But in contrast, conventions of automobile dealers and salesmen are regarded as productive of good play. Perhaps it is not only a difference of temperament. The automobile business seems to offer an example — among many — of an institutionally corrupt business. "There emerges," reports the *New York Times* in a 1975 story on Eastern Chevrolet operations, "a picture of a corporate world seldom encountered by the ordinary consumer. . . . It is a world of kickbacks, payoffs, and favors by wealthy dealers to the much more humbly paid corporate employees who oversee warranty work and thus affect not only the way a consumer's car is serviced but, indirectly, the price he pays for it."[8] Such kickbacks, payoffs, and favors produce dirty money.

We cannot ascertain annual dollar amounts of corruption in American business, government, and organized labor. Along with skimming, kickbacks, bribes, crime, and other sources of illegal funds, these amounts must be considerable, producing vast quantities of dirty money. One estimate is offered by James Henry, a Danforth Fellow in economics and law at Harvard University. He found in 1976 that of the roughly $80 billion in paper currency outstanding in the United States, only one-quarter was made up of singles, fives, and tens.[9] Nearly $30 billion is in $50 and $100 denominations. Since large bills are rarely employed in everyday commerce, and since banks hold as little liquid cash as possible (". . . about one fifth of the currency in existence and less than five percent of the paper denominations of over $50") Henry infers that, even allowing liberally for all obvious legitimate users of currency, at least $40 billion remains unaccounted. He concludes that the money — dirty money — is mainly in the hands of those engaging in activities which depend almost exclusively on large, untraceable, noncredit transactions such as profit-motivated crime and tax evasion.

It seems reasonable to infer that many, if not most, high rollers are possessors of such dirty cash. Some high rollers, to be sure, are gambling post-tax income. But, given what must be the vast amounts of dirty money in America, it is inconceivable that this money is not particularly attracted to Nevada's gaming tables. Thus, whatever the sensual attraction of the Nevada casinos, they offer in addition an extremely valuable commodity in a society containing the fruits of institutionalized patterns of corruption. That commodity is discretion.

Legalized gambling in Nevada treats both crime and social deviance on the precedent of illegal deviance. Just as the illegal bookmaker does not inquire about the source of his customer's funds, so also does the legal casino owner refrain from making such inquiries of his customers. One casino manager told me the following illustrative story: "A couple of our regular customers came in with $60,000 wrapped in neat bundles, to be put in the cage for safekeeping in their name. We noticed the money was slightly burned at the edges, and pointed it out.

"'Oh,' one of them said, 'That's nothing, the torch was a little too hot.'

"We took the money anyhow," said the casino manager. "Las Vegas is a place for fun. We don't run detective agencies in the casinos."

6

The player's casino is thus what the player makes of it. Although it would scarcely be confused with a church picnic, it is easy to accommodate the sensibilities of those who have attended such picnics. Several large casinos maintain child-care facilities, some of which might serve as models for other segments of American enterprise.

Even where casinos permit hookers to work openly, the casinos are improperly interpreted as anything but conventional. The major sexual attractions of the Nevada casinos are the extravaganzas featuring bare-breasted dancers. Such shows are perhaps a bit risqué for little old ladies (who nevertheless attend the shows and apparently enjoy them). Hookers are not conspicuous in the casinos. They are not permitted to flaunt themselves, and the average customer is wholly unaware of their presence. A male drinking alone at a bar might become aware of the proximate presence of a smiling, attractive young woman, who is either dazzled by his appearance, or is looking for business. Anyhow, hookers represent a traditional form of conventional sexuality. They exist not for those familiar with novel sexual life-styles, but for the tired businessman for whom sex represents another purchasable commodity. Prostitutes are commonplace at conventions all over America.

The difference in Nevada is that the major action and attraction is in the casino, not the bedroom. A typical convention hotel maintains a relatively quiet lobby, and noisy parties in rooms. By contrast, the Nevada casino and showrooms draw conventioneers out of their rooms, because the casino is not only a place of games, but also of human congregants. The real "downtown" of Las Vegas is the casino area. Just as drinkers behave more decorously in a casino than in a bar, so do conventioneers. Ultimately, the visitor is captured by the seriousness with which other human beings take the casino enterprise, and it is a rare one who ignores totally the slot machines and the gaming tables. As one casino executive explained: "What attracts players to the casino are other people playing." And people *are* attracted. As a comedian wise-cracked at the MGM Grand: "On weekends Las Vegas is the only town in the world where people stand in line ten deep to have their money taken away from them."

But is that true? One way of interpreting legalized gambling in Nevada is as a gigantic confidence game, where by various promotions and strategies, the general public is lured into visiting what has become a resort with gambling. Las Vegas hotels discreetly advertise their casinos. They stress entertainment particularly — there is no doubt that the Nevada gaming industry also serves as the major live entertainment industry in the United States — plus restaurants, tennis, sunshine, golf, swimming. All of these claims are valid. But there is also no question that these are appendages to the gaming industry, and that the combination of the legitimacy of the gambling industry offered by legalization, plus the outstanding resort features, brings millions of visitors who are — what word is proper? — lured, enticed, beguiled, attracted to gamble.

The confidence-game metaphor is not altogether false, especially when we consider that confidence games rely not only on a false respectable front, but also on the inherent greed of the mark. Even the suckers — those who are utterly unaware of odds differentiation — perhaps most of all the suckers, hope to break the bank, to hit the jackpot, to enjoy the bliss of a costless vacation, made free by gambling winnings. Some do walk away winners, only to be absorbed into the con game by going back home and advertising their good luck to friends and neighbors, who will later contribute to the overall percentages in the house's favor.

At the same time, not all players are suckers. Some are knowledgeable and perhaps compulsive gamblers who eventually succumb to the edge enjoyed by the house; while others — many others — are extremely sophisticated. They put the resort-gambling combination to many uses: as a way of having a good time; of laundering dirty money; of enjoying anonymous extramarital sex, either through affairs or liaisons with prostitutes. These people — the regulars, the high rollers — generally are not naive and are experienced in gambling somewhere. Whatever their motives, casino managers welcome them as a mainstay of the business, and the business depends upon both volume and the capability of management to exploit the potential profit of that volume.

5

Casino Games

ANY ESTABLISHMENT THAT OFFERS A CASINO GAME IS PRESUMABLY A casino, so if a gaming establishment were to have one 21 table it could employ the label. There are casinos in the state of Nevada that maintain one or two 21 tables and perhaps a keno game. Usually these are located in outlying towns and are patronized by the local residents, or such tourists as hunters and fishermen.

One of the political considerations in the legalization of casino gambling is whether to employ zoning restrictions. The state of Nevada has never employed geographic or aesthetic criteria to determine casino location, only narrowly moral ones, such as proximity to churches and schools.[1] Geographic and aesthetic criteria would make social sense and political trouble. Outlying casinos generate little revenue and are costly and difficult to control. Gaming Control Board agents cannot give the attention to casinos in Tonopah and Wells that major revenue-producing casinos in Las Vegas, Reno, and Lake Tahoe attract.

Slot machine operations are, however, evident statewide, and it is common to find a couple of these slot machines in a local luncheonette or motel lobby anywhere in the state. Politically, gambling profits cannot be restricted to a few selected areas or entities. Yet the political problem in Nevada is not only to legalize gambling, but to legitimize gambling among the voters and citizens of the state. By providing a widespread, non–geographically restricted, segment of voters with a direct financial interest in legal gambling, the commercial is transformed into the cultural, and the grocery store slot machine becomes an acceptable ornament rather than an intrusive anomaly.

The larger Nevada casinos — in Las Vegas, south Lake Tahoe, Reno, Sparks, Carson City — usually offer five "pit" games: 21 or blackjack, craps or dice, baccarat, roulette, and the "wheel of fortune," plus keno and slot machines. European casinos offer the major pit games, although craps and 21 have historically been known as American games and roulette and baccarat as European.[2]

It is easy to understand why roulette is relatively unpopular among Nevada casino gamblers, but not so easy to comprehend why the managers at Nevada casinos have deliberately made it so. Roulette is a very simple game to play and popular in Europe because the odds are better. The Nevada roulette table consists of a wheel with 36 numbered metal pockets, plus a zero and a double zero. There are all sorts of betting variations in roulette, and it would be tedious to describe each of these. The simplest is the single-number bet which pays off at odds of 35 to 1. Since, with a zero and a double zero, there are 37 possibilities, the house advantage in Nevada is 5.26 percent. In Europe, which offers 36 possibilities, the home advantage is halved. Moreover, European roulette also frequently offers a bet called the *en prison*. Here, when a zero appears the player only loses one-half the wager, reducing the house advantage to 1.35 percent.

It's a good question why Nevada casinos employ the double zero. The gaming authorities do not require it and any Nevada casino proprietor would be free to introduce European roulette with its single zero. But the double zero seems to be an American tradition. Indeed, in a book published in 1857 Jonathan H. Green, a reformer of his day, describes a layout that contains not only a double zero but also an "eagle" to offer the house yet an additional advantage. "Ask these men what advantage there is in their favor," Green writes, "and they will answer, about 5 percent. They will explain to you that if the ball runs into the eagle, or the double o, or single o, you lose; these they will say are all the advantages possessed by them; but this is all false; for, besides having color for color against you, they have the eagle and the single and the double o, and in addition to all this, the *secret springs,* which they always have it in their power to use: with these odds, it is plain that a man can never win when the keeper chooses that he shall lose."[3] The "secret springs" are of course a cheating device. Cheating at all forms of gambling was common during the 19th century. Some in Nevada say things haven't changed much.

The theme of the cheating in roulette is found also in a book by John Phillip Quinn, another Victorian reformer.[4] Like Green, Quinn discusses roulette and shows layouts that contain the "eagle" as well as the double zero, but he also describes the newer layouts, and particularly the western ones, with simply the double zero. One can speculate that since gaming was illegal, roulette wheels and layouts were relatively complicated sets of equipment and those who operated them felt that they at least needed the edge of the double zero, if not the advantage gained by cheating.

Cheating aside, the tradition of the double zero prevails in contemporary Nevada. I have discussed this anomaly with casino operators and they say it is not a very popular game but that that's the way it's played and that none of them really wants to lose the additional advantage of the double zero. Yet the Europeans have done very well with the single zero because the smaller house percentage is more attractive to players and produces more winners.

It is a paradox of the gambling industry that winners are necessary for the business to continue. If the only outcome were to lose, players would soon stop gambling. Gambling operators like nothing better than the occasional big winner who will provide word-of-mouth advertising. The whole point of a bank is that it does not operate on the basis of a limited number of chance occasions. The more play there is the more likely are chance outcomes to appear. So if the house has an edge of only two or three percent it can do very well, provided that the volume of gambling is sufficiently large. Nevertheless, the double zero prevails in Nevada gaming casinos and relegates roulette to the least popular of the casino games while baccarat, the other European game, has become increasingly popular.

2

Actually, baccarat is not so popular as it is spectacular. The baccarat game offers the Nevada casino an opportunity to show off European flair and elegance. Until November 1974 baccarat games were the only ones played in Nevada with cash instead of chips. Part of the excitement was to see players seated with stacks of hundred dollar bills in front of them. Partly because of this, and partly because of the attempt to attract the big player to baccarat, the game is usually partitioned off from the rest of the gaming area. The baccarat table is oblong with six numbered seats on each side. A caller sits in the middle of the table with six players on his right and six on his left and with two dealers opposite. There will also be one or more supervisory people, both checking the action and checking on credit.

Baccarat dealers don't look like other dealers. Characteristically, they are dressed in formal dinner jackets, or some flashier version of a monkey suit. There usually are beautiful women seated around baccarat tables who are obviously shills: pretend players hired by the house to entice real players into risking their money at the game. Ordinarily, shills are not hookers, although on occasion they may be. They are paid a flat rate and are there primarily to draw attention to the game.

Given all the fanfare, baccarat is nevertheless the easiest game to play and to bet, since no decisions are required of the player. In all situations, the play of the game is clearly spelled out by preordained rules. The object of the game is for the player to get a hand closer to the value of nine than the banker's hand. Tens, jacks, queens, and kings count as zero. Aces count as one and other cards count according to their face values.

Of all the casino games, baccarat offers the best odds to the average bettor. The bettor always has a slight advantage if he bets with the bank rather than with the player. Apparently mathematicians disagree on exact percentages for bank-hand casino advantage, but the disagreements are slight. Bill Friedman has checked out various mathematical approximations and goes along with the Epstein approximation of bank-hand casino advantage of 1.16 percent and player-hand casino advantage of 1.37 percent.[5] Baccarat enjoys increasing popularity because of its simplicity, and because the player gets a very good deal, as well as because of its grandeur. A number of casinos have eliminated the grandeur and are dealing baccarat at a smaller table about the size of an ordinary 21 table with only one dealer. This game, called mini baccarat, operates on exactly the same rules, but its less pretentious setting makes the game available to the ordinary player who might be betting one or two dollars a throw at a blackjack table, while the typical minimum wager at the big baccarat table is usually $20.

3

Twenty-one — blackjack — is the most popular game in Nevada and it is increasingly popular in Europe where roulette and baccarat still prevail. Perhaps that's because it is a deceptively simple game to understand, with just enough strategy involved to make it interesting. There is no question that a sophisticated player can employ strategies to shift the odds in his favor.

The idea of the game is for the player and dealer to get as close to a card count of 21 as possible, without "breaking" (going over that number). The most straightforward way to reach 21 is by drawing an ace (which counts either as 11 or 1) and a 10-card (either a 10 or a picture). The two-card 21 is called "blackjack" and thus the game is often called that as well.

A 21 table is the shape of a semicircle, characteristically with a leather edge and a blue or green felt layout. The layout contains seven wagering places. If we think of the dealer as a pitcher, as in a baseball game, and the player as a batter, then the box directly across from the dealer would be where home plate is. The one farthest to the right would be at first base, and the one farthest to the left would be at third base. First and third bases are significant positions for knowledgeable players and cheaters, partly because of the information they offer and partly because they lie on the periphery of the dealer's vision.

In Nevada clubs, elemental items of information are routinely offered to players on the layout, two of which are critical and the others merely enticing. The critical items are: ties are a standoff, and the dealer must draw on 16 and stand pat on 17. (In translation, the player is not playing against the other players but only against the dealer; and the dealer is totally lacking in discretion.) If the dealer draws ten and a six, the dealer must draw. Therefore, a player need not concern himself with other players' hands. The only thing that counts is the relationship between his hand and the dealer's.

The game is played either with one standard 52-card deck or with up to four standard decks which are dealt out of a device called a "shoe." The purpose of the shoe is to prevent a quick-fingered dealer from making illegal sleight-of-hand moves to cheat the player, or to cheat the house. (Actually, most 21 cheating occurs between a dealer and a confederate whom the dealer allows to win.) Although the shoe provides protection for both the house and the player, moderately experienced players often don't like to play with it. Most regular players employ some form of counting, that is, keeping tabs on discards so as to know which cards are remaining in the deck and to alter betting so as to maximize the probabilities of winning according to the remaining cards; and find it easier to count down one deck than two or four. Very sophisticated players are relatively untroubled by two- or four-deck games. They employ a "running count" providing them with continuing ratio of player disadvantage cards, of which there are 36, vs. 10-value cards, of which there are 16, for a ratio of 2.25. The richer the deck is in 10-value cards, the lower the ratio, and the lower the ratio, the more the player is advised to bet.

If 21 seems a rather simple game, that is because its action — unlike the action in craps, discussed in the next section — is relatively easy to follow. There is a basic strategy for playing 21, which has been determined by various computer experts, and this strategy is the correct one for the first deal of a newly shuffled deck or for a deal from a deck where unknown cards have already been played out and discarded.[6]

Most players don't employ sophisticated counting techniques

because the more complex the counting method, the more it requires concentration, memory, and numerical ability all within the confines of a fast-paced, quickly dealt game. But sophisticated players can and do count.

Generally, casinos are on guard against counters, especially as the basic betting unit rises. But the two-dollar unit counter, who may raise his bet to $10 or $12, is not going to be observed so carefully as the $10 bettor who raises his bet to $50 or $60.

When a bettor starts winning in the hundreds of dollars, he attracts the attention of various casino personnel. The question becomes one of accounting for improbable outcomes. Some intervention other than chance will be suspected and guarded against. If counting is suspected as the principal cause for improbability, casino authorities who understand counting will be brought in to observe the pattern of player performance. (Since maximum information is gained by sitting at third base, a counter who wants to disguise himself sits somewhere else; or modifies bets so as not to maximize advantage.)

Counting is not illegal, but Nevada casinos arguably can bar players. So from the player's vantage, the idea is to avoid being caught. The casino can employ other countermeasures. The simplest and most effective is reshuffling the cards, but this measure is also costly. Casinos make money on the volume of play. Volume explains why a game like blackjack, with something around a four to five percent house advantage over the average player, manages to throw off gross gaming revenues amounting to 20 to 25 percent annually. The average player keeps rebetting until the house advantage beats him several times. It is not uncommon to observe tourists, who play so as to offer the house a high advantage, keep playing with $50 or $100 until they lose it all.

Ultimately, the counter may be barred from the casino, and the casino will be supported by gaming authorities. Thorp writes that in the 1970s, when he was winning thousands of dollars with his counting methods, some would send in dealers to cheat him, but most would simply bar him from play.[7]

The really sophisticated counter is, thus, required to develop a strategy for achieving invisibility. The most elaborate is the "count team."[8] Here, a counter bets according to the basic strategy, an even-money proposition. When the deck is particularly favorable, he signals an accomplice to make a larger initial bet. Since this is the player's first bet, casino personnel do not suspect they have a counter on their hands. Besides, a high first bet tends to legitimize betting variations. The principal player plays for from 20 to 30 minutes; the second, third, and fourth players are introduced, under similarly favorable circumstances. That way, the team makes four highly advantaged initial bets, and the disguise of the sizable first bet permits sophisticated counting for a profitable time period. By going from club to club, such a team can win several thousand dollars during a weekend, and arouse little suspicion.

The gaming authorities find themselves in a characteristic dilemma over the issue of "counting." Privately, they regret the avariciousness and short-sightedness of the industry, especially when players are roughed up by security guards. Still, the authorities recognize that when a major newspaper like the *New York Times* publishes a lead Sunday magazine article on the problems of "counters," the article serves as an advertisement for gaming, whether intended or not.[9] From Thorp through Ken Uston — who teaches counting methods — the message is two-pronged: one is, Nevada casinos violate the "rights" of counters;[10] the other is, if you learn to count, you can win at blackjack.

But few players enjoy either the ability or the bankroll to turn the percentages around, and to exploit the advantage of the edge. Casinos win because of volume. An individual player can lose in an evening, even with an edge. Thus, in the long run, so-called "negative" publicity benefits the casinos by drawing players to Nevada who are not skilled counters, but think they are. The presence of such players provides the clubs with a population that makes the edge prevail.

4

Craps is generally acknowledged to be the most action-packed game in the Nevada casino. In contrast, it is in England a relatively slow game, although the rules are not significantly different. In part, this has to do with the general quietude of the British casino, but also the British have not yet produced a large enough group of knowledgeable craps shooters. To play the game quickly requires knowledge of the game and constitutes a precondition for excitement.

Imagine a group of Englishmen at the Superbowl attempting to comprehend the significance of fourth-downs, time-outs during the last two minutes, and the point equivalent of different scoring possibilities; or a group of Americans at their first soccer match. Boxing is the only truly international sport because — despite the finer points of hooks, crosses, jabs, combinations and footwork — it doesn't require much prior knowledge to understand what it takes for one man to beat another to the ground. But there are many knowledgeable craps players in Nevada, and a "hot" craps table, where a player is making point after point and *not* rolling a seven, is the most exciting game in the Nevada casino.

Craps is an apparently simple game and those who have played some of its simplest versions can scarcely appreciate the complexities of the layout. It takes years to become a really capable craps stickman because one needs to be able to follow all the different bets quickly and, most importantly, make collections and payoffs quickly and accurately.

The sheer variety of possible bets bewilders the newcomer and encourages sucker bets. The most obvious sucker bet on the Nevada table, not allowed on the English layout, is the "big six" or "big eight." True odds against rolling a six or an eight before rolling a seven are 6 to 5. The big six and eight are paid off at even money, but since their true odds are 6 to 5, the house maintains an 18 percent advantage. Players can bet against the shooter as well as with, and in fact the odds are slightly better against than with. But most players prefer to bet with the shooter because the action at a craps table creates a very quick informal group allied against the house. So when a player is making passes, avoiding sevens and making points along the layout, tremendous excitement can be generated. But it's an excitement not easily understood the first or even the 10th time somebody participates in a craps game.

5

Keno is at the opposite end of the odds structure from craps. A bingo-type game, keno disadvantages the player by approximately 20 percent. So why do people play keno? Because, unlike craps, one risks relatively little to gain relatively much, the basic attraction of most insurance games. If somebody were to risk $2 to win $25,000, and won, it wouldn't matter all that much to him if the proper payoff ought to have been $30,000. Keno enjoys, therefore, the advantages of "shallow play." Its advantages suggest the complexity of discussions of the rationality of gambling. For example, gaming-guide author Allan Wilson writes that his interest in keno died as soon as he estimated the basic odds. There was no way for him to overcome the 20 percent edge, so he never has purchased a keno ticket in his life. "It is," Wilson writes, "positively the worst sucker game in the house."[11]

But there is another way to analyze keno, not so much on its mathematical rationality as on what it offers to the relatively impecunious player, who can bet as little as 60¢ in a keno game as opposed to the $2 minimum blackjack or craps bet. Granted, keno isn't usually a game for serious gamblers, but in some ways it is the casino game that conforms most to the recreational gambling model. A modest-betting player can occupy a keno seat for an hour for around $10. The seat is comfortable and many casinos will be fairly generous in dispensing drinks during that time. So, although from the point of view of mathematical logic, keno is the biggest sucker game in the house, from the point of view of social logic, it may be one of the most sensible. The average keno player isn't going to lose more than $20 to $50 in an evening and will have a few drinks and some entertainment for that.

6

Until 1975, pari-mutuel wagering could only be done at small operations downtown and on the Strip. After 1975, the gaming industry and control authorities decided that pari-mutuel wagering in casinos would not unduly damage the small books' business, and would instead attract a new customer to sports and race betting.

Race and sports betting differ sharply from each other. Horse race results are obtained from a race wire service licensed by the gaming control authorities. Each race at major tracks is shown on large boards in the book area. Ordinarily, winning wagers on races are paid at full track odds on wagers up to $100 each for win, place, or show. In excess of $100, winners are paid at track odds up to 20 to 1 on a win bet, 8 to 1 on a place bet, and 4 to 1 on a show bet. There is a maximum payoff limit of 100 to 1 for a winning daily double, exacta, quinella, or parlay wager.

Sports information is received from the major wire services. Wagers are accepted on football, basketball, baseball, and occasional boxing matches.

In football wagering, all winning straight bets are paid at a ratio of $10 for every $11 wagered. The bookmaker's goal is to balance the books as nearly as possible by having an equal sum wagered on each team, leaving $1 for the bookmaker's services. This is done by giving the underdog team "points." The "point spread" for each contest is developed by the casino's sports handicapper, who uses the wire services and other news publications for statistics and information. Sometimes point spreads are "borrowed" from other casinos, if their handicapper is considered more knowledgeable. For basketball, winning wagers are paid at a ratio of $5 for every $6 wagered. Baseball betting is similar.

While those bets represent the majority of the wagering done in a sports book, a player may make another kind of bet: the parlay wager. This involves picking the winner of two or more events, and the payoff is at a predetermined ratio depending upon the number of winners picked. The bettor's payoff for each dollar wagered is greater than it would be if wagered on only one event, but the chance of losing is greater in a parlay situation.

Bookmaking is subject to laws and regulations of both federal and state governments to which casino gambling is not subject. While federal law prohibits transmission of wagers across state lines, Nevada gaming regulations authorize acceptance of wagers by telephone from persons within the state. Nevada law permits no wagers on any election, on amateur events in Nevada, or on events outside the state where the participant represents a Nevada institution.

7

No description of the Nevada casino would be complete without discussing slot machines, which the British authorities, unlike those in Nevada, consider "one-armed bandits." I recall an applicant for a gaming casino license who was temporarily denied approval by the Nevada gaming authorities solely because he wanted to call his club — as a joke — "The One-Armed Bandit." Anticipating no problems with licensing, the applicant invested several thousands of dollars on such promotional materials as TV commercials, billboards, matchbooks, and so forth. But the gaming authorities were not amused, and regarded the suggested name of the club as an affront to Nevada's image.

If the casino is an adult playground, the slot machine section is the portion reserved for the unsophisticated gambler. Among gambling devices — slot machines are strictly speaking not a game — slots appear to possess extraordinary allure. Unlike cards and dice, even the simplest slot machines do something. The reels turn, presenting a blurred imagery of expectations. The player anticipates the reward of matching symbols, as well as the sound of coins tumbling out of the machines; and should the player hit a jackpot, the siren or the bell announces to surrounding and envious onlookers the special fortune of the jackpot winner.

Who is captured by such a seemingly regressive activity? Only millions of visitors — and some residents — who left in 1977 gross slot machine revenues amounting to $580 million.[12] People seem to love to play slot machines, and they seem especially to enjoy playing them in crowds.

The placement of slot machines is carefully thought out by casino managers who operate successfully on slightly differing variations of types of machine and types of payoff. There is an underlying psychology to the slot machine business — really a social psychology because the attractiveness of machine types, locations, and ambience must be related to such variables as social class and ethnicity — but to my knowledge nobody has ever systematically studied it.

Nevertheless, it is there, and casino managers play with it sometimes by consulting with professional psychologists about reward schedules and sometimes by following the ancient homilies of the business: the slot machines should be near the coffee shop, the slot machines should be near the street, near the lounge show, and so forth. All such marketing formulae sometimes seem to work. So long as people play, the machines will win for the house.

A slot machine is made up of reels, traditionally three, but sometimes four or more. Each reel is marked with symbols, usually 20 although some machines now operate with 22 or 25. Slot machines entice players by two simple thrusts at their psychological defenses. One is to place significantly more jackpot symbols on the first and second reels than on the third (the third reel in the classic machine contains only one jackpot symbol while the first has four, and the second five). Generations of players have pulled slot machine handles and produced jackpot symbols on the first and second reels, seemingly just missing out on the jackpot. What happens is this: Because of the differential placement of jackpot symbols, players wrongly — though not necessarily consciously — believe that jackpot odds are something like $4 \times 5 \times 5$ (100 out of 8,000), while in fact the odds are $4 \times 5 \times 1$ (20 out of 8,000).

The other device employed to entice players is a reward schedule, a concept familiar to students of behavioral psychology. Thus, machines pay off not only when the player hits a jackpot, but also when other combinations appear. Traditional slot machines vary the probability and size of reward. Smaller rewards, of course, are programmed to occur with greater frequency.

The state of Nevada does not require that payoff percentages be posted, or that they be above a certain minimum. The state requires only that the payoff schedule be conspicuously displayed — e.g., that 2 cherries and a bell pays off at 2 to 1 — and that the reel settings be recorded and available to state gaming control agents.

Nobody has systematically studied payoff percentages. It is commonly supposed that the more plush the casino, the higher the advantage in its slot machines. Thus, Strip casinos are generally believed to operate at around 15 to 20 percent house advantage, while downtown casinos will give the customer a lower disadvantage, operating at from 10 to 12 percent. However, state gaming agents who have examined payoff schedules tell me that the opposite is true: downtown casinos usually maintain higher house percentages, some as high as 35 percent. Whatever the percentage average for a particular casino, it will usually not operate all its machines at the same percentage. On the contrary, it will usually mix higher and lower payoff machines, often placing them side by side, one to attract customers, the other to maximize the take.

During the mid-1970s, traditional single-coin, three-reel machines were losing popularity to the more complex machines such as coin-multipliers and progressives. Coin-multipliers are machines in which players can deposit one to five coins of a designated denomination. Three rows of symbols are visible in such machines and payoffs can be made on any of the three rows as well as diagonally from left-to-right or right-to-left. Obviously, coin-multipliers are more efficient machines, since they take multiple rather than single coins, and therefore are more profitable.

Perhaps the most popular innovation in slot machines is the progressive, particularly the double progressive. A progressive machine has at least one, and sometimes two, jackpot payoffs that grow, usually at the factory-set rate of 10¢ for every dollar played in the machine. The jackpot payoffs are visible, and, as the payoff grows, the machine is constantly in operation. In 1978, a machine at Harold's Club finally paid off in excess of $200,000; and payoffs of $25,000 and $40,000 are not uncommon. Such "shallow play" machines, where the customers risk a few dollars in the hope of collecting thousands, are extremely popular. Uninitiated slot machine players may not, however, understand the machines, and will drop as much money into a machine yielding a jackpot of $120 as one offering $12,000.

The advantage of the double progressive for the house is this: The house can set different payoff schedules so that one progressive line can build up faster than the other. The player cannot select the higher payoff, but must play a few coins in the lower payoff line, for the opportunity to reach the higher one. Of course, the house never loses — except to slot cheats, a serious problem to be discussed later — and a machine that pays off $40,000 will likely have had at least $50,000 pressed into it by avid jackpot players. But the one who wins — ah! There is no thrill, I have been told, comparable to hitting a major jackpot.

This chapter and the preceding one have examined the casino mainly from the player's perspective, without yet focusing on controls. I have tried to suggest what players find attractive in the casino and to a degree to indicate how management arranges for players to find it so. One could also write a small book on casino-hotel management — even just on selecting and negotiating for casino entertainment. That is big business in Las Vegas. So is food, liquor, linens, towels, even cosmetics. All of this business must be thought through by management, down to the purchase of detergents for cleaning the hotel and casino floors.

But the gambling casino makes the Nevada hotel distinctive, not the swimming pools, or food, or hookers, or balladeers. These ordinary resort attractions can be found in Honolulu or Miami Beach; and while such attractions pose management problems in any resort hotel, it is the presence of a casino that makes the difference between an ordinary resort and a sensitive industry — one that demands special sorts of surveillance, both by management and by the state.

6

Controlling the Pit

WHATEVER THE CASINO REPRESENTS TO THE PLAYER, TO THE MANAGER it is a place of potential but uncertain profit. Despite the casino's "edge" in the gambling games, which to the outsider seems to insure a substantial return on investment, the casino is not a routinely moneymaking enterprise. The casino requires management combining seemingly inconsistent qualities: the easygoing warmth of the genial host with the analytical frigidity of the cost accountant.

Even the famed casino at Monte Carlo was once struggling to survive. Not until the mid-19th century, when Francois Blanc assumed leadership at the request of Prince Charles, did Monte Carlo become a legendary success story. Blanc was a man with lively entrepreneurial ideas. He built a railway line between Nice and Monaco, a new hotel, and to attract players lessened the bank's advantage at roulette by reducing the number of zeros from two to one — thus establishing what has since come to be known as European roulette. In addition, Blanc possessed other qualities needed for successful casino management: access to capital for expansion, an understanding of how to attract and cater to players, and the experience to set up internal casino controls to protect the casino's bankroll.[1] Assuming that a casino can draw players, it must also be able to withstand systematic and frequently ingenious attempts at theft, swindling, embezzlement, and numerous other ploys aimed at undermining the integrity and apparent solidity of the house percentage advantage in the casino games.[2]

It would perhaps be an overstatement, but not by all that much, to describe the business side of the casino as a totalitarian state where the citizens — the employees — enjoy few if any rights, and where the organization and location of activities is intended to maximize the possibilities of surveillance. The goal of casino management is total control. This aspiration is rarely achieved in practice, but the necessity for control is an axiom of the casino gambling industry, as well as the gaming control and law enforcement authorities. In this chapter and the next I shall describe the working relationship between the industry and the authorities, and shall point to instances where their interests diverge. From my point of view, the management of the casino eventually became more interesting than its obvious entertainments. Friends who knew I was undertaking this study would ask whether I spent much time gambling. And I replied, quite honestly, that I rarely played the games, because it was more diverting to watch the play standing behind the dealer than in front of him.

2

The elemental casino control measure is to introduce chips instead of currency at the gaming tables. Chips lend themselves, because of regularities of size and color, to being more readily and accurately observed. By introducing chips, the casino finds itself honoring two types of currency: those of sovereign governments such as the United States, plus its own.

In Nevada, casino managements and the Gaming Control Board have allowed the exchange of chips from casino to casino. With an appropriate nod to the concept of territoriality, chips from other casinos are labeled "foreign" chips. Casinos prefer not to accept many of these but they do as a courtesy to the customer and advantage to the casino owner. Were holders of foreign chips required to redeem them in the casino of distribution, the holder might decide to risk them at the foreign tables as well.

Casino chips are difficult to counterfeit — about as, or more difficult to counterfeit, I am told, than paper money. Operative chips are stored in a chip vault, a small separate room within the cage area, occupied by a vault cashier. Some casinos store a separate set of chips of different design elsewhere as a control measure. The casino manager will introduce these chips — unexpectedly — into the vault if he suspects substantial theft or counterfeiting of normal chips. The vault itself is a control measure designed to maintain the integrity of the main bank. The vault cashier never deals with the general public, only with the window cashiers and the casino departments — roulette, 21, keno, and so forth.

Gambling tables in major Nevada casinos are not arranged haphazardly. Rather, they are arranged in rows, back-to-back, so that supervisory personnel can observe several tables at once by standing or walking between them. For control purposes, every casino table is numbered so that responsible parties can be identified by game, table, and shift.

The in-between area is known as the "pit." The pit is the casino floor's action and control center. The reverse hierarchy of authority there is the dealer; the floorman, who will be responsible for two to four blackjack tables; the pit boss, who will be responsible for all the blackjack tables; the shift boss, who will be in charge of all the pits; and the casino manager, who will be responsible for the operation of the entire casino, but who usually concentrates attention on the casino games. Generally speaking, the higher the amount of money bet, the higher the level of authority attracted to observing the game. For example, two blackjack tables with $5 minimum bets will typically be assigned to one floorman; these may also draw the attention of the pit boss, if the size of the betting increases.

When a table loses it attracts surveillance; some pit bosses will change the dealer just to be on the safe side, even if they don't seriously believe that the dealer is cheating the house. People in the gambling business believe deeply in the house edge; they also believe deeply in fraud, especially when they can't figure out why the table is losing.

Some cheaters are actually as skillful as magicians. You can suspect that a trick is being played on you, even if you cannot figure out how it is being done. Probabilities and deception aside, some pit personnel also believe in luck, and will change dealers on that account. Dealers normally work for 40 minutes with 20-minute rest periods each hour. With reason. They work hard. Aside from standing nearly six hours a day, dealers are constantly being watched by higher-ranking pit personnel and are not supposed to make mistakes.

3

At the beginning of the shift the table will have begun with an empty drop box and an assortment of chips valued at a predetermined par, say, $15,000. Players may purchase chips at the cage, but characteristically they "buy" them at the gaming table. When a player buys, say, $500 worth of chips, the cash is immediately pushed into the drop box. A table wins or loses a certain amount for a given shift. The calculation involves various items — currency, cash, fill slips, credit slips — but for simplicity the win or loss is arrived at by calculating the difference between the dollar-equivalent amount begun with, on the table and in the drop box, and the dollar-equivalent amount at the end of the shift. The table count is made by incoming and outgoing shift bosses for each table, and the drop box contents are counted later in the count rooms.

Suppose a player begins betting $50 on each wager, using two $25 chips. Suppose he wins. The table may soon run low on $25 chips (which would in the vernacular be called "quarter checks" as $5 chips would be called "nickels" or "nickel checks"). So as to insure enough chips to continue the action the floorman will either call the cage or complete a fill requisition slip for a stated amount and chip denomination, say forty $25 chips amounting to $1,000.

The transfer of chips from cage to table or table to cage is a key control point in casino management and both the state authorities and the casinos have developed procedures to prevent theft. Two basic control mechanisms are employed. First, fill slips — noting the transfer — must be consecutively numbered and made out in triplicate. One copy remains in the machine at the cashier's cage, and is forwarded to the accounting department; one copy goes in the locked drop box, and one copy remains at the cage. In addition, many casinos keep a running count of fills, credit, and cash, and can offer fairly accurate records of how much each table is winning or losing at any given time.

Fill-slip procedures are designed to prevent mistakes or deception by cashiers and pit personnel. The three copies of the fill slip are reconciled by the accounting department, a precaution that effectively defeats embezzlement by a vault cashier. If there were not three copies, a cashier could raise the amount of the cage's copy of a fill slip from $500 to $1,500 and pocket the $1,000 difference. But with three copies, the accounting department should be able to catch the discrepancy. Assuming that there is no systematic conspiracy between cage and accounting personnel, no single employee can obtain access to all copies of the fill slip.

A more likely conspiracy would involve undermining the second control measure: the requirement that four signatures — cashier, runner (usually a security guard), floorman, and dealer or boxman — verify the amount of the fill. I've heard of several instances where the four signatories conspired to steal by the simple method of pocketing the difference between large sums signed for and small amounts delivered.

The idea behind the control measure is simple: the more people required in a conspiracy, the more difficult it is to engineer one. The control measure is an entirely sensible but scarcely thief-proof procedure. So an additional measure is in general use: further surveillance of fills. Most casinos maintain an "eye in the sky," a large overhead room permitting observation of each table from above through one-way mirrors to aid in detecting various kinds of cheating.

The basis of casino control is thus to be found in creating conditions of regularity and visibility. Regularity means simply that certain acts are always performed in certain ways. For example, dealers in blackjack games are not supposed to change the denomination of chips given to a player without permission of a floorman. The dealer is supposed to announce the color change and receive a floorman's nod before making change in the new denomination, which will of course be marked by a color change in the chips. The interaction takes place so quickly that most players are unaware that a control event is occurring. In fact, in a well-controlled casino, dealer moves are ritualized as much as possible, including the angle at which the cards are held in the hand while dealing, the order of collection of discards, the placing and spacing of chips when making change, and the pushing of currency into the drop box. Since it is difficult to impose regularity on handheld dealing, many clubs are turning to devices called "shoes" to insure honesty.

One part of a floorman's job, like that of an experienced police patrolman, is to observe deviations from normality. By an experienced patrolman, what we really mean is one who possesses an acutely developed sense of the normality of ordinary situations. Without such a sense, one is resistant to perceptions of the extraordinary. For example, an electric light burning to illuminate a room is a commonplace. But if the room is in a warehouse, the policeman must understand whether that commonplace event should be regarded as normal or extraordinary. When we acknowledge that a patrolman is experienced, we mean that he is capable of making such a distinction.

In gaming, dealing is ordinary, collecting discards is ordinary, exchanging chips for cash is ordinary. By programming the dealers' moves, casino management transforms the ordinary into the normal, and deviations from the norm are transformed into extraordinary events to be registered by the knowledgeable observer. So to be registered the events must be interpreted by someone who possesses a rather highly developed understanding of normal dealer and player behavior. I know of two casinos that employ former cheats in responsible management positions not only because they are aware of standard or well-known deviations from normality, e.g., dealing second cards or "flashing" or a whole universe of cheating ploys, but also because they presumably possess an acutely developed conception of normality and therefore of abnormality.

The ritualization of action — through programmed movements, color coding of chips, and so forth — contributes as well to other aspects of the pit or shift boss's responsibilities. For example, the pit boss is not only a policeman, but also a salesman promoting business. Suppose a player at a $5 minimum table is playing with $25 chips. Such a player warrants observation. He may be cheating or simply playing at high risk. Most likely, he is perfectly honest, and play is to be encouraged. An alert pit or shift boss will try to engage the player in conversation, ask his name, perhaps offer him a complimentary dinner, in the hope that the player will risk further money to recoup losses; and will do so at this club, rather than another. This is salesmanship.

The balance between salesmanship and control is, of course, difficult to strike. Even the most perceptive people seem more skilled at sales than at control. For control purposes several electronics firms have been attempting to develop devices to record every wager and every payoff. The idea of such a device is commonplace in sports betting. For example, a pari-mutuel system records and receipts every wager and every payoff. (Keno was once called horserace keno because the bettor received a slip akin to a pari-mutuel ticket. The difference is that the odds on a horse race are calculated according to the amount bet on various horses, with the track advantage and taxes figured in to produce the odds on a given horse, while keno odds remain constant.)

So far, no device has been devised to record every casino game wager. This means that control must depend upon the human eye, even when electronic viewing devices are employed, since these essentially merely permit the table to be viewed from a distance. The advantage of an electronic device is that its findings can be recorded and later studied. This feature offers the advantage of an impersonal record of impropriety, should it occur. If further control were to be introduced with a computer recording every wager and every error made at the table certain advantages would accrue, but also disadvantages.

The advantages are obvious. Employee stealing would be more easily detected, and the figure for the handle — the total amount wagered — would be available. At the same time, various taxing authorities would be sorely tempted to tax the handle, as it is taxed in horseracing, thus altering the entire existing odds and profit structure. Indeed, the Internal Revenue Service has for years maintained that the handle ought to be taxed, rather than gross gaming revenues, but nobody can figure out how to recount it accurately.

4

Lacking knowledge of the handle, casino managers concern themselves with three basic figures: the "drop," the "win," and the "hold." The drop — the contents of the drop box — consists of five items: currency placed in the box when a customer buys chips; fill slips, reporting chips received from the cage; foreign chips, exchanged for those of the local casino; "chip" credit slips, reporting chips returned to the cage; and "name" credit slips, reporting customer IOUs, given in exchange for chips. The drop is thus a measure of the amount customers are willing to risk at a particular table. But it is an imperfect measure: What of the customer who exchanges currency for chips, and plays the majority of those at a different table?

The win is a more exact measure. The win is a measure of the difference between the value of a table's bankroll at the beginning of a shift — this will be in chips — and the value of the contents of the drop box. The difference between the two constitutes gross gaming revenue.

While the win is an absolute figure, the hold is a percentage — sometimes it is called the win percentage. Recall that the handle — the total amount wagered on a given shift — is always unknown. Casinos are interested in knowing what percentage of that unknown wagering handle they actually are realizing or "holding." If that percentage fluctuates a great deal (particularly, I have noticed, if it diminishes), they worry. The win percentage is calculated by dividing the win for a shift by the drop. My own limited observations suggest that downtown casinos "hold" a greater percentage of the handle than Strip casinos, varying from a craps percentage of 24 to 16, on the average. There is no certain explanation for this difference. A plausible interpretation is: grind joints attract a less sophisticated population of gamblers, and so the operative odds are more favorable to the casino.

Whatever the experience of a given table at a given shift, the integrity of the contents of the drop box is critical for casino profits and state and federal taxes. Anytime the true contents of the drop box are altered, either through employee theft or owner manipulation, the entrepreneurial and legal control systems have been seriously impaired.

5

To prevent this, casino and state authorities rely once again upon the basic control mechanisms — multiple responsibility, visibility, and regularity. First, the drop boxes are supposed to be removed at specified times. Failure to do so violates gaming regulations. Gaming Control Board investigators whom I have accompanied are especially alert to this possible violation, probably because such a breach is so easily detectable. At the same time, it is relatively easily defended, and may portend nothing other than administrative inadequacy.

Drop boxes are locked securely to the tables, and are typically removed by a security guard who has signed out the key from the cage. All the transporting is required to be done in public, so as to maximize the opportunity of casino and Gaming Control Board agents to view the transfer.

The drop boxes are usually deposited within a "count room" in the cage, although one club maintains a glass-enclosed count room in the middle of the casino floor, both as a control measure and as an attraction to bring customers into the casino. The more usual count room, however, is in the cage area, with two corridors of visibility: a one-way mirror, and a closed circuit TV camera with videotape for playback.

The count room is where owner-skimming presumably used to occur. To prevent this, gaming regulations require that casinos with sizable revenues (exceeding $200,000 quarterly from pit games) employ a count team of at least three persons, independent in authority, and approved by the Gaming Control Board. Thus, the count team might consist of someone from hotel management, another from the business office, another from a restaurant. One casino I studied employs a count team entirely drawn from persons lacking gaming experience — a former schoolteacher, a former bank cashier, and a serviceman's wife who was trained for the job. The idea is that with all the controls possible — the videotape, the requirement that empty boxes be shown to the TV camera, and so forth — stealing is improbable; and is rendered even less likely by a counter's lack of prior association with casino gambling.

Whenever casino departments — craps, 21, roulette, keno — are counted down, their revenue is transferred to the cage, where its value is recorded on a bank control sheet. This document presumably should reflect the inventory and equal the cage cash count.

In major casinos, management is provided with a daily breakdown of the drop, win, and win percentages (holds) for each casino department. These can then be compared on a daily, monthly, and year-to-date basis to offer rough ideas of operating trends in the casino. These statistical controls provide another set of norms from which to interpret deviations. Should the trends in a particular department seem out of line, management can call for more detailed reports where departments are broken down by table, and by each shift, as to drop, win, and win percentage (hold) on a daily, monthly, and year-to-date basis. Deviations may generate additional surveillance, supervision, and auditing of records.

Perhaps the most sophisticated statistical controls are available to the slot machine and keno departments through the use of computers. For example, computer analysis makes possible detailed reports on the operation of every machine on the casino, with the capability of comparing the actual yield of the machine against theoretical yield in line with reel settings. If the variation is sizable, management is alerted to some flaw in the machine's operation, either through machine breakdown or cheating. Statistical controls never demonstrate the cause of variation, just its existence. Only observation and inference can point to causation.

6

If a casino is a house of games, it is also, especially in the larger casinos, a house of credit: in some ways like a bank, in other ways like a department store, and in still other ways, unique. Like a bank, casinos make loans to players; but like a merchandising establishment, casinos make loans only for a single purpose — to facilitate merchandising the product of the business.

Unlike department stores, casinos do not loan their customers money to buy merchandise; they loan money to play casino games. Nor do casino banks charge interest. Indeed, one cheating arrangement introduced by a couple of high-credit roulette players was to pretend they did not know each other, with a prior arrangement to play red against black. Since they seemed each to be using the loan properly — to play the game — they at first aroused little suspicion. At the end of the weekend, they would cash in, at a slight loss determined by the casino advantage. It turned out that the loss, based on a casino advantage of 5.26 percent, was less than these businessmen would have had to put out for short-term loans of $20,000 at prevailing high interest rates. Eventually they were discovered.

Casinos share three problems with other lenders: one is determining the criteria to be employed to justify the loan decision; the second is to insure that the money loaned will be employed as intended, i.e., to play casino games legitimately; and the third is collecting on loans, a problem made somewhat more difficult — but not exceedingly so — by the fact that gambling debts are at common law and even in the state of Nevada, treated as unenforceable. The stigma associated with gaming thus shows itself even in the state of Nevada.

But the legal strictures on the collection of gaming debts are not as consequential as they might seem offhand, although they are not meaningless either. As with banks and department stores, debt collection is related to credit judgment, and every lender strongly prefers to make credit judgments that avoid collection problems. Even those who make illegal loans at high and unregulated interest rates — "loan sharks" — must, contrary to most gangland novels, prefer the painless collection of principal and interest to breaking arms and legs. How much, after all, is a debtor's broken leg worth to a creditor, even to a "loan shark"?

Gaming casinos do not encourage bad debts, and make every effort to avoid them. Such debts can arise from two sources: bad checks and overextensions of credit. Suppose a customer wants to cash a check at a cage? One way, the simplest, is through recognition and sponsorship. The customer who knows a casino executive will encounter no problems. Gaming casinos are, comparatively speaking, a model of organizational controls with a minimum of red tape, even on larger credit decisions. Accountability is not to form but to substance, and personal knowledge is sufficient to justify decision.

But suppose the customer lacks personal acquaintanceship with casino personnel? The first question asked by a cashier — "Do you have credit here?" — really means, "Do we know you? Are we experienced with you?" The customer who answers negatively will be asked to fill out a check-cashing application, the most severe formality ever required of a casino customer. If the customer answers affirmatively, the cashier scans the customer's check-cashing record, seeking out deviations from check-writing norms. Customers normally write checks for roughly the same amount, and within their limit.

A progression pattern is one of the commonest indications of suspect customer motivation. One who writes increasingly larger checks may have been attempting either to defraud the casino by establishing credit for the purpose of writing a large unsecured check and walking away with the cash; or, impulsively, to write an unsecured check in the hope of clearing prior gambling losses. If the check-cashing pattern appears sound, the cashier must initial the check; uninitialed checks are unaccountable and permit dishonest cashiers to slip in bad checks and pocket the cash.

Casinos are more careful about cashing checks for new customers than for old ones. Old customers may be as likely as new to cash bad checks but, the reasoning goes, the casino has made a profit on the old customer; the new customer's check is being drawn on casino bankroll.

A new customer who asks to cash a check must present a credit document, plus identification (usually a driver's license), plus information on the application form. The information will be telephoned to Central Credit, Inc., a private check-cashing agency maintaining up-to-date information on customer check cashing in subscribing casinos in Nevada and in foreign countries. Central Credit compiles information on the customer's date of birth, physical characteristics, driver's license number, and residential address. It also maintains records on any derogatory check-cashing information as well as on bank addresses and reports, highest and last action, application dates, amounts requested, and limits granted.

Unless derogatory information is found, a casino usually will cash a customer's first check. If it doesn't, and is a subscriber to Central Credit, it is obliged to reveal why, since its derogatory information might prove useful to other casinos faced with the same question. Perhaps Central Credit's most important capability is in preventing thieves and forgers from negotiating sizable quantities of checks. Armed, for example, with the latest reports on all lost and stolen traveler's checks, Central Credit will be alerted whenever an individual makes consecutive attempts to cash traveler's checks in several casinos. When Central Credit picks up such a pattern, it notifies the police to pick up the check-casher — a process which has pinpointed scores of thieves attempting to pass lost, forged, or stolen paper.

7

Presumably, a check does not constitute credit, since it is backed up by cash in the bank; and where large sums are concerned, casinos will telephone banks to determine whether that is true. From the point of view of a casino, whether or not a check is good is a simple issue. Casinos would have relatively little difficulty in protecting themselves against bad checks or even bad credit risks. The more complex and realistic issue is how to develop a credit strategy that minimizes noncollectibility, while maximizing action on the tables. Too tight a credit policy will result in a reduction of play, while too loose a policy will result in an unprofitable rate of uncollectable debts.

Collectibility is only partly related to the legal status of gambling debts. At common law, gambling debts were legally unenforceable, and so they remain in the state of Nevada. When promissory notes are contested, the issue is whether the loan actually was made for the purpose of gambling. In the ordinary transaction, where a gambling house accepts a promissory note to enable the maker of the note to gamble, the note is unenforceable. It is possible, and does happen, that a customer will sign a marker or cash a check, and then on returning home refuse to pay or stop payment on the check.

Practically speaking, should the holder of the note sue — and the holder will in time be a collection agent — all the writer of the note need testify in a court is that he or she cashed the check; received money for the check; turned right around, bought chips and gambled them away at the tables. If testimony proves that the debt incurred was a gambling debt, the writer of the note or check bears no liability in Nevada or in other states of the Union. This is not true in Puerto Rico; or in England, where gambling debts are collectable, almost as *quid pro quo* in return for other restrictions placed upon the casinos.[3]

The Nevada legislature could have made gambling debts legal, but has never done so. The gaming industry itself is split on the issue — a split particularly evident between that portion of the industry in northern Nevada which favors the present restrictions; and that portion of the Las Vegas branch of the industry which opposes such restrictions. Those who oppose maintaining present restrictions feel that it is inconsistent to legalize gambling but not gambling debts; and that if the state of Nevada does not recognize gaming debts, it should not expect other states to do so.

Those who favor the *status quo* recognize these arguments, but are not persuaded by them, resting their opposition to change mainly on two grounds. First is the ever-present issue of Nevada's national image. They fear the consequences of the publicity surrounding casino owners and collectors who will go hard after a man in his home state. Successful casinos, they argue, do bear well the burden of making credit judgments. It will be mainly marginal operators who will need to resort to the courts; and when they do, it will create the impression that Nevada is a place for losers. Such tactics, they fear, will in the long run reduce revenue.

They also recognize that the change in Nevada's laws would only marginally influence other states. California courts, for example, might not enforce gaming debts contracted in Nevada, no matter what the change in Nevada statutes, and the gaming business depends upon out-of-state residents for the overwhelming majority of the annual handle.

Still, the granting of credit in a casino is complicated by the nonenforceability of gambling debts and renders casino credit judgments more subtle than those occurring in virtually any other lending agency. One can scarcely imagine a bank lending $5,000 without security; or a merchandising establishment or automobile dealer loaning the money to purchase the automobile without the purchase object serving as security. Yet casinos comfortably loan gamblers money to attempt to beat the casino, confident that, given enough play, the money eventually will revert to the casino.

Besides, the casino maintains other controls on credit. A player who enjoys a $5,000 line of credit will not be given $5,000 in cash. Ordinarily, the credit is offered in bits and pieces at the table. A player is given $500 or $1,000 at a time, in chips. A main job of a pit boss at a major casino is observing that the credit player actually plays with the chips and does not cash these in. "Walking" with chips is a classic form of credit cheating — although on busy nights pit executives find it difficult to observe players who roam. Players are entitled to change crap tables or to move to 21 tables and the credit action in the pit can be so time-consuming that the pit personnel may lose track of the player's gaming action.

It is not at all unusual for a player to make six or eight credit transactions in an evening of betting, paying off debts after winning, borrowing after losing. This sort of "credit action" involves club personnel in some pretty fast bookkeeping: recording markers, tearing them up, keeping up to date a running sheet on the players' credit, plus keeping track — again with appropriate documentation — of the transfer of chips back and forth from the cage, as well as of the transfer of the promissory notes. On busy nights, pit personnel are scarcely able to observe betting action as markers are written, recorded, called back, destroyed. So-called premium-player business is largely a credit business and the size of individual tabs at a hot craps table can fluctuate with astonishing rapidity.

No hard figures exist on the percentage collectability of gambling debts. During the course of my field work I was often told that the industry average on bad debts ranges from two to four percent, figures which seemed to portray gambling debtors as models of fiscal responsibility. Additional inquiries revealed the figure to be correct but misleading. It is based upon *all* markers written and then paid. But recall that most markers are paid directly at the gaming tables: gamblers are expected to pay off debts with the chips they win.

One casino executive with more than 20 years' experience felt that the only true baseline for interpreting debt was "departure credit." Here the question would be: "What percentage of markers remain unpaid of those held after the player has left the casino?" These figures are not computed, but they would be much higher, more like 25 to 50 percent. Generally, the older the marker, the less likely it will be paid. Several casinos regard markers older than one year as uncollectable — which doesn't necessarily mean they don't keep trying. Moreover, casinos pay taxes only on cash collected, not on the basis of accrued "receivables," an accounting term that is precisely ambiguous since it refers — in the gambling business — to a legally unenforceable debt and does not suggest the actual probability of receiving. Since the success or failure of a gaming establishment may well depend upon collectability rather than receivability, this is no small matter.

8

Although smaller casinos do not offer as much in the way of credit as the larger Las Vegas casinos, they do not necessarily experience fewer control problems. Effective casino control seems inversely correlated with size. The smaller the casino, it appears, the more difficult it is to control. Managers of small casinos usually do not possess the skills of managers of large ones; a dealer who wants to cheat customers is more likely to escape knowledgeable surveillance in a small casino. Small casinos also tend to lack sophisticated electronic controls, and the pinpointing of problems provided by computer analysis. A large casino ultimately relies upon a system of relatively independent checks to provide balance. Size tends to generate bureaucracy, which engenders regularity, consistency, and a sharper vision of deviation, as well as the experience to employ that vision. Besides, small casinos simply do not generate enough revenue to attract the concentrated attention of state control authorities. That does happen occasionally, but not with the regularity the state authorities would prefer. Small, in a casino, is not beautiful.

7

Controlling Premium Play

THE MAJOR LAS VEGAS HOTEL SHOWROOMS PRESENT MORE, AND MORE expensive, live entertainment than those of any resort in the world. Nevertheless, the cabarets and the legendary entertainers are not an end in themselves, as they might well be elsewhere. From the perspective of casino management, this major entertainment industry exists solely to promote action at the gaming tables and slot machines. The entertainers themselves are pleased to perform in Las Vegas, for its audiences are sophisticates who seem to enjoy special rapport, especially with old favorites like Dean Martin, Frank Sinatra, Sammy Davis: show-biz personalities whose lifestyles reflect an affinity with the gambling resort, and particularly its *premium* customers.

Such customers are induced to gamble, either as individuals, or as part of a group. A player will be offered — in addition to thousands of dollars worth of credit — airfare, complimentary room, beverages, and entertainment for several days, provided that he, and it usually is a he, risks a sufficient amount of money to justify the cost, usually a minimum of $5,000. Those on "junkets" will be offered much the same set package of "comps," with one exception. The junket is a charter operation, occupying either an entire airplane or a portion of it, resulting in a lesser expense for the sponsoring hotels. Both individual premium business and junket business are based on credit extensions, although such extensions are usually higher when individuals are involved. In any event, premium play poses a special set of control problems for both management and the state which I shall begin to explain in this chapter, and will examine further in later chapters, especially those concerned with the Gaming Control Board's Audit Division.

The premium gambler is usually offered credit and complimentaries by a casino executive, often called a "host," who makes the decision. Casino hosts also take care of their customers, obtaining premium tables at the best shows, reservations at the best restaurants, a choice of rooms, and so forth. Many are former sports or gambling figures, with wide connections among high rollers. So it it no surprise that premium players often extend their loyalty to a host rather than to a particular casino; if a popular host moves from the Tropicana to Caesars Palace, so may a lot of players.

One of the most delicate issues in the casino business is responsibility for collecting debts for credit extended by the host. Usually, primary responsibility lies with the casino's collection department, but hosts will aid in credit collections, either by telephoning "their people," or by taking airplane trips around the country. Hosts are characteristically affable and outgoing — warm personalities. They will ask the player who has been tardy in payment not to embarrass them — not to damage their credibility as credit offerers, and their integrity as credit collectors. It is, however, possible that the player who doesn't pay might be in league with the host to defraud the casino. And sometimes hosts can discourage payment for other motives. One major casino, in financial trouble, became even more deeply troubled when hosts and hostesses — figuring that they would be seeking affiliation with other casinos — began discreetly to suggest to their players that they might take their gambling debts less than seriously.

Complimentaries offered by hosts can and do pose a problem for casino profits, but not for state taxes. The state of Nevada has introduced a sensible system of business taxation that might usefully be adopted for federal income taxation. The state taxes gross gaming revenue, not net profits. As a result, the state evidences no direct interest in complimentaries, although it is continually influenced by the indirect interest of maintaining the profitability of the industry. A major casino will give away complimentaries of $10 to $20 million annually and the size of the complimentaries can seriously affect net profits.

A casino executive can give away extensive complimentaries, for example, inviting a player's wife to join the player on his trip and enjoy complimentary room, food, and beverages; but state law forbids returning unpaid markers without reporting the existence of these markers to state authorities, and explaining why these have not been paid. When the casino can prove — as it often can — that the player actually refused to pay, no tax is levied. But if the casino makes a business judgment to settle the face amount for less, it must pay Nevada gaming taxes on the entire amount (but not federal taxes based upon net income). The state authorities regard such "settlements" as promotional items, akin to complimentary room, food, and beverage, since at least a major part of the casino's motivation for settling a gaming debt is to promote the good will of the player, who presumably will be more likely to gamble in this casino rather than another. This is one area where state and management interests diverge.

One illustration: A top executive of a major club told me that he was having a discussion in one of his restaurants with the chairman of the Gaming Control Board. An Asian woman, who was a major premium player, offered to settle her account of close to $250,000 with $200,000 in cash, which she would deliver immediately. He said that, as a business judgment, he decided to accept the cash, partly because $200,000 in payment is preferable to $250,000 in markers when a club is currently holding more than $30 million in markers; partly because the woman was very rich and not the world's most skillful gambler. If she thought she was getting a "bargain" she would continue to play at his club rather than at its surrounding competitors. In the long run, he felt, her good will would more than pay off the difference. The Gaming Control Board chairman, he said, did not disagree with his business judgment, but pointed out to him what they both knew: that the Nevada legislature requires the payment of taxes on gross, not net, gaming revenues. The chairman, he said, conceded that the legislative enactment might not be altogether wise; but as long as it remained he was required to enforce it.

This story illustrates what might be considered a legitimate question about tax policy: whether the state should tax gross gaming revenues when these are actually unrealized. The other side of the argument is that other executives might take advantage of their positions and "settle" gaming debts for friends and others — perhaps organized crime elements whom they owe a courtesy — in the name of good business practice. The question of a payoff to so-called organized crime elements aside for the moment, the following case, taken from Gaming Control Board files — with names disguised — illustrates the problem of controlling "settlements" in the gambling industry from the point of view of the interests of minority stockholders in gaming casinos, and the state of Nevada.

2

On a spring evening in the 1970s at approximately 3 A.M., Bill Friedlander, a hotel owner, arrived at the blackjack pit accompanied by Mel Samuels. Samuels was a long-term friend of Friedlander, enjoyed strong political connections, and headed a sizable bank from which Friedlander had hopes of borrowing money.

Shortly after Friedlander arrived at the blackjack pit, Samuels began to play. Friedlander remained at the blackjack table during most of Samuels's play. Both were drinking heavily and were, in the shift boss's judgment, "plastered." The shift boss stated that because of Samuels's inebriated state, he would have terminated Samuels's play had he not felt that such a move would have angered Friedlander.

Samuels played with cash until 3:30 A.M., when he requested credit and Friedlander responded by instructing the shift boss to give Samuels "anything he wants." Credit was then extended by the pit boss and continued until Samuels passed out at the table at approximately 7:00 A.M. By that time Samuels had accumulated markers totaling $104,000. Either during Samuels's play or when he finished, Friedlander instructed the shift boss not to record

Samuels's $104,000 credit play either on the table card or the pit master credit record. In addition, when Samuels's play was concluded, Friedlander told the shift boss to remove the marker buttons that evidenced the $104,000 in credit extended to Samuels. When the buttons were removed, the pit boss, conforming with the standard control procedures, routinely proceeded to fill out a marker slip.

Before he completed the marker, the pit boss was told by Friedlander to "forget it" and that he, Friedlander, would take care of it. The pit boss accordingly voided the marker.

The casino manager learned of the casino's failure to record Samuels's credit play. He told Friedlander that a marker and related table and pit card entries had to be recorded and that if such entries were not made, Friedlander would be guilty of "skimming." Friedlander told the casino manager to see that all the appropriate entries were made to record Samuels's play. The manager returned to the casino and instructed the day shift boss to fill out a marker for Mr. Samuels in the amount of $104,000 and to make the appropriate entries in the pit and credit records. This was done.

Nevertheless, the Friedlander-Samuels transaction was clearly in violation of gaming regulations, since some 12 hours had elapsed from the time the credit play was initiated and some 8 hours from the time that play was concluded before any entry was made on the pit master and table cards. The combined irregularities of failure to make timely recording of the individual transactions when the credit was extended, removal of the credit buttons from the table without having first received appropriate credit slips, and subsequent mishandling of the markers suggested that Friedlander intended to violate the spirit as well as the letter of Gaming Control Board regulations stipulating regular handling of all credit transactions.

In this instance, the "boss" was caught, but only because gaming authorities had access to a casino employee informant, who reported Friedlander's conduct to the Gaming Control Board. Otherwise, Friedlander's conduct would not have been uncovered. The authorities warned Friedlander about his actions and assessed him for the taxes on the $104,000. Here, Friedlander's conduct illustrates what might be called a "friendly skim" on the part of the casino owner who was evidently not deliberately intending to defraud the state. His primary motive was to do a favor to someone who could contribute to other business enterprises. But Nevada authorities do not intend the casino to be used instrumentally. Still, the authorities are not that well served by informants; it is rare to catch an equity holder.

3

Of all the casino operations, the junket is the most precarious. It involves extension of credit outside of Nevada and therefore occurs beyond the purview of gaming authorities. Junkets are put together by "junket masters" who may be casino employees earning annual salaries comparable to those of top executives — upwards of $100,000 annually — or individuals who receive a certain amount per player whom they bring to Nevada, usually from $50 to $100. Moreover, junket representatives do not undergo the same licensing procedures involved in reviewing the suitability of key owners or casino employees.

Junket representatives are not totally unregulated: they are required to submit a personal history record and fingerprints to the Gaming Control Board. But compared to investigations of key owners and key employees (later to be explored in detail) those of junket representatives are relatively superficial. Since there are hundreds of such representatives — usually between 600 and 700 operate in any given year — the Gaming Control Board appears to possess neither the resources nor the information for licensing junket representatives. Instead, after a cursory investigation, the board will send a very carefully worded letter to the hotel that proposes a junket representative. The letter includes the following statement: "We have completed our investigation of Mr. X and we find no objection to him as a junket representative." The theory behind this, which works to a degree in practice, is simple. As one member of the board told me: "This way we still have the chain and if we need to, we can jerk it."

Nevertheless, it must be repeated that the junket representative works beyond the purview of the gaming authorities. One Miami junket representative, who was found unsuitable because of an alleged association with underworld figure Meyer Lansky, was defended before the board as follows: ". . . a junket representative," his attorney argued, "is a person whose job is to get people out here . . . high rollers, high players. You don't run into them in church and you don't run into them by going into the bank or law office or something. You find them by going to the places where those people frequent, which is at the race track, at the jai alai, at other places in Miami. Now surely he's going to run into some people who might be unsavory characters there."[1]

Occasionally, the characters who populate junkets, as well as the junket representatives, can be unsavory indeed. In Las Vegas, the term unsavory (or any comparable epithet) is obviously not intended for people who gamble, or drink, or who are hedonistically inclined. Moreover, the word changes its meaning depending upon context. In the licensing context, the term would ordinarily suggest someone who has a criminal record or associates with allegedly criminal figures. In the casino management context, such associations would be relevant to players only if it was believed the player was contemplating or had engaged in criminal activities directed against the casino. Otherwise, the only relevant question would be the quality of the player's "action," particularly in the context of junket participation.

Players are actually graded from A to F, depending upon their patterns of gambling. Of course, just as the criteria for grading by college professors are variable, so too is the grading of gamblers' play. Roughly speaking, an A player is one who spends a number of hours at the gaming tables and who makes minimum bets of $10 to $25. (Inflation might raise that figure.)

Casino executives entertain no objection to a player who wins making such bets. They are, however, uneasy about certain patterns of play. Someone, for example, who doubles bets when winning and rolls ten straight passes can walk away with a sizable chunk of money. That sort of player will likely lose the money back eventually, but not necessarily in the same casino. Paradoxically, from the house point of view, the most desirable player is the cautious one; who bets a steady amount of money and pockets winnings. Such a player cannot beat the house too badly.

Junkets are evaluated not only according to the play of the

individual gambler, but also of the group. There is a continual interchange of information between junket representatives and casino executives over both individuals and groups. For example, regarding an individual, there is always a wariness of overextension of credit to those who become deeply involved in play. "What makes credit policy so interesting," explained one of the more knowledgeable junket executives, "is that there is a point in everybody's mind beyond which they cannot assimilate different amounts of money. Take a man, for instance, who has consistently been given $2,000 worth of credit. All of a sudden, he comes to us and says, I want $4,000. Suppose we give it to him and he loses and he goes home and now he owes $4,000 instead of $2,000. He doesn't necessarily stop to think, OK, now I won't go to Vegas for twice as long. All he knows is that he owes more money than he can handle emotionally.

"Besides, people come here usually on junkets as part of a social group. Suppose somebody is at a point where he owes more money than he can pay, say $20,000 or $30,000. He is a man with a lot of influence in his social sphere. When his group gets together and starts talking about what they are going to do for the New Year, he's not going to suggest coming to this hotel. He'll either say, let's go to another hotel down the strip where he doesn't owe anything; or he'll suggest going to Palm Springs or to Miami Beach. So when we overextend credit we not only lose his business but we also lose the business of six or eight people around him, which in the aggregate can result in the loss of $50,000 or $60,000. Our job is to understand, through financial records and through word of mouth, who can handle what size of loss."

In this way and in others, the individual player becomes defined as part of a social group and as part of a junket. On some occasions, where 100 or so individuals are brought out on a junket, the house really doesn't care how most of them gamble, provided that five or six are really first-rate risk-takers. Some casinos have given up on junkets entirely, preferring to cater only to those five or six and to leave the rest at home.

At the same time, junkets provide a party-like atmosphere that brings many people to Las Vegas who might not otherwise come. There is an obvious reassurance in numbers of people undertaking any activity. Those who ski, for example, often find that they are able to muster the courage to ski more difficult slopes when accompanied by six or eight other people. Psychology is replete with experimental examples of the effects of group pressure upon perception and behavior, and the junket is no exception to these pressures. If anything, this sort of group activity demonstrates once again how effectively group pressures can operate to reinforce ambivalent feelings and motives.

But because of the physical distance of junket organization from Las Vegas — a major hotel with a major junket program might have as many as 20 to 25 junket representatives in the field — junkets are a continual source of anxiety and of problems of control to both management and the gaming authorities. In any situation where credit is systematically offered, the possibilities of genuine theft always exist. The following case, drawn from Gaming Control Board records with appropriate disguises, is not typical of junket operations but is typical of the control problems involved in the extension of credit on junkets. This, then, is a case of a characteristically structured deception — employing imposters — although deceptions are not characteristic of junket operations. If they were, the casinos would close.

4

This kind of scam, as with most, requires the collusion of casino executives, who pretend not to notice the imposters. If owners are not involved, they are victims and the executives are embezzlers. If owners are involved, they are conspirators in a skimming scheme. When any agent of the casino is involved in a theft of gaming revenue, or an embezzlement of gaming revenue, the casino remains responsible for the payment of taxes on that revenue.

The discovery in this case was made during an audit in 1974, but the actual junket took place in late 1972. Sixty-three people were on the junket, of whom 43 obtained credit totaling $284,500. As a result of the audit, "confirmation" letters were sent to many casino customers asking that they confirm the marker balances on the date of the junket in 1972. Those to whom the letters were sent denied having been in Las Vegas on that day, or having signed the markers in that particular hotel.

What had happened? A person whom I shall call "Carlo Ianni" had been able to secure, evidently by theft, a list of persons scheduled to come out on a junket with a long-standing and legitimate junket representative and had used that list to arrange a phony junket. One of the phony junketeers was later arrested and told Clark County police the following story of the organization of the junket. I shall call the phony junketeer "Don Kautsky."

Kautsky came from Buffalo, New York to stay with his cousin Ann in California. Arrangements had been made to fly Kautsky and another man, known to him only as "Bud," to Las Vegas. Ianni told Kautsky he had arranged for him and Bud to go into the "El Greco" Hotel as members of a junket. They were to receive credentials of previously established players, whom they were to impersonate. The persons they were to impersonate had already been cleared for various amounts of credit and the impersonators were to be given 10 percent of whatever portion of those credit amounts they could "take off." For example, Kautsky was to impersonate Sid Minsky, who had established a $5,000 line of credit previously in other local casinos.

The operation was arranged for late August 1971, and, according to Kautsky, the entire junket with only two or three exceptions contained phony junketeers. The audit evidence showed that there were only three legitimate write-offs on this junket out of approximately 50 people.

Kautsky was flown to Las Vegas where he was met at the El Greco and, with about 10 others, was ushered into a suite in the rear of the hotel. Here Kautsky and his group were introduced to a man known only as "Al" and were briefed as to the arrangements and to the plan. Every junketeer was handed a credit application that had been previously filled out by the legitimate person they were to impersonate. The imposters were instructed to memorize as much information as possible as contained on the card. They were also instructed to fill out a duplicate card using the name of the established player.

The imposters were then given other identification to assist in establishing their identity. (There is an important control point to be noted here. Ordinarily, on a junket, identification cards are employed, but in addition if there is any question as to who the person asking for credit really is, the junket master is called in physically to identify the person requesting credit. In this case, of course, the junket master was heading the deception.)

The imposters were also told to be difficult to deal with, to insist on the best of service, and to try to resemble a well-to-do or a good-playing difficult customer. They were also advised to drink very little and to play, but to keep their actual play to a minimum.

Kautsky said that he became very nervous, took his 10 percent share, and left Las Vegas. He took a cab to the airport and a plane back to California. But he also took with him, when he left Las Vegas, the legitimate credit application and the driver's license he had been given by Al at the El Greco.

Sometime later, he was located in California by one of the initiators of the phony junket in a bar. This man took Kautsky outside and gave him a severe physical beating. He then took the driver's license away, but never took the original credit application, which was still in Kautsky's possession when Kautsky was arrested by the police. When the beating was administered, Kautsky says he was told: "There was once a guy named Benny who had tried the same thing you did and is probably dead in the desert by now." Kautsky became terribly frightened and left his residence in California immediately.

Such imposter schemes have been accomplished a number of times since in Nevada. Once qualified as a junket representative, with the loose qualifications that implies, a con man is in a position to swindle a hotel for several hundred thousand dollars, provided that he possesses either the active collusion or the nurtured indifference of one or more casino executives. Accordingly, hotels running major junket programs try to be very careful in their selection of junket representatives. Since a busy junket representative can earn upwards of $100,000 a year, he is not likely to turn to fraud as a way of making a quick killing.

Still, two other kinds of actual cases reveal the problems of controlling junkets. One involved Caesars Palace in a widely publicized case in 1975; and another involved hotels running junkets out of Hawaii with established junket representatives.

In July 1975, the Tokyo District Public Prosecutors Office charged three persons who had organized gambling tours to Las Vegas with extortion and attempted extortion. According to the prosecutor's office, these three persons had organized "casino tours" on six occasions between September 1973 and January 1975, in which a total of 83 persons participated. Of those who took part in the gambling tours, 40 persons lost an estimated $1½ million. Two of the losers, Japanese businessmen, complained to the police that their lives had been threatened for failure to make good their Las Vegas markers. The Gaming Control Board dispatched two investigators to Tokyo to review this situation. They were given little cooperation by Japanese authorities, who refused to permit any examination of the original documents, because the documents were being held as evidence for trial. In general, this situation occurred at about the same time as the film *The Godfather* was being run in Japan, and from the point of view of the Japanese the entire affair appeared to have been engineered by organized crime interests.

The agents, who had already done considerable investigation in Las Vegas, were convinced that the hotel — Caesars Palace — which had commissioned the junkets had had no idea that this was to be the method used to collect the markers. The organizer of the junket was actually a Japanese film producer who had met the president of the Las Vegas hotel when he had gone to Japan to begin to stimulate business. The president of the hotel had thrown a party for people whose names he had learned from a variety of sources, including major entertainers who work in Nevada. It was the producer's idea, he told the gaming authorities, not his own, to employ these men as collectors, and he himself would never have sanctioned the use of physical threats.

His story seemed believable. From the point of view of the casino it would be far more desirable to write off hundreds of thousands of dollars in markers rather than to discourage an emerging program of Asian junkets, particularly Japanese junkets. Still, he did not have to know what sort of methods were being used to make collections in Japan, precisely because junket operators work at such a considerable distance from the home casino. Thus, casino operators can remain untainted by any implication that they employ intimidating collection methods, while remote agents, literally unknown to them, do employ such methods.

5

Junkets to Las Vegas have been, in Hawaii, the basis of considerable gangland activity. For example, on February 13, 1970, the body of a man I shall call "Harry Monari" was found strangled in the trunk of a car on a downtown Honolulu street. Monari had worked on a commission basis at a Honolulu travel agency where he was a sales representative. In that capacity, he had organized numerous gambling junkets into Nevada during several preceding years. Monari's death was one of a series of underworld-related killings which had occurred in Hawaii up to that time. There was in Hawaii extensive publicity surrounding the Monari murder and this publicity resulted in a temporary suspension of all Hawaiian junkets by Nevada authorities. Once the publicity faded, however, normal junket activity from the Hawaiian Islands was permitted to resume.

According to the Hawaiian police, the Monari murder was carried out in gangland style. The intelligence information of the police in Hawaii suggested there had always been extensive gambling activity in the islands, but not until the early 1960s did word filter back to the authorities about "juice payments," i.e., tribute paid by gamblers to various underworld figures. Gamblers, bookmakers, lottery managers, and cockfight operators were all considered fair game for strongarm extortionists.

The gamblers retaliated by hiring their own bodyguards. During the 1960s a power struggle resulted in shakedowns, threats, shootings, and bombings. One former lottery operator seemed to emerge from the violence as the first real gangland boss of the islands, and one of his lieutenants became known as the chief enforcer and strongarm operator.

When the junket business into Nevada began around 1967, those who ran junkets were required to pay extortion, a dollar or two for each person they took to Nevada on a junket. In effect, then, if the junket representative was receiving $50 to $100 per person the extortionist was obtaining a small but significant percentage of the take. Eventually, the Nevada authorities called the junket representatives in for a hearing.

Although most reluctant to testify, several finally did admit that extortion was occurring. One, in particular, expressed anger at the extortionists and gave a great deal of evidence. Less than two years later he was found dead in his automobile in the garage of his girl friend's home, presumably a suicide. Whether he had actually committed suicide or, as his girl friend testified, was driven to death by depression resulting from continued harassment, seems almost a moot question.

Both the Japanese and Hawaiian junket ventures suggest how distance from control authorities, casino managers as well as legal authorities, undermines the possibilities of control. As we shall see later in some detail, the casinos are audited and their practices watched rather carefully. At a certain point, however, when the actors become remote enough, there is scant possibility of control. For example, there must be numerous instances where gamblers who have participated in junkets have borrowed from loan sharks to pay their gambling debts.[2] The loan sharks can use force or the threat of force to collect the debts, and neither the casinos nor the gaming authorities need be any the wiser.

6

The basic problem of casino management, as it is of many recreational and service businesses such as tennis camps, ski resorts, and restaurants, is to maintain controls over expenditures and vulnerabilities without diminishing the hedonistic attractions that draw a clientele. But if casinos perhaps enjoy an advantage in displaying a rare talent for promoting pleasure — even better, for making sin acceptable — they also offer a rare opportunity for guile and deception. The previous chapter and this one have attempted to portray some of these opportunities and the measures taken to protect against them by both casino management and gaming authorities.

Gaming authorities rely on casino management to promote business, even though the authorities themselves maintain a steady and acknowledged interest in the amount of business generated. The success of the agency is not measured directly by the amount of gaming revenue generated by all casinos or even by one casino. There is no legislative statement defining the pecuniary involvement of the gaming authorities with the casino, but such an involvement is obvious from the fact that the state derives a sizable percentage of gross gaming revenue, which in turn provides an even more sizable percentage of the state budget. The state is, in effect, a partner in all gaming enterprises and state officials sometimes act like real business partners, suggesting ways of improving profits and actually being pleased when casinos are crowded, fretful when they are not. As the Nevada Gaming Control Commission chairman said in 1975: "Conceptually . . . it is the people of the state of Nevada that are in the gaming business. These people are simply our licensees."[3]

Moreover, the gaming authorities and casino managers and owners share a common interest in the exercise of controls over business operations and promotion. Business volume is a necessary but not sufficient condition for business success. Volume must be tempered by control in order to produce both gross receipts and net profit. So both state authorities and gaming managers share a mutual interest in developing control systems based on regularity, visibility and statistical probability.

But the interests of owners and the state are not necessarily identical. The owner seeks to maximize the profitability of a particular casino or group of them, while the state tries to maximize the interests of the industry, within a framework that may far transcend those of individual owners. To take a single example: It would be in the interests of an owner to "skim" a portion of gross gaming receipts, to shelter these from the tax claims of both state and federal government. So the question is not whether the state involves itself in casino management, but how it involves itself. To understand the character of the state's involvement requires some review of the history of legalized gambling in Nevada, an even closer look at the rise of state control, and a very close look at the day-to-day administration of these controls. The rest of the book will undertake to explore these topics.

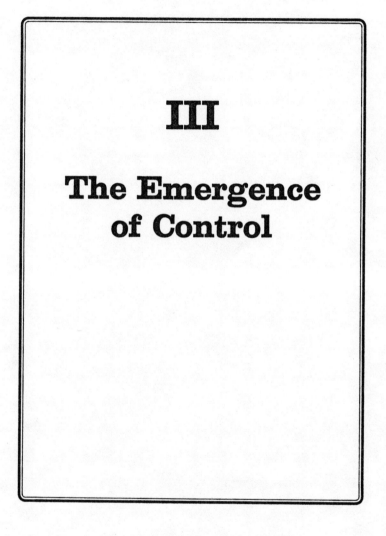

III

The Emergence
of Control

8

The Rise
of a Pariah Industry*

It isn't a very laudable position for one to have to defend gambling. One doesn't feel very lofty when his feet are resting on the argument that gambling must prevail in the State that he represents. The rest of the world looks upon him with disdain. . . .

—SENATOR PAT McCARRAN, *personal letter to a Reno publisher, July 3, 1951.*[1]

CASINO GAMBLING, LIKE DRINKING ALCOHOLIC BEVERAGES, OFFERS A splendid example of "labeling."[2] The activity under consideration can be defined either as acceptable recreational diversion or immoral and corrupting. When the voters of New Jersey legalized casino gambling in Atlantic City in 1976, and therefore redefined the moral status as well as the legal status of the activity in that state, it was no longer officially considered a deviant activity. According to journalistic accounts, general jubilation prevailed in the area in anticipation of tourist spending and economic growth.[3]

* This chapter was co-authored by John Dombrink.

As this book is being written, Atlantic City has a long way to go before it develops its gambling industry on the scale of Las Vegas, if it ever does. Still, it is not surprising that casino gambling was legalized in New Jersey. On the contrary, it is more surprising that until the bicentennial year of the United States, only one of those, Nevada, had legalized it — and even that one not consistently throughout its relatively brief history. Legal casino gambling still remains something of a pariah industry. Why did Nevada embrace gambling? How did gambling achieve respectability in Nevada and not elsewhere? How did early attempts at control over gambling evolve?

2

In the beginning, Nevada did not embrace gambling out of economic need or advantage. That came later, much later. At first, the dry land now identified as the state of Nevada scarcely seemed fit for human habitation. Indeed, the state was found inhabitable by non-Indians only in recent times, and then only in restricted areas: Las Vegas in the southern tip of the state and Reno–Carson City in the north. The first migrants saw Nevada as a barrier to be hurried across on their way to California. Of any of the states between the Rockies and the Sierra Nevada, Nevada offered the least to migrants. In the 1820s trappers and religious groups — members of the Church of Jesus Christ of Latter Day Saints, or Mormons — made inroads into Nevada. The explorer and fur trapper Jedediah Smith crossed the territory in 1827 on his way to California. In the 1830s and 1840s other explorers, including John C. Fremont, passed through the area. "The trappers," one historian observes, "came in small numbers and rarely settled or remained in any one place for any length of time."[4] Following the signing of the Treaty of Guadalupe Hidalgo in 1848, by which Mexico ceded the territory including Nevada to the United States, Brigham Young and his Mormon followers began to settle Nevada.[5]

In 1849, the discovery of gold in California drew westward thousands of prospectors eager to gamble on the possibility of striking it rich. A Mormon trading post was set up at a place later called Genoa, and a small strike of gold was made nearby. While not a rich strike, the gold encouraged others to prospect.

"In 1858 silver lodes were discovered in 'Carson County,' and then," writes Mark Twain, "the aspect of things changed. Californians began to flock in, and the American element was soon in the majority. Allegiance to Brigham Young and Utah was renounced, and a temporary territorial government for 'Washoe' was instituted by the citizens. Governor Roop was the first and only chief magistrate of it. In due course of time Congress passed a bill to organize 'Nevada Territory,' and President Lincoln sent out Governor Nye to supplant Roop."[6]

Silver-mining communities formed and grew near Virginia City. At this time the population of the territory was about 12,000 or 15,000, and rapidly increasing. Hotels, general stores, and dozens of gambling hall-saloon-bordellos lined the streets. Gambling had not been prevalent in the straitlaced Mormon communities, but it now came into its own, bringing a predictable divisiveness between conservative Mormons and carefree gold diggers.[7]

Gold prospecting did not draw men seeking stability and long-term work. The affinity between gambling and prospecting for gold is clear. Either way, one is seeking to strike it rich. Besides, in the 19th-century mining towns there wasn't much else to do. Men without families could drink, whore, gamble, and fight; and they did all of these. For the gold miners, cowboys, and other adventurers who scratched out a living from what the parched desert offered, gambling was a major activity after a day of strained backs and saddle sores. In the dusty little mining towns which constituted Nevada gambling became the principal form of recreation for male members of the community. Thus, the residents of the Nevada Territory adopted gambling as an integral part of life.

3

The first official restrictions on gambling in Nevada came in 1861, when the Nevada Territory was formed. James Nye, the territorial governor and a political ally of President Lincoln, was a firm advocate of law and order. In his first speech to the territorial representatives, he left no doubt as to where he stood on the gambling issue. "Of all the seductive devices extant, I consider that of gambling as the worst. It holds out allurements hard to be resisted. It captivates and ensnares the young, blunts all the moral sensibilities and ends in utter ruin."[8] Under Nye's governorship, running a gambling operation was made a felony, and betting a misdemeanor.

A $100 bounty was offered to district attorneys for each gambling conviction they could obtain. Despite such attractions to enforcement, convictions were virtually nonexistent. Gambling was as much a part of Nevada life as were the mines, and no group of representatives in Carson City could manage to change that solely by the passage of legislation, even if they really wanted to — and many did.

4

Nevada achieved statehood in 1864. One of the more interesting questions is why this sparsely populated territory of Mormons and miners was given independent statehood, instead of being incorporated into the Utah Territory. The answer is twofold: First, Nevada's precious metals from the Comstock Lode, amounting to nearly $300 million, were crucial to financing the Civil War for the Union, and Congress was grateful. Second, President Lincoln needed another Republican state to assure passage of the 13th Amendment, and he moved to create one out of Nevada.[9] The result was to assure that this sparsely populated territory would in perpetuity command the representation of two United States senators.[10]

In 1864, the first session of the legislature of the state of Nevada repealed the 1861 gambling law, and replaced it with a less rigid one.[11] The more realistic sanctions bespoke a legislature more in touch with the realities of Nevada life than its territorial predecessor. Operators of gambling places were now guilty only of misdemeanors. Essentially, local gambling establishments were free to pursue their business as they pleased, subject only to an occasional fine.

A strong movement to legalize gambling crystallized in the passage by the 1865 legislature of a bill to license gambling. But the governor, Henry Blasdel, called gambling "a vicious vice," and vetoed the legalization bill. In 1869, Blasdel vetoed another bill to legalize gambling. This time, however, the state senate and assembly overrode the veto, and gambling became legal. According to a state publication, some of those who supported the bill believed that by requiring a license fee, they had devised an ingenious scheme for the elimination of gambling.[12]

The law demanded a $250 to $500 quarterly fee from gambling establishments, and barred gambling in the front room of the first floor of any building. Gambling might be legal, but it was — contrary to the glaring neon of contemporary Nevada — kept out of sight. Despite official predictions, the new law enabled gambling to flourish in the back rooms of saloons or gambling halls as long as the gold and silver mines remained productive. Still, gambling during this period was, in the most literal sense, a back-room industry which excluded the participation of women and played no part in the normal life of the community.[13]

From 1880 to 1900, as the mines were largely depleted, the state lost one-third of its population. By the turn of the century, more than $1 billion worth of gold and silver had come out of the Comstock Lode. It was responsible for creating many millionaires and multimillionaires. But most beneficiaries took their wealth to San Francisco or other places more attractive than the Nevada desert. Virginia City became the West's most illustrious ghost town.

Despite the serious depression that began in 1880 with the decline of the Comstock Lode, the state's gamblers seemed to continue in relative prosperity.[14] The closing decades of the 19th century saw a fair amount of statutory action in the gambling field as the legislature enacted or amended provisions dealing with the punishment for failing to procure a license, the amount of the license fee, the duty of sheriffs to enforce the licensing law, the prohibition of minors from gambling, places in which gambling business could be conducted, the rights of debtors to gamble, and the times for opening and closing of gambling houses. In general, however, the statutory scheme remained largely unchanged in its major focus, and compliance was a simple matter. Enforcement apparently caused few problems and virtually no court cases.[15]

A mining boom from 1900 to 1910 followed the bust period. The so-called Second Comstock was the discovery of gold in Goldfield, silver in Tonopah, and copper in Ely. Nevada was once again the object of a great precious-metals rush, and the state's diminishing population doubled from 42,335 to 81,875.[16] Tonopah and Goldfield in central Nevada became the new centers of mining activity, and revived the looser life-style mining had brought earlier.

Stakes grew, gambling became more serious, and the larger gambling houses alerted themselves against trickery. The legislature, aware that illegal play was a major threat to one of the state's more important pastimes, passed a law in 1879 making it a misdemeanor for gambling licensees to allow cheating.[17] Still, cheating was as important a part of the game as luck to the dedicated gambler; the artful gambler sought to do it with style and sophistication.

As gambling became more widespread and popular, the Nevada legislature adopted a more liberal attitude, repealing restrictions on first-floor gambling rooms, as well as on opening and closing hours. The legislature also redirected the funds derived from gambling licenses into county and city treasuries.[18]

Although reformers had attacked gambling since its legalization in 1869, they had no real success until the early 1900s when gambling became a target of the puritanical reform movement that eventually resulted in national prohibition. Fired up by women's temperance organizations allied with prominent Nevada officials — the governor, a United States senator, the president of the university, and a supreme court justice — the 1909 legislature acted. "In the exercise of its powers over the policy and morals of the people," it prohibited all forms of gambling.[19]

The new law made it a felony to operate a gambling game and authorized the police to break down doors, and seize and destroy any gambling equipment found on the premises. Criminalization drove Nevada's gamblers underground. It was a repeat of the experience of the 1860s, during which gambling had for four years been officially illegal, but, in fact, remained widespread. Gamblers were still around; they were just more discreet.

5

The seemingly tough new antigambling law did not have the effect its sponsors had intended. The law attracted underworld gamblers skilled in the arts of cheating and of bribing public officials. Not only was public revenue from licensing lost, but a chain of surreptitious joints began to develop that conducted every known game without controls and corrupted public officials to stay in business. Under the circumstances, few criminal prosecutions actually arose under the act. Nevada's citizens tolerated the new gambling law under the assumption that it would soon be repealed. In 1911 the legislature moved in that direction by legalizing some card games, such as poker. But another act in 1913 outlawed all gambling; and yet another act in 1915 somewhat relaxed the gaming prohibition.[20]

We must remember that in Nevada, as elsewhere, public attitudes on "morality" were changing with great rapidity; and besides, publicly expressed attitudes were not necessarily consistent with behavior. It was not unheard of for someone — particularly a legislator — to attend church and support prohibition; and also to drink whiskey and gamble in the speakeasies that emerged in Nevada during the 1920s, along with those in the rest of the country. The 1915 law seemed to have no effect on the illegal games, which increased in size and number each year. Bribes to allow unmolested games were so widespread that they were considered little more than a form of license.

This law remained in force for 16 years, and it was either ignored or poorly enforced. The games allowed in the licensed houses had little appeal to the gambling public, which patronized instead numerous undercover resorts. State and local revenues from license fees declined year by year while the illegal houses multiplied.

By 1930 the antigambling fervor in Nevada had little force. There was still opposition. The same women's groups who supported the prohibition of alcohol remained opposed, as did the clergy, but support among the citizenry was fading after two decades of experimentation. Besides, the antigambling laws had no real effect. No mining camp or cowboy town had ever been without its gambling hall. Thus, despite opposition from clergy, reform, and women's groups, the legislators' appreciation of the potential economic effects upon a Depression-ridden state carried the day. The *Nevada State Journal*, in an article prior to the passage of the 1931 legalization bill, stated, "there is a strong sentiment, particularly in Southern Nevada, that some state or municipal revenue should be derived from the games which now run on every hand with apparent sanction of public sentiment. . . ."[21] Assemblyman Phil Tobin, who introduced the legalization bill, argued that widespread, illegal gambling had long been a fact of life in Nevada, with the nearly bankrupt state gaining nothing beyond a growing incidence of corruption.[22] There was also hope that gambling would spur businesses suffering during the Depression.

6

The bill that Governor Balzar signed in March 1931 legalized all forms of gambling, including bookmaking and sports betting. A schedule of license fees for all games and machines was established, and the counties assumed the responsibility for the licensing and the collection of fees. Twenty-five percent of this revenue went into the state's general fund, and the remainder stayed in the county for city and county use.[23]

County sheriffs were responsible for the administration of the law. A five-member board, including the sheriff, district attorney, and three county commissioners, had license-granting authority. There was no enforcement at the state level.[24]

A related effort to enhance business culminated in the 1931 passage of a six-weeks divorce bill. Although the gambling bill was ultimately of greater importance to the state, the six-weeks divorce bill was of more immediate economic benefit, attracting those affluent enough to travel to Nevada and establish residence for six weeks to end their unhappy marriages.

Gambling first acquired respectability in Reno. In 1936, when Las Vegas was a small railroad city of about 5,000, the Smith family opened Harolds Club in Reno. William Harrah opened his club in 1942.[25] The Smiths and Harrah were essentially promoters.

From the outset, their aim was to erase the stigma of gambling and make it acceptable morally as well as legally. The Smiths decorated their casino with bright lights and colorful trappings to counter the idea that gambling should be done in a smoke-filled back room. They lowered the stakes to attract small bettors and provided transportation home for players who went broke.

Harrah added modern technology to the Smith technique. He commissioned a research firm to point out his likely clientele and how to attract it. When the results indicated the elderly and low-income who owned no cars were that clientele, he provided bus service to 31 nearby cities. He opened up his gambling rooms to full view from the sidewalk, creating the impression that there was nothing to hide.[26]

Keith Monroe captures the atmosphere Harrah created: "Through Harrah's efforts," he observes, " — and those of his imitators — the Nevada side of Lake Tahoe, once a drowsy summer resort, has become a bustling, year-round Monte Carlo for average Americans. . . ."[27]

Although Harrah and the Smiths would not share directly in future Las Vegas growth, they provided foundations to legitimize the legalized gambling industry. They treated gambling as any other legitimate business requiring market research and advertising. The Smiths' advertising program (the covered wagon sign with "Harolds Club or Bust" on the side) brought business to Reno and made Harolds Club and the Reno gambling industry itself not only a functioning part of Nevada's social and economic life, but an acceptable part as well. What had been a pariah industry was slowly evolving into a respected one as economic advantage transformed vice into virtue.

7

When gambling was legalized in 1931, Las Vegas was not quite a third as large as Reno in population, and was then much less concerned than Reno with the economic possibilities of the new gambling act. Las Vegas was more interested in the Boulder Canyon Project which began at about the same time as legalization. It became evident that the United States government's project on the Colorado River would do more for Las Vegas than any gold or silver mine had ever done for a Nevada town.[28]

Hundreds of workers traveled from the dam site to Las Vegas to buy supplies or to be entertained. The city responded to them and to tourists by creating a lively entertainment industry based on gambling and floor shows. Thus, besides bringing an adequate water supply to the southern tip of Nevada, the Boulder Dam project heightened the importance of the federal government in Nevada during the 1930s. That importance grew as World War II stimulated the state's economy by placing heavy demands on copper and other minerals. As the Pacific Coast became a point of embarkation for troops and supplies to battle stations in the Far East, and as military bases were established in Nevada, traffic through the state grew.[29]

Legalized gambling, easy liquor sales, and red-light districts made Nevada towns attractive to soldiers on leave. Between 1931 and 1941 gaming revenues had increased just 50 percent. In the next three war years, 1941 to 1944, these were to rise 56 percent, an unprecedented average of 19 percent for each of the three years.[30] Those three years mark the dividing point between the early history and the modern history of gaming in Nevada, and the growth of Las Vegas marks the turning point of that history.

The World War II gambler was not the same breed as the frontier gambler. Many persons were now interested who might never have participated in illegal gambling. Often they were wealthy visitors from nearby California, who now found Nevada attractive for more reasons than its easy marriage and divorce laws. More than working-class miners gambled in Nevada now; the state also attracted affluent tourists seeking extraordinary excitement and unusual experiences.

The year 1941 saw the first signs of what was to be Nevada's big entertainment industry, when an Elko casino owner brought in a prominent orchestra to play in his hotel-casino. Casino owners in Las Vegas and Reno copied the innovation, and growing crowds came to hear the music. As new casinos opened throughout the 1940s, recognized entertainers presided over the festivities. By 1946 it was obvious that the war had created new economic patterns in Nevada and that most of them favored Las Vegas and the southern part of the state.[31]

Downtown casinos had thrived since the construction of the Boulder Dam. Six clubs opened in Fremont Street downtown, a short walk from the railroad station. Still, they were small operations, catering to the masses. They were hardly striking, physically or otherwise.

Major hotel developers from throughout the country began to build entertainment complexes on the outskirts — the Strip. In 1941, Thomas E. Hull from California built the El Rancho Vegas, and Texan R. E. Griffith added the Last Frontier in 1942. But it was Benjamin "Bugsy" Siegel and the Flamingo Hotel that were to change the face of Nevada's gambling industry.

8

Benjamin Siegel has been called "the man who invented Las Vegas."[32] Siegel's Flamingo Hotel, built in 1946, on the highway to Los Angeles, just outside the city limits, became the prototype for the contemporary Las Vegas casino. It had been Siegel's ambition to build a luxurious complex that would offer gambling, recreation, entertainment, and other services catering to the area's increasing tourist trade.

Siegel was one of the legendary gangsters. His most famous — or infamous — associates included Meyer Lansky, Frank Costello, and Charles (Lucky) Luciano. Siegel was dispatched to the West Coast by these Eastern crime figures, and for ten years he moved in Hollywood social circles. He solidified organized crime connections in Los Angeles, particularly those involving bookmaking and offshore casino gambling. But California authorities closed down his gambling ships off the coast of California, and a 1945 bookmaking indictment added to Siegel's embarrassment.

Siegel wanted to become legitimate, and the attractions of Nevada's legalized gambling were too strong to resist. Even more than the gold rush miners described by Mark Twain, Bugsy Siegel and the Mormons were certainly strange bedfellows. Still, there were similarities in the attention both gave to success in business:

"Seen from the surface," according to David W. Toll, "the *entente cordial* between an alleged Eastern gangster like Siegel and the straight-laced Mormons of Southern Nevada was an incongruous alliance. But the underlying realities were like those in other states where a bootlegger-Baptist alliance keeps a county dry. For one thing, the Mormon population of Southern Nevada had already been severely diluted with Gentiles. . . . Nevertheless, the Mormons represented the largest cohesive political force in Clark County."[33]

Confronted with Siegel, the Mormons in Clark County in 1945 adopted attitudes similar to the ones their grandfathers had shown toward the 19th-century miners. They saw the advantages in the presence of a large capital investment and a continuing payroll and need for supplies. Siegel's unsavory reputation was earned in the East. In Nevada, he proposed nothing illegal. Thus, he should be given his chance like anyone else. Besides, his success would benefit everyone.[34]

Siegel had persuaded the crime syndicate that he could transform Las Vegas into a legal gambling oasis for organized crime, and received their backing in 1943. With their support, he started to work on his initial venture — really the first of the major Strip hotels — the Flamingo, now owned by the Hilton Corporation. It didn't concern Las Vegans that the famous Bugsy Siegel of Murder Incorporated was going to put up the Flamingo. As one veteran spectator remembers: "The only attitude I ever got out of the town at the time was, 'Hooray! He's going to bring money into the town.'" The Flamingo, according to Martin Gosch and Richard Hammer, "was Siegel's preoccupation, to the exclusion of almost everything else. Though he saw huge profits flowing from the legal gambling games, despite Nevada's taxes, he was realist enough to understand that he would have to provide more than the tables to woo customers from Reno. He planned to lure them with the finest food and best wines, the most luxurious accommodations and the biggest Hollywood stars — all at such low prices that no one would be able to pass Las Vegas by.

"As the Flamingo rose, anything Siegel wanted, he got, through the influence and muscle of his underworld partners. In these first postwar years, construction materials were difficult to find, but pressures were put on suppliers and on the underworld-dominated

Teamsters Union for the trucks to haul those supplies to the desert."[35]

Long delays in construction and expensive cost overruns angered Siegel's backers, who believed he was skimming from his building budget. He was slated for death — outside of Las Vegas. The mob was careful to protect Las Vegas's reputation as a peaceful place, and had Siegel murdered in California, in his mistress's Beverly Hills mansion in 1947.

The news of Siegel's death created enormous publicity around the country, and probably attracted additional business for Las Vegas casinos. Even today, tourists still visit Las Vegas hoping to rub shoulders with "gangsters." Las Vegas was to become the biggest gambling center in the world based on the Flamingo model. Siegel's murder gave the Flamingo enormous publicity nationwide: "even in death Bugsy Siegel helped turn a chunk of Nevada desert into the now famous Las Vegas strip. . . ."[36]

In the decade after Siegel's death, Las Vegas was to grow more than it had in the entire preceding century. In 1947, when Siegel opened the Flamingo, Nevada casinos reported gross gaming revenues of $32 million. Siegel said in 1947, predicting the growth that was to engulf Las Vegas: "What you see here today is nothing. More and more people are moving to California every day, and they love to gamble. In ten years this'll be the biggest gambling center in the world."[37] In 10 years' time, Siegel's prediction was vindicated, as the casinos reported $132 million. But Siegel was long dead by then. Perhaps not even he would have predicted that 30 years after he spoke, the Nevada casinos would gross gaming revenues of $1.2 billion.[38]

9

Until 1945, gaming control had been the responsibility of local and county officials. The 1931 state law that legalized gambling after 20 years of various prohibitions, had established county license fees based on the number of games operated. Revenues were allocated to the state, counties, and cities, and the counties assumed the responsibility for the licensing and collection of fees. Twenty-five percent of the revenue went into the state's general fund, and the remainder stayed in the county, for city and county use. The county sheriff, district attorney, and three county commissioners had license-granting authority.

The 1945 law moved these powers to the state to facilitate tax collection. Applicants were required to obtain licenses from the state tax commission as well as from the county boards. In addition, the law imposed on gambling operators a state tax of one percent of gross earnings.[39] The bill was strictly a revenue measure; nothing was said about control of a privileged industry. Since it was a revenue matter, the tax commission was chosen to administer the controls.

To say that the state began control in 1945 is itself an inadequate observation. To assume that such control was thorough, or even well-funded, would be mistaken. For the first year of state jurisdiction, the state tax commission had only one employee for gambling matters, whose main function was to find out who were the state's gambling operators.[40]

The tradition of county licensing created special difficulties for the new state gaming control effort. Even when the state was handed licensing power in 1945, the law required that an applicant for a state license would apply first for a county license. The tax commission arranged for this to be changed by the legislature in 1947, after finding that the regulated chose to view the county licensing process as the major legal requirement for opening a casino, and were upset at state efforts to differ with a county approval of a licensee.[41]

Moreover, in the rapid growth of Las Vegas as a gambling center, the business practices of the new casinos thwarted gaming control licensing procedures. As the tax commission began its licensing function, it operated under a rule that applicants should not apply for a license until short periods — usually a couple of months — before the casino was ready to open. This created obvious problems for the regulators, especially in a state that unquestionably depended upon the casino business to support its tax base. Thus, by the time an applicant appeared for licensing, the casino building was usually nearly completed, investment was already substantial, and loans had been committed. Under such circumstances, to deny a license would amount to revoking it.

Not until 1949 did the legislature specifically write into the law that the tax commission could investigate the antecedents, habits, and background of an individual seeking a license. Starting then, the commission began to develop an administrative staff for gaming control. In 1953 the legislature set out the state's power to license "so as to better protect the public health, safety, morals, good order, and general welfare . . ." of the inhabitants of Nevada.[42]

The legislature also tried to write in some specific prohibitions for a gaming license applicant — certain acts that would deny him a license. "We were beginning to run into appeals from applicants who came in to the Commission with their attorneys demanding more specific reasons for denial," former tax commission Secretary Robbins Cahill recollects. "It was more and more treated as a court of law, and they were trying to develop a degree of proof to somewhat the same degree as would be developed in a court of law."[43] They began with the provision that a license be denied to anyone who had been convicted of a crime in the previous five years. The rule stayed in effect for two years, but the authorities, in fact, wanted to license some who had been convicted — for example, of illegal bookmaking — but not others. They found it difficult to remain consistent within the rule. "Eventually," writes Mary Ellen Glass, "[t]he inexperienced tax agents came to realize that they often needed professional assistance in order to know the differences between and among members of the new crowd of gamblers. With gross revenues from gambling more than doubling from 1950 to 1955 . . . Governor Russell asked the legislature to give the state more police powers and a regulatory staff. The lawmakers responded with the creation of a full-fledged gaming control agency within the Tax Commission, in 1955. Nevada was moving into the regulation business."[44]

10

In retrospect, unique aspects of Nevada's experience have contributed to its growth as a gambling center. Three of these distinguish Nevada from large states like California. First, because of its small resident population, the bulk of the money won by

Nevada's gaming industry is won from visitors to the state, rather than from the state's residents. Gambling in Nevada is, therefore, not merely a method of obtaining revenues for government through a redistribution of monies within the resident population, but it is truly an industry providing a substantial positive cash flow into the state's economy and employment for many of its citizens.

Second, and closely related, the distance between Nevada's casinos and any urban population center has restricted Nevada's gambling to persons of substance who can afford to make the trip. This "discretionary money," as the source of the industry's income, is an important concept for industry and tourism executives; for it is evidence that gambling does not prey off the income of those least able to afford it.

Third, Nevada enjoys relatively small tax needs. While it is impressive to note that half of the state's budget comes from gaming taxes and fees, in 1970 that budget was only $84 million, and by 1978 it had risen to $221 million, a substantial rise, but still a small budget.[45] Nevada ranked fifth among the states in revenue from gambling in 1976, behind New York, California, Florida, and Illinois.[46] When we distinguish Nevada from states like New York or California — with a 1978 budget of $15 billion[47] — we must understand that in these states casino gambling would neither be so central to the state's budget nor so benign for the state's population. In a large state, the gambling industry would not be a major employment source. On the contrary, it might well exploit the resources of urban populations, particularly of the working class and the poor.

Other small states can be distinguished from Nevada as well. As we have seen in this chapter, Nevada became a state as a result of an unprecedented and short-lived event — the discovery of the Comstock Lode in 1859. This discovery sets Nevada off from other states. For, mining aside, Nevada never really has had an alternative economic base. (Other sparsely populated states are characteristically agricultural.) Because of Nevada's mining history, it also developed a unique cultural heritage which accepted the legitimacy of casino gambling. Casino gambling has been legal in Nevada since 1869, except for the period of prohibition from 1910 to 1931: Nevada, then, has approved legal casino gambling for 88 of its 114 years as a state.

This cultural heritage shaped Nevada's evolution into the gambling spa of the nation. Still, much of the foundation of the Las Vegas casino world and its control was laid in the years before the Nevada legislature would create a separate gaming control agency in 1955. The El Rancho Vegas, Last Frontier, Flamingo, Thunderbird, Desert Inn, Sands, Sahara, Dunes, and Riviera all opened before or during 1955. Illegal gamblers from Texas, California, Ohio, and Kentucky converged upon the one state where casino gambling was legal. Without a population of legal casino operators to draw from, Nevada casinos were to be operated by gamblers with notorious pasts and associations that ran the width of organized crime in the United States. Voicing the major criticism of Nevada's legalized gambling experiment — that it gave gangsters a "cloak of respectability" — the federal government began a long history of scrutinizing Nevada gambling casino owners and operators.[48]

In general, the early years of state gaming control, 1945 to 1955 — before there was a separate gaming agency — were to set the scene for most of the problems of the years to come. To have rid the state of organized crime figures or their associates would in that period have meant the end of the industry. So even as gaming control moved from local to state jurisdiction, and began to be more strict, it did not clean house. Instead, those who were already operating were permitted to remain. By "grandfathering" in large numbers of illegal gamblers with connections to organized crime in other states, Nevada's gaming industry cemented its image as a stigmatized operation, a pariah industry.[49]

As the Kefauver Committee stated the problem after its hearings stopped in Las Vegas for one day in 1950: "Yet — and the committee found it a fantastic situation — the Tax Commission promptly granted licenses to the same hoodlums who had been established in Nevada, including several with felony convictions."[50]

Its major conflicts outside the state — with federal law enforcement agencies and banks and other major lending institutions — were to be found in different visions of business respectability.

A new Nevada set of norms would be applicable and a study of the licensing procedures of the gaming control boards in Nevada would show the development of such a new normative order. Federal agencies thought Las Vegas contributed to the continuation of the spread of organized crime, and major lenders thought Las Vegas gamblers lacked business acumen and used inadequate internal controls. Thus, if the modern Las Vegas casino and the success of the gaming business can be attributed to Bugsy Siegel and others like him, so can the major control problems. The dilemma of Nevada gaming control, particularly after 1955, was how to maintain revenue generated by the gangsters while dissociating the state from their disrepute.

9

The Search for
Revenue and Respectability*

WHEN FRANK COSTELLO WAS SHOT IN NEW YORK IN 1957, AND figures for gaming revenue at the Tropicana Hotel were found in his pocket, it was clear that the rudimentary controls instituted by the state of Nevada had failed to screen hidden interests.

The authorities were aware of the problem. Two years earlier the Nevada Tax Commission had tried to suspend the license of Las Vegas's Thunderbird Hotel, contending that one of the hidden owners was Jake Lansky, the brother of Meyer Lansky, known as the financial genius of the underworld.

The allegation of hidden ownership was made on the basis of a loan Jake Lansky had made for hotel construction. Nevada's Supreme Court refused to uphold the suspension order. The court made a tortured argument to find that the hotel and casino were separate entities.[1] Since Lansky had loaned money for hotel construction, the court found, he did not participate "in the business." The Thunderbird case suggested how difficult it would be to eliminate organized crime figures from the Nevada casino business.

* This chapter was co-authored by John Dombrink.

The lessons learned in the Thunderbird Hotel case were responsible for a general change in the Nevada approach to control of the gamblers that legalization had attracted. It would now become difficult for anyone to possess a hidden interest through an undisclosed loan such as the one Jake Lansky made to finance construction. If interests were to be hidden, they would have to be more cleverly hidden, because of a change in the control structure.

In 1959, the Nevada Gaming Commission was established to wield the power formerly held by the tax commission. The gaming commission could grant or deny any application for a gaming license. It could enact gaming regulations and act as the collection agency for all gaming taxes. The commission's regulatory and investigative powers were expanded to insure that criminal elements, mobs, or syndicates had neither interest in nor control of existing businesses.

Still, membership on the gaming commission required few qualifications. A commissioner couldn't be a member of the legislature, hold elective office in state government, or serve as an official of any political party. And, no person actively engaged in or having a direct financial interest in gaming activities could be a member of the commission. No more than three of the five members of the commission could be of the same political affiliation as the governor, who appointed them.

From 1945 until 1959 the governor, as chairman of the tax commission, had a direct hand in the issuance of licenses and disciplinary action. The 1959 act, one of the first actions of newly elected Governor Grant Sawyer, removed the governor from direct authority over gaming control. But, of course, the commission would be appointed by the governor, and he would scarcely lose his influence.

The Gaming Control Board was established as the working arm of the agency — investigating applicants for licenses, enforcing the gaming laws, and auditing to collect taxes. No longer would the chairman of the Gaming Control Board serve as the secretary of the tax commission. Sawyer's term thus began with a new structure and a nearly new board and commission, a practice that the following two administrations would follow.

A few of Sawyer's appointees were ex-FBI men, who brought

a law enforcement atmosphere to gaming control. One of the earliest attempts of the board to control organized crime influence — the Black Book, or list of excluded persons — illustrates the crudity of early attempts to control and the tensions inherent in Nevada gaming control, especially the constitutionality of control tools.

2

Who first proposed the Black Book is unclear. In 1960, a loose-leaf binder was compiled by the Gaming Control Board with the names and pictures of 11 men the board thought to be of "notorious or unsavory reputation," and therefore potentially harmful to Nevada's attempts to portray a clean image for its gaming industry.

The thrust of the book was simple: Nevada gambling casino operators were to keep certain underworld figures off their premises, or else face revocation of their gambling license. Such exclusion seemed to be within the mandate of the board, for it had broad powers to regulate every aspect of a gambling operation.

Still, the Black Book was of questionable legality, especially at a time when civil rights were receiving increased attention in so many areas. Application of the terms of the Black Book — excluding the 11 "unsavory" men from the hotel casinos — led to a court challenge of Nevada's ability to regulate its unique industry.

The case, *Marshall v. Sawyer*,[2] was not resolved until 1966, but the events leading up to it began in the fall of 1960. One member of the 11 on the Black Book list had already challenged the board when John Marshall arrived in Las Vegas in October 1960. While staying in a motel that had no gaming facilities — and thus exempting himself from the provisions of the Black Book — Marshall visited hotels up and down the Strip, dining with casino operators and entertainers. Obviously, Marshall was on familiar terms with many people in the industry. Marshall's long evenings, with visits to many casinos, began to wear on the gaming control agents and frustrate board chairman Ray Abbaticchio. He and a host of agents descended on the casinos that had entertained Marshall that night, picking up dice and cards from the tables — a standard board procedure — with special fervor.

After a few days of following Marshall, and arguing with casino operators, the board was able to have Marshall put out of Las Vegas. He went immediately to Los Angeles, to the attorneys who had brought the first Black Book suit, and prepared to sue the governor of Nevada and the gaming control authorities.

The board's actions were not well received at all levels of Nevada law enforcement. The state attorney general, for one, expressed dismay at the tactics: "My criticism is that gaming officials have illegally raided and harassed resort hotels in Las Vegas, creating a false nationwide impression that the raided casinos are cheating." He expressed doubt about the constitutionality of the Black Book prohibition, and added, "I believe in strong gambling control, but not in muscle tactics by state agents."[3]

Governor Sawyer publicly supported the board's actions, saying: "I agree with any measures to keep hoodlums out of Nevada. . . . We might as well serve notice on underworld characters right now. They are not welcome in Nevada and we aren't going to have them here."[4]

Marshall's lawsuit came in December 1960 in federal court. He asked for money damages, and included as defendants the governor, the members of the Gaming Control Board and the Nevada Gaming Commission, and one of the casinos from which he was ejected. Marshall alleged that the board and commission conspired to discriminate against him and others listed in the Black Book. Further, he charged that the labeling of him and others as "undesirable" was done without any notice or hearing.

An important matter of jurisdiction needed to be settled early. Should the trial be held in federal or state court? In arguing their motion for federal abstention, the Nevada lawyers pointed out that gaming was a peculiarly local industry. Understanding and regulating the unique business of gambling was, they averred, a matter for Nevada, not federal courts.[5]

The state charged that purely local rights dependent on state law are not federal civil rights, that the right to be in a Nevada gaming establishment is a local right. Since the majority of the United States prohibited casino gambling, there could be no argument that civil rights had been denied Marshall.

Marshall's lawyers acknowledged the state's power to grant gaming licenses, but not their power to regulate who could gamble or occupy rooms in a hotel-casino. What had been violated, they charged, was not a right connected with a unique and state-regulated industry, but was a basic, federally guaranteed human right. Such a challenge, they argued, should be heard in federal court.

The federal court upheld the state's argument for local jurisdiction. Marshall's case was appealed to the United States Court of Appeals for the Ninth Circuit in San Francisco, and it in turn reversed the federal district court in 1962, and remanded the Marshall case for trial in federal district court.

Marshall won the jurisdictional question, but lost on the merits. While it was of the opinion that the case should be tried in a lower federal court, the circuit court outlined the conclusions the lower court judge should reach: Marshall was entitled to no relief. Moreover, the court supported a strong state effort in gaming control.

The court took judicial notice that control was essential to the state. "[T]he problem of excluding hoodlums from gambling places in the state of Nevada," the judge wrote, "can well be regarded by the state authorities as a matter almost of life or death."[6]

The court also disputed Marshall's contention that he should have had a hearing before being placed in the Black Book. Since he had been convicted of a felony, and was not included in the Black Book solely because of his reputation, the listing, the court concluded, could not be reasonably attacked.

The case went to trial in 1964 in federal district court in Las Vegas. The district court decision finally came, nearly four years after the filing of the suit. Nevada's use of the Black Book was judged to be a valid exercise of the police power reserved to the states by the 10th Amendment. Marshall's inclusion in the classification of persons of notorious reputation was judged proper, and he was assessed the costs of the suit.

But the Black Book (which in 1976 was renamed "The List of Excluded Persons" because a black citizen complained that the title constituted a racial slur) was never really effective. It was more a public-relations stunt than a serious control measure. In any event, its existence did nothing to reassure the federal authorities and others that Nevada had succeeded in expelling organized criminal interests from its casinos.

3

Federal pressure on Nevada, which had begun with Kefauver, but was muted during the Eisenhower administration, began again when John Kennedy was inaugurated president in 1961. His brother Robert, at age 35, was appointed attorney general of the United States. Robert Kennedy had become interested in organized crime and labor racketeering in his work on the McClellan Rackets Committee. As the chief law enforcement official in the land, he would cite the destruction of organized crime syndicates as a central mission of his office.

Unimpressed by local efforts to control "gangsters" and "hoodlums," he had urged in his book, *The Enemy Within*, the need for a national anticrime effort: "Only through a nationwide network can we fight the widespread penetration by criminals into our economy."[7] As a result of his investigations of Jimmy Hoffa and the Teamsters Central States Pension Fund, Kennedy perceived Las Vegas as an organized crime base, and initiated a campaign directed at that state.

Shortly after Kennedy became attorney general, numerous magazine articles and newspaper stories appeared alleging that untaxed profits from Nevada casinos were being siphoned to the underworld for legal as well as illegal activities throughout the nation and abroad. Many of these newspaper stories and magazine articles were attributed to the attorney general or to unnamed sources in the Department of Justice.[8] The exposés that were to occur during Kennedy's tenure at Justice were among the most vituperative that Nevada's legalized gambling industry had encountered in its 30 years of experience since Prohibition.

The differences between Kennedy and the Nevadans, one gaming industry official recalls, were fundamental.[9] Kennedy was confident that the Eastern underworld had taken over Las Vegas gambling, while Nevada authorities insisted that only a few undesirables had infiltrated the state, and that most of these had been forced to sell out. Kennedy believed that Nevada's impact on organized crime had national consequences through the exportation of hundreds of millions of "skimmed" dollars. Nevada's governor argued instead that skimming was light, and represented only small incidents of tax evasion.

Victor Navasky, who has written the most comprehensive study of Kennedy as attorney general, sets out four goals of Kennedy's organized crime strategy: (1) to educate the nation through speeches and articles to the dimensions and urgency of the "Cosa Nostra" threat; (2) to give new status, personnel, and money, and a top priority to the Department of Justice's Organized Crime Section; (3) to win the cooperation of other government agencies, especially employing his closeness to the president as a selling point; and (4) to mobilize a group of centrally based prosecutors who would investigate, indict, and try cases against key rackets figures. Organized crime was Kennedy's number one priority.[10]

Kennedy's organized-crime strategy combined novel organization, toughness, and an assumption about the incapacity of local officials to handle the problem. As the head of the newly formed Organized Crime and Racketeering Section explained: "Our idea was to set up a group of centrally based prosecutors who would do everything. They would conduct investigations, they would go before grand juries and try cases, and where we thought state and local authorities were unreliable, we'd figure out a theory of federal jurisdiction and do the job ourselves."[11]

In May 1961, Kennedy's office contacted the attorney general of Nevada, and asked that 65 agents of the federal government be deputized as assistants to the Nevada attorney general for the purpose of making a simultaneous raid on all major Nevada casinos. Kennedy was planning to clean out what he called the "bank of America's organized crime," and failing that, "he would press Congress to close down gambling."[12] Kennedy explained that the effect of his agents would be greater if, in addition to being federal police, they were also Nevada police. The attorney general of Nevada, who was in line for a federal judgeship at the time, and didn't particularly care to alienate the Department of Justice, suggested that the law wouldn't permit their becoming deputy attorneys general, but thought they could, by law, be named special agents of the Gaming Control Board.[13]

In any case, the Nevada attorney general did not have the time to apprise Governor Sawyer — a Democrat — of any of this until after he had made the suggestion to Kennedy that the federal agents be made special agents of the Gaming Control Board.

Sawyer became apprehensive. He called in some of his closest aides and gaming officials, and decided that he would go back to Washington to see the president. For three days, the Nevada gaming officials argued with Bobby Kennedy and his assistants at the Department of Justice. By the third day, the Sawyer team managed a reprieve: Kennedy would call off the big invasion. An agreement was reached between the state and the federal authorities to cooperate in any effort to determine the existence of organized crime. What the contemplated raids would have accomplished, other than disastrous publicity to the state of Nevada, the gaming officials said, was never explained.[14]

When Sawyer returned from his meetings with the Kennedys in Washington, he met with the casino owners, and told them that Nevada now "stood alone," that Congress could be moved to end its gambling. Kennedy's interest thus forced a new policy for the Las Vegas gamblers: "They might compete for Dean Martin, Barbra Streisand, or Sinatra, but they knew they must now be as close as oil companies, as well-knit as the farm lobby." Moreover, they would have to become discreet, subtle, and self-disciplining businessmen.[15]

A few weeks after the 1961 meeting, Kennedy dispatched two assistants to meet with Governor Sawyer and members of the Nevada Gaming Commission and Gaming Control Board, to elicit state cooperation for what was said to be a unified effort among the various federal investigative agencies to crack down on syndicate racketeering. State cooperation was assured, despite gaming control beliefs that the federal emissaries displayed a lack of working knowledge about underworld figures.[16] One gaming official explained: "It became evident that the guys from Washington just didn't know what the hell they were talking about in names of people and things like that."[17]

The state gaming control authorities reluctantly agreed to take on a couple of federal agents as undercover men to accompany Gaming Control Board agents into counting rooms. Kennedy's men took the plane back to Washington, and the board never heard any more about it. Next, the FBI was asked to make a total investigation of Nevada gambling. The bureau assigned a young investigator who spent six weeks going over formal records provided by the state. The investigator, who would later return and work for the board, compiled a two-volume report for FBI Director Hoover.

Within six to eight months, various federal agencies began to investigate Nevada's legalized gaming industry. The FBI, the IRS, the Bureau of Narcotics, the Immigration and Naturalization Service, the Alcohol and Tobacco Tax Unit, and the Department of Labor were all involved. The FBI force was tripled in Nevada. The IRS opened an office in Las Vegas staffed by 30 or 40 agents recruited from around the country. The gaming commission later concluded that it was doubtful any gaming licensee escaped the scrutiny of these agencies.[18]

4

The federal authorities were concerned directly with concealed casino profits — skimming. Such unreported earnings would violate law in at least four ways. First, the state of Nevada would not be able to tax skimmed revenues. Secondly, undeclared personal income would violate federal income tax laws. (Nevada has no income tax, thus there is no state counterpart to that particular crime.) Third, authorities assumed that the unreported earnings were turned over to hidden underworld owners of Las Vegas casinos. Finally, it was assumed that the skim would be used to finance other illicit activities of the underworld.

In June 1966, a federal court case involving a Desert Inn casino boss put on the public record for the first time FBI secret surveillance of Nevada casinos. The FBI had, it was revealed, initiated surveillance in 1963 on Nevada gaming operators, and listening devices were installed in the homes and offices of an unknown number of Nevada residents, including but not limited to various casino executives. The bugs were placed by the FBI, without the knowledge either of the IRS agents or operational Department of Justice personnel working on the federal investigations in Las Vegas.[19]

The surveillance provided the federal government with hard evidence of skimming. The evidence was illegally obtained, but not destroyed. For many years these records have served the law enforcement intelligence community and largely account for their certainty as to individuals being "Mafia connected," although the evidence of crimes would not be usable in a court nor would it be regarded as an ethical law enforcement practice by critics.

In 1966, Alan Barth wrote in *The New Republic*: "Whatever was said in the executive suite, whether it related to personal and supposedly private affairs or to thoroughly legitimate business dealings — and it should be remembered that gambling is legal in Nevada and that the men under investigation were not then charged with any crime — the snoopers sifted out and filed away for possible use."[20]

Governor Sawyer was outraged. He called upon Nevada district attorneys to prosecute federal agents for violation of Nevada's antiwiretap law.[21] On July 15, Sawyer called for an investigation of the bugging. The casino boss involved demanded that J. Edgar Hoover produce the tapes, arguing that they would prove that he had not extorted, for which he was on trial.[22] Sawyer called for the "evidence" to be turned over to the state of Nevada, and to the gaming control authorities. He said it appeared strange that the FBI would boast privately of evidence which it refused to divulge to the state of Nevada or the IRS. He charged the Department of Justice and Attorney General Nicholas Katzenbach, with waging a vendetta against Nevada's chief industry, of having declared "silent warfare" against Nevada by alleging underworld casino rakeoffs and refusing to reveal electronically obtained evidence. Katzenbach replied that the data from the case, which he would not call "evidence," was "raw" and "unverified."

Sawyer also claimed that sensational news stories in out-of-state newspapers appeared to be deliberate leaks from the FBI or the Department of Justice. "To learn what J. Edgar Hoover found in Nevada," he said, "you have to read the *Chicago Sun-Times*. His men leaked all their information, not to Internal Revenue or to the Nevada police, but to a Chicago newspaper."[23]

While the governor demanded the "evidence" from the electronic surveillance, the federal agencies were reluctant to cooperate with a state investigation the Nevada Gaming Commission had undertaken after the FBI testimony. The reluctance to testify was attributed to several factors. Some federal officials lacked confidence in state gaming control authorities. Other federal agents said they might risk key undercover agents or informants and secret investigative techniques by giving the state skimming data. Finally, it seemed that if federal officials revealed information obtained by bugging, they might strengthen private or state legal cases against FBI agents or hinder any further federal legal action.[24]

In fact, such civil cases against the FBI strengthened the hand of defendants in the skimming cases, although the federal government at the time denied any connection between the light penalties agreed to in the criminal cases and the settling of the civil cases. According to former Department of Justice officials,[25] the electronic surveillance did not provide evidence for the skimming cases. That evidence resulted from two to three years of IRS undercover observation of the "drop" in the casinos. The IRS agents were furious with the FBI, which not only destroyed their cases, but revealed their methods of observation.

Because of the limitations of illegally obtained evidence, the federal government was able to penalize participants in only one skimming case that occurred during the 1960s. In January of 1973, Miami Beach hotel man Morris Lansburgh and some of his partners pleaded guilty to entering into a conspiracy with six codefendants in 1960 to conceal Lansky's continuing financial interest in the Flamingo, and to conceal true casino receipts by understating $4½ million annually from 1960 to 1967, for a total figure of $36 million. The skim involved credit extended to junketeers gambling in Las Vegas, who would repay IOUs which were not entered on casino records.[26]

In addition, the government estimated that those involved were stealing $11,000 per shift, or $33,000 per day, from just six casinos:

the Fremont, Sands, Flamingo, Horseshoe, Desert Inn, and Stardust, for a total of over $12 million annually.[27] The defendants did not plead guilty to that charge. Nevertheless, the amounts involved, if correct, suggest that "skimming" is a misnomer. The term implies taking the cream off the top. The conspirators were allegedly drawing off most of the milk as well. As *Chicago Sun Times* reporter Sandy Smith wrote in a 1967 series for *Life* magazine: "A recurrent problem for Lansky's Las Vegas front men and accountants has been the reconciliation of the interests of a casino's owners-of-record, who hoped to profit, and its secret gangster owners, hungrily awaiting their skimming dividends."[28]

Government experts credited Lansky with the development and refinement of skimming, and believed that the processing of untaxed revenue through Swiss banks opened the way for Lansky's investment of millions of dollars in real estate. The indictment also said that Lansky received large fees from the 1960 sale of the Flamingo to Lansburgh's group, and the 1968 sale of the hotel by that group to Kirk Kerkorian.

Lansburgh served five months in prison for his guilty plea. Lansky never stood trial because of his absence in Israel; and later because he claimed ill health. Lansky's physician, Dr. Howard Grumer, supported Lansky's lawyer's motion to dismiss the skimming charges on grounds that Lansky was ready for a massive stroke which could result from the anxiety associated with the trial. Lansky's physician's letter portrayed a doddering invalid suffering from recurrent episodes of intermittent confusion, transient visual loss, vertigo, small strokes, chronic bronchitis, emphysema, and duodenal ulcer disease. United States District Judge Roger Foley, sitting in Las Vegas, in August 1974, removed the case from the calendar and chided the Department of Justice for not dismissing the charges. He concluded: "The court finds it is almost a certainty that this elderly and seriously ill defendant will never be well enough to undergo the rigors of the trial of this complex case."[29] Judge Foley formally dismissed the case in October 1976.

Five months later a *Miami Herald* feature article marking the occasion of Lansky's 75th birthday reported that "Lansky maintains his contact with organized crime figures, continues in other questionable associations and has frequent encounters with at least one public official. . . .

"Lansky now takes morning walks with his dog along Collins Avenue and is a regular at opening nights at the Miami Beach Theater of the Performing Arts."[30]

5

From August 9 through 27, 1966, the Nevada Gaming Commission met in special session to discuss the federal charges. The hearings were inhibited by the refusal of federal agents to testify, claiming "executive privilege."

In the "Skim Report" prepared as a result of this session the gaming commission denied that casino money was going to the underworld, and accused the Department of Justice of harassment, betrayal, and blackmail. It pledged to devise a more sophisticated method of observing money handling in casinos, utilizing the latest electronic devices and accounting methods.

But it was the attack on the FBI, both in the report and Sawyer's cover letter to Katzenbach, that was the major issue of that summer and fall. The strongest allegation was that during Robert Kennedy's term as attorney general, the FBI conducted, in violation of Nevada law, ". . . a morally reprehensible program of domestic espionage upon the citizens of this state."[31] Sawyer reviewed the Kennedy and Katzenbach years at the Department of Justice and depicted Nevada as ". . . besieged by an onslaught of federal agencies, some of whom subjected the gaming industry and private citizens to what amounted to harassment." The siege and harassment, he added, violated a "mutual agreement of cooperation between the Justice Department and the state in the fight against the criminal syndicate."[32]

Sawyer chided the FBI for overstepping its mandate, for abusing its law enforcement mission: "The chief law enforcement agency of the federal government is charged with enforcement of the law. The use of illegal or unethical means by this agency is unconscionable."[33]

The wiretapping, leaking of documents, refusal to turn over information to the state, and the continuing investigation by federal agencies, all without indictments, amounted to, Sawyer concluded, a "shocking story of espionage and harassment against the state ... determined to damage or destroy the major business of this state — without regard to morality or law."[34]

By mid-1966 Nevada had reached an impasse with the federal government. Governor Sawyer, seeking an unprecedented third term, was vulnerable to criticism regarding his adversarial relationship with Hoover and the federal government. By contrast, young Lieutenant Governor and Republican Paul Laxalt promised to make peace with the FBI.

Some Nevadans felt that the gaming commission's skim investigation had been poorly conceived. Laxalt was one of these, contending that people outside the state would consider the report a "whitewash." The Las Vegas Sun thought it unusual that the gaming commission could look at the same thing the FBI saw, and one would only see white while the other saw black.[35] During the controversy, a former gaming control official was quoted as saying: "Until the investigation started, the commotion amounted to nothing more than the same sort of exposé stories that have been printed so many times they become monotonous ... Now there is something official to hang them on."[36]

The 1966 gubernatorial campaign was touted as the "race of the century" in Nevada. The campaign discussed Nevada's pressing problems — an expanding population, schools, water shortage, inadequate state services, dependence upon one industry. But with gambling under attack, the other issues faded, and the governor's race was transformed into a debate over relations with the federal authorities.

Laxalt took the offensive. Saying that it was time to mend fences with the FBI, he promised, if elected, to seek a personal meeting with J. Edgar Hoover. Laxalt accepted casino industry money for his campaign, and at the same time castigated Sawyer's "war policy with the FBI" for endangering the future of the gambling industry, the state's economy, and the livelihood of the state's residents. "We have to erase the image that we are in bed with hoodlums," he said. "We must prove to people across the nation that we are an honest state, operating above-board and out in the open."[37]

Some observers attributed Laxalt's victory as much to Sawyer's attempt for an unprecedented third term, as to the conflict with the federal government. Besides, it was unclear what Laxalt would do, once elected, since his largest campaign contributors included those who troubled Hoover most. But Laxalt was rescued from his dilemma when, late in 1966, a private train secretively brought one of America's wealthiest men to Las Vegas. The arrival of Howard Hughes, who was to buy within the year three of the hotels reputedly controlled by organized crime, was a watershed for Nevada. If the state had "grandfathered" in those seen as organized criminals by the federal government, it needed someone like Hughes to buy them out.

10

Investment Capital: Widening the Base*

THE BEGINNING OF NEVADA'S CONTEMPORARY GAMING HISTORY AND the developments leading to the control system to be discussed in detail in the next chapter and those following, can be attributed to the entry of Howard Hughes. Hughes reversed the direction of Nevada. "Back in 1966," as an industry newsletter reported, "Nevada had hit a new low. Its gambling was under unremitting attack from Washington and Nevada was under ultimatum to straighten out, to get rid of certain hotel managements. This might have taken years except for the sudden appearance of Hughes who bought three in five months. . . . By getting into the gambling business he convinced millions that gambling can't be dirty or Hughes — genius of helicopters, space vehicles, electronics — wouldn't get into it. It was a public relations breakthrough for Nevada that could not have been delivered by Madison Avenue for $50 million."[1]

What Nevada saw in Howard Hughes is clear. What remains murky is what Howard Hughes saw in Nevada. While some viewed

* This chapter was co-authored by John Dombrink.

his purchases of Las Vegas casinos in the 1960s as standard business investments, others saw them as participation again in a flamboyant industry for the man who had been a pioneer in motion pictures and aircraft. Some even theorized that Hughes wanted available cash in large quantities to speculate in world gold or mineral markets. Always, three traits — quite consistent — seemed to dominate: He needed to be powerful and to exercise power; he was constantly fearful of being undermined, by "germs" as well as people; and he eventually became totally dependent upon the staff over whom he exerted direct power. Above all, he was very rich, and thus could indulge fantasies and phobias.[2]

Born in 1905, heir to the Hughes Tool Company his father had built as the leading supplier of oil well drilling bits, Hughes had been a Hollywood playboy, movie producer, and crack pilot. After World War II he built his aircraft business into a successful electronics giant and sold his TWA stock in the 1966 bull market for over $584 million, a sale he was pushed into by dissident stockholders.[3]

This was the largest sum ever to come into one man's hands at one time, and Hughes proceeded to use a portion of it to buy into Nevada, as though it were a giant Monopoly game. He was frequently seen at Las Vegas resorts before his decision to seek seclusion in the 1950s, and had made large real estate purchases in the Las Vegas area around that time. Around Thanksgiving 1966, he arrived in Las Vegas furtively, and took up residence in the Desert Inn Hotel. Moe Dalitz, then the principal owner of the resort, would testify later that Teamster leader Jimmy Hoffa had been partially instrumental in arranging Hughes's stay at the Desert Inn.[4]

In March 1967, Hughes purchased the hotel for an estimated $13 million. Four months later he added the Sands Hotel to his holdings, for a reported $14.6 million; then the Castaways for $3 million, and the Frontier for $14 million.[5] His holdings were purchased in the name of the Hughes Tool Company, of which Howard Hughes was sole stockholder. In early 1968, Hughes prepared to purchase the Silver Slipper and Stardust. Those six casinos would give Hughes roughly 25 percent of the business done in Las Vegas, and about one-seventh of the state's gaming revenues. More importantly, he would capture more than a third of the gross gaming revenue along the high-income-producing Las Vegas Strip.[6] To some it appeared that Hughes was purchasing control over one of the states of the Union.

Others, evincing more provincial cares, were worried that Hughes could dictate employment and gambling policy by building a controlling interest in Strip ownership. He could even change the odds in games and force other operators to follow. Nevertheless, the response to the billionaire was overwhelmingly positive; his presence was perceived by most officials as good public relations for the state. The "Hughes Effect," as the *Wall Street Journal* termed it, had boosted the sagging Las Vegas economy, attracted a new class of tourist trade, and sparked an influx of corporate investors who followed Hughes's example and bought up casinos owned by groups believed to have mob connections.

The Laxalt administration gave Hughes pretty much what he wanted. Laxalt, who was later to become United States senator, was a favorite tennis partner of Robert Maheu, Hughes's Nevada administrator. "The Laxalt administration," according to James Phelan, "proved remarkably suggestible. The state gambling control agency waived most of the rules to avoid intruding on Hughes's "privacy." He was not required to furnish a contemporary photograph, to appear before the gaming board in person to be finger-printed, or to provide a detailed financial statement. Once when he wanted a license in a hurry for a newly purchased casino, the control agency members, scattered around the state, gave their approval in a few hours by 'meeting' via a conference telephone call."[7]

Under Lyndon Johnson, the Department of Justice anti-trust investigators were nevertheless concerned and moved to block his state-approved purchase of the Stardust. Hughes, always wary of a legal tilt with the federal government, which would mean opening his private affairs to scrutiny, withdrew from the Stardust deal. When Nixon became president, Attorney General John Mitchell overruled the Department of Justice's Anti-Trust Division chief without consulting him, and permitted Hughes to acquire the 30-story "white elephant" Landmark on the Strip, and Harolds Club in Reno.

"This federal about-face," according to Phelan, "coincided with the secret delivery by a Hughes aide of $50,000 in cash to Nixon's close friend, Bebe Rebozo. Rebozo received two such packets of $100 bills from Richard Danner, a one-time FBI agent turned Hughes casino manager. Rebozo said later he understood the $100,000 was a "campaign contribution." Instead of putting the money into any campaign, he claimed he put it in his safety-deposit box. He returned it to Hughes three years later when a swarm of IRS and Senate investigators began examining the money-passing."[8]

This, and other stories Phelan reports about Hughes, suggests that he was no less inclined to bribe and corrupt public officials than a Mafia chieftain. Possibly, because of his more secure position as a "respectable" big businessman, he was even more inclined. In any event, post-Watergate revelations regarding major corporate bribery suggest that Hughes's practices were in keeping with prevailing corporate ethics.

The Senate Watergate Committee pondered the theory that in 1973, the Watergate break-in may have been committed to determine how much Democratic Chairman O'Brien, who had worked for Hughes, knew of the $100,000 "loan" Hughes had channeled to President Nixon through Nixon's friend Bebe Rebozo. The White House "Plumbers Unit" supposedly broke into the safe of a Las Vegas newspaper publisher, seeking such information.

Nobody knows exactly what Hughes expected from the loan, but in 1969 Hughes had instructed Maheu to begin negotiations toward purchase of the Dunes Hotel, despite previous anti-trust problems. Richard Danner was sent to Washington and met three times with Mitchell. Nobody has been able to learn exactly what went on in those conversations. Mitchell denies having assented to a Dunes purchase, but Mitchell is scarcely a credible denier. In any case, the deal fell through on business grounds, and the Dunes remained in the hands of its owners. Nevada officials had been concerned that with the amount of money Hughes could afford to contribute to political campaigns, state and local candidates would be beholden to him and inclined to set Nevada policies and adjust regulations to favor his interests. It appears that Hughes's national influence was comparable to or exceeded his influence in Nevada.

Hughes's life in Nevada was closely guarded. As a result of his death, the revelations of his staff, and conflict over his will, details of his life after 1966 are gradually emerging. Thin and aging, his long hair and fingernails giving him the appearance of a ship-wrecked sailor, Hughes was surrounded by elaborate security and a crew of male secretary-nurses, predominantly Mormon, who ministered to his comforts and eccentricities. The man who was among the wealthiest in the world bottled and stored his urine, watched mediocre movies on his own projector, injected himself with mysterious drugs, and went on bizarre eating jags.

2

For four years Hughes conducted his unique life-style from his penthouse atop the Desert Inn. Then, around Thanksgiving 1970, Howard Hughes quietly stole away from Nevada. His departure came amid a power struggle between competing executives and lawyers in Hughes-controlled companies.

Ten days after he left Las Vegas, Hughes ordered the dismissal of his chief executive, Robert Maheu. At that point, the faction opposing Maheu moved their personnel into the casino cashier cages to take over the money and records. They retreated only after a Las Vegas judge found their action improper, and granted Maheu an injunction. When Maheu challenged the authenticity of Hughes's signature in court — on a proxy granting power to the Davis-Gay forces — Hughes telephoned Governor Laxalt and expressed his support for Davis and Gay.[9]

As the fight for control continued in court, more amazing facts turned up. Maheu testified that he had never seen Hughes face to face in a 17-year association. Instead, they had communicated by telephone, through messages phoned by the secretary-nurses, and in the now-famous handwritten messages that were always on yellow ruled sheets, and delivered by a security guard. Maheu was ousted, but he eventually was awarded nearly $3 million in damages for false accusations made by Hughes, reportedly on the representations of his California executives seeking to wrest control of the Hughes empire from Maheu.[10] (On December 28, 1977, after Hughes had died, the 9th U.S. Court of Appeals reversed the damage award and sent the case back for a new trial on the grounds that "the trial court's one-sided characterization of Maheu came close to directing a verdict in his favor, thus denying Summa a fair trial.")

The firing of Maheu put Hughes once again in the spotlight. Spurred on by the Hughes publicity and aided by a Hughes aide's unpublished memoirs, author Clifford Irving produced a bogus Hughes autobiography for McGraw-Hill. Irving maintained that he had surreptitiously met Hughes in motel rooms and parked cars at a time when Hughes was refusing to meet with Nevada gaming authorities to authorize changes in his casino management.

While Hughes could have let the fake autobiography pass, he could no longer afford to offend the Nevada officials. Unless he denied meeting repeatedly with Irving, he could hardly continue to refuse meeting with Nevada authorities. On January 7, 1972, from his Bahamas hotel suite, Hughes conducted a telephone interview with seven newsmen who had interviewed him previously. His denial of the Irving book was front page news across the country. He disclaimed tales of his wild appearance, said he would fly again, and spelled out his plans to return to Nevada.[11]

In 1972, the gaming commission appointed by Governor O'Callaghan denied an application for the Hughes organization to alter its corporate structure, until the recluse agreed to meet personally with some state officials. Basically, the governor and the gaming officials wanted to know whether Hughes existed, whether he sounded reasonably coherent, and whether he supported those who claimed to be his representatives. In March 1973, O'Callaghan and his Gaming Control Board chairman flew to London, for a two-hour private meeting with Hughes on the future of his Nevada gaming holdings.

Hughes met with them in his London suite at 2:00 A.M. Hughes appeared in a bathrobe and slippers, wearing an old-fashioned hearing device, which he would point in the direction of the speaker. His appearance was neat but frail.

Hughes spoke in great detail about the oil drilling bit that served as the springboard for the Hughes fortune. "He seemed," according to the gaming board chairman, "eccentric but articulate."[12] The only agreement made by the governor and the gaming board chairman was to keep the details of his appearance secret. Since

Hughes looked reasonably "normal" the request seemed harmless enough, and was honored. Years later, James Phelan was to report that hours were spent getting Hughes in shape for the meeting, in particular trimming his shoulder length hair and several-inch-long fingernails. As a result of his representation to the governor and the gaming board chairman that he wanted new management representatives, the gaming commission approved them.[13]

Hughes's entry into Nevada changed the course of legalized gambling in that state. Publicly traded corporations followed his lead in investing in casinos. Hughes was eccentric, but, especially during the 1960s, he was a leading and respected businessman. He certainly captured the good offices of Governor Laxalt, who made no apologies for the special privileges accorded to Hughes. "Mr. Hughes's involvement here has absolutely done us wonders," Laxalt enthused. "I just returned from a trip to the East where I spoke to some industrialists in mid-town Manhattan and their questions no longer are concerned with the Mafia, the skimming, the underworld. . . . People come here now feeling they can come here in respectable, safe circumstances."[14]

Between 1966, when Hughes came to Nevada, and 1976, when he died, the gross gaming revenues of the state's casinos tripled: from $336 million annually to $1.18 billion annually. After his death in 1976, Nevada officials debated Hughes's worth to the state. Not only had his concentration of power threatened the state's economy, but materially he had done little for the gaming industry. He bought existing properties, did little to improve them, and built no new resort hotel complexes. He promised space-age casinos and a medical school, but did not deliver. Hughes had not expanded gaming directly, but, by bringing some respectability to a pariah industry, indirectly promoted investment. For this alone, Nevadans were grateful.

3

When Nevada's gaming industry was still small, most of the business enterprises conducting gaming were organized as sole proprietorships and partnerships. As the industry grew, and the average casino increased in size, larger investments were needed and more investors involved.[15]

The corporate form, while not expressly prohibited by the state, was not encouraged. The 1931 legalization act had permitted ownership of gaming facilities by corporations. But a provision in 1955 that each stockholder be licensed effectively kept publicly traded corporations from owning gaming facilities, because neither the corporation nor the state had the means to prequalify ownership in a stock market with daily trading.

From the early 1950s to the mid-1960s, Nevada gaming authorities emphasized the goal of knowing who the owners and operators of the casinos were, in the hope that holding every one of them accountable would achieve the goals of honest and accurate tax accounting.

From time to time corporations did form to operate a casino, albeit with only a few stockholders. Hughes, for example, was sole stockholder of his corporation and the board of directors was responsible to a lone stockholder. A few publicly traded corporations did manage entry into gaming. By forming an independent Nevada corporation or partnership, a limited number of officers of a publicly traded corporation could enter the gaming industry. In some cases, such corporations entered as landlord to another newly formed entity which conducted the gaming.

Nevada casinos have never rated high with conventional financing institutions. Traditional lenders have been wary of the casino business with its heavy cash flow, opportunity for skimming, precarious reputation, and lack of standard business procedures among the casino managers.

One outcome has been a troublesome and inordinate reliance for investment capital on the Teamsters Central States Pension Fund. According to figures released by the fund's director at the close of 1976, a total of $269 million was invested in Nevada casinos out of $1.4 billion in total fund assets.[16] Teamsters fund loans to Nevada casinos in good part precipitated a Department of Labor investigation of the fund in 1976. Still, it has been very difficult for the state to bar such funds, partly because it needs them, and partly because a pariah industry cannot afford to be fastidious with a pariah lender, provided that the lender is an acceptable legal entity.

Moreover, there is an ironic quality to the situation existing between the state of Nevada and the Teamsters, since the Teamsters have to a degree earned their disrepute because they have loaned so much money to casino gambling, which the state of Nevada insists is a legitimate and respectable activity. Were the state to prohibit casinos from borrowing from the Teamsters, it would not simply be a case of the pot calling the kettle black. In this instance, others call the kettle black because of its associations with the pot.

The Teamsters loans are part of a large investment capital problem, which, by the 1960s, began to emerge clearly: that a broadening of the investment base in the gaming industry was absolutely essential to the growth of the industry. Loans necessary for the construction of a new establishment or expansion were not available from conventional sources. Reputable financial institutions were unwilling to lend the huge sums required to a small group of investors and very few individuals could afford the heavy personal investments necessary. Hughes, of course, had proved an exception.

A 1966 study of the gaming industry commissioned by the Nevada legislature came to a conclusion shared by many of the financial analysts and bankers: the major casinos had to enlarge or face severe financial problems. Department of Justice officials believed that a good deal of the financial problems could be traced to skimming. Still, the effects of rising labor costs, the war in attracting top-name, top-salary entertainers, the changing nature of the Nevada customer, and the possible saturation of casinos had moved casino owners to add rooms. A new economic strategy was developing along the Strip: hotels needed more customers — a higher volume of play by a new type of customer who played modestly, and who would stay at the hotel.

The Corporate Gaming Act, conceived of and lobbied for by the Resort Association, took three legislative sessions for passage. Corporate gaming had been proposed in the 1963 and 1965 legislative sessions, but the state had balked, fearing the possibility of having to license every stockholder in a publicly traded corporation. One major obstacle to acceptance of the corporate gaming concept was the position of the northern Nevada casino owners, who had resisted the move for several years. The northerners didn't look forward to the competition that publicly traded corporations would bring. They argued that the large corporations would dwarf established operations, and set standards and policy for the industry. Conversely, Las Vegas was desperate for investment money.

More than economics separated the two groups. Nevada, like New York and California, has a north-south antagonism rooted in the physical and historical differences between Reno and Las Vegas. Vogliotti writes: "The old Reno/Tahoe section looks down upon Las Vegas as bush, noisy, vulgarish, criminalish and baffling for its ability to capture glamour and earn millions. The south reciprocates, describing the north as stodgy, dull, third rate and capable only of such entertainment as you find in Balkan villages."[17]

More legislators began to favor the concept of a law that would provide money to speed up the sale of the "problem" casinos, as statements from Washington alleging gangster ownership intensified. They needed to devise a means of providing equity capital and insuring wider investor participation, while still maintaining the necessary controls over the operations of the gaming establishments.

Then-Governor Sawyer also feared possible intervention by federal agencies concerned with corporate control. In a 1976 interview he was to say: "Another fear of mine was that we would just call down the feds upon the state with all kinds of controls upon the corporations. The hostility of the Federal Government to Nevada gaming was such that I felt that we would never get a fair shake."[18]

Still, the nationwide ownership of Nevada gaming casinos, through wide ownership of publicly traded securities, would broaden the support base of Nevada gambling and decrease the possibility of adverse federal legislation. Finally, in 1969, the Nevada legislature was able to write a bill enabling publicly traded corporations to own gaming operations without licensing each stockholder.

Nevada authorities believed that the emergence of corporate gaming would further the control of legal casino gambling in several crucial ways. It was hoped, first, that SEC disclosure requirements, their scrutiny of publicly traded entities, and the involvement of federal law generally would deter hidden control. Moreover, SEC filing requirements, proxy regulations, and rules for reporting would serve as a valuable backup to the state's requirements for determining control.

Second, publicly traded corporations would seek to avoid negative publicity, fearing adverse effects upon stock prices. Thus, the corporations would try to demonstrate to a large audience — the SEC, the stock exchange, stock analysts, investors, and stockholders — how well-protected their corporate assets and revenues are. They began by installing the most sophisticated security systems the casinos had yet seen.

Third, as a general rule, the casinos owned by publicly traded corporations are the larger hotel-casino complexes, and as such would stand to lose more should they be caught cheating. The Hilton Hotels Corporation owned or managed 163 hotels in 1976. Of these, the Company's Las Vegas hotel-casinos accounted for approximately 43% of its income before interest and dividend income, interest expense, write-down of investments and sales of properties, and income taxes in fiscal 1975 as compared to 29% in fiscal 1974.[19]

Fourth, the impact of publicly traded corporations would, it was thought, be greatest and most positive in the area of accurate tax accounting. In casinos owned by publicly traded corporations, management and ownership are presumably separated, and ownership is interested in effective internal controls to protect the assets and revenues of the corporation. Thus, the interests of the publicly traded parent of a corporate gaming licensee and those of the gaming authorities coincided in the development of accounting procedures and controls that minimized the possibility of revenues being diverted from the corporation.

The Corporate Gaming Act was the last major addition to the legal structure of gaming control in Nevada. As we shall see in the next chapter, its details were still being examined and reformulated in 1977. As with previous control measures, this one was particularly intended to remedy the major problems begun by Siegel and others who originated the Las Vegas gambling casino business; that is, to locate socially respectable sources of revenue, who would also pose fewer control problems. Still, as later chapters will show and discuss, the optimism expressed by advocates of corporate gaming would not be borne out in practice — the legal form of the enterprise would not prove as significant as the individuals operating the casino. The development of corporate gaming might reduce the investment capital or skimming problems of the industry, but it would not eliminate them.

11

Contemporary Control

THE INTERSTATE COMMERCE COMMISSION, THE FEDERAL TRADE COMmission, the Securities and Exchange Commission, and the National Labor Relations Board are all administrative agencies created by Congress to control commercial and industrial activities. The growth of these agencies has been perhaps the most remarkable governmental development since the Roosevelt administration. They are also a social scientist's dream because administrative agencies are governments in microcosm.[1]

An administrative body may be called a board or an agency, commission, division, authority, administration, or any other such designation the active mind of legislators or their assistants can invent. It doesn't really matter. What counts is the actual authority given and the discretion exercised in carrying out that authority. Administrative agencies are themselves regulated by law: what they can and cannot do, how they should and should not act in making these governmental decisions.

Scholars disagree whether the substance of these laws can legitimately be called a "field" of law. More importantly, there is increasing recognition that bureaucratic, political, and social interests count far more in determining administrative agency actions than formal legal considerations. "Most administrative agencies," writes Richard B. Stewart in the *Harvard Law Review*, "act in a highly charged field of political forces. . . . The policies adopted by the agencies, the energy and effectiveness with which they are pursued, and the agency's ultimate impact on the world may all be far more a function of these factors than the formal apparatus of administrative law."[2]

These "factors" — and how they really influence gaming control — are the principal subject of this book. This chapter is an introduction to the gaming control agency as it functioned during the period I studied it, 1974 to 1977. The chapter is intended to accomplish a number of things: to introduce the structure of the agency and the breadth of its authority; to introduce some of its key people; to illustrate some of the dynamics of control, especially two sets of relations — the formal legal one obtaining between the legislature and agency, and the informal problems of authority generated among various segments of the agency and persons working in it.

Finally, the chapter discusses an overriding issue affecting the agency's capacity to do its job fairly and vigorously: What kinds of measures, if any, are appropriate to restrict future employment in the industry by agency officials?

2

The Gaming Control Act delegates strong and broad powers to the *Gaming Commission* and *Gaming Control Board*. The two together constitute the "agency." The agency licenses every Nevada business having anything to do with gaming, from the most major casino, to the grocery store harboring a few slot machines.

The formal structure of authority does not, however, represent the reality of the gaming control enterprise. The statute technically delegates all power to the commission. Moreover, the commission, sitting at the top of the structure, apparently controls the subordinate board. (See Chart 1.) But that is not always accurate.

CHART 1.—ORGANIZATION AND FUNCTIONS, NEVADA GAMING REGULATORY AGENCIES*

NEVADA GAMING COMMISSION
- 5 part-time members appointed by Governor; not more than 3 with same political affiliation; no more than 2 with same profession or association; no political activities; staggered terms opposite Governor's term.
- Final authority to require, issue, deny, suspend or revoke gaming license.

GAMING POLICY COMMITTEE
- 7 part-time members with Governor as chairman; 1 member of the Gaming Commission, 1 member of the Gaming Control Board, 2 members representing gaming industry, and 2 members representing general public.
- Makes advisory recommendations regarding gaming policy.

STATE GAMING CONTROL BOARD
- 3 full-time members; 1 with administrative background, 1 accountant, and 1 with legal or law enforcement experience.
- Conducts background investigations on license applicants and recommends issuance or denial of gaming license to Gaming Commission.
- Enforces gaming laws and regulations.
- Collects gaming taxes, fees, and penalties.
- Inspects premises where gaming is conducted.

Investigation Division
- Conducts all field investigations needed for processing applicants for gaming licenses.

Enforcement Division
- Protects the honesty of games and gaming establishments from cheaters.
- Investigates customer complaints.

Audit Division
- Conducts regular and unscheduled audits of gaming establishments.
- Monitors internal gaming controls and security measures.
- Enforces accounting regulations.
- Investigates loans to licensees.

Tax & Licensing Division
- Issues and updates licenses.
- Collects gaming taxes, fees, and penalties.

Securities and Economic Research Division
- Collects, analyzes, and publishes financial information relating to gaming industry.
- Maintains a reporting system on publicly traded corporations with casino interests.

* From the Commission on the Review of the National Policy Toward Gambling, *Gambling in America* (Washington: U.S. Government Printing Office, 1976), p. 85.

During this study, the commission enjoyed real power, but the board, which supervised 156 full-time employees,[3] maintained the capacity to shape the direction of that power.

The commission was composed of five persons, each appointed for a term of four years. Commissioners were not permitted to hold office in a political party, or "hold a direct pecuniary interest" in the gambling industry. Thus, a lawyer serving on the commission could not retain clients in the gambling business. This sort of restriction might not mean much anywhere else, but in Nevada it is financially consequential, and tended to exclude from the commission most of the leading attorneys in the Las Vegas area, and increasingly, in the entire state.

The commission met at least one day a month, and sometimes more often. Unlike the board, it was composed of volunteers who, by law, were compensated at $40 per day.[4] (One commissioner was a Standard Oil dealer for Las Vegas; another a small town newspaper editor; a third a nongaming motel owner on the Las Vegas Strip; a fourth, who replaced a Las Vegas lawyer, a Las Vegas accountant.) The commission was apparently supposed to take into account the broader business interests of the state, while the board functioned primarily as an investigative and policing agency.

The commission chairman enjoyed a lucrative personal injury law practice. Although someone other than a lawyer might function effectively as chairman, a skilled lawyer can exercise exceptional control over both the board and the industry, whatever the structural limitations placed upon him. Yet the commission operated under two principal legislative constraints. First, in licensing decisions, a negative vote by the board required a unanimous commission vote to overrule. Second, commissioners were part-timers with other interests. Accordingly, the board controlled day-to-day operations. It, rather than the commission, was the operative portion of the agency. I shall describe board members in greater detail because, if social and economic groups and interests influence administrative agencies, their force is mediated by the quality of agency personnel. Who occupies an administrative position may be equally, if not more important, than whether there is one.

3

The board chairman, whom I shall call "Tom Walker," presided over a sizable staff of investigators, law enforcement officers, and auditors, with a chief as head of each of these three major divisions of the agency. When a government official can draw upon a sizable staff, with ample resources and facilities, he can emerge a significant figure. The chairman of the Gaming Control Board enjoys the resources to be the second most powerful man in the state, next to the governor. Tom Walker was regarded in Nevada as a strong and powerful chairman, without doubt the key figure in the agency.

Walker was born in Montana in 1934, graduated from a Catholic high school in Reno, where he starred on the football team; and turned down an athletic scholarship to Princeton to stay — among friends — in Nevada. He played football at the University of Nevada, joined the service, abandoned the idea of a law school education when his wife became pregnant. After some time as a juvenile probation officer, he became director of the Nevada Health and Welfare Department. When, in 1971, Mike O'Callaghan became governor, O'Callaghan appointed Walker to the chairmanship of the Gaming Control Board.

Whatever criticisms might be made of Walker — and for years one heard remarkably few either from his staff, the industry, or the press — there was no question about his administrative ability. His critics suggested he was power-centered and dominating, perhaps too close personally to a number of owners and executives. Nobody suggested, however, that he was less than sharply intelligent. "He is," as one put it, "an old fox, and you've got to be careful you're not one of his chickens."

Normally, the board chairman works out of Carson City, the state capital, where the main offices of the board are located, along with the governor's office, the legislature, and other agencies and bureaus. Carson City is to Las Vegas what Springfield is to Chicago, Albany to New York City, and Sacramento to Los Angeles. But given the remarkably small population of Nevada, Carson City, unlike Las Vegas, is really a small town, not only in population but in feeling. One can drive through it along the main thoroughfare in about three minutes flat; and the bar where high-ranking government officials drink after work could survive nowhere except perhaps in such other Nevada towns as Ely and Tonopah.

Walker worked closely with the other board members, one of whom was Pat Tracy. Like Walker, Tracy also worked in Carson City. By statute each board member is supposed to be specially qualified in one of three areas: public administration, finance, or law enforcement.[5] Walker held the administrative slot, while Tracy occupied the position designated for someone experienced in finance. Tracy's formal financial qualifications derived from prior experience on the tax commisson. He represented an earlier era of gaming control, and his formal credentials were slighter than his informal ones as an old-timer liked and trusted by Nevadans throughout government and the gaming industry.

The statute was interestingly ambiguous about the qualifications it mandated for the position of *fiscal director*.[6] That person need not, as the chart drawn by the National Commission on Gambling suggests, have been an accountant. The gambling commission's error is understandable. The qualifications were drawn in seemingly strong language, e.g., that the fiscal director shall have a comprehensive knowledge of the principles and practices of corporate finance. But the statute allowed an undercutting alternative — that the fiscal director may be an expert in gaming. In any event, Tracy, the occupant, was not a CPA.

The state required the third member of the board to be experienced in *law enforcement*. It did not require that the third member or the staff be located in Las Vegas. Yet this exercise of administrative discretion — that there be a set of offices comparable in size to those in Carson City — was more consequential than the formal requirement that the third member possess a background in law enforcement. These sorts of requirements are broadly stretched and therefore rather easily met, although not quite meaningless. For example, Walker could if necessary have fulfilled the law enforcement requirement.

The board's law enforcement slot was occupied by two different people during my research. The first, Kimball Bixbe, had been a deputy sheriff in Washoe County before going back to college and then to law school at the University of Utah, where he rose to become managing editor of the law review. Bixbe's elevation to the board, if seen as a political appointment, represented the administrative equivalent of an Eastern "balanced ticket." For Bixbe, a Mormon, and his successor, a Jew, law enforcement credentials were necessary by statute but not sufficient by politics. The commission chairman was of Basque descent (as is Senator Laxalt). Basques constitute a significant political constituency in northern Nevada. Walker was Catholic, Tracy Protestant.

It is worth discussing further the presence of an active Mormon (Bixbe) on the board, because Mormons constitute a sizable and historically influential portion of Nevada's population. Although it is unlikely that the Church of Jesus Christ of Latter Day Saints would call for the prohibition of casino gambling in Nevada, the choice of a Mormon to sit on the Gaming Control Board was nevertheless politically advantageous. Mormons are willing to accept the necessity of casino gambling, but they are not enamored of it. While the Church of Latter Day Saints totally forbids its active members to engage in casino gambling, it does permit limited participation in casino management. It also opposes the extension of legal gambling to other states. A Mormon on the board, particularly one who is a devout and active member of the church, reassures the Mormon population not only of representation on the board, but also of a certain kind of representation. If Mormons must abide gambling in the state, at least they can feel it will be administered by men of probity.

4

The appointment of a Mormon also symbolizes integrity. The agency is very concerned about its reputation for integrity with the law enforcement intelligence community. This includes agencies associated with the United States Department of Justice such as the FBI, various United States attorneys' offices, and organized crime strike task forces; other federal agencies such as the Internal Revenue Service, the Securities and Exchange Commission and the United States Immigration Service; plus a wide variety of state and local police agencies such as the attorney general for the states of Illinois or Michigan and the Los Angeles Police Department's organized crime unit. The gaming control authorities cannot function without considerable cooperation from these other agencies.

Law enforcement officials who deal with organized crime are apt to be even more suspicious than ordinary police, who are suspicious enough. I have elsewhere developed the concept of the symbolic assailant to describe the stereotyping that patrol police, like the rest of us, engage in when walking the streets and making assessments of the potential dangerousness of individuals. Patrol police develop a perceptual shorthand to identify gesture, language, and attire that police recognize as a prelude to violence. The judgment that someone symbolizes potentially violent behavior in the street is based on a rather simple symbolic code involving age grading, demeanor, dress style, and racial, and cultural characteristics. A young, black male in a white middle-class or business neighborhood may symbolize the threat of violence to an observing patrolman, even if the young man has never committed a violent crime in his life.

Is there an organized crime counterpart to the "symbolic" assailant? Not really. B movies and TV series to the contrary notwithstanding, no policeman would claim that he could walk into a Las Vegas gambling casino and pick out the organized criminals on the basis of their appearance. Indeed, one who skims does not possess a standard symbolic stereotype, even in fiction, where the hired killer always looks tough and mean and brutish. Real life is very different. One gangland assassin most feared by police is deceptively mild-mannered and pudgy.

If appearance is the most important symbolic representation to be attended to by the street cop, the organized crime cop works with elusive and intractable data. Big-time hotel casino gambling was started in Las Vegas by a Jewish gangster. Does that mean that every casino owner or employee with a Jewish background should be suspected to be linked with organized crime? Obviously not. As we shall see later, in many cases, certainly the hard ones, the organized crime designation takes law, both criminal and administrative, into the area of character assessment based upon life history. As the street cop responds to appearance and behavior, the organized crime cop responds to life history and prior associations. He is more of a clinician than a technician in a legal setting where the clinical judgment does not hold much weight.

A Catholic, especially one whose last name ends in a vowel, may easily earn the suspicion of possessing an organized criminal affiliation. So may a Protestant, and so surely may a Jew. But Mormons seem different. The Mormon religion suggests moral purity, which is one reason Howard Hughes surrounded himself with believers in the latter-day saints of Jesus Christ. Similarly, when a Mormon presides on a board regulating an industry stigmatized both by the antigambling view held by various churches and many citizens, as well as by the notorious history of gangland connections in Las Vegas, the Mormon projection cleanses. In this respect, Kimball Bixbe's presence on the Gaming Control Board performed latent services perhaps not wholly appreciated by those affiliated with the gambling industry.

5

Actually, Bixbe functioned very much as a lawyer on the board. One of his main lawyering tasks as a board member was to interpret the regulations in writing, something strongly advised by leading experts in administrative law.[7] Bixbe and other board members also spent considerable time orally interpreting regulations to those working in the industry. His successor did this often enough to consider employing a high-level assistant to help make these interpretations, so as to afford him more time to think about major policy issues.

As a lawyer, Bixbe also served as a liaison to three other very important staff members — deputy attorneys general assigned by statute to the board and commission as legal counsel.[8] Two were permanently assigned on a full-time basis. They advised and counseled the board on areas that might be particularly sensitive to future litigation. They also represented gaming officials when suit was brought against the board or commission — most commonly in connection with denial of license or the imposition of a disciplinary sanction. A third deputy attorney general was a securities specialist deputized on a fee basis to advise the board and commission on securities law. As indicated in the previous chapter, this area of law became increasingly important as publicly traded companies penetrated the gambling industry. The Corporate Gaming Act is a key part of the edifice of control. Its history reveals much about relations between the Nevada legislature and the gaming authorities. Its interpretation suggests the deep and often hidden suspicions the board and staff hold in assessing the action and motives of commission members. Indeed, later on, under a new commission chairman, suspicion rose to outright hostilities. I shall illustrate these dynamics from a complex case involving Frank Sinatra and his lawyer.

6

Recall that before the Corporate Gaming Act of 1969 was enacted every owner of every share of stock was required to be individually licensed. It didn't matter whether somebody held stock in a gaming casino merely to earn money, to fill out a portfolio that might include General Motors and IBM stock along with San Francisco municipal bonds; or along with holding stock, was actively involved in running a casino. All stockholders — active or passive — required licensing. Then, for reasons earlier discussed, the legislature changed the law, and created regulatory problems concerning who should be required to undergo a licensing investigation.

Publicly held corporations permit an expansive industry to attract investors who don't want to work in it and who don't want to be licensed — but who do want their capital to produce income. Such "passive" investors also demand liquidity should they wish to transfer their capital to another investment. As a Nevada securities attorney put it in a memo to the gaming authorities: "They will not invest in a company by purchasing shares in a public offering unless they know that they can sell the shares without being hassled."

So with the passage of the Corporate Gaming Act, the state of Nevada created a problem. The state was for the first time required to distinguish between those who controlled casino operations and needed to be licensed; and passive stockholders — investors who should be allowed to trade their shares freely. In principle, this meant also that the state lost control over the passive stockholder. A well-known Mafia figure, e.g., Sam Giancana, could have owned shares in the Hilton Corporation and received benefits of such ownership without being licensed, provided he did not own a "controlling" share. But since he could never have met the licensing requirements, prior to the Corporate Gaming Act, he could not have held *any* stock in a corporation involved in gaming.

The legislature tossed the problem of distinguishing between an active and a passive stockholder to the gaming authorities and passed two statutes to handle the transfer. One statute said that each officer and employee of a publicly traded corporation who is or is about to be active in administering or supervising gaming activities "must be found suitable . . . and may be required to be licensed. . . ."[9] The other gave the commission the power to engage in general rulemaking to "impose on any publicly traded corporation any requirement not inconsistent with law which it may deem necessary in the public interest. . . ."[10]

But power given is not always power taken. We often hear about power-grabbing in government. A more commonplace problem, especially in police agencies, is the reluctance — for various reasons, including overwork, incompetence, laxity, corruption — to employ authorized power. Evidently, subsequent legislatures were dissatisfied with the failure of the board and commission to expand its authority to enact new regulations. So the 1971 legislature firmly directed the gaming authorities: "The Commission shall," it declared, "with the advice and assistance of the Board, adopt regulations to implement the provisions of . . . [the Corporate Gaming Act] and shall thereafter maintain such regulations in conformity thereto."[11]

The agency adopted regulations (15 and 16) effective on September 1, 1973. Under these, the old rules requiring prior approval for transfer of securities were maintained for operating corporations and closely held corporations. But new rules prevailed for corporations traded on the major stock exchanges and over-the-counter. For the first time, *control* rather than *ownership* of a corporation became the focus of regulatory action, creating a new set of questions: What is regulatory action? How should and do the gaming authorities decide what constitutes "control"?

That issue was raised most dramatically in September 1976, when the Del Webb Corporation was called in for a hearing to discuss whether Frank Sinatra and his attorney Milton Rudin, both stockholders, should be required to undergo a licensing investigation because together they controlled 6½ percent of Del Webb's stock. The board chairman outlined the issue. He pointed out that there had been erroneous discussion in the press suggesting there was a mandatory requirement that a person or group owning five percent of the stock of a publicly traded corporation be required to undergo licensing. "In our regulation," he added, "it basically states . . . that if you acquire five percent or more of the voting shares of a corporation, there is a requirement for licensing, unless there is an absence of control. That language is extremely important because it apparently provides for a rebuttable presumption; that is, if a person can show that by holding the stock he does not maintain control or he does not acquire control, then, he would be in a different posture with respect to the State."[12] Thus, a close analysis suggested that where there was no actual control of the company, licensing was not mandatory. (At the end of 1977, the legislature required that a holder of 10 percent beneficial ownership would be required to be licensed, regardless of control.[13] But it remained discretionary with the commission as to whether one holding 5 percent would be so required.)

During the testimony, it developed that Sinatra wanted to undergo licensing, but he wanted the Del Webb Corporation to pay for the costs — in his case that could run into hundreds of thousands of dollars. The Del Webb Corporation resisted on grounds that Sinatra and Rudin did not own enough stock to elect even one director to the board; had nothing to say in the operation of the corporation or its casinos; and that it would be an unnecessary expense to Del Webb and its stockholders to require that they pay for Sinatra's investigation.

The *board* was persuaded that Del Webb had rebutted Sinatra's presumption of control. The regulation stated that the commission may, "upon the recommendation of the Board," determine that an individual needs to be brought in for investigation or licensing.[14] In this case, the *commission*, led by the chairman, did not wait for the recommendation; and determined independently that Sinatra needed to be called in for licensing.

Privately, the *board* members and members of the staff were annoyed, feeling that the *commission* had found control where none existed. They speculated unflatteringly about the commission chairman's motives in what they considered a premature and arbitrary action. Some felt he entertained political ambition; others attributed his conduct to ego needs — he would be known as the official responsible for calling in Frank Sinatra to be licensed.

In March 1978, the issue was mooted. Sinatra, his attorney, and publisher Hank Greenspun sold their 629,799 shares of Webb stock to Ramada Inns, Inc., a nationwide motel chain. Sinatra's publicized interest in Webb had made the stock more valuable. The sale reportedly netted the three an estimated $6 million profit.[15]

Whatever the merits, the whole affair showed gaming authority in Nevada to be a complex regulatory structure, "in a highly charged field of political forces" with wide margins for interpretation and disagreement among constituent parts. Officials judge each other, as well as the staff, whose opinion influences both commissioners and board members.

When one observes the Nevada gaming control enterprise in action, one is reminded of Tolstoy's observation on military command. "The activity of a commander in chief," he writes, "does not at all resemble the activity we imagine to ourselves when we sit at ease in our studies examining some campaign on the map, with a certain number of troops on this and that side in a certain known locality, and begin our plans from some given moment. . . . The commander in chief is always in the midst of a series of shifting events and so he never can at any moment consider the whole import of an event that is occurring. Moment by moment the event is imperceptibly shaping itself, and at every moment of this continuous, uninterrupted shaping of events the commander in chief is in the midst of a most complex play of intrigues, worries, contingencies, authorities, projects, counsels, threats, and deceptions and is continually obliged to reply to innumerable questions addressed to him, which constantly conflict with one another."[16]

In an administrative agency, shifting events result in shifting perceptions of the agency's authority and competence. As new issues arise, at least three sorts of perceptions about agency policy and practice shift: one, about those practices and policies able to be remedied within the framework of existing authority; two, about those requiring modification by the legislature; and three, about those awaiting clarification by the judiciary.

A paramount question always at issue is the independence of the control authorities from the industry. Do they genuinely decide on the merits or are they significantly influenced by other concerns? The struggle for independence is a continuing problem and dilemma for the Nevada gaming control enterprise.

7

Where discretionary decision-making is so important, as it is in this agency and in others, conflict of interest is projected into an overriding structural problem. In Nevada, the agency could be affected in all its functions — licensing, law enforcement, and auditing. The Gaming Control Board experiences a continuing problem familiar to other administrative agencies: the industry pays better than the government. This generates two issues: the legitimacy of competition between industry and government for qualified personnel; and the question of conflict of interest for those who enter the industry from the agency.

Kimball Bixbe, for example, left the board not because he didn't enjoy his work, but because he felt he could no longer afford to remain. He had five children and a wife to support. Given their deeply held commitment to the church, he and his wife both tithed, among other contributions of time and energy, an annual donation of 10 percent of his $23,000 salary. The salary was scarcely commensurate with Bixbe's abilities or needs.

The casino gambling industry was not unhappy with Bixbe's departure. Bixbe could be a warm and likable personality, and for the most part his colleagues on the board, the staff as well as the members, liked him and enjoyed working with him. Nevertheless, the gambling industry representatives felt uneasy with him, uneasier than with a man they could sit down and have a drink with and talk things over.

When Bixbe's seat became vacant the governor appointed "Bob Grossman," a man personally unknown to the governor. Grossman was both a lawyer and a CPA, who had directed an organized crime unit in the Clark County District Attorney's Office. He was willing to undergo a pay cut from his job with the district attorney's office, but he was not naive about how his appointment might benefit his career. In an interview, Grossman said that in the future he "will be uniquely qualified to sell his skills to those wishing to enter the gambling industry or to foreign governments wishing to establish or police their own gambling industries."[17]

Grossman's CPA credential rendered him especially qualified for appointment. A knowledge of accounting was becoming essential to the investigative and audit functions of the board.

By 1975, it was also politic to appoint to the board someone with a visible Jewish identity. Grossman, like most Las Vegas Jews, was a cultural rather than a religious affiliate, yet his name and associated ethnic identity might bring some small comfort to those who felt the board and its agents represented an alien force. In fact, Grossman's Judaism made no difference in the way either he or the board operated. Nevertheless, an ethnic distinction makes a representational difference even if not an operational one, and who would argue that political symbolisms can be entirely lacking in the appointment of government officials? Grossman's appointment made clear another fact. In 1975, in Nevada, it was still not perceived as a political necessity for a Democratic governor to appoint a black or a woman to the board.

8

When Bixbe left the board, he thought carefully about resuming his law career. Before joining the board he had briefly worked in the most prestigious law firm in Nevada — a firm headed by a former governor and a state supreme court justice. Like Grossman, he was well aware that the value of his services as a Nevada lawyer would be enhanced by his experience as a board member. But he felt that he could not seriously consider rejoining his firm. While Bixbe had been a member of the board, the firm had represented several important licensees and applicants. Street rumors, embarrassing to Bixbe, suggested that favorable rulings were eventually to be repaid with a partnership in the law firm. For this reason and others Bixbe chose instead to try to negotiate a partnership with a small, prosperous Reno law firm, which claimed no gaming clients. Bixbe's role would be to develop a gaming clientele in Las Vegas. Bixbe saw nothing wrong in this. He believed his experience as a board member could benefit both the state of Nevada and potential clients.

The negotiation with the Reno firm fell through because the parties failed to agree on salary and perquisites. Bixbe negotiated another arrangement with the law firm of one of the commissioners, who was also considering resigning as a result of statutory proscriptions forbidding board and commission members from holding gaming clients. This commissioner — whom I shall call "Fred Collins" — was generally respected. He enjoyed the capacity to comprehend complex technical issues, and the courage to raise in public questions that might prove embarrassing to the gambling industry or to gaming authorities.

Yet his departure, and Bixbe's, raised interesting if not serious questions of conflict of interest. Immediately after they left the board and commission, their new law firm held itself open to accept gaming clients. Within a few months the firm, and particularly Bixbe, represented several such clients. One of his gaming client accounts was both lucrative and suspect; it was thought by several law enforcement agencies to be linked with organized crime.

Nobody really doubted Bixbe's personal integrity, but some questioned his judgment in avoiding the appearance of impropriety. Most important among these was the commission chairman, himself a lawyer. He publicly said he saw nothing wrong in Bixbe's representation of the particular gaming account, but he also publicly challenged Bixbe's participation in one matter, a questionable loan that had been made by Bixbe's client while Bixbe and Collins respectively were serving on the board and commission. Neither of them knew of the loan and thus it did not fall technically under the American Bar Association's ethical restrictions, as a matter in which the lawyer "had substantial responsibility while . . . a public employee."[18] Still, whether Bixbe was or was not guilty of a technical ethical violation mattered less than appearances. Bixbe seemed to place himself in the position of Hamlet's mother, who remarried while her late husband's funeral meats were still warm. Eventually, in early 1977, Bixbe discontinued representing this client. He refused public comment, but confessed privately that he had begun to entertain serious doubts about his client's business ethics and associations.

9

Potential conflicts of interest trouble every administrative agency charged with regulating an industry. Both the federal government and various states have tried to remedy the conflict of interest problem by imposing a two-year prohibition on former public employees in representing certain kinds of cases or matters before public agencies. But the problem is particularly acute in Nevada, where the gaming industry is so dominant.

The idea behind conflict of interest regulations directed at former employees involves an idealistic presumption rarely met in practice: that all citizens should be afforded equal consideration of their claims before governmental agencies, equal hearings, and equal access to the agency. Administrative officials invariably begin to prefer certain client representatives over others. These preferences need not be motivated by dishonesty. There are perfectly legal and honorable ways to get on the good side of an administrator. An attorney who understands the formal legal constraints governing an agency, plus the informal perspectives and history of the agency, can save an administrator time and irritation, and earn his gratitude. A former official or employee, especially one who enjoyed the confidence and respect of colleagues, would be particularly advantaged by past connections. No matter how scrupulous present occupants of official positions may be, it is difficult to see how they can avoid favoring formerly close colleagues and friends. By then, of course, such friends are no longer representing the general public, but are advocating the special interests of a client.

The question of conflict of interest was raised publicly at a meeting of the Gaming Policy Committee in 1972.[19] The policy committee is also a formal part of the control structure.[20] It is composed of the governor as chairman, who appoints the members. These include one member of the commission and board, usually the chairman of each, two members to represent the gaming industry — usually one from the south and one from the north — and two members of the general public, also usually distributed geographically.

The Gaming Policy Committee is supposed to air such basic policy questions as whether casinos should be allowed to accept bets on sporting events; whether licensees should be permitted to hold interests in gaming establishments outside of Nevada; and whether board members and employees should be allowed to move freely between government and industry. Its recommendations are passed on to the legislature.

At the meeting on conflict of interest, board Chairman Walker opposed the governor's recommendation that rules comparable to those imposed on federal employees govern the conflict of interest of gaming board members with respect to post-regulatory employment within the industry. He made the obvious and perhaps compelling point that the control agency and the industry are so closely tied as to be indistinguishable. Therefore, he reasoned, it would be unfair to limit employment. "Many, many of the people we hire, we hire from the industry," he said. "If they don't earn enough money working for the State, or if there's a change of administration, or if they don't like working for us — for whatever reason they wish to leave State employment — I think it's grossly unfair to attempt to prohibit them from going back into the industry and earn a living in perhaps the only way they know how. . . ."[21]

Walker was seconded in his position by the commission chairman, at that time "Paul Steigler," a widely respected northern Nevada lawyer. "I gave up two or three clients involved in the gaming business when I became a member of this Commission," Steigler said, "and I'll tell you very frankly, if I were restricted in any way from going back after I leave this job and again taking up their representation — maybe not of these people but other clients in the gaming business — frankly, I would just throw up my hands right now."[22]

In practice, however, the key issue in the conflict of interest area is the *extent* of the prohibition. Should a former commissioner generally be allowed to represent those about whom he has made key decisions? Or should the constraint apply only to matters the commissioner — or board members — acted upon while in office, with freedom to undertake representation on new matters? For example, the United States Code prohibits former employees from engaging for two years in prosecuting a claim involving a matter with which the former official was directly involved.[23] That is very different from prohibiting the former official from appearing before the agency entirely.

10

Conflict of interest problems were prominent in the legal literature during the early 1960s but interest in that issue waned during the late 1960s and early 1970s. The Watergate affair renewed interest in the whole question of integrity in government.

In 1976 the Ethics Committee of the Washington, D.C. Bar Association proposed a really tight and consequential conflict of interest restriction: that an entire law firm be barred for two years from appearing before an agency, if the firm hires a lawyer who worked for the agency. Such a restriction really contemplates an arms-length civil-service bar at the federal level. Depending upon how well it was compensated — through pay, job-security, free time, and so forth — it might or might not draw fewer first-rate attorneys. Presumably, the faculties of major law schools, as well as judges, could earn more in private practice, suggesting that a civil-service bar could prove competitive provided it offered appropriate inducements.

Conflict of interest laws are designed to prevent abuses, but they also create a dilemma. The *New York Times* quotes ICC Chairman Daniel O'Neal as saying: "You have to weigh the danger of conflict against not getting quality people in government jobs."[24] If conflict of interest laws create a dilemma in Washington, they are particularly problematic in a state like Nevada that is dominated by a single industry. When drawn too restrictively they discourage the most qualified applicants from serving on regulatory bodies. When drawn too loosely, they invite those who serve to exploit their agency experience for personal gain. In Nevada, however, not only do agency personnel consciously use their appointments as stepping stones to more lucrative jobs in the regulated industry; the agency in effect encourages them to do so. The head of the audit division would tell potential recruits that, while the pay is low relative to the industry, board work is more interesting. In addition, an accountant's value to the gaming industry, he would point out, is enhanced by association with the board.

When Walker left as chairman, he took a vacation, and then accepted a position as executive director of a major group of casinos. Obviously, his value included his experience as board chairman. Walker had always argued for freedom to move into the industry from the board, but many in Nevada thought the move inappropriate — including the governor who had appointed him in the first place.

11

Behind the conflict of interest issue, behind the entire structure of authority and rules, is the more fundamental and persistent issue of the agency's capacity to regulate the industry, and the industry's capacity to use the agency to legitimize its needs. To the extent that agency representatives are contemplating future jobs with industry while employed by the agency, some question must be raised about conflict of interest with present employment. Moreover, such conflicts must be seen in the light of what has now become an axiom of administrative law: that, as Kenneth Culp Davis puts it, "Regulation which appears to be against regulated parties is sometimes in fact sponsored, nurtured, and controlled by them."[25]

As we have seen, agency regulations are characteristically vague and subject to broad interpretation and direction. So the legal regulation of casino gambling has to be significantly tempered by the character of those doing the regulating and their relationship to the regulated. Given the right relationship, an edifice of regulatory control can be redirected so that the legally controlled actually manipulate the control structure.

Kenneth Culp Davis quotes from a letter written in 1892 by the United States attorney general to the president of a railroad, assuring him that the Interstate Commerce Commission was good for the interests of the railroads: "The Commission . . . is, or can be made, of great use to the railroads," the letter reads. "It satisfies the popular clamor for a government supervision of railroads, at the same time that the supervision is almost entirely nominal. Further, the older such a commission gets to be, the more inclined it will be found to take the business and railroad view of things."[26] The letter was apparently persuasive. "The railroads realized they needed the protection of the Federal Government," writes Gabriel Kolko, "and they became the leading advocates of federal regulation on their own terms."[27]

Similarly, the gaming casinos advocate regulation — on their own terms. The industry understands that the regulatory role is cast as paternalistic — to keep the industry healthy and growing in the interest of the general welfare of the state. Given the omnipresent "image" problem, those in the gambling industry welcome the appearance of a strong control structure. Individuals within the industry even welcome the reality provided it isn't directed too harshly at them.

Control is supposed to be achieved through licensing of applicants for an equity interest or as key employees in the industry; law enforcement of the daily operations of the casinos; and auditing the relations between casino management and the government (including not only collection of taxes, but also conformity with the regulations on a variety of activities ranging from issuing stock in corporations to paying off jackpots). An agency official — board member, commissioner, agent — who contemplates working for a particular business entity, or even within the industry as a whole, may be tempted to be less than vigilant. No doubt in individual instances the temptation is often overcome. But the expectation of industry employment can scarcely strengthen the integrity of legal control.

Additionally, whenever a member or employee of the Gaming Control Board or the commission takes a position with a gaming corporation, either as an officer or trustee, he brings with him knowledge of materials submitted in confidence, and protected by statute. The advantages of such access seem unfair; but these of course would fade and eventually disappear as time elapsed between industry employment and official authority.

The answer to the conflict of interest problem is perhaps unclear, but probably lies in two directions: The easiest and cheapest involves prohibitions against regulated industry employment. Some measure of time should elapse between agency and industry employment — a year perhaps. But the easiest and cheapest method is not necessarily the best. If the state is serious about control, at any governmental level, it must also make work with the government more attractive.

Nicholas Katzenbach, for example, earned $25,000 annually as attorney general of the United States; in 1976, he was paid nearly ten times as much by IBM. Inflation aside, the discrepancy between the earning power of a top corporation lawyer and the attorney general of the United States is appalling. In Nevada, a similar discrepancy exists between the earning power of a gaming board member and a top private attorney appearing before the board, to say nothing of the earning power of high-ranking casino personnel. Under such circumstances, if the only problems that arise are *appearances* of impropriety, the state should perhaps count itself lucky.

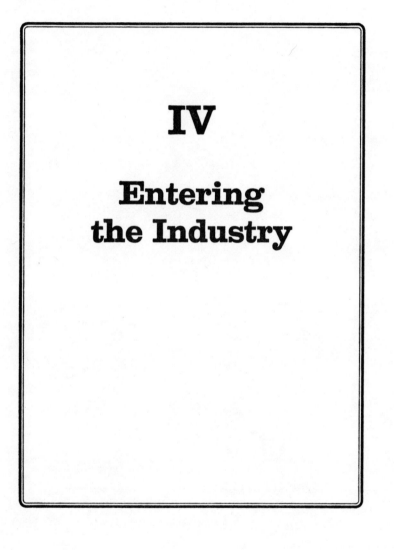

IV

Entering
the Industry

12

Licensing: The Sociology of Suitability

THE HOMESTEAD IS THE AMERICAN DREAM. ONE SETTLES ON A PIECE of land, works it, and grows crops and raises livestock. Success depends upon hard work, ability, and favorable weather conditions. One's character is perhaps demonstrated by outcome; but a government board doesn't decide, after applications and review of one's social and professional character, that one is "suitable" to work a farm. In contrast, licensing inevitably suggests a formal and unfree system of occupational control. The market is not permitted to decide whether you will be successful or not, unless the government decides that you are fit to enter the market. Given the broad discretion accorded government in the licensing area, it would appear that licensing boards and processes represent the most developed form of modern governmental bureaucracy.

Sometimes the licensing judgment is made on broad economic or social grounds. The community, nation, state, city, already has enough of what you would like to be or do — operate a liquor store, drive a taxi, open a gambling casino. Assuming that it is economically or socially acceptable for some individual to open a new gaming casino or liquor store, the focus shifts to qualities of the particular applicant. In contrast, small, nonindustrial societies do not require agencies and bureaucrats to assess social character. The immediate family and larger kin-network serves as a moral litmus test reflecting, however inaccurately, the moral worth and integrity of those within it.

As societies grow, religious affiliation may serve as the litmus. Max Weber visited the midwestern United States around the turn of this century and noted that sectarian Protestant churches served indirectly as credit investigators. One who could qualify to join a Baptist or Methodist Church would prove a likely candidate for a bank loan.[1] If religious affiliation of this sort did not guarantee virtue, it at least supported it.

As societies become larger, more complex, increasingly urban and mobile, it becomes increasingly difficult to judge people by outward appearance. Thus individuals have, in our time, become defined through dossiers of achievement or its opposite rather than by their family or religion. Again, there are exceptions. When a family is rich and powerful and *known* as, for example, the Rockefeller family, it achieves more than a *prima facie* case for social worth and reputability. But once licensing is required by law even the rich and powerful are subject to formal scrutiny. Thus, licensing merges the traditional social task of character assessment with the procedural formalities of legal governance.

In many instances, as in Nevada which has made a business of the "quickie" marriage, licensing implies little more than registration, and some minimal competence associated with age. In the United States, the states may generate other requirements, e.g., that applicants show they are free of venereal disease, as indicated by a mandatory blood test. (In this day and age such requirements are scarcely effective, since they assume that only married persons engage in sexual intercourse.) Some nations still require that applicants for marriage be of the same race — a requirement of course no longer constitutional in our country, but once thought sufficiently important to have been passed by the legislatures of 39 states at various times in United States history.[2]

A license to drive an automobile is considerably more restrictive than a marriage license since the applicant must pass a driving examination. Up to a point, driving ability can be judged and scored. Still, many contemporary drivers, particularly in the eastern United States, owe their licenses to the size of their wallet, rather than their ability to handle an automobile. Even performance tests do not altogether protect against corruption. Neither does the visual test and the examination of knowledge of driving rules and regulations. Nevertheless, the competence demanded of a driving license applicant is fairly straightforward. The standards of driving ability, age, and knowledge are fairly objective even when abused.

Corruption aside, licensing becomes most problematic when the standards employed are subjective, stressing social character over competence. Competence is a much more ascertainable, if not measurable, quality than character. A young man who refused to serve in Vietnam was morally despicable to some, heroic to others. In 1961, the New York state legislature passed an act suspending and revoking the driver's license of anyone convicted of advocating the overthrow of the federal government under the Smith Act. Assemblyman Paul Taylor, the bill's sponsor, explained that driving licenses were not a right but a "privilege." The Smith Act communists, he pointed out, were convicted of advocating the overthrow of the government by force, violence, or assassination. Thus, he reasoned, they were not concerned about the rights of others. Since being concerned about the rights of others "is a prerequisite of being a good driver," he concluded that those convicted should be denied a driving license.[3] In short, the concept of "good moral character" is relative and therefore peculiarly susceptible of abuse.

2

The qualifications for a Nevada gaming license are no exception. The abilities needed to run a gambling business are not easily measured, although attempts have been made — not very successfully — to prescribe, and by inference to have measured, bankroll requirements for the operation of casinos. Whatever, the gaming license standard is vague and subjective. The applicant bears the burden of demonstrating to the board and commission that he or she is a "suitable person . . . having due consideration for the proper protection of the public health, safety, morals, good order and general welfare of the inhabitants of the State of Nevada. . . ."[4]

Ownership or operation of a key aspect of a gaming casino is not considered, as it could be, something that any entrepreneur might do. True, one needs to be sophisticated in the arts of gaming to run a casino, but specialized knowledge is not subject to such strict examination in many other business ventures. Particularly in a nation and state where free enterprise is so highly touted, it seems at first glance incongruous that one should have to prove one's business ability, and more importantly, social character, before being allowed to risk one's skills and capital in the gambling business. But gaming authorities in Nevada rely upon licensing as the mainstay of the control apparatus. Licensing is intended to insure that revenue is reported, taxes paid, rules followed.

Being neither dense nor vindictive, the authorities recognize the potential for abuse of the licensing process. Their reliance upon licensing is thus doubly interesting. It suggests how assessments of social character are still thought to be more significant than such technical skills as surveillance and audits in controlling human misconduct.

Is the gambling business so special that those holding key positions within it really require licensing? Milton Carrow has developed the concept of "sensitive" businesses, namely "Those which have inherent potentialities for abuse and where self-corrective forces, economic or otherwise, are not effective."[5] He lists a variety of such businesses, ranging from temporary ones — auctions and liquidation sales — to those with fiduciary responsibilities — banks, trust companies, securities dealers, and insurance companies. "Good moral character" is required in these as well as in other occupations and businesses where it is assumed that the consumer cannot fully understand the complexities of the transaction and, particularly, where the consumer might sustain uncompensable injury. Thus, physicians, pharmacists, engineers, architects, and lawyers are licensed on some standard of competence plus "good moral character."[6]

Sociologically speaking, licensing in the gambling business constitutes a formal affirmation of nondeviance. One cannot participate in it without being investigated, reviewed, and found acceptable. Licensing is not required in the gambling business because high status attaches to the profession. On the contrary, gamblers are required to be licensed because gambling lies at the other end of the honorific spectrum, is thought likely to attract scoundrels, cheats, and worse — sophisticated criminals nurtured in conspiracy and intrigue, willing to employ brutal coercion, and capable of systematically corrupting authority to gain positions of vast and hidden power.[7]

So it is that the statutes governing gambling in the state of Nevada have been permitted to be broadly drawn. In 1977, the Gaming Control Board could recommend to the commission that an applicant be denied "for any cause deemed reasonable by the board," an enormous, striking grant of power.[8] A recommendation for denial based on that standard could be overruled only by a unanimous vote of the commission.

3

An applicant for a "nonrestricted license," i.e., one permitting the operation of gaming equipment involving more than 15 slot machines — which means any of the table games — must submit a variety of forms and information to the Gaming Control Board.[9] They include, in addition to the application itself, a personal history record inquiring after the applicant's family, marital status, arrest record, military service, residential history, occupational history, and prior connections in the gambling business. (The euphemism of "gaming" for "gambling" is not used on the personal history form since, presumably, an applicant could claim he didn't know what "gaming" was and that's why he neglected to state that he was a former bookmaker.) The applicant must also file two completed fingerprint cards; an affidavit stating that the applicant has fully and accurately disclosed all information requested; a statement to a bank or banks releasing information sought by the board; a statement releasing the board from all claims against it resulting from the investigation, and a check, money order, or cash amounting to $250 per applicant, to cover the investigative fee. When the investigative fee for agent time and travel exceeds that amount, as it frequently does, the applicant must pay it. The fee could amount to thousands and even hundreds of thousands of dollars.

Of all the forms required of an applicant, none is more important than the "Invested Capital Questionnaire," which not only requires a complete statement of assets and liabilities, but also requires the applicant, if asked, to turn over income tax returns for inspection by board agents. The ICQ, as well as a history of prior employment, is intended to permit review of the applicant's experience in gambling and other businesses. From the viewpoint of the licensing authorities gambling is not a sport or recreation but a business; and the history of an individual's business experience must indeed be counted as a salient licensing consideration.

Yet gambling is a very special kind of business. Since casino gambling was long outlawed in every state in the Union except Nevada, the licensing dilemma has always been how to reconcile knowledge of gambling practices and procedures with legitimacy, especially for key employees in the casinos. It is possible for an owner, as in the case of a Hughes or a Hilton, to be someone whose prior experience and source of income are clearly traceable to businesses other than gambling. On the other hand, it is difficult to locate an experienced key casino employee of whom the same can be said. Even where it *is* possible to find an occasional young casino executive who has been trained exclusively in legalized gaming places such as Nevada or England, the dominant norms of the working casino setting are laid down and reinforced by experienced gamblers; which means, for interpretive purposes, gamblers who gained their experience in illegal settings, or were trained by those who themselves learned the business in illegal settings. Gamblers learn to mind their own business and to protect their bosses.

Licensing cannot erase the normative influence of the illegal gambling business. An incident I witnessed will illustrate the point:

The president and major stockholder of a leading casino decided to test the integrity and loyalty of his employees by requiring them to submit to a lie-detector test. He undertook to do this because a friend in a retail clothing business had elicited confessions of theft by employees who had submitted to the test. In this instance, the test consisted of two questions: Have you ever stolen from this casino? Do you know of anyone who has stolen from this casino?

The casino manager was distraught over the test even though he had passed it. He had, it turned out, actually lied, although the test had not caught the lie. The casino manager, along with several other employees, believed that the casino president had been tapping the poker receipts for several thousand dollars a night and had "lied" when asked whether he knew of anyone who was stealing from the casino. The manager had learned the gambling business in pre-Castro Cuban casinos that were run by various organized crime figures, where you did not "report" to anyone what your boss was doing, particularly if it was illegal, and where you were expected to cover up for him.

The casino manager in question had been licensed by the gaming authorities and was thought well of by them and by others in the industry. He was considered to be industrious, capable, and honest in the day-to-day operation of the casino. There had never been any question of removing this man's license and the whole incident was known anyhow only by a few people — and not by the gaming authorities. Besides, there is no question that whatever the integrity of this casino manager, it was certainly not lesser, and probably was greater, than the integrity of most other casino managers in Nevada. As another high-ranking individual in this gambling casino explained to me: "Irv is a totally honest guy doing his job as he saw it. And that's why he's all torn up over this." The president, incidentally, was at first outraged that his casino manager could think he was stealing, and later was persuaded that loyalty had indeed been the operating motive. In fact, poker room receipts had declined. But casino presidents are immune from investigations from below. That poker room receipts had declined would signify little to a state auditor without prior knowledge of the casino manager's suspicions.

This incident suggests why, although licensing is of limited use as a control mechanism, it continues to be regarded by the gaming authorities as the key to the control structure. The answer lies in the distinction between reliance and confidence. *Reliance* implies doing the best with available resources. *Confidence* suggests that those resources are actually accomplishing what they were set out to accomplish.

The other blocks of the control structure are law enforcement and auditing. As we shall see, these control mechanisms are problematic. Thus, the informal norms of casino employee behavior, combined with the acknowledged limitations of law enforcement and auditing control mechanisms, which shall be discussed later, encourage reliance upon licensing. Consequently, the moral character of those who own and operate gambling casinos stands as the linchpin of the control structure. It is indeed a house of cards.

4

The investigation process begins when the proper forms have been filled out (a set of additional forms is demanded for the licensing of corporations). The forms are reviewed by the director of Applicant Services who prepares a check sheet for the file, listing the appropriate documents the applicant must supply. Once processed, the file is relayed to the Investigations Division chief in Carson City, who reviews it and sends it on to an agent, selected for reasons of competence, availability or both.

Every case presents background details suggesting scrutiny — business, credit, or law enforcement agencies to be contacted. Scores of agencies could be contacted during an investigation. In addition, the five personal references the applicant provides upon filing will be contacted by the agent. Agents always try to verify the financial assets and liabilities listed by the applicant to determine whether the applicant possessed the money claimed, whether it was where it was said to be, and if it came from the sources listed on the application.

Before the late 1960s, investigations outside of Nevada were farmed out by the board to private investigative firms. During this study the board sent its own agents out of town. Such a use of the board's own agents, as opposed to out-of-town investigators hired on a fee-for-service basis, permitted closer supervision. Moreover, and perhaps more importantly, this policy was thought to eliminate the possibility that local influence would modify information gathered in the applicant's home territory.

5

Routine cases produced a routine agenda for monthly board and commission hearings. But whether the agenda was routine or not, once it was set, it guided the work of the agency. The day before the board hearings, always held in Carson City, usually on the second Wednesday of the month, the board assembled in the office of the chairman, to review the next day's agenda. These meetings, called "rump sessions," were tense even when the agenda was fairly straightforward. They were tremendously nerve-wracking for those involved in significant and problematic cases. The rump session, followed by the board meeting, followed by the commission meeting, produced high drama. (The rump session, it should be noted, was neither statutorily required nor authorized. But these secret sessions were possibly the most significant of all in shaping the thinking of board members and the outcome of cases, with some exceptions to prove the rule. Whether they violated Nevada's Open Meeting Law is a close question, later to be discussed.)

It's something of a toss-up whether rump sessions were tenser for investigators or for board members. The investigators feared that some alleged fact or interpretation included in their written report would be found inaccurate or incomplete by the board members. The board members feared that inaccuracies might be overlooked only to be revealed unexpectedly in the public meeting, while the work of the investigator became the direct responsibility of the board. On balance, the investigator bore a heavier emotional burden during the rump session than the board member. Although the board member anticipated possible criticism the following day, the investigator experienced his challenge during the rump session, where board members were free to express occasional anger and sarcasm.

Investigators were required to conclude whether the applicant or applicants should be licensed, to point to the evidence supporting that conclusion, to develop a logical argument as to how the evidence supported the conclusion, and to put the entire train of evidence and inference into clear written form. The development of an argument through the medium of words on paper is ripe with possibilities for ambiguity and error, even for a professional writer. The task sometimes seemed particularly arduous for the former policemen comprising the bulk of investigative division agents.

6

Investigations Division agents — to repeat, mostly former police — were best at routine investigations and those involving small fry. If, for example, an applicant for a slot mechanic's license was rumored to associate with known slot thieves, Investigations Division agents were adept at checking out such reports. As ex-cops they could draw upon years of street experience, as well as contacts with casino employees. In contrast, when more sophisticated financial investigations were demanded, accountants were required. Indeed, before 1973, accountants routinely were assigned to conduct financial investigations.

In 1973, the task of conducting routine financial investigations was transferred from the Audit Division to the Investigations Division. The Audit Division was, as a result of its investigative responsibilities, falling behind on audits required by statute. The Audit Division, which was closely knit, considered the transfer a mistake. They believed that a balance between audit and investigative work offered a more attractive working environment, and contended that the balance raised the quality of recruits to the Audit Division. Moreover, they questioned the ability of the lesser paid Investigations Division agents, mostly qualified by police background and occasionally by bank credit experience, to conduct financial background investigations.

For the purposes of licensing, a financial investigation focuses upon determining the source of an applicant's investment funds. Essentially, the question is whether the applicant is actually indebted to a source unacceptable to the gaming authorities, who might exercise control over the applicant should he become a licensee. Control, on the other hand, might mean many things, ranging from having a determinative voice in the selection of key casino personnel to recommending a purveyor of food or liquor; from recommending a line of credit to offering complimentary room, food, and beverages. This sort of leverage amounts to hidden ownership, and might result in various fraudulent schemes. Simply stated, a financial investigation seeks partly to verify how the investment money has been accumulated; and partly to determine whether the applicant's representation of how it was accumulated stands up as well.

To exemplify the problem: An applicant might attribute $200,000 of his investment to a bank loan. Upon checking, the investigator might indeed find a loan from the XYZ bank for the amount. But the applicant might have been told by an organized crime figure to borrow $200,000 from the bank, in return for which the applicant will be given a piece of property worth $100,000 plus a deposit of $100,000 to his bank account. (By this device, the bank becomes the apparent source of funds, while the true source, the organized crime figure — and the nature of his interest — remains hidden in the background.)

The metaphor of money "streams" into and out of a financial "lake" characterizes both the complexity and methodology of a source-of-funds investigation. The applicant points to an outflow stream — the casino investment — and attributes it to a particular income stream — e.g., a bank loan. The financial investigator must dredge in the lake to determine whether the designated income stream actually accounts for the outflow. The applicant's balance sheet, showing numerous assets, is his "lake." Although, theoretically, a source-of-funds investigation involves checking all assets, in practice, investigators are told to set priorities. Investigators are neither expected nor encouraged to take the time to clear a $5,000 asset for an applicant contemplating a $1 million investment.

In addition to an asset's size or value, the investigator is instructed to weigh its character. Suppose stock is put forth by the applicant as collateral for a bank loan. In addition to verifying whether the loan exists — it probably will — the investigator is supposed to check to find out if the applicant (rather than a hidden investor) actually owns the stock. If the applicant does, the investigator conducting an adequate financial investigation should press on to determine the source of funds used to purchase the stock. If a check was used, the investigator should inquire where the money came from in the bank account. If from the sale of a piece of property, he should find out who was the purchaser. A competent financial investigator will keep pressing until the original source of the funds is discovered.

Within the agency, there has been persistent rivalry between the Audit and Investigations Divisions over responsibility for source-of-funds investigations. The Investigations Division maintains that it is increasing its capacity to carry out adequate financial investigations, but the auditors remain skeptical. They are quick to point out the inadequate accounting knowledge and experience of agents and supervisors in the Investigations Division; and low morale resulting from their perceived but unacknowledged inadequacies. The auditors maintain that an investigator without an accounting background cannot review and comprehend the complex financial transactions one would find in the records of large corporations with diverse holdings.

7

After the investigative reports have been reviewed at the rump session, applicants are characteristically afforded a hearing the following day. In some instances, where a major application is involved (as it would be when the application calls for an equity interest and active participation in running one of the major hotel-casinos) the board may conduct an investigative hearing.

These hearings are usually attended by members of the board who are themselves transformed into investigators, perhaps one or more attorneys general, the applicant, and the applicant's attorney. The applicant is placed under oath, and a transcript is recorded and usually later made public. Often, the materials that are developed at the investigative hearings could have been developed during the public board hearings. But investigative hearings may take several hours, and one of the problems for the board is to complete its monthly agenda in the one day allotted to it. Only in rare instances is one day's agenda permitted to extend over a second.

Consequently, the investigative hearings serve as a device for conserving the time of applicants who might be sitting around waiting for days for their hearing while a time-consuming applicant is being considered. (I wish I could reprint the transcript of an investigative hearing, but if I did there would scarcely be room left in this book for anything else.)

Investigative hearings and rump sessions are followed by public board hearings. An agenda for the board and commission meeting usually has several sections. One involves applications for "nonrestricted gaming licenses" (meaning that the applicant may own or manage an operation consisting of more than 15 slot machines. As I have already mentioned, any operation having even a single 21 game is required to apply in the "nonrestricted" category).

There are generally about a dozen nonrestricted applicants in a given month, and twice as many "restricted" applicants. In addition, there are usually a couple of applications to introduce new — usually electronic — gaming devices. The board maintains and relies upon an electronics expert to test these machines to see that they will do what they say they will do. By the time these devices come up for licensing, their defects, if any, have been checked out by the electronics expert.

There are also likely to be several applications to transfer interest among those already licensed, usually as the result of a purchase between established casino operators. If all the parties are licensed these applications are ordinarily routine. Besides, licensees usually consult with members of the board before pursuing a purchase that might appear problematic. Some licensees own interests in several casinos, and frequently they bring expertise to a questionable operation. But the board and commission have become increasingly wary of multiple control of casinos, in the Howard Hughes model, since such control commands so much power.

8

Two sorts of licensing applications present no problems: the *clearly suitable* and the *clearly unsuitable*. The requirements for a restricted license are fairly simple, and no deep personal investigation is required for one who seeks to operate a few slot machines in a grocery store or motel. Of the dozen or so applicants for nonrestricted gaming licenses in any month, the overwhelming majority are acceptable. Some applicants have previously held licenses, and require only routine investigation. Others — key employees — have worked for years in the industry, and are personally known by the investigators and the board. Other applicants, associated with such major hotel corporations as Hilton and Hyatt, are presumptively innocent of organized crime ties. Even if such ties existed, they would normally be so well hidden as to be beyond the skills of even the most intrepid investigator. Clearly suitable applicants are thus prosaic for the board, for this writer, and for the reader. They tend to be routinely successful business people, who are discussed perfunctorily, if at all, at rump sessions.

Clearly unsuitable applicants are more interesting, particularly in light of Nevada's gaming history. One becomes clearly unsuitable through a confusing but fascinating labeling process.

First, an applicant is ineligible to be licensed if he or she is believed to be an organized crime figure. No formal procedure exists for determining who is an organized crime figure. A criminal record is neither necessary nor sufficient. The absence of a felony criminal record does not exclude an applicant from being considered an organized crime figure; and the presence of a felony record certainly does not define one as an organized crime figure: numerous ex-felons are licensed in the state of Nevada.

So what does? An organized crime figure is somebody who (a) is reputed to be one; and (b) is unwilling to make the effort to disprove the allegation. Meyer Lansky has, for example, been judicially "noticed" by the Nevada Supreme Court as an organized crime "leader," while his brother Jacob was said to be an organized crime "figure."[10] Quantities of books, testimony, and magazine articles have been written about Meyer Lansky and other so-called organized crime figures.[11] Since an applicant for a gaming license bears the burden of demonstrating acceptability, these allegations are admissible as investigative evidence. The applicant must then attempt to disprove them, although ordinarily the applicant is not presented with a bill of particulars setting out the problems the board — following its investigation — has with the applicant. Besides, widely heralded organized crime figures ordinarily do not apply. Those possessing such a reputation would scarcely be disposed to undergo the deep investigation triggered by the gaming application. In part, they understand that they don't stand a chance to be licensed, simply on the basis of their reputations; and in part their reputations are based on sufficient fact so that a discrediting negative judgment could easily be sustained against them, were it to be challenged in court.

But what of the applicant who arouses board suspicions, even though he is willing to undergo investigation? During this study, the most interesting and important example I encountered was an applicant whom I shall call "Jacob Cantor," who applied for a controlling interest in the "Pyramid" Hotel. I shall describe the Cantor case in some detail. It was the most complex licensing investigation undertaken by the gaming authorities during the period of this study; and I became deeply involved in it because it raised the major issues involved in the gaming licensing process: (1) Is the hearing procedure fair? (2) How is an applicant's reputation and image to be assessed, and once assessed how much weight should be given to it? (3) What is the proper method for conducting and interpreting a financial investigation? (4) How legitimate have the applicant's relations with public officials been in the past? (5) Has the applicant's past business history been tarnished by criminal or ethically questionable activities? (6) What is the reputation of those with whom the applicant maintains business and social relations? (7) Do any of these relationships suggest the presence of undisclosed hidden interests in the casino? (8) Ultimately, given a set of facts, supposed facts, and inferences drawn from these, what can be predicted about the future conduct of the applicant as a licensee?

13

The Problematic Applicant

I BECAME AWARE OF JACOB CANTOR WHILE HE WAS BEING investigated. So many agents were working on his investigation, from different parts of the agency, that a highly confidential meeting was called in Carson City to discuss the status of the investigation. One of the deputy attorneys general called it a "squaring session" — "So we can get everybody squared with everybody else to see what they are doing." I was invited to the meeting along with chiefs, deputies, and key agents doing the investigating. From the meeting I learned that the board and its agents wanted desperately to keep Cantor from being licensed in the state of Nevada. They were especially worried about their relations with other law enforcement agencies who believed that Cantor was deeply involved with organized crime.

They also were aware of and feared Cantor's brilliance. His business arrangements had been described by an investigative reporter in *Life* magazine as "labyrinthine schemes which dazzle and befuddle the government. . . ." The board had collected and reviewed newspaper and magazine articles written about him over many years. Even the most favorable of these stories raised questions about Cantor's association with underworld figures and his business ethics. One article, unusual in that Cantor was favorably portrayed as an immigrant who had worked hard for success and given freely of himself and his possessions for numerous charities, acknowledged also that: "The image generally painted of this great criminal lawyer . . . is that of a shadowy, devious character with arteries to the underworld."

Cantor telephoned the board during the squaring session. Bixbe took the call and reported that Cantor was making what was to prove to be the first of a number of legal jabs at the licensing procedure and the board's prerogatives — some of which stung, some of which didn't, and some of which threatened to sting.

Agents from the Audit Division had been instructed to walk into Cantor's office and search his office safe on the spot. Cantor objected. They told him they were under orders to search his safe, sealed it so that Cantor could not open it without the agents' knowledge, and advised him to call Bixbe and settle the issue with him.

Cantor did call. And during the call Cantor objected to a search of the contents of his safe on grounds that he was a lawyer, and that much of the material in the safe pertained to the affairs of clients. He was concerned about one client in particular, the late James R. Hoffa, and argued that he should not be obliged to violate his client's confidence on behalf of the requirements of the gaming authorities. Bixbe told Cantor that he would call him back within an hour after he had a chance to think over Cantor's objection and to discuss it with other members of the board.

Bixbe returned to the meeting and raised the issue, particularly whether, if Cantor was denied a license on grounds that he refused to cooperate fully in the investigation by withholding the contents of his safe, Cantor could later sue for relief on grounds that the licensing procedure discriminated against a class of persons — lawyers — who would not be licensed unless they were prepared to violate the confidences of their clients. The lawyers present discussed the issue and felt that Cantor would not have a strong court case. They agreed on a compromise. Anything pertaining to his labor-leader client could be put aside as outside the board's authority. But Cantor's business affairs were also the board's. If he felt he could not distinguish his business affairs from his legal responsibilities, he was told, he would have to make a choice between being a lawyer and having a gaming license.

The board was hoping that Cantor would refuse to open his safe and would sue instead. Not only was it confident that it could win in court, but also it felt that a lawsuit would prove so time-consuming that Cantor's plans for financing the remodeling of his hotel would be thrown into disarray. Its hopes to the contrary notwithstanding, Cantor agreed to open his safe.

Two apparently incriminating items were found within it: One showed that Cantor had obtained a 1947 Oldsmobile for "Oswald Benson" in 1946 when automobiles were in short supply. According to a newspaper article, Benson was at the time chief auditor of the post-review section of the Revenue Bureau in Washington, D.C. Two of Cantor's clients were under investigation in 1948 for possible evasion of $65,000 in income taxes. The newspaper stated that when the case was submitted to Benson, the idea of prosecution was soon abandoned. When interviewed by Cantor's home-town newspaper in 1950, Benson said that he had paid for the automobile, that Cantor had done him a favor by selling it to him, and that the favor had nothing to do with the case against Cantor's clients.

The second item concerned Cantor's relations with "Harry Freid," first assistant United States attorney in Cantor's home city. Freid served in that capacity for 23 years, until his death in 1958. The position was powerful and important. Fried's duties included authorizing or declining the cases presented for federal prosecution by various federal and state agencies. Agents of the board found three notes in Cantor's safe, payable to Cantor from Freid, amounting to $3,750. The notes bore dates of June 25, 1947, December 3, 1947, and May 27, 1948. During this period Mr. Freid's annual government salary was $6,600.

2

When the board finally completed the Cantor investigation it found that it had had to employ nine agents over six months to look into the relations among 60 separate business entities at a cost to the applicant of $152,000. Actually, as shall become evident, Cantor's licensing cost at least double, probably triple, that amount in his investigative, lawyer's, and witness fees. Yet, as a knowledge-able insider remarked at the time, it was worth it. "The expenses are billed to the corporation, and $500,000 won't break a hotel that gives away $10 million in complimentaries annually." To compre-hend Cantor's enterprises, the auditors finally had to draw a chart of interconnecting businesses so large and complex that Cantor himself said it was the first time he had had his whole portfolio laid out before him.

Even his application showed this complexity. Cantor owned 100 percent of AJK, a Nevada corporation initialed after his late partner, "Arthur J. Korn," a southern California land developer who had over several years acquired, with Cantor's assistance, almost $150 million in loans from the controversial Teamsters Central States Pension Fund, originally set up by James Hoffa.

Cantor had represented other union leaders as well on criminal charges. With his friend and partner, Korn, he had obtained sizable loans for real estate ventures from other union pension funds besides the Teamsters. Indeed, during the investigation the board learned that federal authorities were planning to indict Cantor in connection with a $6½ million loan from a midwestern pipe-fitters union pension fund. The loan was to be secured by real property which had a reported value of approximately $8½ million, belonging to a land development company jointly owned by Cantor and Korn. A review of the loan documents and further investigation by federal authorities had revealed that the escrow holder, the Title Insurance Company, had been prevailed upon by Korn, who was a major customer of the title company, to fail to disclose, or "write-over," the existence of $1,182,000 in prior liens on the property.

The "write-over" was perceived by the federal authorities as a fraud on the union pension fund, since the land employed as collateral would not — with liens upon it — be worth as much as had been contended. The board relied upon the federal authorities and believed the latter had hard evidence to show Cantor's participation in a shady, and probably unlawful, business practice. The board thought Cantor would claim that Korn was directly responsible for the transaction. Still, Cantor was, with his partnership interest, a beneficiary of what appeared to be a fraud.

Korn's business interests in California, operating under the name Pico Industries, were, while monumental, highly leveraged, with borrowings high in relation to investment, and requiring substantial monthly cash flow in interest payments alone to keep the whole structure from collapsing into bankruptcy. Cantor had in 1969 become a 25 percent partner in Pico. Early in 1973, the Teamsters Central States Pension Fund decided to take an "equity" or ownership interest in Pico, dividing it up three equal ways to Korn, Cantor, and the pension fund, with Korn to continue to manage Pico, and with Cantor to be responsible for the entire pension-fund mortgage remaining after the redistribution.

Then Korn died unexpectedly, of a heart attack. Since Cantor was intimately familiar with Korn's enterprises, the pension fund turned to him to assist in "working out" the Korn-related mortgage problems. Cantor was given as his one-third interest four major properties, with AJK Nevada to be used as the vehicle for borrowings to facilitate the repair of Korn's business difficulties. In addition, Cantor was promised a $17 million loan from the pension fund to purchase and expand the Pyramid Hotel.

So in 1974, Cantor owned 100 percent of AJK Nevada. In turn, AJK owned 37 percent of Midwest Industries, Inc., a company with valuable electronics and shipping interests. Midwest Industries in turn owned 100 percent of B & A Inc., a corporation established to enjoy the tax advantages offered to corporate business by the state of Delaware. B & A Delaware owned 100 percent of B & A Nevada, a "closely held" corporation — one where stock is not available to the general public — that did business as the "Pyramid," an elegant but fading Las Vegas casino-hotel. The Pyramid was proximate to several of the largest and most successful hotels on the Strip. If left as it stood, it would increasingly suffer by comparison, and increasingly decline. If it were to expand, add more rooms, and refurbish those it had, it might well attract players from its neighboring casinos, as well as attract more on its own.

3

Cantor's financial situation was more than complex: it was not only labyrinthine and dazzling and therefore difficult to put together, but once you put it together (assuming you actually had), you weren't sure how to identify it; and once you thought you'd assembled and understood it, you had to wonder why it had been put together quite that way.

Cantor's case presented facts so complicated, ambiguous and encompassing as to raise all the basic problems of licensing. The board was presented with a 130-page, single-spaced document, plus appendix and index, from the Audit Division, citing 14 separate problems.

The size and complexity of the document presented a procedural dilemma. Previously, based on the investigative report, the board would in a public hearing raise questions to the applicant about problems it might have. The chairman was distinctly inclined, in the Cantor case, to follow his usual procedure and confront Cantor, at the public hearing, with problems on a piecemeal basis. Besides, the chairman was confident that he would never vote to license Cantor, on the grounds that Cantor's image, particularly his reputation with federal agencies as well as with the general public, was opposed to the interests of the state of Nevada. In a closed private meeting, which I attended on the Monday morning prior to the Wednesday public hearing, the chairman pointed to a letter in a Reno newspaper criticizing the Democratic candidate for lieutenant governor for having accepted a $1,000 contribution to his campaign fund from Cantor. The letter-writer claimed former residence in Cantor's hometown, and charged that he was known there as a political fixer and organized crime associate.

The chairman asked me — jokingly referring to me as his due process consultant — whether the letter alone wasn't enough to deny Cantor a license, on grounds of his image, regardless of the truth of the allegations? I replied that the particular political candidate happened to enjoy a reputation for integrity. I thought it would be neither fair nor prudent to introduce such a letter to deny Cantor, pointing out that Cantor might justifiably argue that the letter sustained a contrary inference, namely, that the acceptance of a contribution of that size by a man of the candidate's reputation suggested only that Cantor was liable to be smeared by false charges.

Besides, I argued further, a letter to a newspaper written by a person otherwise unknown to the board seemed a thin twig on which to hang so important a licensing decision. Cantor could surely produce several letters from persons better known, who would attest to his character. The proper procedure, it seemed to me, would be for the board to assemble and interpret its evidence, and to summarize it. Then each board member would be free to present Cantor with a written statement of those aspects of his background and character that seemed most troubling. Cantor would have been given "notice" of the grounds the board was considering in possibly denying him. After considerable discussion, which continued on an airplane ride from Las Vegas to Reno, the chairman indicated he was inclined to agree but wanted to sleep on the suggestion.

During the discussion, the chairman advanced three related concerns. The first was practicality. Like most organizations facing deadlines, the gaming board often finds itself a bit behind schedule, struggling to keep even. The auditors had presented the board with their investigative report several days later than all — investigators and board members — had hoped. The report was long, detailed and complex. Board members had received it on Friday and had spent the weekend reading it. Here it was Monday, with the hearing scheduled for Wednesday, and with other applicants scheduled to be heard as well. It was clearly a task of some magnitude to digest the contents of the investigative report, summarize it, and write the summary presentably. I thought it could be done by Tuesday midnight, and offered to work with the staff on it from early Tuesday morning to midnight. For me, I explained, this seemed an ideal opportunity to advance my knowledge of the board and its procedures.

Precedent and administrative prerogative were the second and third closely related concerns raised by the chairman. He and Bixbe and I had earlier spent, and would continue to spend, countless hours discussing the appropriate procedural requirements for fairness in judging applicants for gaming licenses. We have as a nation, especially during the tenure of the Warren Court, developed high standards for the administration of criminal law. But are the due process standards of the criminal court applicable to the administrative hearing? Mr. Justice Frankfurter, a highly regarded teacher and scholar of administrative law, wrote in an early opinion that differences in the idea behind the origin of administrative agencies, plus the way they were supposed to function, would "preclude wholesale transplantation of the rules of procedure, trial, and review which have evolved from the history and experience of courts."[1]

But if wholesale transplantation is not the answer, what is an appropriate measure of partial transplantation? There is no question that there has been a tendency to judicialize administrative procedures in the United States. According to Judge Henry Friendly, English judges and scholars "consider that we have gone simply mad in this respect."[2]

That opinion often seemed to be shared by the chairman of the Gaming Control Board, who feared that a presentation of the board's "problems" in the Cantor case, formally and in writing, would create a precedent that might be insisted upon by other applicants. Such a precedent, he felt, might serve to weaken the discretionary authority of the board. The statute creating the board puts the licensing burden on the applicant. If the board was required to set out its problems in every case, and if the applicant could meet the enumerated problems, then the board might have no choice but to grant a license. This, he believed, would constitute a subtle shifting of the burden from the applicant to the licensing authority. Besides, he argued, the board is not so much akin to a judicial body as it is to a prosecutorial one. It merely recommends to the commission, and the commission can overrule its recommendations.

The problem with that argument, as he quickly but ruefully acknowledged, was that a recommended denial by the board required a unanimous vote by the commission for the applicant to be licensed. Particularly in a case like Cantor's, where the investigative report was so complicated, and where the candidate for licensing was so controversial, it seemed inconceivable that the commission would unanimously overrule the board, particularly if the board voted unanimously to deny the application.

In practice, the board employed its own voting pattern as a signaling code to the commission. In cases where the board split 2-1 in denying an applicant the commission had come to understand that the board did not mind if the commission overruled it. The board's stance was that, as the investigative and prosecutorial arm of the agency, it did not want to appear soft and yielding. The commission, which theoretically represented both the judicial arm of the agency and the voice of the citizenry, should, if anyone should, be the yielding arm of the agency.

Actually, the prosecutorial argument made by the chairman was stronger than I realized at the time. If one considers the realities of the criminal justice system, rather than the due process model alluded to earlier, a very different picture emerges. In fact, criminal defendants are subject to two substantially different sets of procedural standards, depending upon the stage of the proceedings. The due process model applies to the *trial* stage, but the overwhelming majority of criminal accusations never reach trial. Large percentages, anywhere from 10 to 40 percent of criminal accusations will be dismissed, because of lack of evidence or procedural inadequacies or merely on the basis of what the prosecutor considers to be in the interests of justice. Of the cases remaining, the prosecutor in most urban American jurisdictions will plea-bargain more than 90 percent. During these proceedings, which, statistically at least, are more significant than those that go to trial, the defendant is subject to decisions more hidden, more discretionary, and likely less carefully considered than those rendered by Nevada's Gaming Control Board.

Nevertheless, Chairman Walker was finally persuaded, after sleeping on it, to set out the bill of particulars, apparently for several reasons: First, it seemed to be possible. Second, it was useful for the board. The investigative report was unusually complicated; unusual for its size, number of problems, and complexity of problems. It needed to be summarized for the board's benefit, so the members themselves could understand what they really believed with respect to Cantor's licensing.

Finally, it was fair. Bixbe took the position that the Cantor case should be decided on the evidence; and that Cantor should have the opportunity to contribute to illuminating the evidence. He could do that only if he was aware of the board's problems. In short, Bixbe early on adopted a more judicial stance toward the proceedings. In the discussions, he was supported by the deputy attorneys general, the legal eagles, as Walker was apt to refer to the lawyers present.

Walker's attitude toward law and lawyers is worth a comment. It was at least multi-faceted: it reflected interest in legal issues, scorn for their outcomes, and appreciation of the adroitness of the minds of the lawyers; plus some deprecation of the lawyers' ability to inject what he considered "technicalities" into what he considered "common sense," as well as of their capacity to advocate the cause of any paying master. When he could be persuaded that a procedure was fair in terms of his personal sense of fairness he could willingly comply. When he believed a procedure amounted to a technical and needless burden, he would resist. But even when he was most apt to dismiss the law as, in Mr. Bumble's phrase, "a ass," he remained regretfully aware that it was a powerful ass.

This last consideration was probably dispositive in deciding to issue the bill of particulars to Cantor. Walker shrewdly perceived that in this case, as in others, the prerogatives of the board were most likely to be tested in the courts by capable and substantial applicants. Whatever doubts the board might have entertained about Cantor's character, there was none about his capacity to assert his rights in a courtroom. The effect of this perception of Cantor and others was to develop — however imperceptibly, unconsciously and surely — a set of de facto procedures favoring legally competent applicants.

4

When the board presented Cantor with its bill of particulars, he was astounded. He went on, almost ritually, with his prepared presentation stressing his plans for developing the Pyramid Hotel. He and his lawyers asked for and received a two-month continuance to respond to a document setting out a pattern of allegedly improper relations with public officials, questionable business ethics, and questionable business and personal associations. Cantor's defense was to take place on January 15, 1975.

When I arrived in Carson City on Tuesday, January 14, I joined the board in its conversations with Cantor's lawyers. By now, these included former governor Grant Sawyer who, technically, was representing the other stockholders of B & A, the closely held corporation doing business as the Pyramid, but whose presence lent credibility to the image of Cantor as a potentially respectable licensee in the interests of the state of Nevada. The lawyers and the board were discussing the logistics of the hearings, and were informed that Cantor was prepared to produce 40 material witnesses to discuss the specific issues, and 26 character witnesses, mostly from charitable organizations, religious groups, and bar association groups. The Cantor party occupied two floors and suites at the largest hotel in Carson City. The room, food, beverage, and transportation bills alone would have sustained several average American families for at least a year.

During the hearings, as in affidavits, Cantor's character witnesses would testify that he was generous with money and, more significantly, with the time and interest he invested in people. Implicitly, they developed a portrait of a certain ideal of manhood, the Jewish ideal of *mensch* as contrasted with the Latin ideal of *machismo* that has become so strong in traditional frontier western culture. The *macho* ideal of manhood calls to mind a tough, fearless, carefree, resourceful, but ultimately irresponsible high-rolling stud. This is the image of the professional gambler and the image the state of Nevada tends to project throughout the world. The image attracts visitors, but sits uneasily with law enforcement authorities.

The image presented of Cantor, by himself as well as by others, was, appropriately enough in the licensing context, exactly the opposite. Cantor nowhere near fitted the stereotype of the professional gambler, a close kin to the stereotype of the gangster. He did not even approximate the flinty-eyed, fast-talking lawyer who represents gangsters. On the contrary, the board was presented with a portrait of a resourceful lawyer, sound businessman, and family man who managed to combine shrewdness, energy, ambition, and intelligence with kindness and personal warmth; in short a *mensch*, a man of knowledge, capacity, maturity, and responsibility. It is not an unpleasing projection to present to an administrative body concerned with images of respectability.

The most interesting prehearing event revealed the complex relations, assumptions, and courtesies obtaining between the board and other law enforcement agencies. Sometime after Cantor's lawyers left, Walker received a telephone call from an FBI agent assigned to an organized crime strike force. The agent told Walker that the strike force believed it finally had a strong case against Cantor and that an indictment would be drawn. Furthermore, Walker was told, the strike force intended to subpoena the board to produce the transcripts of the Cantor hearings, since testimony taken at the hearings, which are conducted under oath, might prove relevant to any legal proceedings to be taken in the future by the federal government against Cantor.

This telephone call highlighted the continuing problem of the board acting in its double role as a *judicial* and *investigative* agency. When a judge or an arbitrator decides a case, he presumably does so on the record before him. When a jury is not involved, a judge need not follow strict rules of courtroom evidence. Still, the evidence is presented in a courtroom. Were the judge to be briefed by federal agencies before and even during the hearing — civil or criminal — the procedure would be considered outrageous. But an investigative agency like the Gaming Control Board does just that. When the board members discuss the investigation with their agents, they are privy to allegations and beliefs that not only violate rules of evidence, but that never become public. These may stem from law enforcement officials or others who are unwilling to step forward and say what they know.

If a board member were to believe that the federal government were about to indict, and quite possibly convict an applicant, that information could scarcely fail to influence the board member as an adjudicator. And because the information had been received outside the hearing of the affected party (*ex parte*) it might not be fair to use it. At the same time, a theorist of administrative law with a more discretionary orientation, like Justice Frankfurter, might argue that in an administrative licensing hearing, the possibility of a forthcoming indictment ought to be known to the board, if the purpose of the agency is to protect the industry from having in its midst persons who are likely to be subject to indictment by the federal government. Obviously, the federal government would then be in a position to employ its indictment powers to harass an applicant.

Just as obviously, the board might well be entitled to take into account potential harassment by the federal government, particularly in an industry so fragile and uncertain in its relationship to federal authority. In fact, the board did take into account the potentiality of an indictment, but did not think it mattered that much. Besides, the board was aware that the facts behind the indictment would be tested during the licensing hearing.

5

There is no room here to describe fully the Cantor defense. The Cantor hearings were continued into the next week and lasted over three days. On two of them the board sat for 15 hours, not even taking a break for dinner. The audience, including writers and Cantor's entourage and attorneys, surreptitiously gnawed on chicken and hamburgers smuggled into the hearing room by enterprising and hungry observers during break periods. The board, never faltering, maintained its dignity and careful attention throughout. The testimony presented by Cantor's witnesses was thoughtful, detailed, often informative and occasionally brilliant.

Yet the rest of the agenda also needed to be heard. Thus, a full agenda was heard on Wednesday, January 15, and the Cantor hearings, with witnesses present from all over the United States, were held over and scheduled for Thursday morning at 8:00 A.M. Following the Wednesday agenda, the board and relevant staff who had worked on the Cantor investigation retired for a quick dinner and returned to work for five additional hours, until 1:00 A.M., reviewing the investigative materials, with the investigators and with each other, to prepare for the 8:00 A.M. hearing.

This meeting proceeded as any other rump session, except for the complexity of Cantor's affairs. Every few months a case might arise presenting some materials as complex as these, but none presented 14 separate issues of comparable difficulty. Five hours was not enough time to review the investigative report, and 50 might not have been enough either. Board members, having sat all day, were tired, irritable, but surprisingly alert and attentive. Besides, they had a new problem to worry about. Would Cantor later argue in a court of law that the meeting they were holding violated the provisions of Nevada's Open Meeting Law?

Nevada adopted its Open Meeting Law in 1960.[3] Modeled after California's "Brown Act," the law mandates that meetings conducted by public agencies, such as the Gaming Control Board and Commission, be open to the public. Board and commission hearings are open, and ordinarily pose no problem. In Cantor's case, however, two problems were raised. The deputy attorneys general were aware that "investigative hearings" which the Gaming Control Act permits to be "conducted in private at the discretion of the Board" were possibly unlawful and in conflict with the Open Meeting Law.[4] The attorney general had issued a booklet in 1974 giving his formal legal opinions on the Open Meeting Law, and while courts are not obliged to follow the opinions of attorneys general, such opinions carry weight.[5] Anyhow, the deputies assigned by him to act as counsel to the board had to take account of his opinion.

The attorney general had offered an interpretation of the Open Meeting Law that was generous to the public and restrictive to public agencies. The booklet cites as governing law a California Court of Appeals decision: "To 'deliberate' is to examine, weigh and reflect upon the reasons for or against the choice," the decision reads. "Deliberation thus connotes not only collective discussion, but the collective acquisition or the exchange of facts preliminary to the ultimate decision."[6]

Clearly the investigative meetings of the board involved collective discussion of acquired facts preliminary to the ultimate decision. The two Nevada statutes were evidently in conflict. The remedy would be either to modify one of the statutes, or, more sensibly, to alter the structure of the board to separate its investigative (or prosecutorial) functions from its deliberative or judicial) ones. In any event, the board decided to call its pre-Cantor hearing meeting an "investigative" one, and hoped for the best.

6

During the hearings, Cantor's most impressive witnesses were attorneys who testified regarding (a) the "write-over" that was to be the subject of the federal indictment, and (b) his relations with the two government officials revealed by the materials found in his safe. One important witness who testified about the write-over was John Hetland, a California law professor acknowledged to be the state's leading expert on this sort of question, who regularly taught courses on secured transactions in real estate, and who had himself argued several of the cases he was about to cite before the board.

During Professor Hetland's testimony, he was asked whether he was there because of his great love and affection for Mr. Cantor, or whether he was a paid consultant. "I'd better be paid," he answered. Amidst laughter, he continued, "No, I have never met Mr. Cantor, and that's true right now. I still have not met him. I saw him in the room, but I don't know him, and I have never met him."

Essentially, Hetland testified that it really wasn't the lender's business whether liens existed or not on insured property held as collateral. The property was there to be sold in case the borrower defaulted on the loan. Sometimes, in default situations, the sale of property does not bring in enough to cover the loan. In contrast, if a loan is covered by title insurance, the lender can count on being paid by a defaulting borrower. The heart of the testimony is contained in the following exchange:

Q: Then would it be your opinion that whenever a lender takes real property as security for his loan and he accepts a title policy, that he is in effect waiving any defects in the title, relying solely upon the title policy as security for his loan?

A: Absolutely. That's all he asks for in here. That's all he wants. He wants a policy of title insurance and he isn't waiving any defect. There are no defects. If you have a solvent title company — T.I. is the largest in California — and you have a policy saying there are no senior encumbrances, the truth is, there are none. It can have absolutely no effect at any time on anything having to do with the parties. The title company is able to pay it off and is obligated to pay it off immediately upon any kind of default.

When the professor concluded his testimony, the chairman remarked that he wanted to thank him and to thank Mr. Cantor "for providing you here to give us this seminar on real estate law." The audience broke into spontaneous applause. Hetland's testimony had not only scored heavily with the board, but had also undermined the legal basis for the projected indictment by the federal government. Hetland was unaware of the proposed indictment but did mention in his testimony that there are lawyers who believe, wrongly, that lenders really have a legal interest in property held as collateral "as opposed to their real interest . . . to get paid." Evidently, the federal government's lawyers were among the false believers.

7

The materials found in Cantor's safe, though old, were serious if their implications — that he corrupted public officials — could be sustained. Cantor himself testified on the Benson matter. He said that to the best of his recollection, Benson had never been in a position to influence whether Cantor's clients would be prosecuted in the government's tax case. Moreover, when he sold Benson the car, the man was no longer actively employed by government. He was on extended leave, using up vacation time acquired prior to retirement to take a cross-country automobile trip. He had telephoned Cantor just to say hello, and Cantor had invited him to dinner. During dinner, when asked how he was getting along, Benson said that he was enjoying his trip, except that his automobile wasn't working well. He would like to have replaced it, but new cars in 1947 were hard to find. Cantor testified that he had bought a new car months earlier, but found he didn't really need it, and had been thinking about selling it. He offered, Cantor said, to sell Benson the car at the same price he had paid for it. It was, Cantor said, a friendly arms-length transaction, with Benson acquiring the car he needed; and with Cantor selling an unnecessary used car for the price of a new one. The sale, Cantor argued, was certainly no bribe since Benson (a) did not get something for nothing; and (b) was not now nor had he ever been in a position to show favoritism to Cantor's clients.

George B. Crowley, an imposing figure and well-known Chicago attorney, corroborated Cantor's testimony. He testified that he had personally been in charge of the Department of Justice's prosecution of Cantor's clients on casino skimming–tax evasion charges, and that the evidence simply wasn't there, so the charges were dropped. Benson wasn't at all involved in any decisions. His job was strictly a technical accounting one, according to Crowley.

Furthermore, Crowley testified that he had known Cantor for years, that he worked with him on a number of bar association committees, and that he would gladly put his unqualified endorsement on Cantor's character. To disbelieve Cantor, then, one would have to disbelieve Crowley, not merely on whether he was responsible for dropping the charges against Cantor's clients, an alleged fact which could be checked, but whether Crowley had dropped the charges legitimately. There was no evidence or suggestion that Crowley was anything but honorable — except the generalized stigma carried by Cantor. So much for the first item found in Cantor's safe.

8

To answer the second item — the suggestion that Cantor had possibly bribed Freid, his hometown United States attorney in charge of criminal prosecutions — Cantor testified that he argued few federal cases in those days and that Freid was a close personal friend. Freid asked for a loan to resolve some family health needs, Cantor said — his child required an operation. And the loan had been repaid.

Cantor was pressed to explain the presence of notes in his safe for a repaid loan. Cantor testified that this was a friendly loan and that Freid had never asked for the notes back. It would never occur to Freid to think that Cantor would sue on a note already paid. Besides, Freid had died years earlier. There was really no point in having kept Freid's note. It had lain there in the safe all these years because Cantor was less than compulsive about cleaning out his safe. The agents, he admitted, had shown him up as an untidy safekeeper, but nothing more.

Several possible inferences were open to the board. One was to infer that Cantor's explanation was accurate. Another was that Freid had died without repaying the loan. It was not an outright bribe, but an indebtedness. That perspective suggested a third interpretation: that it might not matter whether the loan had been repaid or not. Was Cantor the sort of man who would seek to create indebtedness in public officials? Surely, it would not be proper for Cantor, the licensee, to loan the chairman of the Gaming Control Board half a year's salary in the year 1975, even if the chairman was to repay it. Was it proper in 1948 for a practicing criminal law attorney to loan half a year's salary to a United States attorney?

Cantor produced the ideal witness to respond to this question. He was Samuel Dash, chief counsel and staff director of the Senate committee investigating Watergate, who had flown with his wife Sarah to Carson City to answer questions on legal ethics and to offer testimony on behalf of their friend Jacob Cantor. Whatever negative associations alleged by law enforcement to Cantor, it was to turn out that a number of prominent persons, most notably Samuel Dash, were willing to testify to his high character, commitment to the legal profession, and charitable impulses and activities.

When I asked Dash why he had testified, Dash explained that the Dashes and the Cantors were friends; that they had met, as he testified, through his and Cantor's activities in the National Association of Criminal Defense Lawyers and the American Bar Association's Criminal Law Section. To the best of his knowledge, Dash said, Cantor was a man of integrity and professional responsibility. He had thought twice before coming out to testify, but felt it was important to tell what he knew about a man whom he considered to be outstanding, and to interpret Cantor's conduct to the board in the light of legal ethics, a subject he had taught and worked on for years.

Dash testified that the ethical sensibilities developed by Watergate would certainly preclude loans between a criminal defense attorney and a prosecutor. He also testified that he had served as special consultant and reporter on an ABA committee, headed by then Judge, now Chief Justice, Burger, to set out standards of

conduct for the prosecution and defense functions. The committee was formed in the 1960s to answer these kinds of questions; in fact, the relationship between defense attorney and prosecutor was unclear. Lawyers were forbidden to make loans to judges, hearing officers, or tribunals, but the relationship between lawyer and prosecutor was never clear. Lawyers were never specifically excluded from making loans to prosecutors, and the climate of the 1940s, as Cantor had testified, did not frown upon such activities. Affirming Cantor's testimony, Dash testified that at the time, 1948, lawyers — prosecutors and defense attorneys alike — were considered to be a fraternity. They could eat, drink, and socialize together and presumably make the sorts of loans friends might make to one another. At the time, he testified, neither ethical canons nor common practice suggested impropriety.

Dash was obviously a powerful witness, partly because of his testimony and partly because he personally symbolized official integrity. The board could not fail to be moved by the fact that a man of his stature would travel from Washington, D.C. to Carson City, Nevada to testify for Jacob Cantor.

But Dash never could totally erase Cantor's stigma. Part of the reason was — is — related to the *ex parte* evidence available to an administrative agency that conducts its own investigations. For example, in the Cantor case, several persons who were unwilling to testify — perhaps because their testimony would not withstand public questioning, or because they feared offending Cantor — had spoken differently to the board than Cantor's witnesses about Cantor's professional character. Indeed, several witnesses had told stories to the board privately that directly contradicted their public testimony.

The board grudgingly granted Cantor a license. He had responded vigorously and well to the various allegations, well enough so that the record created a reasonable doubt as to whether his alleged misconduct was in fact misconduct. He had not proved, regarding Mr. Freid, that he had done no wrong. But in order to deny Cantor a license, the board would have been required (as Bixbe pointed out in explaining his positive vote) to draw negative inferences in each and every instance where an alternative was possible. The commission also voted unanimously to license Cantor,

with the stipulation that Cantor would not make loans to any of his other corporate interests from the company operating the Pyramid.

Stipulations aside, the Cantor licensing investigation and hearing were unprecedented in their complexity and importance. There really was no turning back after that. The authorities had become, however reluctantly, educated to constraints imposed on officials by legally competent actors in a constitutional democracy.

14

The Applicant Fights Back

LATE IN 1976, THE CHAIRMAN OF THE GAMING COMMISSION, HIMSELF a lawyer, publicly attacked corporations employing high-powered lawyers to challenge the gaming control apparatus in Nevada. "The new group of gamblers — many of them corporations — are now talking about rights," he said. "It would be impossible to administer gaming if we adhered to their philosophy."[1] The chairman's comments were made in the wake of a Nevada district court decision overturning the gaming authorities' denial of a license to applicant Frank Rosenthal, who was applying to be director of casino operations for the Argent (Allen R. Glick Enterprises) Corporation, which at the time held five major casinos. Glick, who had moved into Nevada in a major way just a couple of years earlier, had become, as another commissioner put it over drinks one evening, "our number one problem." Allen R. Glick Enterprises — and I shall here use real names because a major law case is involved — did indeed embody the dilemmas of the legalization of casino gambling and the process of their resolution.

One facet of the dilemma involves "the issue of calculation." As Erving Goffman puts it: "When a respectable motive is given for action, are we to suspect an ulterior one? When an individual supports a promise or threat with a convincing display of emotional expression, are we to believe him? When an individual seems carried away by feeling, is he intentionally acting this way in order to create an effect?"[2]

The issue of calculation is further complicated when interpretations are being made in a legal and economic setting. An individual involved with another in a purely social relationship may attribute dishonorable motives to the other and simply close out the relationship — perhaps by refusing further social contact. But an official must defend the attribution process both personally and legally. The two acts may not and often do not coincide. Thus, it is not enough for a gaming official to suspect or even to come to believe in an ulterior motive. To act, he must construct a set of legally defensible reasons for attributing such a motive. He must cite evidence, to be sure. But the ultimate issues are: what sort of evidence, how gathered, how presented, how available to challenge, under what rules of disclosure and openness?

He must also carefully weigh the variety of consequences of acting or failing to act on his assessments of character and motivation. Will the agency's future control position be strengthened or weakened by his acts? Will the industry benefit or be harmed economically? Will he put himself in a position of legal liability?

Still, assessments must be made. Inaction is a form of action. The tactics of gaming control are not clear when attributions of character and motive are uncertain. As the remainder of this chapter will show, however, once judgments of character take shape, the dilemma moves toward resolution. The gaming authorities, the courts, the legislature, and the industry join together to reject those who contribute to the "pariah image." The community takes care of its own out of fear of outside intervention. In Nevada, the ultimate deviant is one who threatens the independence and profitability of the gaming industry. Allen Glick and Frank Rosenthal were eventually to occupy this unenviable position.

2

Allen R. Glick's meteoric rise to financial prominence was investigated as carefully and thoroughly as possible by the board and its agents, who could find no specific grounds on which to deny him a license, although board members were deeply troubled by aspects of his rapid accumulation of wealth and power. At the age of 27 Mr. Glick, an Ohio-educated attorney and army captain, had completed a tour of duty as an intelligence officer in Vietnam. After he left the service, he was earning $800 a month selling apartments and condominiums. Five years later, Mr. Glick held a total of $146 million in loans from the Teamsters Central States Pension Fund for properties in California and Texas, and five Nevada casinos.

Mr. Glick's first step up the financial ladder was his association with a California real estate company located in San Diego. The chief executive of this company — Saratoga Development — found Mr. Glick's services so valuable that he sold him a 45-percent share of the company for $2,500. At the time, the company, for which Mr. Glick had worked 1½ years, was worth between $4 and $5 million. Mr. Glick was the beneficiary of a $2 million bonus for 1½ years of work in a $2,000 per month executive assistant's job. The man who gave the money was interviewed by board agents, who found him both unfriendly and unimpeachable. He insisted that how he spent his own money was "his own damned business," and that if he felt Mr. Glick was worth it, he was.

The same company also financed Glick's first Las Vegas venture, the purchase of a controlling interest in the Hacienda Hotel in 1973 — a loan that had still not been repaid in 1977, a year after the company went into Chapter 11 bankruptcy proceedings following a series of defaults on loans. Mr. Glick had severed his connections with the company in 1974.

While still with Saratoga, Mr. Glick learned of the availability of the Stardust and Fremont casinos, then held by the Recrion Corporation. According to a deposition by Mr. Glick, he met with a Mr. Todd Derlachter in a coffee shop and Mr. Derlachter told him of the availability of the Las Vegas properties. Mr. Derlachter was well paid for his services in pointing Mr. Glick toward Recrion. He received a $422,000 finder's fee, plus a seven-year, $10,000-a-month consulting contract with Argent.[3]

Recrion's principal stockholder, financier Delbert Coleman, had been a defendant in a Securities and Exchange Commission civil suit charging him with massive and improper stock manipulation of the shares of Recrion's predecessor, the Parvin-Dohrmann Company.

Mr. Coleman agreed to sell Mr. Glick his 31-percent interest in Recrion. Mr. Glick agreed to acquire nearly all of the remainder, partly because Mr. Coleman's consent decree with the SEC bound him not to make a transaction of this nature unless all the other Recrion stockholders were comparably benefited, and partly because Mr. Glick wanted to merge Recrion into Argent, so as, according to Glick's attorney, ". . . to have complete control of the entire venture and ultimately to eliminate the dual corporate structure."[4]

The entire acquisition would cost Mr. Glick almost $62 million, and he went to the Teamsters Central States Pension Fund for financing. The Teamsters approved Mr. Glick's request for a $62.7 million loan since he was well connected there, having already borrowed more than $15 million. He knew assets manager Alvin Baron, who was indicted by a federal grand jury in 1976 on kick-back charges. Mr. Baron pleaded not guilty and at the time of this writing the case was unresolved. Mr. Baron was a close associate of Allen Dorfman, a special consultant to the fund until Dorfman's conviction in 1972 on loan kickback charges.

The gaming authorities were well aware of and disturbed by additional Teamsters loans coming into the state, as well as by Mr. Glick's relations with Messrs. Baron and Derlachter. The authorities conferred privately, talked over lunch and drinks, held extensive public hearings, and concluded that although both Mr. Glick and the Teamsters were questionable, they could not prove, any more than the federal government could, that there was anything legally wrong with Mr. Glick or with his relationship with the Teamsters. Board member Kimball Bixbe expressed the disturbed and ambivalent feelings of the authorities. "I've been bothered by this whole transaction," he said. "I've been bothered by the fact that Allen Glick is a young man who is almost too good to be true. His success is beyond that of many more accomplished people who have been wheelin' and dealin' for a long time. But since we've been unable to uncover any evidence — and I think we've been back and forth across the country and up and down and covered it in every direction trying to find out if there is any evidence that there's something evil about the way you managed to reach the level at which you now find yourself, I have to be fair and vote with what the evidence says and ignore this feeling — this unquieting feeling that I have in my stomach that, down the road, I may be proved to have been right."[5]

Glick obtained two more Teamsters loans in October 1974, on particularly favorable terms. These, for a shopping mall in Oakland, California and a dormant land-development project in Los Angeles, totaled $32 million. In December, he borrowed another $25 million for Argent, and in August 1975 he refinanced the original $62.7 million loan into a new one for $73.5 million, making a grand total of $146 million in Teamsters borrowings, most of which was for Nevada casinos.

After Mr. Glick was licensed in 1974, the gaming authorities began to recast him into a new image. Allen Glick, having been licensed, began to be considered a respectable and even desirable licensee. Sour grapes began to taste sweet.

To be sure, when one of his dissident business associates, Tamara Rand, was murdered in San Diego, Glick was linked by newspapers and the law enforcement intelligence community with the murder.[6] But nothing ever came of the allegations, and he vigorously denied any connection whatsoever. The board investigated as well and was not entirely persuaded by the associational inferences drawn by other agencies in the law enforcement intelligence community.

The information in this case looked like yet another instance of what I have come to think of as the "adverse premise–circular information" phenomenon that pervades the law enforcement intelligence community. One begins with an adverse premise about an individual's moral character, a premise which is reinforced by the exchange of information among intelligence agencies. The validity of an item of information is enhanced by the number of intelligence agencies it passes through, thus leading to an adverse conclusion. The conclusion may or may not prove to be correct, but it achieves creditability through circulation. If the conclusion proves to be correct, the process of inference tends to be affirmed. This is, of course, a non sequitur, but an understandable one.

Glick's diminished image with the gaming authorities, as well as with others in the industry, came about less from his prior business and social associations than from his active sponsorship of Frank Norman Rosenthal to be his director of casino operations.

3

Frank Rosenthal is recognized in the gambling world as a top-flight professional gambler, and has been one for most of his adult life. In this respect, he resembles many who began and continue to occupy positions of authority within the gaming industry. There is some question as to whether Rosenthal was ever an illegal bookmaker. He was indicted by the Department of Justice for being one, but the indictment was later dismissed. Rosenthal himself denies ever having been a bookmaker. He says he was principally a sports bettor, one so knowledgeable that his bets often helped to establish the odds and the point spreads on major sporting events.

Actually it doesn't matter much. A man who bets across state lines with illegal bookmakers, or who was himself one, does not fall beyond the licensing pale. A nice distinction is employed here: the question is, did he behave ethically while he was behaving illegally?

The Gaming Control Board had long been uneasy about Frank Rosenthal. He had received a work permit through the sheriff's office in Clark County and was employed, in a presumably minor position, in a legal race and sports bookmaking establishment in Nevada. At that time, bookmaking was legal, but not terribly consequential (because the federal government's 10 percent tax discouraged bettors from betting with legal Nevada bookmakers).

Rosenthal and another man, Elliot Paul Price, were arrested by federal agents in December 1970 on illegal bookmaking charges. They were acused of running a separate illegal book out of the legal establishment; the federal agents seized their work permits. Had Rosenthal and Price continued to work without permits, both they and any employer would have been subject to criminal penalties in Nevada. While the federal case was pending, Price applied to the Clark County sheriff for another work permit and received it. The Gaming Control Board was notified of this fact, and the sheriff was instructed to repossess the work permit.

Price sued on grounds that his application for replacing the original permit, in possession of the federal authorities, was not a new application, but merely a replacement for one that had been lost. He argued that the board could not take away his work permit without a separate hearing. The Nevada Supreme Court upheld Price and admonished the legislature for not specifying a procedure for revoking a work permit.[7] (Since then, the legislature has introduced such a procedure.)

As a practical matter, the Price decision, which was handed down on January 31, 1973, helped Rosenthal. Having lost an important Nevada Supreme Court case, board members became wary of going after somebody's job without legally acceptable procedures. By this time, Rosenthal was employed in the Stardust Hotel, apparently assuming increasingly greater responsibilities.

This point is important, for it has been and continues to be difficult for the gaming authorities to draft either legislation or regulations defining who is a key employee, i.e., subject to being licensed — particularly if the controlling stockholder or stockholders and the employee seek to evade the licensing process.

Let me offer one illustration: In 1977, Frank Sinatra held the gaming status of a revoked licensee. At least two major casino corporations held entertainment contracts with him, at sums far exceeding the $40,000 annually that the regulations define as the point at which someone becomes a key employee. I mention Sinatra, because he is so obviously a bona fide entertainer, and probably had little to do with how the casinos he worked in did business — how they extended credit, hired dealers, offered complimentary food and beverages, and so forth. On the other hand, entertainers do make such recommendations, and if the casino cares about their good will the recommendations will be taken seriously. In the vernacular, top-flight entertainers enjoy lots of "juice" in the industry.

Should top-flight entertainers be required to be licensed as key employees? Whether they should or not, it is inconceivable that the gaming authorities would ever attempt to do so, even if they could draw a technical case for licensing. There would be an uproar in the industry over any such attempt and the governor who appointed such a board would fear being voted out of office at the next election.

In contrast, should the entertainment or food and beverage or sales and conventions director of a major hotel be required to be licensed? This is a gray area, and one that Frank Rosenthal occupied for a long time.

Actually, a letter was sent to the Stardust on January 6, 1972, asking about Rosenthal's duties, authority, salary, and so forth. But the Stardust and Rosenthal requested postponing formal licensing until the federal indictment could be cleared up. They felt, and the board believed, that the case against Rosenthal was weak and would eventually be dropped, as it indeed was.

Besides the Price case and the indictment, a third factor was operating to delay Rosenthal's licensing. So far as the board could tell, he was on his very best behavior. Indeed, at one time he was operating as an informant for the gaming authorities. Later, they were to express serious reservations about the quality of the information received from Rosenthal, but at the time he was regarded as someone with a questionable past history — and also with an extraordinarily knowledgeable approach to gaming.

Little by little, Rosenthal's character was becoming rehabilitated — an asset to the industry, a respectable gaming man. When Glick began to rely more and more upon Frank Rosenthal (ultimately he came to be "Director of Nevada Operations and Special Consultant to the Chairman" of the Argent Corporation), the gaming board members were not entirely dismayed. They and the commission members did, however, insist that under the circumstances Rosenthal simply had to be licensed.

As the investigation progressed, Mr. Rosenthal began to appear increasingly unacceptable as a candidate for a Nevada gaming license, particularly as director of an entity of the magnitude of Argent Corporation, with its four casinos and with Teamsters loans totaling over $100 million.

4

Recall that a gaming investigation involves, among other aspects, a check of law enforcement agencies. By its very nature, such a "check" involves taking secret information of varying authenticity. Thus when the evidence is being taken, the person about whom it is being offered has no opportunity to challenge it, to confront witnesses, to correct rumors, and so forth. In this respect, a gaming investigation is much like a security clearance investigation, where the applicant waives his or her right to challenge those making statements.

Frank Norman Rosenthal is a name known to organized crime investigators at federal, state, and local levels. Among these investigators, Mr. Rosenthal is not considered to be a man of exemplary moral character. In part, Mr. Rosenthal's reputation stems from a lifelong association with Anthony Spilotro. Mr. Spilotro was described by the executive director of the Illinois Crime Commission as one of the syndicate's most dangerous gunmen and a specialist in the invasion of legitimate businesses by the mob.[8] *Time* magazine was more direct, calling Spilotro a "Chicago Mafia triggerman."[9]

A Las Vegas resident, Spilotro was thought by federal authorities to be the watchdog for mob-connected interests in Las Vegas. These authorities believed that the acknowledged social connection between Rosenthal and Spilotro involved business connections as well, although Rosenthal denied that at his hearings. Nevertheless, as one of the board members pointed out at the hearing, the Rosenthal–Spilotro association would pose "image" problems for the state of Nevada, even if the relations were purely social.

Rosenthal's relationship to Spilotro goes back many years. Evidently, the Rosenthal and Spilotro families had long been close friends, because Rosenthal testified that he knew Spilotro "before he had been conceived." Moreover, he was deeply indebted to Spilotro who, he testified, had once saved him from a bad beating at the hands of FBI agents. Speaking of an encounter on a Florida roadside, Rosenthal testified:

> This was at nighttime, and [the road] wasn't heavily trafficked, kind of quiet.
>
> And as Frank Rosenthal, that's the way I am, I walked back to that car. They didn't come to me, I walked back to them, and we had a few words. I reminded [the FBI agents] about some of the members of their family, kind of a nasty thing, back and forth. With that they got out of the car. One was out and one was in. The one was in, got out, and they pushed me off, physically pushed me off to the side, and the one agent said, "We finally got you. We are going to give you the beating of your life, you son of a bitch." . . .
>
> They tried to get me a little further into the bushes. There was no contest. They were two big agents, they were armed, and I wasn't that big.
>
> With that, another car pulled up very quickly, and two fellows jumped out of the car, and one of them was Anthony Spilotro, and he wasn't armed, and there were just a couple of words went back and forth, just a couple, very, very few. He is about five foot two or five foot three, and they got back in their car. . . .[10]

If there had been nothing else problematic in Mr. Rosenthal's background besides his association with Mr. Spilotro, he conceivably might have squeaked through the licensing investigation. Law enforcement officials could speculate about the business side of the Spilotro–Rosenthal connection, but they could prove nothing.

The most comprehensive theory of that connection was based on the premise that the Stardust Hotel had never really changed hands, in that it had always been controlled by the Chicago underworld. The Stardust had been built by a man named Tony Cornero, who ran gambling ships off the coast of California. He had died before the structure was completed and his family had sold the hotel casino to a group headed by Moe Dalitz.

During the 1960s the state was under pressure by the federal government to rid the industry of old timers like Dalitz, one of the original members of the Cleveland group that invested in the Desert Inn. He had grown up in Detroit, moved to Cleveland during the Depression, and allegedly operated illegal gambling clubs in Ohio and Kentucky before moving to Las Vegas. His group also owned one of the leading Strip casinos — the Desert Inn — until 1967, when it was sold to Howard Hughes.

Around Las Vegas, Dalitz is spoken of nostalgically as a man who kept his word and was financially generous, especially to local charities and residents. In the eyes of many of his contemporaries, Dalitz represented "the good old days" of gambling and the achievement of a new respectability in Nevada's permissive climate. A group of journalists investigating the murder of reporter Don Bolles in 1976 interviewed Senator Barry Goldwater's brother Robert, an Arizona businessman, in connection with his relationship to Dalitz. "I have no way of knowing [if the mobster description is accurate]. . . . I know of two dinners given in his honor by the people of Las Vegas — testimonial dinners attended by the attorney general, the governor, senators of the state of Nevada."[11]

In any event, Dalitz, in 1968, sold the Stardust to Parvin-Dohrmann, a firm also beset by federal troubles. Parvin-Dohrmann sold to Delbert Coleman and Recrion, and Recrion sold to Glick.

The theory — that the Stardust was always controlled by mob interests, who could from time to time produce new and acceptable purchasers, plus financing from the Teamsters — is perhaps plausible, but no law enforcement body has been able to demonstrate its validity in a courtroom. The Spilotro–Rosenthal connection was consistent with the theory, but certainly did not confirm it. Standing alone, it would have proved a questionable ground for denial of a license to Frank Rosenthal.

5

More important was a pattern of "unethical" illegality. Evidence existed to substantiate a charge that Frank Rosenthal was at some point in his life a fixer of sporting events, particularly collegiate basketball and football games. As indicated, it doesn't necessarily matter in Nevada that you have been an illegal gambler or bookmaker, or have run illegal gaming casinos, although such acceptance of illegality might change in the future as legal casino gambling becomes institutionalized. The legal gambling industry has always had to contend with the problem of reconciling expertise with illegality and has done so by imputing standards of morality to illegal conduct. Thus, it is acceptable to have been a bettor or bookmaker, but not acceptable to have fixed the games you were betting.

In 1962, Rosenthal was charged by a North Carolina court with attempting to bribe a New York University basketball player in a game between NYU and West Virginia to be played in Charlotte, North Carolina. Rosenthal did not contest the charges and paid a fine of $6,000, plus court costs.[12]

During his licensing hearings, Rosenthal claimed to have been the innocent victim of an associate who turned state's evidence to save himself. Such protestations of innocence are rarely convincing by one who pleads guilty. In Rosenthal's case, they were particularly unconvincing since they were coupled with charges by another college athlete, an Oregon football player named Mickey Bruce, that Rosenthal and his associate David Budin offered him $10,000 to fix a football game with the University of Michigan. The charges were made in September 1961, before the McClellan Senate subcommittee investigating organized crime. On the advice of his attorney, Rosenthal refused even to tell the subcommittee whether he knew the Oregon football star. He invoked the 5th Amendment privilege against self-incrimination, and reportedly glared at Bruce during the hearing.

Bruce's testimony stands very strong on the record. Senator McClellan, who knew how to twist the knife once he had stuck it, said to Bruce:

I have no reason to believe that the testimony you have given is false, but if there is any error in it in any way at all, before you leave this stand, correct it. I don't want any injustice done to this man. You are a young man. You know exactly what happened. If there is any error in your testimony, any mistake that you can think of at all as you have given it, I wish you would point it out before you leave the stand.

Mr. Bruce: I am absolutely positive that what I said is true.

The Chairman: You have no doubt. You know that this is the man that was present?

Mr. Bruce: That is the same man.

The Chairman: You identify him, and you could not be mistaken about it?

Mr. Bruce: I could not be mistaken, sir.

The Chairman: Very well.[13]

In addition, there was testimony at the same hearing by two Florida police officers that, while they were arresting Rosenthal in his North Bay Village (Florida) apartment, Rosenthal admitted that he had been paying off other police officials to keep from being bothered. In connection with Rosenthal's Nevada hearings, an affidavit was taken from Martin F. Dardis, one of the arresting officers, who said that on December 31, 1960, Rosenthal was arrested for being a bookmaker. The affidavit goes on to say:

Whereupon, Mr. Rosenthal said he could not understand it because he (Mr. Rosenthal) had been paying off $500.00 a month not to be harassed. Mr. Rosenthal then asked me if I had been "short changed" and stated, "didn't you get your piece," referring to the $500.00 monthly payment. . . . I interpret Mr. Rosenthal's comments as indicating that Mr. Rosenthal was paying money to law enforcement officers to keep them from interfering with his gambling operation.[14]

Finally, as a result of the testimony by the Florida police officers and the football player at the McClellan hearing, Rosenthal was barred from racetracks and pari-mutuel operations in Florida.

At the end of Rosenthal's hearing, the testimony and the evidence were discussed. Rosenthal's application was denied by the board, and the denial was upheld by the commission.

Rosenthal expressed considerable bitterness at the decision. At the time there was merit to both points of view. From Rosenthal's perspective, the board and commission had acknowledged that he had done nothing during his tenure as an Argent employee to cast doubt on either his competence or his integrity. Although he did not admit to an organized crime connection, he had never made a secret of his friendship with Spilotro, or of his North Carolina conviction, or of his background as a professional gambler. He never claimed purity, only familiarity with the world of professional gamblers. In effect, he attributed to himself nothing more or less than the moral character of a professional gambler and challenged the state that had legalized professional gambling to find something wrong with that.

Ironically, when Rosenthal's licensing hearing took place, a major embezzlement at the hotels he supervised had not yet been uncovered and thus was never to become part of the legal record. Had it been, doubt would surely have been cast upon either his competence or his integrity. He might have claimed, as he did, that he knew nothing of the theft. But he could not also have sustained a claim that he was an extraordinarily able director of casino operations.

Indeed, he was evidently thought to be so unusually competent that, *before the hearing*, Allen Glick rewarded him with a 10-year contract at $250,000 per year *whether or not he was licensed*. Argent's annual report to the Securities and Exchange Commission showed that in 1976 Rosenthal received compensation of $579,636, including salary, land, and a home outfitted with various electronic devices designed to permit him to review aspects of the casino operation from his home base in a fashionable section of Las Vegas.[15] There was no question that the gaming board's denial of a license to Frank Rosenthal was a serious economic blow. The question to be resolved in the courts was whether the blow had been lawfully administered.

6

Rosenthal appealed the gaming authorities' decision to a Nevada district court. In a blockbuster decision, the court ruled the entire gaming control structure unconstitutional, essentially on two grounds: first, that the statutes are void of standards; and second, that the process used in invoking them is unconstitutional under the Due Process Clause of the 14th Amendment to the United States Constitution. The court laced into the structure full force. It called the statutes "facially unconstitutional . . . wholly without rational basis and essentially arbitrary. . . ."[16] It pointed out that Rosenthal was not notified of the charges against him, was not given sufficient notice to oppose any such charges, did not know the claims against him since the proceedings relied on confidential material. Furthermore, it pointed out that, since subpoena power does not exist extraterritorially, the football player who had testified at the McClellan hearings could not be brought to Nevada to be cross-examined, nor was Rosenthal given the right to cross-examine.

The decision was extraordinary for a Nevada court. In the past, Nevada courts had been generous in their interpretations of the Nevada control statutes, but this court seemed almost gratuitously to undermine the authority of the legislature and the control agency it had created.

Some months later, the judge, Joseph Pavlikowski, of the Clark County District Court, was found to have been given a $2,800 write-off on a bill for his daughter's wedding reception in February 1974. In an interview with a *Los Angeles Times* reporter, the judge explained that he had not disqualified himself because the bill had been paid by an earlier management. The judge did not acknowledge — perhaps he hadn't known? — that when the wedding took place, Frank Rosenthal was employed in public relations at the casino.[17]

7

Initially, board members were upset by the decision. In a short time, however, with the advice of their able deputy attorneys general, both relatively recent law school graduates, they began to perceive that the Rosenthal case was tailor-made for testing the legal authority of the board and its procedures. The Rosenthal licensing case would go to the Nevada Supreme Court, but this time the state of Nevada would be the appellant and Frank Rosenthal the respondent.

The prestigious corporations in Nevada rallied to the state's defense. For example, the MGM Grand submitted an *amicus* brief supporting reversal of the district court's decision. The brief avoids legal arguments entirely. A paragraph is worth quoting because it succinctly and powerfully summarizes the *economic* and *social* arguments for reversal:

It is amicus' considered opinion that a finding of invalidity of the licensing statutes and regulations could have a far-reaching and adverse effect on the State's gaming industry. Any suggestion that the standards for licensing are going to be lowered will be interpreted by organized crime elements as an invitation to renew their efforts to gain a foothold in Nevada's gaming industry, efforts which have been frustrated by the vigilance and dedication of the Gaming Commission and the Gaming Control Board. It will also serve to undo the industry's efforts over the last decade to persuade the nation's financial community that the gaming industry is a responsible and qualified vehicle for public investment. Finally, it will counteract the industry's efforts to convince the convention industry that Nevada is a desirable situs for major business conventions.[18]

Obviously, the Rosenthal case was not only interesting and significant in its legal issues. On it was thought to rest the future of an industry.

15

The Future of Licensing

THE AUTHORITIES FELT THAT IF THEY COULD NOT WIN THE ROSENTHAL case they could not win any. Still, because Rosenthal enlisted on his side unusually distinguished counsel, former dean of the Harvard Law School and former solicitor general of the United States Erwin Griswold, it was not to be an easy victory. Griswold and his associate counsel presented a learned brief.

To win, they had to persuade a court that Rosenthal had a "property" right under the United States Constitution. The 14th Amendment holds that one cannot be deprived of life, liberty, or property without due process of law. Did Frank Rosenthal, a gaming license applicant, hold a property or liberty interest that would entitle him to United States constitutional protection? Only where a party can show a property interest, as in a job or some form of government largesse; or a "liberty" interest as a defendant does in a criminal case, is an individual entitled to that mysterious but significant blessing of constitutional democracies called due process. More importantly, at least for starters, would the Nevada Supreme Court find such interests?

No precisely analogous case had ever come up before the United

States Supreme Court or any federal court. There had been cases where an assistant professor had sued a university or a policeman a city after having been fired, arguing that they had been deprived of property or liberty without due process of law.[1]

But Rosenthal hadn't been fired. On the contrary, his employer enthusiastically supported him, or at least appeared publicly to do so. And he wasn't an untenured professor or a small-town policeman. He was a professional gambler who had been working in the legal casino gambling business with a work permit. So, the first question, more precisely stated, was: Does an applicant for a Nevada gaming license, *who has held a work permit for several years*, have a property interest sufficient to trigger the protection of due process?

The Nevada Supreme Court did not think so. It found that the legislature distinguished between persons who have been licensed and those who never have. Those with a license, who are being disciplined, have a property interest. Those who have not, don't. The distinction possesses the virtue of simplicity, but it is also simplistic. Surely, different property interests prevail as between, on the one hand, someone applying for a new license to hold an equity interest in a casino, and, on the other, an applicant who has held a work permit for several years, and is being promoted to a position requiring licensing. That sort of advancement in a career already underway seems to suggest a property interest stronger than a new applicant's.

Although the Nevada Supreme Court did not recognize such a distinction, it nevertheless went on, as courts are inclined, to consider the hypothetical question of whether the decision would have been sustained if Rosenthal had had a property or liberty interest.

2

One route to understanding due process is social and philosophical. The other, and inherently connected, route is legal. A legal analysis would examine those cases most analogous to the one at hand. Depending upon which adversary position a lawyer was arguing, he or she would try to show that in like cases individuals were granted, or the government was required to offer one who was about to be deprived of life, liberty, or property, due process —

such procedural protection as the right to counsel, or the right to a public hearing, or the right to appeal, or the right to cross-examine, or the right to be given notice.

The other adversary, normally government counsel, would attempt to distinguish the present case from those preceding. Perhaps the two United States Supreme Court cases most relevant to the Rosenthal proceeding were *Board of Regents v. Roth* and *Bishop v. Wood.*

In *Board of Regents v. Roth* an assistant professor, who held a one-year contract without tenure, was fired without any reasons being given. The court found that since Roth did not have tenure he did not qualify as one with a property interest; and since reasons were not given for his firing, his reputation wasn't harmed, and therefore he had not been denied a liberty interest.

As a matter of constitutional law development, the case was significant because it finally disposed of the "right–privilege" distinction in constitutional law and substituted a new formula: Only if a liberty or property interest is at stake will an individual be entitled to due process of law.[2] But on the question of what constitutes a property interest for a gaming employee seeking a license as a key employee, it was only remotely applicable. With Roth, questions of academic freedom were involved. Roth was fired from an impermanent job. Rosenthal was hired to a semipermanent one. Roth was not denied employment by a regulatory agency. Rosenthal was, and one given broad powers by the legislature.

A later case, *Bishop v. Wood* was not much more analogous to Rosenthal's, but it is nevertheless important for understanding the future of licensing because it further restricts the concept of a property or liberty interest.

Mr. Bishop was a small-town North Carolina policeman. He was fired by the city manager. The city manager told the policeman in private why he was being fired and also put the reasons in writing in answer to interrogatories (a set of written questions to be answered in writing) in the lawsuit challenging the dismissal. A majority of justices found that the city ordinance of Marion, North Carolina did not grant Bishop a property interest. The manager was therefore entitled to fire him without interference by the federal courts.

In my opinion, if one reads the ordinance one can find a property interest or not, depending upon the philosophy of the proper relationship between federal courts and local authorities. That seems the key to this case and to the question of future interpretations of the breadth of permissible administrative discretion at the state and local level. For example, Mr. Justice Stevens writes, offering broad discretion to local authorities under the United States Constitution:

The federal court is not the appropriate forum in which to review the multitude of personnel decisions that are made daily by public agencies. We must accept the harsh fact that numerous individual mistakes are inevitable in the day-to-day administration of our affairs. The United States Constitution cannot feasibly be construed to require federal judicial review for every such error.[3]

In contrast, Mr. Justice Brennan answers in his dissent:

However, the federal courts are the appropriate forum for ensuring that the constitutional mandates of due process are followed by those agencies of government making personnel decisions that pervasively influence the lives of those affected thereby; the fundamental premise of the Due Process Clause is that those procedural safeguards will help the government avoid the "harsh fact" of "incorrect or ill-advised personnel decisions."[4]

But another issue was left unresolved by both these cases. Suppose one is protected by due process of law? What exactly does that mean? Justice Marshall's dissent suggests that due process means only that when somebody is denied "liberty to work" — is fired by government — reasons must be given. Of course, he intends this only as a minimal requirement in the context of answering the argument that to provide procedural due process to all public employees or prospective employees "would place an intolerable burden on the machinery of government."[5]

Of course. But the questions remain, what additional requirements — besides reasons — would put an intolerable burden on the machinery of government, in which contexts, and how should these requirements be balanced against basic considerations of fairness?[6] More particularly, the situation in Nevada is further complicated by the existence of a pariah industry. This changes the general question of requirements to: "What requirements of due process should prevail where there is an historical threat of infiltration by organized crime?"

3

Nevada authorities are disposed to offer as little formal due process as possible, as little as they can legally get away with. This is not because they are particularly authoritarian. Rather, like all officials who enjoy discretion, they prefer not to be constrained either by precedent or resources. Unlike prosecutors, who do enjoy considerable discretion to bring charges or go to trial, the agency — the Nevada Gaming Board and Commission — has become increasingly wary of the rights of applicants and licensees.

Sometimes, as indicated at the beginning of this discussion, authorities become petulant about those who make claims of right, especially those who possess resources and legal competence to assert such claims. The average prosecutor rarely faces individuals as well endowed with resources as those appearing before the Nevada gaming authorities. How many of those charged with offenses for which they might receive substantial criminal penalties are represented by a former Harvard Law School dean who also served as solicitor general of the United States? If Frank Rosenthal was connected with the Chicago underworld, as alleged, his backers demonstrated cultivated legal taste.

In any case, the authorities feel pressure. Nevertheless, there is no good reason why Nevada (and other states seeking to license those applying for gambling licenses or licenses in a myriad of other activities that, presently illegal, might become legal) could not introduce a more sharply defined adjudicative model into the licensing process. The model I have in mind would contain many of the features of the contemporary Nevada one, with a major exception, from which several minor ones result.

The major exception would be formally to separate the investigative from the judicial function.[7] At present, the gaming authorities, both board and commission, are conceived of as a distinct but connected part of an agency that is part watchdog and part big brother. The agency is supposed to regulate the industry in the industry's own interest, but the concept of regulation is neither clear nor enlightening. Distinctions between the board and commission are confused in the day-to-day operations of the agency. For one example, the commission issues regulations that in fact are drawn and enforced by the board and its agents. For another, board and commission share the same legal counsel. In fact, commissioners and board members will even sit down together over drinks or dinner and discuss the problems of the industry and particular individuals within it. I am not suggesting that such behavior is illegal; although it might be under the Open Meeting Law.[8] I am arguing that the *structure* of the agency invites such practices. Nobody is seeking to evade the law. It is simply that its dictates are unclear.

Those who want seriously to consider due process in the gaming control context must comprehend an important reality. This agency investigates. It is inconceivable to maintain an investigative agency which does not receive *ex parte* evidence. The Gaming Control Board cannot first secretly investigate an applicant, then hold an open hearing, in a seemingly adjudicative forum, and not be influenced by the prior results of its own investigation. I once pointed this out to the chairman of the board. His rephrasing states the issue with a clarity I could never hope to achieve. "I see what you mean, Jerry," he said. "You can't be playing the game and tootin' the whistle at the same time." Exactly. Kenneth Culp Davis makes a nice distinction between individual and organizational involvement in judging: "For an individual to serve as both advocate and judge in the same case is obviously improper. . . . But it is not improper even in a criminal case for a large institution, the state, to prosecute through one officer, the prosecuting attorney, and to decide through another, the judge."[9] In Nevada, the same individuals sometimes investigate and judge.

Under the present arrangements, the relationship between board and applicant is unclear to all parties. The board often finds itself torn between adopting a challenging, investigative law enforcement stance toward the applicant; or a more sympathetic, friendly one, especially to those already involved in the industry. Such applicants are understandably resentful when challenged hard and *publicly* by board members. The members themselves sense the conflict of roles and sometimes become less forceful in their questioning than they would be if all their preliminary interrogations were directed toward forming a conclusion to bring to an independent hearing officer or officers.

Under an adversary–adjudicative system the board would assume a more prosecutorial stance, in effect, a quasimagisterial one. Should the board's investigation result in a clean bill of health, the applicant would automatically be granted a license. That is now true, in practice. Under the present system, the board really enjoys discretion to grant licenses. It has never made a positive recommendation that was overturned by the commission. As one board member quipped: "We dispense justice, they dispense mercy."

But when the board has problems, it should not also sit as judge. Ideally, the board would present its problems to a truly independent adjudicator. An adjudicative model would thus dispense with the present commission altogether, since that is the forum where argument and influence are most often blurred. In its stead, a highly qualified and independent hearing officer or panel not subject to *ex parte* communications would make decisions based on the record before it.

It would be terribly naive to believe that hearing officers, any more than judges, invariably consider cases solely on their merits, with no concern for economic consequences. But at least such a system would establish a judicial posture for the hearing officer. For example, when the Nevada Supreme Court considers a case affecting the gaming industry, the court is of course aware that its decision will prove consequential for the industry. An *amicus* — e.g., MGM Grand — may file a brief pointing out those consequences, but it would not be appropriate for members of the court to sit down over drinks and discuss the consequences with the *amicus* or the contending parties. An adjudicative model would insure observance of at least essential proprieties.

The present arrangements sometimes seem unfair and, worse yet, pretentious and confusing. They seem unfair because the same agency — albeit with some separation — is playing the game and tooting the whistle. They seem pretentious because the agency must appear as if it hadn't played the game when it is called on to act as judge. It is one thing clearly to combine investigation and judging in an administrative agency. It is another clearly to separate these functions. But the present Nevada system is a will-o'-the-wisp, sometimes combining, sometimes separating. All too often, the process ends up mainly confusing — to the board and its agents, the commission, and the applicants.

4

Although Rosenthal's brief attacked various aspects of Nevada's licensing procedures, it zeroed in on the *vagueness* of the gaming control statutes as a failure of due process. At the time, the statute granted "full and absolute power and authority" to deny a license "for any cause deemed reasonable." Obviously, such language is terribly vague. The regulations adopted by the commission to clarify the statute were somewhat more specific, but not exceedingly so. The applicant must have satisfied the commission that he or she was:

(a) a person of good character, honesty, and integrity;
(b) a person whose background, reputation and associations will not result in adverse publicity for the State of Nevada and its gaming industry; and
(c) has adequate business competence and experience for the role or position for which application is made.[10]

The brief noted that recent United States Supreme Court cases have upheld catch-all phrases like "character, honesty and integrity" against due process attacks, but these cases all involved "distinct and separate portions of society whose history, customs and traditions have given special meaning to catchwords like character, honesty and integrity." Actually, most of these cases involved professional or allied occupations such as doctors, lawyers, or government officials. The brief argued that gambling did not constitute such a "separate sphere of society."[11]

That assertion was to be the brief's fatal flaw, especially in addressing a Nevada court. It acknowledged that if a separate sphere of society was involved, "catchwords" would be permissible.

But in the past, both Nevada and federal courts had found that gambling is a special area of society, not because its practitioners are likely to be persons whose education and professional expertise place them in positions of trust — like doctors and lawyers — but because they possess distinctive opportunities for criminal activity.[12]

Perhaps the most telling riposte to the argument of vagueness came during the oral presentation before the Nevada Supreme Court. Mr. Griswold argued that under the Nevada statutes a man could be denied simply because he had red hair. One of the Nevada justices, Mr. Gordon Thompson, pointed out that Mr. Rosenthal had not been denied for that reason, but because he had pleaded guilty to the charge of attempting to bribe a basketball player. An "imaginary horrible" quickly fades in a courtroom when countered with a realistic adornment.

The Nevada Supreme Court found that due process was not denied to Mr. Rosenthal and went on to conclude that even if it were, federally protected constitutional rights do not apply in gaming since it is a matter "reserved to the states within the meaning of the Tenth Amendment to the United States Constitution," a legal argument of doubtful currency. Still, given the prevailing philosophy of the United States Supreme Court, such an argument for state control might carry weight, particularly with those justices disinclined to offer federal protection to state violations of due process. In any event, the United States Supreme Court declined to review the decision, and so it stands.[13]

5

Whatever the organization of licensing procedures, and regardless of Nevada's victory in the Rosenthal case, due process considerations have generated and will continue to generate problems in three areas of licensing: (1) exploration of alleged criminal associations; (2) comparative standards of "deviance"; (3) the scope of the licensing authority.

It has become legally tricky, almost treacherous, to explore the relationship between those who do apply and those persons — allegedly organized crime figures — with whom they might be associated. Let us discuss, by example, the case of a woman, "Mrs.

Gregory," who applied to purchase a controlling interest in a major Strip casino hotel. Her husband had applied for licensing several years earlier when he sought to purchase the same interest. He had been denied because of his close association with "John Tommy." Mr. Tommy had, during the 1930s, accumulated an impressive criminal record, including convictions for bank robbery. In recent years he had been seen having dinner with organized crime figures. When Mr. Gregory died, Mr. Tommy became Mrs. Gregory's business advisor. He also took a job as entertainment director of the hotel, a position that ordinarily does not require a license. Two questions follow: Did Mr. Tommy's associations, coupled with his record, still qualify him to be regarded as an organized crime figure threatening the integrity of the state of Nevada? Should Mrs. Gregory, now a widow, be denied a license because of her relationship with Mr. Tommy — in other words, for the same reasons her husband had been denied a license years earlier? Mr. Tommy, it turned out, developed from a bank robber into an admittedly capable businessman who gave Mrs. Gregory substantial and effective business advice and was also listed as the executor of her will.

Mrs. Gregory's hearing was particularly interesting because the board heard testimony from Mr. James E. Ritchie, at the time executive director of the National Commission on Gambling, and formerly a director of two organized crime strike forces. He had been called in to testify by Mrs. Gregory's attorney, Richard Crane, who had recently resigned as head of the Los Angeles Organized Crime Strike Force.

Mr. Ritchie testified that, in assessing the impact of organized crime on the state of Nevada, the board should take into account whether the party in question took orders from or acted on behalf of organized crime; or whether he merely associated on a social basis with organized crime figures. Mr. Tommy, he testified, fell into the latter category, a fact that Mr. Ritchie said he could attest to on the basis of highly reliable confidential information. In the meantime, the board had information from another organized crime expert, unwilling to testify, because he feared exposing his surveillance operation, that Mr. Tommy had been meeting on a daily basis with an organized crime figure. The board was astounded by Mr. Ritchie's testimony, particularly the following exchange:

Q: Mr. Ritchie, you are not saying that you guarantee personally that Mr. Tommy is not affiliated nor has he ever been affiliated, connected or associated with organized crime.

A: I absolutely am. I wouldn't have given an affidavit to that effect otherwise.[14]

Mr. Tommy's standing as an organized crime figure aside, what about Mrs. Gregory? Even if it could be argued that Mr. Tommy was closely associated with organized crime, should her license be withheld, in the absence of any information that she was associated with organized crime? She acknowledged that Mr. Tommy was her advisor and, indeed, gave her very good business advice. She also testified that she was a capable person who could distinguish between good advice and bad advice and that while she appreciated Mr. Tommy's advice on the basis of his record of success, she did not feel obligated to take it if she thought it was wrong or inappropriate.

Despite these protestations, the board voted to deny Mrs. Gregory a license. The commission — by the required unanimous vote — took the unusual step of overruling the board and granted her a license. Between the board hearing and the commission hearing, there was much discussion of her case within the agency and considerable skepticism as to whether the board had been prudent in denying her the license. There was feeling that she might have a good court case were she to be denied by the commission. She could claim that the board and commission discriminated against her as a woman, because it denied her on grounds that she was under Mr. Tommy's influence, an allegation she had repudiated.

Besides, it seemed incongruous to deny Mrs. Gregory a license while Mr. Tommy was permitted to work unlicensed for the casino as entertainment director, while rumors suggested that he exercised considerable control over casino policy. The commission decided, without provoking bitter feelings on the part of the board, to overrule unanimously, and to grant Mrs. Gregory a license. At the same time, the commission called Mr. Tommy up for licensing to investigate his associations.

Nevertheless, the testimony of someone so distinguished as Mr. Ritchie could only serve to undermine the associational basis of license denial. It might in the future be difficult to demonstrate that an applicant works on behalf of, or on the orders of, organized crime, if the only evidence is that the applicant meets with organized crime figures. Board agents learned that both local and federal police were amazed by Mr. Ritchie's testimony, and skeptical of the reasoning employed by the commission to grant Mrs. Gregory a license after it had earlier denied her husband on similar grounds.

Richard Crane, Mrs. Gregory's attorney, also raised what might be called the "comparative standard of deviance" argument before the board. He said that he knew of other people working in the Nevada gaming industry, recently licensed by the board and commission, who were worse than Mr. Tommy in terms of organized crime connections and affiliations. One man he had in mind had been working in Nevada since the days of Benjamin Siegel. The board had recently licensed him because they knew of his reputation within the industry. During that hearing the chairman had publicly downgraded the significance of associations, a statement that was to haunt him when it was read into the record before the commission.

Mr. Crane's line of argument raises a basic question concerning discretionary authority of the board and commission: Do they now carry the burden to show that the party they are denying is of lesser moral character than those persons already working in the industry? The board and commission have taken the position, in a number of cases, that they are indeed employing increasingly stringent standards and have been over the years. Still, the question of comparable suitability will surely be raised again. Moreover, it is not too difficult to distinguish one case of associations from another, under the same standard, if one wishes to. It might be hard to argue that Meyer Lansky should be licensed and Benjamin Siegel denied, or vice versa. But cases with that degree of organized crime affiliation clarity rarely, if ever, appear before the gaming authorities.

6

A third issue is the scope of the licensing authority. From the control perspective, if somebody applies for a license and is turned down, he may well be prohibited from working in the industry in a nonlicensed capacity. The control rationale goes something like this: If a man is turned down to be a casino manager, then, even if he were to work in a different or in a lower-ranking position, he would still be in a position to exercise some kind of hidden authority merely by being on the premises. Moreover, the gaming authorities are always concerned about the issue of "image." Once they find out in a licensing procedure that a person is unqualified because of defects of character, they feel they have the right to prohibit him from working in the industry.

Recently, a district court of the state of Nevada disagreed with them.[15] A young man had been granted a work permit by the county authorities to work in a casino poker room. Within the agency itself various investigators believe that that particular casino — the same hotel involving Mrs. Gregory and Mr. Tommy — is most susceptible to organized crime interests. The applicant first worked in the poker room as a dealer and then as a shift boss. Eventually, he was offered a position as manager of the poker room, a position requiring him to be licensed. The licensing investigation revealed that he had failed to disclose pertinent information — an arrest history, a failure to pay taxes on gambling earnings — and he was denied a license to manage the poker room.

The applicant did not object to the denial of his application to be manager, but to another aspect of the gaming agency's ruling. When the applicant came up before the commission he was in effect told that his work permit was revoked — he was exiled from the industry — because of what had been found out about him during his licensing procedure. He sued in district court and the court upheld his claim that he had been arbitrarily denied the right to work; the court reinstated his work permit. The court said that although the board and commission could deny the man the right to work in a position of authority, they could not deny him the right to work in a lesser position without a specific hearing on that question.

The board has the authority to revoke work permits.[16] This ruling could have serious implications for gaming controls, since it would permit those already denied a license to continue working in the industry unless their work permit was also to be denied. The board was prepared to bring a revocation action against the applicant on the statutory grounds that he had concealed material facts in the board's investigation. But other casinos seemed uninterested in acquiring the applicant's services after the denial, and after his victory in court.

This outcome highlights the limitations of due process victories for small fry. Any court review of gaming authority practices, procedures, and standards poses a threat to the discretionary authority of the agency. Ordinarily, however, the industry will be wary of embracing an applicant who has drawn the disfavor of the board, even if he should win on a technicality. The agency not only licenses; it also monitors the continuing operations of the industry through its enforcement and auditing divisions. Under those circumstances, a court victory may prove troublesome to the discretionary licensing powers of the agency, but hollow to the unemployed victor, since the entire industry is still subject to the enforcement and auditing authority of the board. We shall examine these aspects of control in greater detail in the chapters that follow.

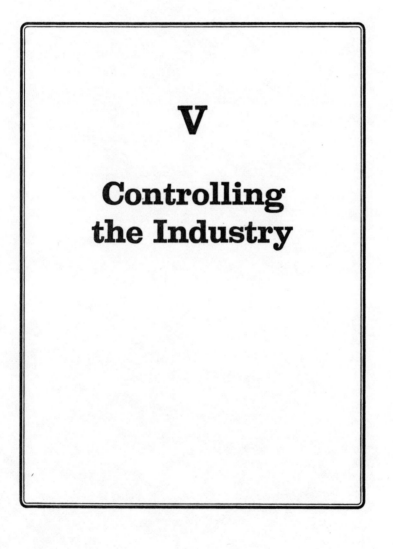

V

Controlling
the Industry

16

Patrolling
the Casino Floor

WHEN ONE OBSERVES THE THREE MAJOR FUNCTIONS OF THE GAMING
Control Board in detail — licensing, policing the casino floor, and
investigating casino management — they sometimes seem to
possess little unity. In what respects are the lofty and abstract
constitutional law issues of due process found in licensing related
to cheating on the casino floor and in the count room?

They are similar, I think, in three ways: First, the board is intended to control a panoply of activities in light of a vision of
appropriate conduct, which the gaming laws and regulations
attempt to spell out. Thus, licensing of equity holders and key
employees is regarded as the linchpin of the control apparatus
because the casino gambling business is especially susceptible to
fraudulent schemes. Consequently, it seems sensible to assess the
moral character of those who enter the industry to eliminate potential tricksters from positions of authority. The overall goal of controlling misconduct accordingly links all three divisions of the
agency.

Second, the control that is exercised is legally authoritative and
therefore limited. One could envision gaming control authorities

who would arbitrarily administer severe punishment to those whom they believed to be miscreants. In a constitutional democracy that is not permitted, and to my knowledge such control tactics were rarely, if ever, longed for as a forbidden fruit in this agency — a situation very different from some police departments I have encountered. But limits imply discretion, and there was throughout the agency a persistent question of how much authority could rightfully be exercised; as is the case with all agencies interpreting rules and regulations, so with the board. Official discretion in daily action is sometimes a troubling, and often quite an interesting issue, especially when higher authorities in the agency evaluate the conduct of those lower down. Any attempt to evaluate in terms of consistency generates precedent, against which to judge the future conduct of all.

Third, the gaming authorities deal with an astonishingly accomplished universe of schemers. As we shall see in this chapter and the ones that follow, merely to call them crooks is utterly to fail to appreciate the cunning and technical sophistication demanded of successful gaming industry defrauders. Licensing presumably eradicates those inclined toward larceny who might occupy positions of casino control. Whether it in fact does so successfully is arguable. In any case, there is considerable chicanery, and it is hard to tell who is involved in schemes to cheat the casino, the state, and the public. All too frequently, but not necessarily, some collusion obtains between casino employees and those cheating the casino.

I shall describe several of these casino-cheating schemes. In this chapter, I shall begin with a description of the most intricate of all to show how gaming miscreants frequently turn out to be not lazy and shiftless, but deft, hardworking, and crafty. Such artistry creates special problems because law enforcement under these circumstances requires unusual access to information on unlawful activities, plus methods and procedures for obtaining that information. Aside from the question of the *efficacy* of law enforcement, there is also the issue of *propriety*. So the agency must decide which methods are legally and morally acceptable in obtaining evidence. These topics will provide the material for this chapter: the scam, the organization of law enforcement to combat the scam, and the dilemmas of obtaining and interpreting evidence.

2

To my knowledge the most intricate scam of them all is, because of its mechanical complexity, the gaffed blackjack "shoe." The "shoe," a small box that holds several decks of cards, is employed to prevent the casino from cheating the player. If, through an accomplice, a player can smuggle in the type of shoe I am about to describe, the player cheats the casino.

An ordinary shoe is fitted with a black plastic bottom that is slanted toward the front above a wooden base. The slant is needed for gravity, to keep the cards moving smoothly to the base of the shoe. Dealing from a shoe is an art form; and some dealers I have seen deal from it with astonishing rapidity.

Between the plastic bottom and the flat wooden base, there is a hollow area of about 20 cubic inches. In the gaffed shoe the base is clear glass with black glass under it, but to the eye it resembles black plastic. Indeed, in every outward respect, the shoe looks legitimate, and thus can be used in play totally without the dealer's or house's knowledge, although it would doubtless require someone working in the casino to infiltrate the shoe into the pit.

Inside, the shoe is a marvel of optical engineering. There is a prism located on the front end of the shoe that captures the image of the corner of the next card to be dealt, revealing its identity. Tiny lamp bulbs surround the prism. The bulbs are lit by a player with a miniaturized transmitter hooked up to a miniaturized receiver inside the shoe. The bulbs illuminate the reflected image of the corner of the card. The illuminated image is then passed through the prism through a set of lenses, approximately midway up the inside of the shoe.

These lenses direct the image through still another set of lenses to two mirrors at the back of the shoe. These mirrors invert and transmit the image back up to a third mirror, in turn reflecting it through a tiny window in the apparently opaque bottom of the right-hand rear of the shoe. With a flick of the transmitter, and by positioning himself at "first base," the cheat can see in the window the illuminated image of the telltale corner of the next card to be dealt. This, of course, provides an overwhelming advantage.

This fabulous gaffed shoe was discovered only by chance in 1976 when an alert and suspicious pit boss wondered why his table was losing, and thought that the shoe felt a bit heavy. He decided to look inside, and found the apparatus described.

The shoe was examined by the full-time electronics expert who works closely with the Law Enforcement Division, and a description was sent out to alert the industry. In the year following, no other such shoe was discovered. The expert nevertheless believed that several lighter and more sophisticated models might be in operation in other casinos.

3

Gaming-law enforcement agents played no role whatsoever in discovering this scam. That fact suggests the considerable limitations of the Law Enforcement Division in policing the casino floor. But perhaps these limitations are comparable to those experienced by urban police departments whose patrols seem no more effective in preventing crime in the city.[1] This comparison makes sense — up to a point — because the Law Enforcement Division does seem to serve as the counterpart to the patrol division in a municipal police agency. In any event, it is worth comparing and contrasting the two, since the patrolling cop is so familiar a figure.

Unlike patrolmen, gaming-law enforcement agents do not wear uniforms setting themselves off from the general public. Rather, like patrolling detectives who are not assigned such specialties as burglary or auto theft, their job is to canvass the territory of the casinos. They are supposed to detect any rule violations that might be occurring within the casino, to develop casino informants and contacts, sometimes to organize stake-outs and other enforcement ruses to catch cheats and thieves, and — like street patrolmen — to react to and mediate claims that the casinos have deceived, defrauded, or otherwise abused members of the public.

This is the main working responsibility of the division and its agents, and in this respect it is most like the patrol division of a municipal police department. In addition, the Law Enforcement Division is assigned a wide span of responsibilities including the review of work-card applications; the counting of slot machines for tax collection purposes; maintaining relations with other law enforcement agencies, particularly to monitor the activity of ex-felons seeking employment in the gaming industry, as well as the activities of itinerant professional gambling cheats.

The Law Enforcement Division does not, except as a tangential matter, deal with other sorts of crime. Routine sorts of crimes do occur in and around casinos. There have, indeed, been armed robberies of the casinos themselves, but these are rare. Law enforcement agents, when interviewed, could recall only one, at Harrah's in 1972 — the thieves absconded with $185,000. More frequently, thieves will scoop a handful of chips and run for it, particularly in the South Shore casinos at Lake Tahoe during crowded summer evenings. Major casinos patrol their parking lots and elevators to prevent muggings. These do occur, in and out of the hotels, and with some frequency.

There is no question that casino gambling invites street crime in two ways: first, it provides moneyed victims; and second, it develops desperate losers willing to steal from motels, gas stations, and other players to make up losses. And some losers claim to have been robbed, rather than admit they lost their money gambling. Gambling losses are not tax deductible, while robbery losses are. But these ordinary crimes are not, in the argot, referred to as scams. Besides, they are usually the province of local law enforcement. The schemes to defraud the casino, and through it the taxpayers of Nevada, fall within the jurisdiction of the Gaming Control Board's Law Enforcement Division.

4

As is the case with ordinary criminal law enforcement, police usually learn little of importance through patrolling alone. Patrolling, to be effective, must be focused. Police must learn usually from informants or contacts such as casino executives or employees secretly moonlighting for the Law Enforcement Division, that some sort of scam is, in the vernacular, "goin' down."

The development of informants follows no set pattern. Yet it is possible to discern a typology of informants from conversations with gaming control agents. This typology breaks down into agency informants, paid informants, voluntary informants, and "made" informants. Agency informants are individuals in both private and public law enforcement who exchange information with gaming control agents. Public law enforcement agencies include a whole variety of federal, state and local police agencies. Private agencies are mainly national and local detective agencies.

The main problem of obtaining information through agencies is developing exchange patterns satisfactory both to the individual detective and agency he represents. Thus, confidential information gathered by the board in the course of investigations and audits is not routinely made available to the FBI or the IRS. In turn, these agencies guard their own information carefully. Both sets of agencies are constrained by statutes and policies within the agency. For example, some police agencies — usually local ones — permit detectives to maintain their own stable of informants known only to themselves, and whose identities are often a closely guarded secret. By contrast, the FBI requires that its agents keep available to superiors a record of informants used. Moreover, once information is turned over to a federal agency, local police, as well as the gaming authorities, fear it may be made public, under the authority of freedom of information statutes.

The Gaming Control Board itself has undergone considerable anguish over its own informant policy. Its former law enforcement chief resigned when detectives were required to reveal the names of informants to higher-ups in the agency. Its present chief defends a tightly controlled informant policy. He believes that even the best intelligence information isn't useful unless it can be used to provide evidence in a courtroom or formal hearing; and it can't be used unless documentation (based upon information produced in the past) indicates that the informant is reliable.

The advantages and drawbacks of each system are reasonably clear. Under the first — really a nonsystem — the agency depends upon the good character and judgment of the agent to control the informant. The idea is: hire the best agents possible and give them free rein. Under the second, the agent is controlled by higher-ups. The system then comes to depend more upon formal documentation (and the good character and judgment of higher-ups).

Private agency detectives are generally regarded as less trustworthy for the exchange of information than those working in public agencies, although the estimate may vary from individual to individual. While this study was being conducted, one agent experienced the unpleasant sensation of being "burned" by a private detective. He had offered confidential board information to a private detective to obtain information in return. It was believed that the private detective used the information to extort money. None of this could of course be proved, but the board agent in question was treated with a good deal of wariness and suspicion by his fellow agents for some time thereafter.

Enforcement agents do pay informants, but rarely. Each agent starts his tour of duty with a sum of state money either to gamble (if the agent can slip into a questionable game) or to pay off informants. The exact amount is not for public disclosure.

Agents and board members are wary of paid informants. Someone who offers to sell information is inherently unreliable, for such informants can generally be bought off by someone else for a higher price. Moreover, since information about gambling scams is such a will-o'-the-wisp — the scam may indeed have been planned but called off — gaming agents are unusually subject to being conned by paid informants with no way of testing whether they were conned or not. With respect to the paid informant, the policeman is placed in the position of a powerless consumer. Policemen do not seem to appreciate that position at all.

In contrast, the policeman is in a powerful position when he "makes" an informant, one whom the policeman is able to place or discover in a legally vulnerable position. Whatever the prescribed informant system, an agent can induce cooperation by ignoring an arrestable incident. Once an arrest is made, the offer to drop or reduce charges must be approved by a superior, thus disclosing the identity of the informant. But under any informant system agents can and do negotiate on their own, thus assuring themselves of a pool of personal informants. Detectives feel inadequate without informants, since informants constitute their only source of regular information.

A final class of informant — the volunteer — is both the most reliable and the least adequate in the long run. This is because volunteers normally turn only one scam for the agents. They are reliable, however, because their motive is sometimes altruistic (though more often self-interested in one respect or another). For example, an ambitious casino employee might seek to ingratiate himself — in the vernacular "build juice" — with management by informing about a potential scam. Management, in turn, informs the board.

Vengeance can also serve as a motive. For example, an agent told a story — perhaps apocryphal — of a change girl who called the board to report a conspiracy to cheat customers she had seen involving several colleagues and her superior. She called, she said, because "the cheap bastards didn't give me a piece of the take." Whether the story is true or not, it nevertheless suggests the structural problem created by the volunteer informant. The authorities do not enjoy the power to coerce such an informant into providing a regular stream of information. This is a serious limitation in the gambling enforcement business, since it is virtually impossible to locate scams through random observation alone. Thus, agents try whenever possible to "make" informants.

5

Of all the scams on the casino floor, those most persistently investigated involve the diversion of revenue from slot machines. The "one-armed bandit" seems extraordinarily susceptible to the two-armed variety. One widespread slot machine scam, invented by obviously intelligent and talented thieves, is comparable in mechanical ingenuity to the gaffed blackjack shoe — and probably more profitable. It is based upon a miniaturized receiver—

transmitter combination, with the receiver implanted in the slot machine by an outside party — usually a casino mechanic. The scam works best at major casinos, where hundreds of machines are operating.

When one opens the door to a slot machine one observes a complex mechanical apparatus. About one-third to half-way up the inside of the door are two small, black, rectangular switches. A unique miniature receiver is built into one of these switches. Most impressive is this: The receiver, consisting of several components including wiring, a diode, a resistor, and a transistor, is hand built around the standard components of the switch, and does not interfere at all with the other wiring controlling the hopper mechanism that releases coins when a winning combination appears. All of this is accomplished in a space of less than one cubic inch.

Once the receiver is installed, a cheat can play until a winning combination — three oranges in a row, for example — appears. Then, with the transmitter, he can engage the receiver and cause the payoff to repeat. Conceivably, the thief could dump the entire contents of the hopper into the tray. A quarter coin machine holds on the average about $250 in its hopper. But these thieves are too clever to empty entire hoppers, or to do anything that might arouse suspicion.

The entire scam is structured to protect its secrecy. First, the transmitter is carefully disguised. (The one obtained by the authorities was disguised to appear as a cigar in a cigar holder.) Second, the thieves will usually take no more than $30 or $40 a week out of any machine. Such prudence prevents detection in two respects. It does not draw attention when the act is being committed, since slot players commonly (a) smoke; and (b) leave their coin winnings in the slot machine tray. An observer would therefore not be alerted by coins dropping into a tray, with a payoff combination visible on the machine. In addition, later on, the percentages would vary so slightly as to blunt the suspicions of those employing statistical controls. Obviously, the profitability of the scam depends upon volume. It is, in effect, a high-volume, low-profit business. Authorities estimate upwards of 200 machines gaffed in the entire state, but conceivably there are two or three times that number. Even the lower figure amounts to $6,000 to $8,000 per week — scarcely a negligible amount of money, even if split six or eight ways.

6

So far, the scams we have discussed involved an outsider — perhaps with the collusion of insiders — cheating the casino. Casino ownership is the victim. But is the ordinary player ever cheated? It is hard to say how frequently this occurs, but it surely does. Usually, it happens without the knowledge of higher management. Why? Owners and casino managers do not necessarily reside on a higher moral plane than those below. Rather, particularly in the larger casinos, management earns more from a larger volume of play. Where play is substantial, the house edge is sufficient to provide generous profit to the honest casino. But the blackjack or poker dealers do not experience similar economic imperatives. Some are accordingly willing to victimize the player and — by casting doubt on the integrity of the casino and its control — the casino owner as well, who has hired the dealer to deal, not to cheat the player.

Cheating is very difficult to perceive and even more difficult to prove in any of the games, but particularly in card games. Cheating occurs even in the largest casinos employing the most sophisticated controls. For example, the Clark County grand jury voted an indictment in 1976 against the manager, a shift boss, two dealers, and several outside confederates of the poker room of a leading hotel. The year before, I had been told by a couple of the law enforcement agents that the poker room in question was one of the few that could be trusted.

Ideally, to combat cheating a secret camera would focus on the dealer's hand, and a slow motion replay would prove whether certain card manipulations had occurred. The problem is that there are many of these, and even the most ordinary are hard to catch.

The most common sleight-of-hand dealing tricks are dealing "seconds" and "bottom dealing." The dealer holds the cards in the left hand. Ordinarily, his left thumb will push the top card forward, to be picked up and dealt with the right hand. When dealing "seconds," the dealer's right thumb darts in and slides out the second card, instead of the one on top. The dealer will have ascertained the identity of the top card by skillful "peeking" and will save it to enhance the hand of a confederate or destroy the hand of an opponent. Bottom dealing requires more skill, but works on the same principle. The difference is that the dealer deals your cards off the top and his off the bottom.

Since all dealing games are vulnerable to cheating, Nevada's problems in this area are inevitable. That the dealer is not part of the poker game is scarcely a foolproof control against cheating. Once the dealer combines with one or two confederates, his interest in the game is established. The action occurs so quickly that unless one is a skilled and experienced dealer, the cheating cannot be detected. I may be extraordinarily dense in these matters, but I have been shown how to deal "seconds" and have observed a skilled "mechanic" deal them in slow motion so I could see them coming. Then he speeded up the action. Even though I knew he was "pushing off" seconds, I could not really spot the seconds from the top cards. Needless to say, in a genuine cheating situation the victims are not forewarned.

Nevada dealers, as a group, are very skilled with their hands. I am not arguing that most Nevada dealers cheat. I am suggesting that most enjoy the ability to cheat, and that some unknown number are inclined to take advantage of that ability.

7

Since cheating is so difficult to detect, and difficult to prove, enforcement is faced with a hard question. What level of evidence of cheating should be striven for by the casino and by the gaming authorities?

The first level of evidence is *rumor*. In any other business, management would be severely criticized for firing an employee on the basis of a rumor. In the gambling business, such criticism might not be forthcoming where the cheating of customers is involved. Still, most casino managers would try to *verify* the rumor, escalating to a higher level of evidence. Suppose they — or the board — employ an undercover agent to check out the rumor, and the agent reports that the dealer in question is cheating. Their dilemma is: Do they fire the dealer on the spot, based on the observations of one agent, who might be wrong in his judgment; or do they try for further verification by sending in a second, or a third agent?

The pressure to establish evidence is based upon a set of values and norms traditional to police organizations. These may be summarized as *the enforcement imperative*. This imperative dictates not only that the situation be repaired — that the cheating stop — but also that the offenders be identified, convicted, and punished. This is a fundamental norm of all operating law enforcement agencies from the Gaming Control Board, to local police and prosecutors, to the United States Department of Justice. There is often a good deal of wheeling and dealing to achieve the end of conviction and punishment — granting of immunity, plea bargaining — but one rarely, if ever, hears the goal unchallenged.

In contrast, *the business imperative* is profitability rather than legal justice. An entrepreneur does not take kindly to interventions that will interfere with the normal operation of his business enterprise. He might prefer a conviction, but will gladly settle for less, provided it doesn't hurt the business. The business imperative operates perhaps most strongly in a tourist-oriented locale — one that depends upon tourists making positive decisions to spend a brief time here rather than there. The moral timidity of tourist-oriented entrepreneurs is legendary. Consider Ibsen's *An Enemy of the People* or Peter Benchley's *Jaws*.

But let me illustrate and elaborate: Suppose a dealer is fired after having been suspected of cheating, or after he's been caught at cheating. In the first instance, there will almost certainly be a cover-up, only partly induced by considerations of fairness. After all, a suspicion is not a fact. Not only will the gaming board not be told; neither will other casinos who propose to hire the fired dealer.

Ordinarily, an effort will be made to protect the reputation of the suspected cheater. I am reliably told by people who hire and fire that the only way to obtain accurate information about why someone was fired is to speak with an executive in another casino, trusted because of a long history of discreet confidences. Only then will the suspicion be voiced. There are several reasons for this. First, the traditions of illegal gambling still persist in Las Vegas in a cultural sense. One does not voice personal suspicions of cheating to any bureaucrat, including a manager. Moreover, one does not wish to incur needless enemies. It is bad enough to fire somebody. One needn't impugn his character and worth as an employee as well.

What about the second instance, where a dealer has been observed to be cheating? Here, too, many clubs are reluctant to invoke an official response for the reasons developed above, but another as well. Suppose solid evidence can be produced and brought to the authorities? Any action would have to be taken in a public disciplinary hearing, where the fact that cheating had occurred at that club would be established. Clubs do not enjoy such publicity, and many would prefer merely to fire the cheater, rather than to bring the cheater to the attention of the authorities. When they do, it is usually as a last resort. Possibly they suspect that a sizable number of people have been involved in a cheating conspiracy and hope that the board will pinpoint who these are.

Finally, some casino executives who elicit assistance from the board express the idea that ferreting out and disciplining cheaters is good for the industry's public relations, since it suggests that the industry and the board stay on top of cheating in Nevada's casinos. There is no way to determine how widely shared that view is, and observation and interview suggests it is not consistently held even by the same people. The attitudes of casino executives, as of other human beings, are often not hardened until a specific event occurs; and may shift as some new situation demands — or at least one that lends itself to being interpreted as being different.

In one instance, for example, both the casino and the board were criticized by people within the industry and the press because, in order to establish a legal case, they sent in observers over a period of several months. The cheating was thus permitted to continue for more than 100 days, with customers as victims, largely because the casino itself began to adopt the law enforcement imperative. Both the board and the casino felt quite uneasy over this decision. Ordinarily, under similar circumstances, unless the board can develop evidence sufficient for an indictment in a week or ten days, the enforcement effort is discontinued. Usually, the suspected cheaters will be fired. Sometimes, surveillance provokes suspicion, and the cheating ceases. Law enforcement decisions in this area are rarely clear-cut.

The commission can take action against cheaters by revoking their work cards; and against gaming licensees who knowingly or through incompetence permit cheating to occur, by revoking their licenses. When a prosecution is contemplated, an even higher standard of evidence is required. For work card or license revocation the standard is "substantial evidence," less restrictive than the "clear and convincing" or "preponderance" standard prevailing in civil disputes and not nearly so restrictive as the "beyond a reasonable doubt" standard prevailing in criminal cases. It appears to mean that where the evidence is conflicting, if "substantial evidence" supporting the revocation action of the commission is introduced, it need not outweigh contrary evidence. Thus, the standard offers considerable discretion to the authorities.

8

The typical cheating case usually occurs in a small casino, in places like Wells or Tonopah or North Las Vegas. The following exchange took place at the Nevada Gaming Control Commission regarding a work card revocation hearing in 1976. The questioner is the deputy attorney general. The answerer is a gaming agent.

Q. Approximately how long did you play this game of twenty-one?
A. Thirty to forty-five minutes.
Q. Was it a continual game?
A. Yes, it was.
Q. During the course of that game, did you observe any oddities in the manner in which that game was dealt?
A. Yes, I did.
Q. Would you describe to the Commission what you observed?
A. I observed the dealer to heel peek on almost every hand that was dealt and on numerous occasions to deal seconds.

Q. Would you briefly describe to the Commission what is meant by heel peeking?

A. That is sliding the top card of the deck, single deck, in a manner as to where the dealer can observe the face value of the top card.

Q. And for the purposes of the record, would you describe what you mean by the term dealing seconds?

A. That is sliding the top card of the deck backwards or to the side, thus, enabling the dealer to take off the second card of the deck or another card other than the top card.

Q. And pursuant to your training as a Board agent, are these techniques cheating techniques as outlawed by our statutes and regulations?

A. Yes, they are.

Q. Do you recall in terms of a specific example on that night of any particular hand or hands that you played?

A. Yes.

Q. Could you describe that to the Commission, please?

A. Yes, I had received a nine and a two, and I doubled down on that hand. The dealer then, after peeking, dealt me a second card, which was a seven. The dealer had a ten up and three in the hole. He then hit his hand with the top card, which I should have received in the first place. The top card was an eight. My total was eighteen. The dealer's total was twenty-one.

Q. You testified just immediately preceding this example that you saw him heel peek on virtually every hand. In terms of the dealing of seconds, during that period of time, how frequently did he deal seconds?

A. I can't say exactly how many times he did, but it was very numerous.

It appears that the stronger the verification sought, the greater the collision between enforcement and business imperatives. Since the Gaming Control Board subscribes to both imperatives, it finds itself in a continuing and enlarging dilemma in this area of enforcement — as in others — as it strives to strengthen its evidence.

9

Evidence in a law enforcement agency can be developed by a process of interrogation and confession in addition to surveillance and observation. When a suspect admits guilt, there is no problem. When a suspect denies culpability, whether in the context of claiming a jackpot or in defending an association with respect to licensing, a hoary law enforcement question arises: Is the speaker telling the truth?

Truthtelling has been a problem for every society, and the idea of detecting lies according to alterations in physical response goes back to early forms of trial by ordeal. (For example, one form of test was based on the observation that fear inhibits the secretion of saliva. To test credibility the accused was given rice to chew. If he could spit it out, he was considered innocent; if it stuck to his gums he was judged guilty.)

But it was not until 1895 that anybody had used a measuring instrument to detect deception. In that year, the Italian criminologist Cesare Lombroso employed a combination of blood pressure and pulse readings to investigate truthtelling. Other researchers began further experiments with blood pressure and with respiratory recordings. John A. Larson, who was a part of a Berkeley group of the 1920s seeking to advance the "science" of lie detection built an instrument which he called a "polygraph"; it combined all three measures — blood pressure, pulse, and respiration. His junior collaborator added galvanic skin response to the list. This machine, with some small changes, is the basic "lie detector" used today by most law enforcement agencies, including the Gaming Control Board.

It so happened that in 1961 I had concluded an intensive study of lie detection as part of my research on criminal justice processes.[2] The research convinced me and continues to convince, that lie detection on the basis of physiological response is fundamentally flawed. The assumptions supporting the relationship between physiological change and lying do not, I contend, survive close analysis.

Whatever the instrument employed, lie detection based upon physiological change makes three basic and questionable assumptions. The first is that lying will be conscious. Somebody who believes he is telling the truth, even if he is not, obviously cannot experience the emotions of a "liar." Don't arguments often occur between two people, each of whom righteously believes the other misperceived?

The second assumption is also questionable: that people who consciously lie not only feel emotion, but a consistent and measurable sort of emotion. Some people experience emotion when they lie, some don't, while others vary, depending upon their personalities and the context of the lie. The classic personality lacking in emotion is the "psychopath" described by a psychologist who studied the relation between autonomic activity — the kind measured by the polygraph — and psychopathy as follows: ". . . a callous, emotionally immature, two-dimensional person who lacks the ability to experience the emotional components of personal and interpersonal behavior. He is able to *stimulate* emotional reactions and affectional attachments when it will help him to obtain what he wants; however, he doesn't really *feel*."[3] People who have been diagnosed clinically as psychopaths have also been demonstrated to show low autonomic activity.

Lie detection's third assumption is this: the emotions felt upon lying are translated into changes in blood pressure, pulse, respiration, and perspiration so consistently and regularly as to dispose of the issue of lying. This assumption is simply wrong, in my view. Nobody has been able to pin down the relationship between emotion and autonomic activity in that measurable and consistent a fashion. If emotion were related consistently to one autonomic activity, the best instrument would be a "unigraph" measuring that activity. Four measures are employed because one does not suffice and the intercorrelations among them are negligible. Because of this, there is no "inter-interpreter reliability" among polygraph examiners. That is, you cannot show the squiggles on a graph obtained by one examiner and ask a second to interpret these, the way you might ask radiologists to exchange x-rays and expect similar conclusions.

Nevertheless, the lie detector has achieved popularity in many law enforcement agencies over the years and the Gaming Control Board is no exception. There are two reasons. First, lie detection examinations produce results, even if the technique is based on flawed scientific assumptions. The first result is in achieving an outcome. Law enforcement officials, no less than others — perhaps more than others — feel uncomfortable with irresolution. Rightly or wrongly, the machine helps achieve a verdict. Even if the subject refuses to take the test, the refusal itself may become a verdict.

The second reason is that lie detection examinations are, if nothing else, interrogations conducted by skilled and experienced questioners who use the threat of the mysterious and allegedly probative machine to elicit truthtelling or confessions which might not otherwise be forthcoming. Like the blackjack, the gun, or the club, the polygraph may prove useful in an interrogation even if not entirely ethical or valid.

In the gaming context, however, the lie detector probably backfires as often as it generates truthful outcomes. The sort of people involved in gaming scams are more likely than the normal population to feel cool under pressure and little emotion when lying. The people who commit gaming crimes are rarely impulsive criminals. On the contrary, the gaming board is faced with a population of the coolest, slickest, most organized and inventive criminals imaginable. Whether they would qualify clinically as psychopaths is hard to say. But they are confident men and women of just the sort who could most likely prove to be false negatives in a lie detector test.

My opinion is that for such people the lie detector test is an advantage. It tends to exculpate them when in fact they are lying; and the gaming board goes along with the charade, not because it expresses all that much confidence in the lie detector, but because it feels it has not that much choice. Law enforcement agencies employing the lie detector often assume the position of the drunk seeking his lost keys under the lamppost — not because he lost them there, but because that is where the light is.

This is a problem endemic to much law enforcement. Vice squads concentrate on small-time user-dealers because of their accessibility. It is very difficult for law enforcement agencies to ascend the criminal hierarchy. Most law enforcement agencies usually encounter relatively unskilled criminals, who lack both capacity and resources to stand up to the agency. Even these are difficult to catch and convict. Those who inhabit the gaming business are far more skillful and capable than the ordinary criminal actor. I am not talking here only about the organized crime variety made so familiar in *The Godfather* and other popular fiction and fact, but of the *resourceful* criminal, who is knowledgeable and professional. Law enforcement in this context requires extraordinary access to information, extraordinary observation and surveillance skills, and extraordinary luck. In short, the odds against effective policing of the casino floor seem scarcely as good as the odds on the games.

17

Corruption and Discretion

"A LEGAL SYSTEM," WRITES PHILOSOPHER JOHN RAWLS, "IS A COERCIVE order of public rules addressed to rational persons for the purpose of regulating their conduct and providing the framework for social cooperation."[1] A law enforcement agency is part of the "coercive order" and operates within a rigging of intertwining sets of rules.

First are rules that forbid specified conduct, otherwise known as the substantive criminal law. Nevada's serious crimes include murder, rape, robbery, and the alteration of a gaming device.

In addition to the law of crimes are rules placing limits on the procedures of law enforcement agents. The best known illustrations of these are constitutional, statutory, and case law setting out limits on police when they search and interrogate suspects.

As governments in microcosm, administrative agencies also have their specialized rules. The counterpart of "substantive law" for the Gaming Control Board are its regulations, e.g., prescribing how drop boxes should be removed from gaming tables. As a law enforcement agency, the Gaming Control Board is governed by procedural rules that apply to all law enforcement officials when a prosecution is contemplated. But the board necessarily issues its own rules and policies on how to enforce administrative regulations.

In addition, every law enforcement agency issues internal rules governing the professional conduct of employees. These rules do not enjoy the grandeur of constitutional and statutory law, but they are terribly significant within the agency. One learns formally how to interpret them, and, in turn, how to evaluate the constitutional, statutory, and case law of the community. The interpretive wisdom relating to these rules is what provides the informally shared knowledge, demands, and expectations of the law enforcement perspective in the agency. When one learns to respond to these, one has been "socialized" into the role of law enforcement agent.

Thus, if one seeks to understand how and why an agency operates the way it does, one must flesh out the commonly held understandings and conflicts about the processes of interpreting agency rules. This task is subtle and difficult. Not only is there no prescription for interpretation; before interpreting you sometimes need to be in a position to observe rules actually being breached; not an easy task when the rule breakers — themselves police — are in jeopardy.

2

The most troublesome rules in any police agency are rules against accepting gifts or gratuities. Even in American police departments enjoying a reputation for being incorruptible and "legalistic," such as Los Angeles's, the taking of commodities is acceptable and a fine line is drawn between commodities and cash. Joseph Wambaugh had years of service as a Los Angeles policeman and detective. In his novel, *The Choirboys*, one of Wambaugh's characters, an ordinary L.A. policeman, "had accepted a thousand packs of cigarettes and as many free meals in his time. And though he had bought enough clothing at wholesale prices to dress a dozen movie stars, he had never even considered taking a five dollar bill nor was one ever offered except once when he stopped a Chicago grocer in Los Angeles on vacation."

Wambaugh explains his character's behavior by pointing out

that "[t]he police department and its members made an exact distinction between gratuities and cash offerings, which were considered money bribes no matter how slight and would result in a merciless dismissal as well as citizen prosecution."[2]

Corruption is a harsh word and few, if any, officials care to think of themselves as corrupt. So although a bribe can be given directly, the offerer is usually more cunning. Discussing the "moral blunders" of employees involved in the Equity Funding Fraud, Seidler, Andrews, and Epstein described the overtures, the sly subtleties, the invitations to rationalize that were suggested to a key auditor. "Bribes," they write, "don't come with labels; they aren't subject to truth in packaging. It takes moral courage, a willingness to step up to the plate, to stamp a bribe for what it is."[3]

A discretionary judgment is not always expected to be correct. If that were the case, such judgments would not be considered matters of choice. When there is a clearly correct answer, judgment cannot be used. But discretionary judgments are supposed to be made on the merits, independently, unimpeded by irrelevancies, such as the fact that a casino owner is a nice guy, or is generous with food, drink, and complimentary tickets to shows.

The problem of bribery is particularly acute in the gaming industry. Unlike the luncheonette owner, whose relationship to the police is primarily that of protectee to a protector, the gaming proprietor is both a protectee and the subject of the policeman's observations. The gaming policeman is not supposed to accept *anything* from a casino. The trouble is that, by refusing the gift or a drink or a meal, the gaming agent establishes himself as a sanctioning figure rather than a protector. Since the agency itself vacillates, as it must, between its roles as protector of the industry and as its policeman, some gaming agents also vacillate, and under the circumstances are drawn toward the magnet of the gratuity.

If agents could control their greed and limit their taking, few problems would arise. But taking can escalate to the point where the taker can no longer function as observer of the giver. For example, a senior agent of the enforcement division was fired because it was discovered that he had accepted moderately valuable gifts — hotel furniture — from a man who was later to figure prominently in the largest scam in the history of the gaming industry. Nobody believed the official was himself involved in the scam. But is was felt that he could not have given this man's casino responsibilities the skeptical attention they deserved while he was taking gifts from the giver.

The problem in Nevada is not so much that the agent will be involved directly in the scam as that his attention will be drawn away from it, or that he will in some other way compromise enforcement. This is demonstrated in the following story, based on the observations of my research assistant, Tom Gray, a former policeman. Gray was trusted enough to see rules being breached. Policemen tend to permit policemen and former policemen to see things others are not permitted to observe. In this case, my assistant participated in a flawed "stake-out" of an alleged poker room scam. A "stake-out" is law enforcement jargon for a disguised observation of illegal activity.

3

Not every casino operates a poker room, but almost all of the larger ones do. In California, where poker is legal at local option, players rent a seat at a poker table for a certain sum per hour. The proprietor is not responsible for the conduct of the games. In Nevada, the house is responsible, at least to the following extent: dealing is restricted to a professional, provided by the casino, who resolves any disputes that might arise and rakes the pot to obtain the house cut or profit on the game.

No fixed percentage goes to the house in a poker game and the maximum rake must be posted. The dealer is instructed by the poker manager to rake a portion of the pot, and gaming regulations permit raking as high as 50 percent. In practice, the rake percentage is usually lower, but the normal rake often renders the final odds against the player worse than they would be at the table games, craps and blackjack, and even worse than they would be at the slot machines. As played in Nevada, poker is, even more than other games, considered by knowledgeable gamblers a dangerous game for amateurs if only because the rake varies, and the average player is not aware of how high a percentage the house is raking. The rake is drawn deftly by the dealer, and many players are unaware that it is happening, to say nothing of being able to follow the percentages while concentrating on their own hands.

Since poker is played with chips, the rake physically consists of chips. These are supposed to be dropped into a slot leading to a locked drop box. Behind the slot is a chip tray, from which the dealer exchanges money for chips. When a dealer wants to steal, he surreptitiously rakes chips across the slot onto the chip tray. As a result, the chip tray, really a fixed bank for exchanging money for chips, will, at the end of a shift, contain more than the original amount. The shift boss picks up the difference while making "fills" and later splits it with the dealer according to a previously agreed upon percentage arrangement.

The stake-out was set in motion by the report of a casino manager (in a casino other than the one previously described) who believed that a shift boss was working together with poker dealers to steal a portion of the rake. Because shift bosses and dealers are aware of house security personnel, new or distant undercover agents are employed during a stake-out. Whenever a man has previously identified himself as a Gaming Control Board agent, a disguise is limited, particularly in an industry where people are trained to observe and interpret deviations from normality. Tom Gray was asked to participate in the stake-out, partly because of his police background, and partly because he was not known to the dealers, as Las Vegas board experts might be. Gray was to be accompanied by two agents who had been brought down from Carson City because they were unknown in Las Vegas and, it was thought, would keep a low profile. In this instance, however, one of the Carson City agents succumbed to the lures of Las Vegas: he was away from home, he liked to drink, and he was aware that discounted fees are traditionally offered to law enforcement agents by Las Vegas hookers. He took advantage of the discount a few hours before the stake-out.

Not only did he let a hooker know he was a cop, but he also, it was later learned, let slip that he had a job to perform at a particular casino. When the stake-out team arrived, the hooker was at the bar, sipping a drink. She smiled sweetly at the agents, who proceeded to observe a poker game conducted strictly by the rules. The head of the law enforcement division learned — I cannot say how — that the agent had been with the hooker just before the stake-out. When the results of the internal investigation were in, the agent was fired. Board agents are not civil service employees, but in this case, such protections probably would not have mattered.

4

In certain respects gaming enforcement is comparable to other forms of policing; it is rather like a combination of patrol work and vice detection. But gaming enforcement takes place in the casino, an environment designed to encourage fantasy and undermine inhibition. The hedonism of the milieu challenges conventional restraints because casino customers are not so socially distant from law enforcement officers in appearance and motivation as to preclude identification between the two.

Unlike the drug addict or the strongarm robber, the player is not an object of scorn. Nor are the pit bosses, the dealers, the bartenders, or the bellmen. The gaming enforcement agent is thus required to become something of a moral schizophrenic in two respects — appreciative of or at least accepting his working environment, while avoiding participation in it; and shifting perspective from controller to protector of the industry.

Corruption is a problem for many police agencies, where it is quite accurately thought to be related to vice enforcement, particularly to systematic payoffs from illegal gamblers. Thus, the victimless crime is correctly thought to provide a socially structured set of motives and opportunities for corruption. But it does not necessarily follow, as many in the past (including, alas, myself) have suggested, that legal gambling eliminates such opportunities and motives. When we observe the discretionary authority of the gaming cop in action, the reasons for corruption become evident. They are not eliminated — just different. Unlike the vice cop, the gaming cop has no opportunity to accept cash in return for overlooking illegal bookmaking. But there are other discretionary decisions that may be quite important to the proprietors of the casinos or perpetrators of misconduct. We have just witnessed how a cop can tip off those being observed in a stake-out. Let me illustrate further by describing one final scam of the casino floor involving slot machines.

5

As we have seen, slot machines are vulnerable when thieves can conspire successfully with casino employees. But the machines can be rigged from the outside as well as internally, and perhaps with even greater payoff. The most pervasive and troublesome scams involve penetration of the machine from the outside with a drill. Several areas of the machine are appropriate for drilling, but I shall concentrate on the one that disables the "clock," a locking mechanism that prevents the reels from running free after they have been set in motion by a handle pull and slowed down as that energy source dissipates. If not for the clock, the reels of a slot machine would never click into place.

The scam involves three people: the "wireman" and the "collector," who work as a team; and the "driller" who performs an entirely separate function, and often works alone. One Las Vegas driller is renowned to the police for the quality of his holes. They are so small as to be virtually invisible to the naked eye and point straight to the clock. I myself have with the agents investigated holes so small that they were still invisible from the outside even after we had learned from an informant the numbers of the drilled machines. The holes were discovered only after we opened the machines, pulled out the mechanism, and searched with a flashlight the inside surface of the steel side opposite the handle. Even then, the holes were difficult to perceive, and the agents had to consider whether these were the fresh holes they had been alerted to or older holes, there for some time.

The casing of a slot machine is made of hard, cold-forged steel that is supposedly able to withstand the most sophisticated drill. But in many respects the technology of the slot machine is akin to the technology of the bank vault. It involves a race between the thief and the security engineer. Develop a better lock and thieves will find a way to defeat it. Develop a harder steel and, it turns out, thieves will find a way to drill it. Thieves presently employ carbide-tipped bits, the size of the smallest dentist drill bit. If an even harder steel were to be developed, there already exist diamond-tipped bits which could drill through it.

Still, drilling demands extraordinary skill. First, the drill must not be visible to security police. For some machines, drillers can use cordless electric drills. For other machines, requiring a reasonably bulky motor, say three inches in diameter and six to eight inches long, the motor must be worn under a coat with a flexible cable running down the sleeve, where the actual implement, not much bigger than a fountain pen, is held in the hand. Second, the hole must be drilled in the right spot, on a line with the clock, while the driller appears to be nonchalantly playing the slot machine: he has to drill the hole without looking at it. Third, he has to work quickly. Drillers are known to a variety of watchers who observe slot machines.

The most able drillers employ a template to guide them to the hole. The piece of cardboard is placed against the side of the machine while an accomplice looks out for security. The hole is drilled within a few seconds. A competent driller can set up 15 slot machines in less than half an hour. Then he leaves the casino and nothing happens for several weeks.

In the old days, drillers worked in groups with wiremen and collectors. But the latter occupations are more unstable than drillers — for reasons we shall presently see — so few gangs remain. Currently, and mostly, the driller is a loner who "sells his holes." For a price, the driller will deliver the identity of the machines containing holes — all slot machines are numbered — and even the template to guide the wireman's hand directly to the hole.

The "wireman" can double as a "collector," but it is more likely that two separate individuals will assume the different roles. Where they work separately the wireman and the collector will together walk into the casino. They will find a progressive machine, ready to pay off at from several hundred to several thousand dollars. The collector will play the machine adjoining the drilled machine. In the meantime, the wireman will insert a slender wire, about six or eight inches long, to disengage the clock mechanism, permitting the reels to run free; then, with a magnet concealed in a hardpack cigarette box, he or she (slot thief teams are not exclusively male) will line up the reels to produce an appropriate payoff symbol. When the wire is pulled, the clock functions once again, and the symbols click into place. The wireman will place the wire along with the magnet in a coat pocket or purse and walk out of the club. The collector then steps over to the set-up machine and claims the jackpot.

What happens next? The simplest outcome is the normal one. The casino executive authorized to make the payoff will check the machine, fail to discover the tiny hole, assume the jackpot claimer is legitimate, and cheerfully make the payoff. Even when a hole is discovered, that fact alone does not prove the jackpot claimer is making a false claim. If the casinos could use that excuse, they might routinely drill a portion of their machines, then challenge the claims of legitimate jackpot winners.

Actually, casinos don't mind paying off, provided the jackpot is legitimate. The payoff is part of the business. Recall that about 80 percent of the money that goes into a slot machine is supposed to go out. Thus, paying off is a routine event, although a major payoff is not. It is hard to say where the line would be drawn, but the higher the amount of the payoff, the greater the suspicion it will generate. A machine that produced a $27,000 jackpot would be opened, taken apart and examined very carefully. Even a several hundred dollar payoff normally draws considerable attention.

When the payoff is made, no problem is created. When the payoff is disputed — for example, when the machine has a hole — a whole series of legal, ethical, and policy problems is created for the gaming authorities, and for the law enforcement agent in particular. These discretionary issues are apparent in the following story of a disputed payoff.

6

"Charlie Briggs" is a former policeman who elected to join the gaming board rather than local law enforcement. His friends, who were also policemen, suggested that the local police agency was inept and riddled with corruption, from top to bottom. Such observations about local Las Vegas law enforcement are common-place, and are seldom contradicted by anybody in a position to observe local law enforcement closely. The accusations are roughly on the order of those heard about Eastern police departments — New York, Boston, Newark — in the pre-Knapp Commission days; the sort of thing everybody knowledgeable claims to know about but is unwilling or unable to document.

My research assistant, Thomas Gray, who teaches and consults with various police departments, spent a month studying the Law Enforcement Division independently of me. We also studied it together, exchanging observations and interpretations. He felt that Charlie Briggs, along with five or six other agents, was savvy, able, and honest. About others, he was not so confident.

One evening, he and I walked around a casino with Charlie. We had previously made a couple of card and dice pick-ups, one of the routine assignments established within the Law Enforcement Division. (Pick-ups are a form of quality control. A gaming board agent walks quickly and unnoticed to a dice or 21 pit, identifies himself to the pit boss, checks the work cards of the pit personnel, and confiscates the dice or the cards for later examination. The key to the system is, of course, surprise.)

Tom and I were treated to plenty of pick-ups when riding with law enforcement agents, since pick-ups are one of the few forms of active law enforcement that agents can easily show off. Like many patrol cops, law enforcement agents spend much time killing time. Ironically, we learned later that an agent whom we had first observed doing pick-ups was later fired because he was believed to have called a casino beforehand with the information that he was scheduled to pick up gambling paraphernalia there that evening. The casino was at the time strongly suspected of containing highly placed thieves on the inside. In any event, the casino was losing far more money than could reasonably have been expected, until the gaming authorities forced a change in management and ownership. The pick-up is, in a sense, the structural counterpart in legal casino gambling to the raid in illegal gaming — and offers somewhat analogous possibilities of payoff.

On this particular night, Charlie received a call on his private "beeper" — a small, receiving unit carried on his belt. The "beep" meant he should call his office. He called, and was told to proceed to the "Lucky Jackpot" Casino, a grind joint featuring slot machines, to investigate another routine event, a jackpot payoff dispute.

When we arrived at the Lucky Jackpot, I was once again astonished by the cacophony of sounds — jingling coins, sirens, bells — accompanied by programmed lights of different colors. (The *son et lumière* apparently attracts people to play slot machines. All this movement is intended to signal to the slot player that this is a place of fast, throbbing, sustained, high-energy action. The action is so blatantly preorgasmic, culminating in the release of the jackpot, that the psychoanalytic interpretation of the link between gambling and sexuality seems justified.) I am also aware that the light and the noise and the movement do nothing to enhance the possibilities of controlling slot thieves. It would prove impossible to hear a drill above the din, and the disorienting features of the normal environment cannot fail to dull the perceptions of casino personnel assigned to be watchers.

Shortly after we walked in, we were ushered into the casino manager's office, cramped and irregular in the shape of the room and its walls, as if it had been put together to fit between more important functions. In a grind joint, the office fits where the slot machines won't, usually next to the cage. The furniture was appropriate to the setting — worn and plastic, the refuse of the casino floor. Tom and I were introduced as consultants to the board to those present. They included the manager, a player — "Mr. Nash" — and two private detectives employed by the "Kennedy Detective Agency."

7

"Charles Kennedy" was formerly a high-ranking detective in a local police department. Within the Gaming Control Board, he and his agency are controversial. Some say that he does an effective job of keeping slot thieves out of casinos. Others allege that if a casino declines his services, he will encourage slot cheats of his acquaintance to bring their business to the casino.

One owner, when asked why he retained Kennedy, was reluctant to discuss him at all, and was particularly reluctant to discuss whether he thought Kennedy was legitimate. "You can write," he replied tersely, "that receipts from our slot machines have increased since we hired him."

The Kennedy Detective Agency offers two principal services: one is a "black book" containing pictures and descriptions of alleged slot thieves; the other is the capability to interrogate jackpot winners, if there is a dispute about the validity of the jackpot. The Kennedy Agency does not assign detectives directly to the casino with which it holds contracts. Instead, they are on call to resolve jackpot disputes or any other problem that casino managers do not care to have come to the attention of public officials. I am told by gaming officials that Kennedy holds contracts with all of the major casinos. His business is clearly profitable.

I once questioned a board member about why Kennedy and his agency were not required to be licensed, since they constituted such a significant aspect of day-to-day gaming control. I was reminded that Kennedy Agency personnel were licensed as private detectives. That seemed to me to be quite irrelevant, and I said so. Lawyers are also licensed to be lawyers, but the gaming board has always stoutly defended its right to license a lawyer who might want to purchase an equity interest in a casino, or to work in an administrative position.

The board member added that the Kennedy Agency could do things the board could not. For example, Kennedy could circulate a list of suspected slot cheats to casinos subscribing to his services. But as a public agency the board could not itself compile and distribute such a list, for two reasons: First, board agents could and should not maintain the sort of relations with the criminal underworld needed to identify individuals as potential slot thieves; Kennedy agents were reported sometimes to work so closely with slot thieves as to be indistinguishable. Second, the board was a public agency. It could not circulate a list of "suspected" slot thieves without inviting legal problems. A private detective agency, representing a client, might offer its opinion privately as to who might be a slot thief. The board, in contrast, does not have clients.

When its information is disseminated, it must be passed along to the industry as a whole — in effect, made public.

In addition, the Kennedy Agency could engage in other investigative practices prohibited to board agents, such as illegal searches. Not that Kennedy ever admitted to or was permitted to make illegal searches. It was simply understood that these might occur, although Kennedy would deny that, if pressed. Thus, the board simply did not inquire too closely as to how Kennedy obtained his information, nor would they inquire closely of any informant. Yet Kennedy's information sometimes proved valuable to the board, providing the sort of intelligence information every policing agency wants and needs. The idea of a private detective agency doing police work that might be illegal, marginal, or inappropriate if done by sworn officers seemed to the board member to be an unsatisfactory solution that made him uneasy, but had not led to action while this study was in progress.

In part, this hesitancy was attributable to the fact that the board is not simply a police agency; that the interests of the industry are also the board's. To illustrate: Although the board sometimes is presented with law enforcement issues as sensitive as those of any agency — for example, the role of organized crime in gaming — it does not see itself primarily as a crime-fighting operation. It does not engage in wiretapping, out of sensitivity to the irritation and fear wiretapping would produce in the industry. Whatever its drawbacks, the Kennedy Agency helps the industry, even when it engages in questionable activities. The presence of the Kennedy Agency, as well as the more general function played by the board, places the board's Law Enforcement Division directly on the horns of a recurring dilemma: its mandate to protect the industry, even as it polices it.

8

In the manager's office, the Kennedy detectives argued that Mr. Nash had collected a jackpot the year before, and was, along with his wife, strongly suspected of being a "collector" in a slot thief gang.

If Mr. Nash was a collector, he was an accomplished one. The collector's role demands the skills of the character actor. He, or she, must claim the jackpot cool as can be, knowing full well of the existence of a tiny, illegal hole in the left side of the machine. Mr. Nash played the innocent claimant's role perfectly. He appeared to be confused, slightly shaken, and utterly innocent of knowledge about drills, holes, and the like. When it was pointed out to him that his wife was also suspected of being a slot thief he became slightly indignant but not overly so. He acknowledged that she had won a $150 jackpot several months earlier in a club down the street, had collected the money as well as a congratulatory snapshot taken by the club to give her as a fond souvenir of her lucky day. Without her knowledge or consent the same photograph provided the Kennedy Detective Agency another winner's likeness for its files.

9

The situation at the Lucky Jackpot was further complicated; an informant had provided a law enforcement agent with the information that 17 machines had been drilled at that casino. (The informant was a slot thief who owed a favor to the agent. But employees of casinos also — most often anonymously — volunteer information that such-and-such a scam is occurring. Sometimes, the scam has already been completed, or has been discontinued because the employees engaging in it feel something has gone wrong, that they have been discovered.)

In this case, the driller had offered his templates for sale to a wider market, and with more information than prudence would dictate. He had identified the club where the drilled machines were located. Such information alone would not be valuable for a slot thief, since the club contains several hundred machines, and the only sure method of spotting the holes is to take the machine apart and to examine its casing with a flashlight. But the information is valuable to the enforcer. An agent passed the information along to the Lucky Jackpot. Once this happened, the club and the gaming board were on the same side. Unless a club management is itself responsible for the scam, it would most certainly be interested in preventing it. Even if it weren't, it would have to make a reasonably serious show of interest, by examining all its machines.

When the Lucky Jackpot machines were examined — the information had been transmitted a day earlier — 17 holes had been discovered in 17 machines. Ordinarily, the machines would have been repaired by attaching a patch of case-hardened steel to the inside surface, against the hole. Unfortunately for the Lucky Jackpot, the manufacturer was out of the steel patch parts; it wouldn't be receiving them for "a few days." Like other mechanical devices of modern civilization, slot machines are often easier to purchase than to find spare parts for.

Worse yet, the management had been told by the board not to operate these machines until they had been repaired. Since the casino manager could not locate the spare parts, he had ordered the club's slot mechanics to attach paper firmly against the inside casing of the machine.

This is an old trick to catch slot thieves. If a wire breaks the paper, the hole is clearly visible, and one can assume the machine has been tampered with. The only problem is, it is not clear who did the tampering. The wireman may have felt the pressure offered by the paper, made the hole, suspected a trap, and left hurriedly with the collector. Several hours later a thoroughly innocent player may then step up to the machine and hit a legitimate jackpot. He is hustled off by two detectives to the back room of a casino, is accused of being a slot thief, and is confronted by a law enforcement agent from the Gaming Control Board.

10

In this case, the question was: Was Mr. Nash a legitimate claimant or a false collector? With that question, the gaming control agent is transformed into part detective, part judge. He is faced with what is essentially an adversary relationship between the casino and the jackpot claimer. How much evidence, and what kind, is needed to decide whether the claim is legitimate? What weight should be given to the fact that the casino, in violation of a board direction, did not in fact repair the machines? What weight should be given to the fact that Mr. Nash's wife had won a jackpot several months earlier; that she appeared in Kennedy's book as a suspected slot thief; and that the machine Mr. Nash had been playing had twice been tampered with, once by being drilled, and once more by being penetrated?

Charlie explained as politely as he could to Mr. Nash that he would have to return to his office, just a few minutes away, and check him out. Whatever the true identity of Mr. Nash, the situation was embarrassing. If Nash was in fact a slot cheat he had been caught claiming a jackpot in a drilled machine — but he couldn't be arrested. Still, the board agent could not assume that Nash was a collector, since the agent was aware the machine had previously been drilled and was still operating. On the other hand, if Nash was a legitimate jackpot winner, who occasionally played in Las Vegas, he was being treated very much like a suspected thief, in a thoroughly confusing, intimidating, arbitrary procedure which seemed to put the Gaming Control Board in the position of being an accomplice to the club in cheating Nash out of his legitimate jackpot.

Charlie returned to the office, called the local police, checked the board's files, and could not find any indication that Nash was a cheater. He called the deputy chief of the division — by now it was 1:30 A.M. — told him about the situation, and asked for instructions. The deputy chief told him the man should be paid.

Charlie called the club and told them to pay the man his jackpot, but the club manager, on the advice of the Kennedy detectives, requested a 72-hour delay to conduct an investigation.

Charlie asked to speak with Mr. Nash. He told Nash the club had a right to conduct an investigation if it wished. At the end of 72 hours, he explained, if the investigation proved negative to the satisfaction of the board, he would personally see to it that the jackpot money would be sent to Mr. Nash, at his address, by registered mail.

I was curious and a bit skeptical. "What regulation," I asked, "gave the club the right to conduct an investigation concerning a disputed jackpot claim?" Charlie was nonplussed. He had always assumed that casinos had that right. He called the deputy chief and raised the question with him. The deputy chief replied that there was no such right, and that Charlie had the discretion to deny the club its 72 hours.

By now Charlie, a decent, warm man, felt a bit embarrassed since his inclination would have been — had he been aware of his discretionary authority — to order that the jackpot be paid off. He had begun to believe Mr. Nash. But, having explained to Mr. Nash that the club had 72 hours, Charlie was disinclined to modify his decision, figuring that Mr. Nash would receive his money in 72 hours anyhow. If he didn't, he had ten days to appeal Charlie's decision to a board member.

The next morning, we learned from agent "Jimmy Brooks" that he had in his possession a photograph of Mr. Nash standing in front of a machine after he had hit a jackpot of $200 at the Lucky Jackpot Casino. Brooks said the photograph had been given to him the afternoon before the jackpot incident by Kennedy, who had identified Mr. Nash as a suspected slot thief. He had neglected or forgotten to pass it along to Charlie.

The photograph had been taken one month earlier. It showed Mr. Nash smiling in front of a different slot machine at the Lucky Jackpot. Mr. Nash had denied, the night before, that he had ever hit a jackpot in Las Vegas, although his wife had. Clearly, the photograph showed that Mr. Nash either possessed an uncommonly inaccurate memory or was lying. Mr. Nash had already left town, effectively escaping prosecution; but he certainly wasn't going to get his jackpot claim. Anyhow, he had been an extremely convincing "collector."

11

The problem of Mr. Nash had been resolved. But the continuing problem of the drilled machines had not. The night before, when he had authorized the 72-hour investigation, Charlie had also advised the manager that the drilled machines would have to be put out of service until they were repaired. When Charlie's shift was over, at 2:30 A.M., Tom and I volunteered to check whether the drilled machines had indeed been taken out of service, and to call Charlie at home with our findings. Checking, we discovered that the machine Mr. Nash had been playing had been taken out of operation, but none of the others had. We relayed our information to Charlie, who in turn called the deputy chief, who left instructions with the morning-shift agent, Jimmy Brooks, to seal the drilled machines.

The relationship between the board's law enforcement agents and the casino is rather like an optical illusion that appears to show one object if perceived from this view and another from that; it is all a matter of perspective. When the player appears to be cheating the casino — and the state — board agents are supposed to favor the casino. But the agents are also responsible for protecting the player from an exploitative casino. Thus, when machines are drilled, agents sense a dual responsibility: one is to protect the public from even the embarrassment that might result from hitting a jackpot in a drilled machine; the other is to assist the casino, in any legitimate way possible, to repair the machines at least well enough to consider them as in working order. In this instance, for example, it was not considered acceptable to the agents, as it was to the casino, to operate the drilled machines with paper fixed to the holes. This could have led to the reenactment of the Nash situation, but involving a truly innocent player.

Still, no formal regulation existed explicitly requiring that under the circumstances slot machine holes could not be papered over. Suppose the agents in this case actually had accepted gratuities from this club, or any other that might find itself in a similar situation? The Law Enforcement Division might have been tempted to permit papering over the holes until repairs arrived. Actually, Tom Gray, of all people, figured out how to fix the drilled slot machines. He thought of inserting and hammering steel needles into the tiny holes, and clipping the edges. But the casino would have preferred, if necessary, to paper over the holes — casinos often fail to distinguish between their own self-interest and that of the industry as a whole.

Ultimately, the latter guideline is supposed to govern the discretionary authority of the Law Enforcement Division. Those in it at least are supposed to exercise discretion in terms of *long-range* industry interests, not *short-range* casino interests. It is thought to be in the industry's — and Nevada's — interest to protect the integrity of the jackpot. When we review the work of the Audit Division, which concerns itself more directly with higher management, we find that conceptual distinctions between industry and casino, and industry and state, are empirically difficult to sustain.

18

Auditing
Casino Management

SINCE THE STATE OF NEVADA'S RELATIONSHIP TO THE GAMING IN-
dustry is ambiguous, occupying the field between the poles of
partnership and policing, one might think that the role of the
Audit Division would be equally uncertain. During the three years
I was involved in this study, I had unimpeded access to gaming
records and personnel, and actually participated in major audits,
in addition to spending hundreds of hours interviewing and working side by side with senior agents engaged in the most sensitive
investigations.

During that time the Audit Division played perhaps the least
ambiguous role in the agency in relation to the industry. The
division chief saw the industry as an adversary from whom taxes
were to be collected; and also as continuously threatened by the
predations of organized criminal elements. His views, however
were not widely supported.

During the mid-1970s two important developments occurred.
One, the division was subtly but inexorably transformed into a
high-level detective division where law enforcement priorities

began to challenge and ultimately to take priority over those of routine tax collection; and two, the legislature eventually recognized and affirmed the functional relationship between revenue collection and intelligence operations. As a result, the division became the largest and, for awhile, the most influential in the agency. But a strong Audit Division can also prove controversial, attracting powerful enemies as well as friends. The aggressive stance of the division eventually led to open and serious conflict with the commission and the industry.

2

Auditors are accountants, people who establish, maintain, and examine financial records. When an accountant examines financial records, such as balance sheets, income statements, and statements of changes in financial position, he is said to have performed an audit. Usually, on the basis of that examination and related verification procedures, the accountant prepares a report confirming that the statements were prepared according to generally accepted accounting principles and accurately reflected the financial position of the audited business entity.

When compared with lawyers and physicians, the accountant occupies a unique, ambiguous, and even contradictory relationship to the client. In theory, the accountant acts as an impartial reviewer of the financial statements of the client and comments favorably or unfavorably on them for third parties such as the investing or lending public. Presumably, the "public accountant's" review is impartial, even though paid for by the client.[1]

In recent years, however, the impartiality of the accountant has been increasingly questioned. CPA firms have been defendants in lawsuits — some involving millions of dollars — claiming that the financial reports of the clients "attested to" by the CPA firms did not actually represent the clients' financial positions.[2]

Even more recently, disclosures of illegal political contributions by major United States corporations, routinely audited by major CPA firms, have renewed interest in the auditor's responsibility for disclosing illegality. According to an article on the subject appearing in the *Journal of Accountancy*, the accounting profession is grappling with an agonizing problem: What is the auditor's role and responsibility when his client commits an illegal act?[3]

The usual answer is that the ordinary audit is not oriented to the discovery of fraud. Indeed CPAs are increasingly modifying their representations in public statements. As Lee Seidler, deputy chairman of the AICPA's Commission on Audit Responsibilities, was recently quoted on the subject: "People tend to think of auditors as detectives. They're not — they're accountants. We train them in debits and credits. Even if they look carefully, auditors will miss many, maybe even most, frauds."[4]

3

Gaming Control Board auditors are Nevada's accounting firm in gaming matters. These accountants are not in the business of affirming the representations of the casinos. On the contrary, their task is to view these with deep suspicion. Depending on the intention of the audited entity, errors may represent honest incompetence, or an attempt to deceive the government. On the whole, gaming control auditors describe their procedures as "fraud audits" or more precisely, as "fraud-oriented" audits. Ordinarily, the auditors do not expect to find fraud by equity holders — owners — but rather by employees who are experienced in the gambling business and are undermining the interests of owners.

Fraud-oriented gaming control auditors employ three tactics ordinarily unavailable to or simply not used by the conventional CPA firm. These include (1) an intelligence network geared to collecting prior information; (2) the capacity to make surprise visits to the casino count rooms and cages; and (3) the legal authority and resources to undertake a detailed examination of assets, liabilities, revenues, and disbursements. These tactics are effective only when combined with genuine independence from the audited entity.

The decision whether to initiate an audit derives from a rough equation and is based on three factors: prior scheduling, an indication of a problem, and the size of the operation. Audits are sup-

posed to be conducted periodically by the Audit Division —
usually about three years separate one audit from the next — but
the decision to initiate an audit is often precipitated by prior
information that something untoward, or possibly illegal, is
occurring in some aspect of the casino operation. Those in
authority at the Audit Division operate on the theory that rumor
may indicate real weakness; and that problems are not isolated.

4

There is a persistent rivalry between the Investigations and Audit
Divisions over capacity to perform intelligence. Investigations
agents, mainly former policemen, think they can do the job
better than accountants, who disagree.

Police training, however, does not especially qualify one to
perform intelligence work in the gaming control business. Much
of the illegal activity in the gambling business involves complex
financial manipulations. Besides, police are principally trained to
be *apprehenders* of known criminals, not crime *solvers*. Thus, Egon
Bittner views the capacity to employ force as the key to the
policeman's role[5] while Jonathan Rubenstein has similarly observed that the policeman's principal tool is his body.[6] The gun
and the club are extensions of the body, which the policeman uses
to control other people.

The detective's job sometimes involves apprehension. Hence it
is appropriate for detectives to be drawn from the ranks of policemen. But intelligence — the gathering of information about crime
— is a separable function. This is especially so in the gaming
control context. Here information about crime or possible crime
derives mainly from six sources.

First, disgruntled employees may confide in an auditor, usually
milder-mannered and seemingly less threatening than someone
with the demeanor of a conventional policeman.

Former financial employees of casinos are another source.
Auditors sometimes learn more about hidden practices at other
casinos where the employee previously worked than about the
entity being audited.

Owners and managers of casinos are a third information source.

They are obligated to answer the technical questions directed by auditors, and are more likely to perceive accountants as intellectual and social equals.

Fourth, auditors conduct special investigations involving lengthy interrogations of casino employees. During these interrogations, they develop future contacts for information and also develop information that might relate to future investigations and audits, in the casino under investigation or other casinos.

Fifth, general intelligence preliminary to an audit is often provided by other agencies of the federal government as well as state and local governments. This generalized intelligence-gathering function was the province of a former FBI agent who possessed an accounting degree, and who maintained a variety of information sources, particularly in the area of organized crime and the casino. Here a police background is desirable, since police agencies generally respond more favorably to those who share this background.

Finally, some (albeit minimal) intelligence is offered to the auditors by other divisions within the agency. At one time, a board member proposed that an intelligence section be established within the agency, pooling intelligence from all sources, with the Audit Division's organized crime specialist in charge. The idea scarcely commended itself to the other divisions.

5

In practice, the most significant audits have begun as a result of prior information — intelligence — directed to the division through an agent, or the division chief, who probably maintained contact with more informants than anyone else in the agency. In the case of one particular audit, the chief had received word through informants that substantial credit of approximately one-quarter of a million dollars had been extended to a minor organized crime figure in a hotel-casino complex I shall call the "Golden Palace." The problem was not that the organized crime figure was thought to own an interest in the hotel. The hotel was too big and he was too small for that. The issue was whether the organized crime figure had built up credit exceeding his capacity to pay and was, with the collusion of a casino executive authorized to grant credit, about to defraud the hotel of a quarter of a million dollars, and the state of Nevada of its tax of $13,750.

The Golden Palace was one of the Strip's leading moneymakers. It was part of a nationally known, publicly traded corporation and was, by Las Vegas terms, highly respectable. Actually, the national corporation had experienced financial difficulties before it purchased the Golden Palace, but had become prosperous as a result of the Las Vegas operation.

The Golden Palace was one of several hotel casinos where the hotel and casino enjoyed independent profitability. This does *not* mean that the hotel would have prospered without a casino. It *does* mean that it was usually not necessary to offer the hotel as a complimentary loss-leader so frequently that the hotel lost money. On the contrary, the Golden Palace's lavish hotel complex earned nearly as much as the casino, in large part because it enjoyed an extraordinary year-round occupancy rate exceeding 95 percent, in what used to be considered primarily a summer and weekend resort.

Since the Golden Palace was a highly valued property, a showcase for the state, the gaming control authorities took very seriously its continued prosperity. It took equally seriously the suggestion of financial difficulty at the Golden Palace — and ordered another audit.

6

Once the decision is made to audit a hotel, a senior agent is assigned to examine a variety of files in the gaming control offices as a background to the audit. These files are summarized to provide a map of the terrain about to be audited, as military officials might review a map of enemy territory about to be invaded.

A number of relevant files are included. In addition to the "intelligence file," the senior auditor reviews files documenting who are the hotel's owners, key employees, and junket arrangers, plus permanent and major leases, loans and contracts, and prior tax returns. (The latter is compiled by a small Economic Research Division, which maintains and analyzes basic data about casino revenues. This division will also provide a computer readout listing licensed games and slot machines.) In effect, these files document financial normality.

Several other files suggest deviation from normality. One is a "compliance letter" file. CPAs hired by the casino are required to indicate violations of gaming control rules found in conducting their audits. Files of work papers compiled during previous audits by gaming control agents are also examined. Another file is checked, showing violations found in the past which management has been required to remedy.

The most comprehensive file review derives from a regulation, perhaps the single most important in the whole accounting control apparatus, requiring that every nonrestricted licensee with gross annual gaming revenues exceeding $500,000 submit a written and diagrammatic representation of its systems of internal controls. The Audit Division drew up a questionnaire to serve as a guide for evaluating the adequacy and effectiveness of the licensee's system and how well the licensee has compiled with other accounting regulations.

The questionnaire asks specific questions, and therefore interprets each aspect of Regulation 6, the Accounting Regulation. For example, regarding Regulation 6.010, the questionnaire asks:

1. Are all table game boxes:
   (a) Marked with a number corresponding to a permanent number on the table?
   (b) Marked to indicate game and shift?
   (c) Marked in such a manner as to be clearly visible at a distance of 20 feet?
   (d) Locked to the table and separately keyed from the container itself?

Finally, there is a file containing undercover observations, the most pertinent of which will have occurred several days prior to the audit.

In preparation for the Golden Palace audit, several members of the division walked around the crowded casino watching for violations of key control measures. (I was present throughout.) We looked to see whether table game boxes actually were marked with a number corresponding to a number on the table. We did not, however, have a formal checklist. At that time, the agents maintained — in their heads — a conception of normal and appropriate responses to the accounting regulations. They would, for instance, have spotted a discrepancy between table number and drop box number. The Audit Division has since introduced a checklist, partly out of recognition of the complexity of internal controls, and partly because so many new auditors have joined the division.

In this casino, at that time, the only observed violation was a departure from the time designated for transferring drop boxes. The transfer started several minutes earlier than stated. That was noted, and followed up with a letter informing the casino of the violation and asking what measures were being taken to bring the casino back into compliance.

7

The initiation of an audit on the casino premises is a tense and dramatic event for the auditors. Since the Golden Palace was a large casino, a staff of five auditors plus the division chief independently arrived at the casino at 3 A.M. dressed in fancy blue jeans and leisure suits, attire that would appear inconspicuous at that hour of the morning in a Las Vegas gaming casino. The agents ambled about the casino, drifted to the bar, played some slot machines to remain inconspicuous, all the while concentrating on deviations from prescribed internal control procedures.

At precisely 5 A.M. the youthful-looking Audit Division chief approached the graveyard-shift boss, a man who was once as they say in Las Vegas heavily "connected" — and looked the part — flashed his badge and demanded entry into the cage. The shift boss at first appeared scornful, towering and glowering over the slightly built auditor. Then his expression changed to apprehension — you could almost hear him wondering why the gaming board authorities had selected his shift for an audit.

Finally, he sighed heavily and motioned the audit chief and several of the chief's colleagues who were also flashing badges to follow. I joined the pack and walked next to the audit chief as the group of which I had now become a part was admitted to the cage by the security guard. My nonexistent credentials were, from an operational standpoint, in order. So long as my presence was accepted by the gaming agents it was satisfactory to those in charge of cage security.

The audit began at 5 A.M. primarily because that is when the count had already begun, according to gaming board records. Counts usually start around this hour partly because the casino's busiest shift is usually the swing shift, running from early in the evening to early in the morning. Casinos operate on the principle that money should be counted promptly. The sooner it is accounted for, the less the opportunity for theft. Moreover, when the count starts early deposits can be made early.

The audit began with a surprise surveillance of both the count room and the cage. Thus, one group of auditors, by prearrangement, split off and began "counting down" the cage to determine that its contents reconciled with prior documentary description; and to see whether the cage procedure conformed to gaming board regulations.

The second group proceeded quickly to the count room, truly a backstage area. While the casino floor is all glitter and hype, the count room is all business. Even in as large and opulent a casino as the Golden Palace, the count room, located behind the cage, is spare. A large table — the counting table — dominates the middle of the room. On one wall are all the swing-shift boxes with money in them. On another wall are empty boxes. The third wall, across from the first, houses a shelf for counting. The fourth wall is constructed as a gigantic one-way mirror.

Two cameras hang from the ceiling. When a box is emptied, the camera must be shown the inside of the box to prove that theft has not occurred. In a casino of this size, the cameras will be video-taping, and the tape can be played back later. The entire set-up is designed to heighten the counter's awareness of sustained surveillance, from all angles.

Ordinarily, five people — three men, two women — occupy the Golden Palace's count room. One counts the money, a second checks that count, a third adds the value of fill slips, and records the amounts on a ledger known as a "stiff sheet." A fourth person packages the cash into bundles. A fifth, who never touches the money, holds the keys to the locked boxes, allows the money to drop to the table, shows the empty box to the camera, and locks the box so that it is ready to be replaced at the table at the next swing shift.

In the count room itself, the audit chief ordered the count stopped. The very first issue in a count room audit is administrative, underscoring the relationship between administrative and accounting controls. Each of the five persons participating was asked to identify him- or herself by work card and driver's license. Each did that satisfactorily. Gaming regulations require another identification mechanism because, conceivably, the work card and the driver's license could be forged. This is a signature list provided to the gaming board of each person who works in the count room. One of those engaged in counting, it turned out, had not signed that list. The gaming auditors are delegated personal discretion to interpret such a minor breach of regulations. As it happened, the counter who had not signed was personally known to two of the auditors, who recorded the violation, but made no fuss over it.

More importantly, the counters were asked to recount what they had just counted, to determine whether there was a discrepancy between the recount and the amount recorded for the original count. There was none at that shift on that day. This finding — based on a surprise sample of one — led the auditors to the presumption that no embezzlement or skimming was occurring in the count room of the Golden Palace. Of course the validity of the presumption was only as strong as the representativeness of the sample.

As the audit proceeded, the auditors examined a variety of records over time. For example, after watching the count-room operation I walked into the cage and observed a senior agent count the checks that had bounced during the past year. The amount, for a casino of this size, seemed surprisingly small. It was under $20,000 and most of the checks were, by Las Vegas gambling standards, for relatively small amounts, from $100 to several hundred dollars.

The relatively small number of bad checks suggests that the credit-checking services available to casinos in Las Vegas operate quite effectively. Besides, many people — especially those inclined to "hang paper" — may believe that extralegal sanctions are available to Las Vegas casinos.

8

Another senior agent was involved in what is perhaps the most important area to be audited, the outstanding markers or IOUs. Recall that in the only proved case of skimming through 1977, the defendants pleaded guilty to the destruction of markers in the casino, and their subsequent collection later on — privately and without tax liability.

The audit of the Golden Palace's markers revealed that millions of dollars' worth of markers were being held not in Las Vegas, but in the New York and Miami junket offices of the Palace. This included the quarter of a million dollars worth of markers that had precipitated the audit in the first place, held against an organized crime figure employing a fictitious name, with the knowledge of the casino management. Las Vegas casino executives do not ask where customers find the money to pay off gambling debts, only whether they will pay off.

The agent was not particularly disturbed that markers were missing. On the contrary, had all markers been present, he would have been surprised. Gamblers who run up sizable debts frequently do not reside in Nevada. Major hotels maintain offices in a number of cities. Usually, the largest are located on the East Coast, with New York and Miami dominating the action. The original markers are held in these offices since a player paying off a marker normally wants it returned, right there, even though the marker might be legally unenforceable.

Of course, copies of the markers are retained in Las Vegas, and considerable information is available for review by the agent doing the checking. In addition to determining the customer's real or purported name, the date of the item, the amount, and whether the original is on file, the auditor will review comments on the marker envelope discussing steps already taken to collect it. He will also check to see whether the marker was actually authorized. The agent will pull the credit card to see whether the player signed it, who authorized the credit limit, whether it was exceeded, and who authorized the excess, if any.

The review, however, can raise more questions than it answers. A player may use either a false name or in some instances two different names. If two names are used, the auditor must be able to check back from the marker envelope to the credit card under both names to follow the history of credit. For example, we ran across one marker envelope marked to a man called "John Hercules." His real name appeared on another marker envelope.

When the auditors checked his credit card they found and photographed the following note, initialed on a typewriter by one of the casino executives (who would later claim that he did not in fact initial it, but that the initials were put on by somebody else). The note read: "Money is in Miami, but we have been instructed to write it off as paid in chips. When money is paid destroy this note." This mysterious note referred to a $50,000 marker. Why was it written? The agent who discovered it considered several possibilities: (1) chips were stolen to pay off the marker and the collectors were embezzling or skimming the cash; (2) a player legitimately won and paid off with these chips; (3) there were no chips involved at all; instead, the marker was paid off in cash, but the records would show it was paid off in chips. Such a deception could have been arranged to avoid IRS tax liability; the player in question may not have wanted the IRS to know he had that much cash, and the casino executive was cooperating.

The intensive scrutiny of markers is ultimately directed towards two goals: detecting crime (whether skimming or embezzlement has occurred); and collecting taxes (whether uncollected markers are to be treated as taxable revenue). When markers are unpaid, the question is basically whether the player refused payment; or whether an embezzlement occurred. The casino is responsible for paying taxes on the latter — it bears liability for the miscreant acts of its agents — but not the former.

Both questions — those of crime *and* tax liability — are complicated by credit business conducted outside Nevada. Thus, what would normally be key auditable entities — original IOUs — are not immediately available during a Las Vegas audit.

Still, the auditors are by no means precluded from conducting a surprise audit of Miami or New York headquarters of Las Vegas casinos. In the instance I describe, for example (in part because the original markers precipitating the audit were missing and in part because of other business in Miami), the audit chief decided to send an auditing team to New York and to Miami, where the original markers were discovered and explained to the auditing team's satisfaction.

The markers, the auditors found, did indeed belong to an organized crime figure. He had already paid some of his liability, and was good for the remainder, they were assured. The debtor only asked that his name not be disclosed. Requests for privacy are frequent in the gambling business.

From the viewpoint of the agency, this response was temporarily satisfactory, since the agency does not concern itself, except in rare cases, as when someone is listed in the "Black Book" as an undesirable, in the social or business character of players receiving credit. This is another instance of the similarity of interests obtaining between the authorities and casinos. Obviously, a state policy requiring that credit holders be selected on grounds other than ability to pay, regardless of where the money came from, would prove counterproductive to the gambling business — and to taxable revenue. As we shall see, however, the auditors did not put the organized crime figure out of mind.

9

The industry and the agency conflict on some matters, notably those involving additional assessments by the agency of the casino. For example, if the agency chooses to send auditors to Miami and New York, who should pay, the state or the casino? The agency actually assessed this casino for the cost of the trip, arguing that the casino was required by statute to maintain its records in Nevada. If it chose, with the state's permission, to maintain records elsewhere, then it should reimburse the state the additional funds needed to audit records properly. The agency likened the audit function in this instance to payments required of applicants for licenses for investigative expenses. When, for example, the Bally

Manufacturing Corporation sought licensing in Nevada, it was required to pay the costs of sending agents to Rome, London, and Australia, where it also operated as a business entity.

The industry maintained otherwise. It took the position that the state had given permission to maintain records outside in order to generate gaming revenues. Since these revenues were taxed by the state, the industry argued that funds required to audit out-of-state records ought to be provided by the legislature just as the federal government pays for Internal Revenue Service audits. The federal taxpayer is not assessed for the cost of auditing business records maintained in different states. The industry sued and won.

The 1977 Nevada legislature amended the gaming statutes to reflect the industry's view, even though the Gaming Control Board chairman asked the legislature to require the industry to pay for the cost of out-of-state audits. The gaming authorities carry considerable clout within the Nevada legislature, but not quite so much as the industry.

When a dispute arises between the industry and the authorities, legislators often find themselves in a dilemma. During the 1977 session, the issue of out-of-state audit payments precipitated a minor crisis between the upper and lower houses. Ultimately, the gaming board chairman, in the interests of amity, withdrew his request to require the industry to pay. From the agency's viewpoint, the important issue was whether the agency would be budgeted to account for the costs of undertaking out-of-state audits. The agency did not really care who paid, only that investigations were not restricted by lack of funds.

10

Size and fame of a casino do not automatically protect it from problems. The Audit Division continually receives information from one source or another about the financial stability of Nevada casinos, particularly the major ones. There is a continual traffic between the Strip casinos and the Audit Division's downtown offices. During my research, several seemed particularly prone to visits. These casinos are in effect the "delinquents" of the industry.

Like kids who move in and out of juvenile correctional facilities, they eventually come to be perceived by the gaming authorities as possessing the business equivalent of characterological problems. Moreover, like such juveniles, they may not actually be more guilty than others, but merely more susceptible to being caught.

One casino, the "Parisien," was plagued by a fundamental problem which successive managements found difficult to overcome. The problem stemmed from the lack of symmetry among four key variables: the economic class of the consumer market, the number of available rooms, the fixed costs of restaurants and showrooms, and the size of the casino. In this instance, large restaurants and showrooms presented fixed costs out of line with the return possible from the relatively small casino area and number of rooms. Furthermore, the casino depended upon a high-rolling clientele who demanded exceptional room facilities. But as the economic crunch set in, the quality of food and service declined. The Parisien found it increasingly difficult to attract the carriage-trade clientele, who were being siphoned off by nearby competitors.

For years, various managements wrestled with the dilemma of either changing the social and economic character of the players to keep the casino filled; or acquiring the financing to expand and refurbish both casino and hotel facilities. As management wrestled — and vacillated — the hotel lost money. At the same time, internal administrative controls suffered, and more money was lost, contributing to the cyclical decline.

Moreover, since junkets constituted a significant portion of the hotel's operation, the casino frequently experienced cash-flow problems. Normally, the house holds around 20 percent of the amount gambled. But winners on a junket win cash, losers lose credit. Losers are expected to pay markers before leaving, but that doesn't always happen, and this casino counted around $9 million in uncollected markers: even seemingly profitable junkets can result in serious cash reserve problems.

Nothing — not even cheating — is taken more seriously by gaming authorities than casino cash reserves, and for similar reasons. When potential players believe they will be cheated, or will not be paid off when they win, the entire industry suffers.

In one respect failure to pay off is even more serious than cheating, because the latter is typically subtle, and subject to being denied. By contrast, if a major casino were to fail to pay off a winner because the casino lacked cash reserves, the nightmare headlines would be printed around the world. Accordingly, the gaming regulations include a formula for cash reserves to back up every game played on the premises.

In fact, the authorities recognize the impracticality of formal reserve requirements because they are based on an assessment of what might happen if players were to win maximally on each game played. So, when reserve requirements are not met, usually not much concern is expressed, provided the authorities feel that a realistic amount is available — whatever that may mean. Usually, nobody looks very hard.

During one weekend, however, the auditors learned that the cash reserves of the Parisien were dangerously low — down to around a quarter of a million dollars; so low that a closure of the entire operation became a genuine possibility. Accordingly, the gaming authorities were faced with a decisional crisis.

The broad discretion enjoyed by the gaming authorities becomes most apparent when the possibility of closing down a major Las Vegas casino is involved. On one side are short-range financial considerations. These include not only the cash bankroll in the cage, but also other assets: cash in banks, casino cash-flow, and such other sources of cash as might reasonably be counted on in an emergency.

Liabilities have to be considered as well. Not only must a winning player be paid off, so must other creditors, such as food and beverage wholesalers, mortgage holders, and employees.

Still, on the other side, an important long-range factor looms in the decisional equation. Were the Parisien to close, approximately 1,000 persons would become unemployed. In a state with a population of around 500,000, where gaming is the major industry, to suddenly close out employment for around 1,000 persons, many of whom have families, would constitute a political as well as a human problem. This is the sort of issue that precipitates concerned telephone calls from the governor to board and commission members.

Furthermore, closing down a major Las Vegas hotel would affect the entire industry. The stability of a number of investments in the Las Vegas area might suffer, as well as the capacity of gaming hotels to obtain financing for expansion.

Finally, the closing of a hotel further undermines its already precarious financial position. In the Parisien's case, the immediate reason for closing was lack of cash, directly traceable to around $9 million in uncollected markers. With that cash in hand, the hotel could pay off its creditors and maintain sufficient bankroll to keep the casino operating. If the hotel closed down, debtors holding already hard-to-collect markers would be disinclined to pay off a new management, to whom they owed no personal fealty.

Under tight circumstances such as the Parisien's, three members of the gaming commission, following a recommendation by the board, can declare that an emergency exists. The declaration of an emergency permits investment in the hotel by persons who have not undergone the deep investigation implied by formal licensing.

When a casino is financially shaky and actively seeking investors, a variety of what the audit chief calls "flakes" are attracted to the operation. In this case, for example, intelligence sources reported that two different Mafia families were developing nominees as investors who could pass a superficial investigation. Control of a Las Vegas casino is apparently prized by Mafia families.

While pressure was being put on the board chairman to recommend that commission members sign an emergency order for investment, he was taking his time. He was not really opposed to declaring that an emergency existed but was merely exercising prudence: he wanted in his own mind to be "damned sure" an emergency actually existed. An emergency, he feared, might be created as a device to introduce equity holders into a casino who would not normally qualify for licensing. Once entrenched, they would prove hard to dislodge.

He wanted documentation and turned to the Audit Division to determine if the Parisien did indeed have cash-flow problems serious enough to demand that an emergency order be issued. A team of auditors worked all night and drew up a financial report attesting to the seriousness of the Parisien's cash-flow problems.

After reading the auditors' dismal findings, the board chairman felt he should recommend issuance of an emergency participation order.

One of the first to come in under the order were a couple of motel owning brothers, "Ted" and "Red Mahmoud." The Mahmoud brothers agreed to form a group of investors, who would raise $7 million in half-million-dollar increments. In addition to Mafia families, various well-to-do people, ranging from businessmen to movie producers, apparently would like to own a share of a well-known Las Vegas casino. For those who are wealthy, with high cash income, such an investment offers considerable tax advantages, as well as the possibility of being treated like an owner, with an owner's considerable perquisites. In this case, there were discussions of involving investors with as little as $100,000. This may seem like a sizable sum, but it is not in these circumstances.

As ownership equity is dispersed, particularly under an emergency order where full licensing is precluded, the possibilities of control diminish. In short, the more "owners," the less the possibility of control. Besides, even if the investor is clearly not an organized crime figure or nominee, he or she will not have undergone the education the licensing process normally provides. Ordinarily, the licensee or applicant is respectful of the authorities: he or she needs their approval, not they his or hers. But when an individual gains entry through an emergency order, he or she realizes that the shoe is on the other foot — in a sense the authorities become supplicants.

The situation would not be so serious if the emergency order worked quickly to restore profitability and cash flow. In the case of the Parisien, the new infusions of cash were soon spent, and eventually the casino was once again threatened with closure. Indeed, one Saturday night the commissioners finally signed an order for closure which they gave to one of their number, acting as representative. He and the auditors counted the cash in the cage, and found approximately $250,000, which eventually was reduced to $210,000. (Sometimes the players win.)

Although the authorities were finally resigned to closing the place down, they engaged in some extraordinary activities to keep it open. For example, one of the assets of the cage was a check, made out to cash, drawn by a gambler whose check was known to be good. A casino host of questionable character — he was then under a federal indictment — was permitted to take the check in return for $40,000 in cash, which he happened to have, and offered to exchange for the check to help keep the casino operating. Furthermore, the commissioner permitted the casino to write a check to another casino for $50,000 which it didn't have — until Monday. The casino was saved by two factors: the house edge ultimately prevailed during the heavy weekend play, and a new investor, a California real estate operator, was coming in with a $2 million investment on Monday.

11

When Monday arrived, the commissioner, the audit chief, two senior agents, and I went to meet the real estate speculator in Red Mahmoud's offices at the Parisien. The speculator enjoyed a reputation for being eccentric, obnoxious, and very rich — reportedly worth between $100 and $200 million. He more than lived up to his reputation. A heavy-set man, thick in the jowls, with beady eyes, his manner was authoritative. What was remarkable was his personality — energetic, explosive, and vulgar. Referring to the previous owner of the Parisien, he shouted: "Take this down, Red. I'm going to cut that cocksucker's balls off. We're going to get that cocksucker." And so forth for nearly two hours.

The commissioner was at once appalled, firm — and conciliatory. He knew how badly the Parisien — and by implication, the state of Nevada — needed the speculator's $2 million, real money, on deposit at a local bank. He therefore humored the man, who strongly hinted that this investment would be the first in a long-range plan to buy gaming property in Las Vegas — provided the state wanted him. The commissioner — a capable lawyer — managed nicely to convey social acceptance without making legally committing statements, other than to indicate approval of the $2 million loan on an emergency status.

For a time, the money kept the club operating, and also helped to settle a battle between two factions for control of the club. The auditors learned that one of the factions — perhaps both — were backed in part by money attributed to known underworld figures. They were not permitted to gain control. Eventually, the $2 million was returned to the speculator, who managed for several months to offend nearly everybody at the club, including Mahmoud, with his antics. Such may be the qualities of emergency investors.

But even a couple of years later, no one in power at the management level had been able to resolve the dilemma of altering the social and economic character of the hotel or financing the cost of expanding the casino and the number of rooms. The frustrations felt by management were shared by the authorities, who felt a responsibility for keeping the hotel going on a sound fiscal basis, and irritation at management for its seeming ineptitude. Even the hotel's lawyer developed a reputation for inefficiency.

The auditors were continually checking the books, the cage, projections for future revenue. So much traffic occurred between the Parisien and the Audit Division that the commission chairman once threatened, jokingly but out of serious exasperation, to charge Mr. Mahmoud for the shoe leather and tires worn out by the auditors in their trips to his hotel.

Eventually, the hotel managed to survive by attracting as principal stockholder an extremely wealthy and somewhat eccentric investor, whose capital declined substantially as a result of the investment. Still, someone worth $40 to $50 million can apparently afford to lose $10 or $15 million without a substantial change in life-style — and less than a significant impact upon casino operations.

19

High Finance
and Hidden Interests

EVEN THE MOST SUCCESSFUL HOTELS REQUIRE EXPANSION AND REFUR-
bishing. The occupancy rate of the newest and biggest hotels is
high, but only because these hotels can present the most elegantly
furnished rooms, the fanciest and most varied restaurants, the
best service, the most sought-after entertainers. All of this costs
hard-to-get capital. The problem is how to obtain it from acceptable
lenders.

It is hard to say whether gambling is, from a financial point of
view, actually more precarious than other businesses. While other
industries have experienced serious declines during periods of recession, the gambling industry has managed to more than hold
its own. During the 1970s recession, Nevada gross gaming revenues
increased by around 15 percent annually. Some of the major publicly traded corporations holding properties inside and outside of
Nevada, such as Del Webb, Hilton, Hyatt and MGM, consider
their Nevada properties to be their prime investments. Gambling
is a tricky business, but it can be very profitable indeed.

Nevertheless, gambling tends to be as much a pariah industry in the world of business and of finance as it is in other ways. I once had a long discussion with a colleague, a dean of the University of California School of Business Administration, about why the financial community is reluctant to make loans to the gambling industry. He carried the question to some banker friends, one of whom introduced nonpecuniary considerations into the conversation. "So far as I'm concerned," replied the banker, "gambling is simply immoral. Under no circumstances—even at 30 percent interest—would I approve a loan to a gambling casino." This statement is supported by the experience of the gambling industry, which has on the whole found it difficult to obtain capital financing from conventional institutional lenders.[1]

2

A pariah industry attracts a pariah lender. Such has been the relationship between the Nevada gambling industry and James R. Hoffa's creation, the much criticized, much investigated Teamsters Central States, Southeast, and Southwest Areas Pension Funds. At an early stage of this study, in 1974, I attended a private meeting of the gaming commissioners to discuss the impact of the fund.

The commissioners were clearly worried about the impact of this lender on the future of the industry. By 1974, under the management of Hoffa and his successors, the fund held 56.1 percent of all loans to Clark County (Las Vegas) casinos grossing annually more than $96 million.[2] (By 1978, out of more than $1.5 billion in assets, the fund had more than $247 million invested in Nevada casinos.)[3] Although there was considerable discussion, and wringing of hands, nothing came of it except deep reservations —the power of a major lender had already exerted itself. The relationship had reached a stage where a public attack on the Teamsters Central States Pension Fund constituted a public attack on the gaming industry.

Paradoxically, because of its association with the Nevada gambling industry, the reputation of the Teamsters Central States Pension Fund has diminished, while the reputation of the Nevada gambling industry has declined as a result of its association with the pension fund. Although at first analysis, this might appear to represent a process of circular stigmatization, the attacks suggest a construct that holds together both as an analytical description of the process and as a serious indictment of the relationship.

The construct contains six principal elements, joined as follows: (1) the pension fund's investment policy; (2) coupled with organized crime domination of Teamsters Union locals nominating trustees to the fund; (3) generated kickbacks to those controlling the fund; (4) who in turn controlled casino management to permit kickbacks involving (5) skimming and embezzlement of casino revenues (6) deposited with organized crime families who influenced the nominations of the trustees. Not all of these elements can be proved with equally strong evidence, but the construct does organize the various indictments and allegations that have been made separately about the gaming industry and the fund.

Let us examine the elements of the construct somewhat more closely since, during the course of this study, much of the special investigative activity of the Audit Division as well as the concerns of the board and commission involved casinos holding pension fund loans.

3

Pensions plans for workers began during the closing years of the Second World War, principally in the garment trades unions, the electrical unions, and, most notably, the United Mine Workers Union under John L. Lewis. The next major expansion was in the steel industry, which struck in 1949 for a $100 monthly pension for workers over 65 with 25 years of service. Other unions followed, with similar plans, the biggest being the United Automobile Workers. During this flurry of activity, Jimmy Hoffa and the Teamsters were doing nothing about pensions for workers. Hoffa did not negotiate his first pension plan until 1955, more than a decade after other unions had started theirs.

Still, other unions had invested their pension fund capital very cautiously; in retrospect too cautiously. For example, the garment trade trustees refused to turn the money over to banks for fear the resulting investments would prove too speculative. They invested instead in government bonds. The United Mine Workers were even more conservative, perhaps irrationally so. In 1962, 40 percent of the reserves were kept in cash.

In contrast, Hoffa was convinced he could outperform professional bankers and investors, and engaged, in 1956, in a bitter struggle to permit direct investments in shopping center developments, racetracks and Nevada hotel-casinos. These were the sorts of investments that easily accommodated themselves to infiltration by organized crime. Whether the fund's flamboyant investment policies paid off — corruption aside — has never been entirely clear.[4] By 1974, while other pension funds held 1.8 percent of their assets in mortgages, 58.3 percent of the Teamsters Central States Pension Fund's assets were mortgages, many of which had eventually to be renegotiated.[5] In any event, the policy of allowing the trustees, instead of professional investors, to select loans resulted in questionable loans being made from the very beginning.

For example, the first investment commitment made directly by the fund's trustees was for a 10-year, 6-percent, $1 million mortgage to the Cleveland Raceways. Robert Kennedy challenged the prudence of this investment and eventually the borrower terminated the relationship as a result of the publicity. Economists Ralph and Estelle James, who completed the most intensive study of Hoffa and the pension fund, comment: ". . . even a racetrack could be hurt by the social opprobrium which became an unintended but intrinsic aspect of a Teamsters loan."[6]

Although this was the first commitment, it was not Hoffa's preferred initial investment. He had actually wanted to purchase the Sands Hotel in Las Vegas, and the trustees passed a motion to purchase. But, much to Hoffa's consternation, the deal fell through. At the time, the fund lacked the cash to purchase, and there was also a move to diversify.

From the beginning, Hoffa dominated the union trustees on the fund. By threatening selective strikes, Hoffa broke the resistance of management trustees, and assumed control in 1955. During the ensuing 20 years, the fund became ridden with scandal and was a favorite target of journalists.

In 1967, Hoffa lost control of the fund and of the Teamsters Union presidency after he was imprisoned on charges of helping to swindle $2 million from the Central States fund.[7] Hoffa disappeared in August 1975. Those responsible were allegedly organized crime figures threatened by a Hoffa campaign to resume control over the union.[8] In his autobiography, published one month after his disappearance, Hoffa charged his successor, Frank Fitzsimmons, with "letting known racketeers into the Teamsters" and "making vast loans . . . to known mobsters."[9]

Jim Drinkhall, investigative editor of *Overdrive*, the largest-selling magazine in the United States for long-distance truckers, described the fund as "The Bankroll for the Mafia" in an article in July 1972, one of a lengthy series pointing up improprieties and criminal conduct. Drinkhall, who was later to become the *Wall Street Journal's* specialist on union corruption, talks of the "long standing Pension Fund rule of kickbacks being no less than 10% of the total of the loan."[10] In 1975, *Newsweek* engaged in an intensive journalistic investigation of the fund, and *Newsweek* reporter Tom Joyce concluded that "the mob's hold on the Teamsters and its finances is as strong these days as it was during the McClellan investigation eighteen years ago."[11]

In particular, the career of Allen Dorfman, whom Drinkhall calls the link between organized crime and the fund, and perhaps its most influential loan arranger, supports these allegations. Dorfman entered prison on March 28, 1973, and served 8 months following his conviction for a kickback involving a fund loan. He was convicted of extorting a $55,000 fee from a textile manufacturer who wanted to borrow $1.5 million.[12] In 1974, Dorfman was again indicted, along with others, on charges of defrauding the pension fund. All were acquitted after a key government witness was killed by gunmen wearing ski masks.[13] Amalgamated Insurance Agency Services, Inc. and other Dorfman-controlled companies continued, despite Dorfman's legal troubles, to process insurance claims generated by the pension and health and welfare funds.[14]

His successor and protégé, Alvin Baron, became the fund's top consultant and chief loan supervisor after Dorfman was convicted in 1972. In November 1976, Baron was indicted by a federal grand jury in Chicago on charges of taking a $200,000 kickback from a California businessman who sought a $1.3 million loan from the pension fund.[15]

On June 26, 1976, the Internal Revenue Service, citing mismanagement and questionable loan practices, revoked the pension fund's tax-exempt status, retroactive to January 31, 1965.[16] This action threatened to render the fund liable for millions of dollars in taxes on its earnings back to 1965. Employers, the sole contributors to the fund, would not be permitted to deduct contributions on federal income tax returns.[17] The loss of tax-exempt status would prove disastrous. The fund was also under investigation by the Justice and Labor Departments, which found many instances of kickbacks and loans to favored Teamsters businesses in real estate and gambling.[18] In 1972, an officer of Bally Manufacturing Corporation gave stock worth almost $100,000 to members of the family of William Presser—a vice-president of the union and reportedly the most influential trustee of the Teamsters Central States Pension Fund after Hoffa resigned. Eighteen months later, Bally was awarded a $12 million loan.[19]

The revocation of tax-exempt status was part of a concerted federal effort to clean up the fund. The federal government made a deal: In return for restoring the fund's tax-exempt status, 11 of the 16 members of the fund's board of directors—trustees nominated by union locals—had to resign.[20] The Labor Department finally even forced the resignation of Teamsters President Frank Fitzsimmons from the fund's board of directors. Yet by May 1978, the fund's trustees had repudiated the agreement with the Labor Department. The repudiation occurred approximately one month after the trustees had fired Dan Shannon, reform executive director of both the pension and health and welfare funds. Shannon reportedly was fired because of his criticism of Allen Dorfman before a Senate committee and his efforts to sever health and welfare fund ties with Dorfman.[21]

During the earlier barrage of federal pressure, the fund had presumably frozen loans to gambling casinos. Still, one major casino (which I shall call "Alexander's Nugget") was able to obtain such a loan through a complex financial arrangement which, coupled with the board and commission's response to it, had several high-ranking staff members shaking their heads in dismay. It was up to the Audit Division to investigate their subterfuge.

4

In the fall of 1976, the "Cordoba" Hotel filed a form required by the gaming authorities whenever a loan has been received. The form was routinely routed to the Audit Division, since the division is responsible for investigating the sources of funds loaned to those already licensed. According to the form, the Cordoba Hotel had received the loan from its parent, publicly traded corporation, Alexander's Empire, which held as the crown jewel of its corporate holdings the famous Strip hotel, Alexander's Nugget. There was no form filed for a loan to Alexander's Nugget.

The auditors asked for more information regarding the source of funds for the loan. They were told, in writing, that Alexander's Empire had received the money from a sale/leaseback agreement relative to its "Honeymoon" Hotel properties in the Adirondack mountains. After paying off the mortgages, the letter stated, Alexander's Empire received a net income of $12,345,678.52. Alexander's Empire loaned $2 million to its subsidiary, Cordoba Hotel, which used most of it to pay off a demand note due a local bank. The remainder of the money would eventually be used to expand Alexander's Nugget.

The auditors still were not satisfied, and pressed for further information. Who had purchased the Honeymoon Hotel? Was the buyer also the lessor? They received a written response saying that the buyer and the lessor were "one and the same." The buyer-lessor was an Arizona partnership called "Sunny Associates." Sunny's address was given as a posh health resort in Phoenix.

The auditors became suspicious, since the letter did not mention the names of the partners in Sunny Associates; and learned—from a Phoenix law enforcement agency—that the owner of the resort was a man named "Seymour Silber."

Silber is a Phoenix accountant on whom the gaming board and other law enforcement agencies maintain full and damaging files. For example, during a trial for income tax evasion in 1969, the FBI was forced to admit that in 1963 it had bugged Silber's office. According to the agent's testimony, Silber was being bugged not because of tax evasion, but because of his meetings with top mobsters, and his possible knowledge of skimming operations at Las Vegas casinos. These buggings, plus others conducted by authorities outside the United States, reveal conversations where Silber discusses Meyer Lansky's affairs and state of health.

The audit chief also has access to an informant, a former underworld figure who now lives under an assumed name and a new identity. This informant gave the audit chief a sworn statement saying it was a well-known underworld fact that dealing with Silber was the same as dealing with Lansky; and that he personally had seen the two of them "walking together often."

A senior audit agent was sent to interview Silber. When he returned he described Silber as polite and quite articulate in defending the transaction with Alexander's Empire. Silber denied that Lansky had any interest in the transaction. Still, from the gaming board's viewpoint, allegations about Silber's reputation cast doubt upon him as a reputable lender or business associate. On balance, he seemed just the sort of man the gaming authorities wanted to prevent from having an interest in Las Vegas gambling.

What made matters worse—much worse—was that the president of Alexander's Empire had engaged in a similar deal with Silber a few years earlier, and had been warned not to have any further business associations with him.

Both deals were marvels of financial complexity. They were also sufficiently ambiguous, as a result of their complexity, to permit several interpretations of meaning and intent. No one doubted that Alexander's Nugget could profitably employ capital for expansion. The question was, as my former political science professor and colleague Harold Laswell might have expressed it: "Who got what from whom with what effect?"

5

It turned out that the partnership, Sunny Associates, was formed expressly to acquire the Honeymoon Hotel from Alexander's Empire, Inc. About 18 days after it was formed, Sunny received a commitment letter from the Teamsters Central States Pension Fund to loan $16 million for the purchase and leaseback of the Honeymoon Hotel. Sunny had three partners, Silber and the sons of another questionable figure, a former president of a Las Vegas hotel, who pleaded guilty and served four months for conspiring to conceal and distribute $36 million in unreported income—skimming—from the hotel's casino. Meyer Lansky was indicted as a coconspirator in the case. (As discussed earlier, Lansky never came to trial, and his indictment was eventually dismissed in a Las Vegas federal court.)

Silber and his friend's sons were already linked in a corporation we shall call Silco. The commitment letter required (1) that Silco guarantee the loan; (2) that Alexander's guarantee the loan; and (3) that the Sunny partnership guarantee the loan.

Unlike corporate stockholders, partners are personally liable for loans to their partnership. Thus, in defense of the loan the Teamsters fund could argue that by making the loan through Silber and his associates, the loan was better protected than it would have been had it been made directly to Alexander's Empire, particularly since the auditors learned that Silber's net worth was around $40 million.

In opposition to the loan, it could be argued that by involving Silco, the fund could scarcely deny making a loan to the sons of a Lansky associate convicted of skimming, whatever the reality of Silber's relationship to Lansky. A pension fund spokesman, part of the new administration, said that the present administration did not know whether those who had made the loan to Mr. Silber had known of his reputed association with Mr. Lansky.

In any case, Silber apparently reaped a handsome windfall from the loan, deriving mainly from the difference between the monthly mortgage payments from Silber to the fund, and the monthly lease payments from Alexander's to Silber. (Silber was required to pay $137,000 per month over 20 years, while Alexander's rent was $188,000 monthly.) In addition, Alexander's agreed to spend $2 million for new construction. Finally, at the end of 20 years, Silber would own the property. The auditors conservatively estimated its worth then at its current $15 million value. If the $15 million sales proceeds received by Alexander's are subtracted, Silber would net a cash flow of $29,012,000 over 20 years.

Since, however, Silber would not receive this cash flow all at once, but over 20 years, the auditors discounted the future cash inflow at the prevailing 9 percent interest rate. By this calculation, they figured, Silber was to receive a present benefit of more than $10 million—simply as a result of the pension fund loan being channeled through him. The auditors thought that this was a pay-off — possibly for a hidden interest by Lansky — to Alexander's Nugget, which had a checkered history.

Yet Alexander's could, and did, argue that the loan was a legitimate business deal, and not a payoff to a hidden interest. Alexander's made three basic arguments. First, they argued, by channeling the loan through Silber and associates it was backed up by Alexander's Nevada properties, plus the Honeymoon Hotel, plus the personal liability of Silber and associates. Without such additional protection, the fund could not have made yet another loan to a Nevada gambling casino.

Second, Alexander's argued that conventional financing, in the form of $15 million worth of mortgage loans to the Honeymoon Hotel, was simply unavailable. A couple of banks had been tried, and had turned down the proposal.

Third, the loan was said to present tax advantages to Alexander's. Had the loan been secured as a mortgage, only interest would have been tax deductible. But under a lease plan, the entire payment was deductible. The auditors calculated, however, that the difference between the mortgage plan and the lease plan over the entire 20-year period amounted only to a negligible advantage. They concluded that the lease plan was in fact costing Alexander's Empire more than $50,000 per month — again adding up to a present-value windfall to Silber of more than $10 million.

While all this was being uncovered, secrecy and intrigue prevailed on the board. A major property was involved in what appeared to be a serious scandal that would make headlines. I became aware of what was happening only because I was at the time working closely with the senior auditors who were investigating the case. They themselves were trying to figure out whether this was a legitimate deal, or a shrewdly conceived arrangement for paying off a hidden interest.

Finally, in a confidential report, the Audit Division concluded that the repeated involvement of Alexander's Empire with Mr. Silber, in spite of at least two prior board and commission warnings, constituted conduct reflecting discredit upon the state of Nevada in violation of the standards contemplated by Gaming Control Board Regulation 5.011, which states general grounds for disciplinary action against a licensee.

The commission did not follow this recommendation for disciplinary action, and treated the entire matter with unusual concern for privacy. Confidentiality statutes were invoked, although there seemed scarcely any need for them, since loans of this size are normally treated publicly. What happened? Apparently, confidentiality prevailed not primarily because of financial considerations, but because the entire situation was a source of embarrassment and discomfort to the higher control authorities. Perhaps other considerations were operating, unknown to this writer. In any event, it seemed a strange piece of business.

6

The loan suggested several weak links in the gaming control structure. Nevada authorities had prided themselves on how well the publicly traded corporation device worked. Here, it backfired. The loan reported to the gaming authorities was from a public corporation to a subsidiary it had been carrying for years. Had the Audit Division not investigated that loan — and it need not have — the gaming authorities might well have remained unaware of the loan between the publicly traded corporation and the Teamsters Central States Pension Fund. (The parent company was not required to report loans, only the operating company.)

The commission did require that in the future, Alexander's Empire report its loans as if it were an operating company. (One highly placed commission representative acknowledged that, since Alexander's Empire was not required to cancel the agreement, this was a case of locking the barn door after the horse had escaped.)

It is understandable that the commission was not overly interested in publicizing the fact that one of Nevada's major casinos — presumably cleansed of prior organized crime influence — was accepting loans through an intermediary regarded by federal and state law enforcement officials to be a close associate of Meyer Lansky. Besides, things needed to be said in private that could not be said in public: That a key official of both the publicly traded parent corporation and the closely held Nevada one had previously been warned by the board chairman not to have any further business dealings with Mr. Silber, and was even still involved with Silber in a personal business venture.

An enterprising reporter, Al Delugach, who was assigned to report on gambling's financial affairs for the *Los Angeles Times*, pressed the matter and did force public disclosure of the outlines of the transaction, plus the earlier deal between Alexander's Empire and the same questionable parties. No attempt was made formally to dislodge the official who negotiated the loan after ignoring prior warnings not to do so. Nor was an attempt made to fine the operating company for its part in the transaction, even though it was the primary beneficiary of the transaction.

The treatment of this loan suggests the weakness of gaming control in the face of a major economic and political challenge. Higher authorities find themselves locked into a dilemma when a prestigious casino appears to engage in hanky-panky. Gaming control is based on the theory that state regulation will handle problems as they arise. Small problems in Nevada are handled rather well. But when major problems arise, the authorities are reluctant to take action, especially public action, in part because public action only compounds the problem of attracting legitimate sources of capital to support industrial expansion.

In this respect, almost any big scandal reflects badly on the financial image and attractiveness of legal casino gambling. In this case, for reasons that were never quite clear, the board and commission not only took light disciplinary action—really a warning about future conduct—but also sought to protect the reputation of the casino as much as possible.

7

The Teamsters loan surfaced in March 1976, approximately two years after I began this study. Naturally, a central and pressing question about gaming control in Nevada was the role of organized crime; particularly whether federal pressures of the 1960s leading to the full development of the contemporary control structure had in fact severed organized crime's connections with Nevada gaming.

As the facts about this loan developed, I realized how important it was to maintain an analytical separation among three discrete issues: one was the honesty of those working within the control agency; a second was how the combined pressure of the Nevada economy, of social relationships between higher agency authorities and industry executives, and of political pressures within the state undermined the overall capacity of the agency to control; and a third was the intractability of the enterprise itself—that the gambling business is particularly and inevitably vulnerable to fraudulent schemes.

The loan pointed to answers in all three areas: The loan showed that certain portions of the agency, particularly the Audit Division, were capable of aggressive intelligence and hard analysis. It also showed that the higher authorities, the board and commission, were institutionally more vulnerable than the agents who worked for them. As in many agencies, so here, the higher authorities ultimately come to represent the interests of the industry, in part because they tend to identify with the industry and give special understanding to its definition of needs and expectations; and in part because the gaming industry is to Nevada what General Motors would like to think it is to America. What's good for gambling, in other words, is thought to be good for Nevada.

Finally, the loan suggested that one reason organized crime influence seems to hang on in Nevada is because opportunities for deception abound at every level of the business. The organized crime influence is seldom apparent, and is virtually never seen on the surface of everyday casino operations. But every once in a while it surfaces, particularly, it seems, in hotels with Teamsters Central States Pension Fund connections.

20

The Ambivalence of Control

IN JANUARY 1976, INFORMATION BEGAN TO TRICKLE IN TO THE HEAD
of the Audit Division from both street and intelligence contacts,
that theft of slot machine revenues involving employees was
occurring at the "Flagship" Hotel and possibly other hotels in the
same chain. (This group of hotels enjoyed nearly $100 million in
Teamsters fund loans.) The audit chief favored moving hard and
quickly on the information.

At the time, two board members believed that the Audit Division had overextended itself in the area of special investigations,
and was falling embarrassingly behind in making standard
revenue-oriented audit investigations mandated by statute. Because
of time constraints the auditors were forced to check mainly for
error, not fraud. Despite protestations by its chief, the Audit
Division was required by the board to cut back sharply on special
investigations, and to perform some 50 audits (that might exceed
the three-year statute of limitations on collecting-error-caused
failure to pay taxes.) Although the audit chief called attention to
information on embezzlement at the Flagship Hotel, the board
insisted that the statutorily mandated audits be completed.

The board's order of priorities was partly attributable to the continuing controversy surrounding investigations and policing activities of the Audit Division. In any event, it was not until the revenue-oriented audits were completed that the Audit Division was able to turn attention to the reported problems of slot revenue embezzlement. When agents became available the audit chief dispatched some to look into the reports. One agent was a former big-city police detective who had been hired by the Audit Division to work with the auditors in uncovering theft. At the time, the audit chief figured that a police-trained presence would enlarge the capacity of the division to deal with major sorts of crookedness, especially involving organized crime.

The trained detective and an auditor were sent to the "Peninsula" Hotel — part of the chain — to make a surprise investigation of the so-called "hard count" of slot machine revenue. The manager of the slot machine operation for the four hotels in the chain convinced the two agents that it was not possible to check on the accuracy of the count in the usual way, i.e., to reconcile the wrapped coin with the count sheet. He convinced the agents that certain transactions had already occurred in the cage to account for any discrepancies they might find between the amount of wrapped coin present and the amount accounted for.

The agents did not pursue the matter, but the audit chief was not satisfied with the explanation, and felt that the agents might have been duped. Moreover, he felt that the visit had probably proved counterproductive because it might well have alerted conspirators to the suspicions of the authorities.

Information pointing to slot revenue embezzlement continued to drift in. The audit chief set up another surprise investigation, this time at the Flagship Hotel. A group of auditors presumably examined and counted appropriate items in all the slot booths, but arrived at the count room too late: all the coin had already been counted and removed. The auditors simply had used up too much time counting everything in sight on the casino floor and thereby missed one of the key artifacts in the scheme to defraud. Scams are oftentimes like magic tricks. Once you discover the deceptive device, you wonder how you could ever have been fooled. But until you actually know how it works, the deception is invisible.

While the auditors had been unsuccessfully making surprise visits, the Law Enforcement Division also had been independently observing the Flagship slot department. They had learned that a conspiracy had been formed to increase reported jackpot sizes. Thus, for example, if a player won a $200 jackpot, the casino employees would give the player the $200, and with the collusion of a couple of minor executives would record the jackpot as $400 or $500, and pocket the difference. The slot machine manager was evidently so busy with his own fraudulent schemes that he had eased up on controlling those subordinate to him.

During the course of their investigation, law enforcement agents learned from employees about a so-called "special fund" that was being used to supply the slot booths with coin money. One senior law enforcement agent in particular maintained good and close relations with the audit chief. The agent checked with him to inquire whether he knew anything about this mysterious fund. The audit chief reviewed the results of the surprise visit taken only a few weeks earlier, and found that no mention had been made of such a fund. He became suspicious, even though he thought it might merely have been an oversight. In any event, he asked if he could talk with the employees.

They described a curious, but not necessarily illegal, practice. Every day, they said, the slot machine manager or his assistant would deposit quarters into an auxiliary booth. The coin in the booth would be used to supply quarters to other booths when they ran out of change. The Flagship Hotel maintained a huge, busy, high-revenue slot machine operation, one of the largest in Nevada. Attendants had been told that the auxiliary coin saved trips to the cage, which, because of its distance from the slot machine operation, made it difficult to renew the coin supply readily.

Furthermore, those manning the booths were told that when they accumulated currency of various denominations, as they normally would in exchange for coin to play the machines, they should take this assorted currency and exchange it at the cage for $100 bills. Then they were to "buy" auxiliary quarters from the booth with these bills. These instructions would not necessarily arouse suspicion since, under them, slot machine personnel avoided trips to the cage to buy quarters. Instead, they carried only bills, and converted these into neat packages of $100 bills — much easier to count than coins. The bills were placed in an envelope, then dropped into a slot attached to the rear wall of the booth containing the auxiliary coin. The $100 bills were picked up daily by the slot machine manager and his assistant, who, it was assumed, were properly incorporating them into casino revenues.

The audit chief and the law enforcement agent returned to the office, and mulled over the report. They were deeply suspicious, but still hadn't figured out what was happening. Finally, it ocurred to the audit chief that somehow coins were being under-counted, and removed to the booth.

2

If this were a scam, and had been occurring over a long period of time, more than a year, possibly millions of dollars were involved. The board members were in Carson City for the monthly meeting. Like other police I have observed in major enforcement efforts, the audit chief decided that, for security reasons, he would play this investigation close to the vest, and not tell anyone about his suspicion. At the moment, he trusted only one person outside his division — the law enforcement senior agent already working on the investigation. He put together a team of four audit agents for a trip to the Flagship Hotel in search of a special bank to sell quarters.

When they arrived at the Flagship, they sought out the shift boss who denied knowledge of a "special fund." His denial seemed genuine, and almost persuaded them to leave. Nevertheless, they decided to bluff their way with the slot machine manager. The audit chief telephoned him, and asked for the key to the "special fund" — the audit chief did not know exactly what terminology was used to describe this change booth. The manager hemmed and hawed, asked for a more complete description and finally said, "Oh, you mean the 'auxiliary bank.' I'll be right down."

When he returned, he led the agents to a locked change booth, and opened it. Inside was $7,000 in neatly wrapped quarters. There was also a record sheet in the booth showing that $10,000 in quarters had been deposited at the beginning of the shift. On the back wall of the booth was a small locked drawer with a slot in it. Given the combination of the record sheet and the $7,000 remaining, there should have been $3,000 in currency in the locked drawer. Nobody present had a key to that drawer. The only one who did, the investigators were told, was the coin room manager.

When several Gaming Control Board agents or auditors begin asking direct questions in a casino, word spreads very quickly. In this case, the audit chief told the slot machine manager to call the coin room manager. "I told him not to tip anybody off," said the audit chief, "but later on we learned that calls began flying all over the place. All over the state, as a matter of fact — to lawyers, to Gaming Control Board members. All hell was breaking loose. We were sitting on $10,000 in stolen coin that nobody could account for. It turned out, in fact, that that was about the average day's take for more than one and a half years — and this was at only one of the four casinos."

The coin room manager lived about one mile from the hotel, but he did not hurry over. In the meantime, the audit chief began checking against possible defenses. He checked out the cage to determine whether an "auxiliary bank" account existed there. It did not. He called the comptroller of the casino, himself an accountant, and asked whether an account existed in the general ledger that might explain the presence of the auxiliary bank. The comptroller could provide no explanation. Shift bosses were interrogated. The assistant treasurer was questioned. Little by little the auditors were able to piece together how the auxiliary bank operated on the casino floor, and who operated it there..

One of the operators was apparently the coin room manager, whom others had observed unlocking the drop box holding the currency. When he failed to show up, audit agents telephoned his house and talked with his wife, telling her that the house was under surveillance. He finally arrived at the casino around 5 A.M., approximately eight hours after he had first been called. He spoke briefly, denying knowledge of a key, an auxiliary bank, or a drawer. He refused to discuss the matter further without an attorney, and requested his 5th Amendment rights. So far as the auditors were concerned, the coin room manager appeared to bear some responsibility for embezzling from the casino.

The other keyholder had briefly been the slot machine manager for the four casinos, but he had a minor criminal record, plus a reputation as a slot thief. The board had earlier forced him out of that position by threatening to bring him up for licensing. An arrangement was made to place him in a position not requiring licensing, as something less than a "key employee." He was made assistant to the treasurer of the publicly traded corporation in charge of casino construction, provided he would no longer have anything to do with the day-to-day slot machine operation. News of the auditors' presence and questions soon reached him at the home of a casino executive, where he was visiting. His reaction to the events was more dramatic.

He never showed up at the casino. The board learned from law enforcement contacts that he had fled to and was residing in Mexico. About a year after his disappearance, his son visited him there and returned to Las Vegas. Several days after returning, the son was found dead in his own bed. His head was described as "crushed." It was not clear whether the motive for the murder was anger at the father for not having turned over the proceeds of the embezzlement as he was supposed to or anger at the son for having double-crossed somebody on his own. In any event, the father was clearly guilty of embezzlement. The remaining questions were: How did he do it, and who were his accomplices?

3

The first question was easier to answer than the second. The Audit Division engaged in a massive investigation, not only because the case was unusually significant, but also because there was slight physical evidence to rely upon. To find out who were the conspirators and to build a case against them, the auditors were forced to rely upon testimony from casino employees who for the most part had not been involved in the conspiracy, who had observed only discrete portions of it, and who had thought that what they had been seeing was lawful.

The investigation was meticulously organized around the outlines of the scam. Its details were complicated but the principles were simple enough: find a way to siphon off thousands of dollars worth of coins in the count room; and find a method — the "auxiliary bank" — for converting those coins into high denomination currency for ease of transportability. No one, not even a slot machine manager, can easily carry $10,000 worth of quarters daily out of a casino without being noticed. Even if he could, they would eventually prove too bulky and visible for interstate transportation. But $100 bills are just right, and the casino cage offers a perfect setting for the transformation.

The scam was built around the basic method of accounting for coins in the count room. First, the coins are weighed, and converted by the scale to a dollar amount, then wrapped. The wrapped coin is counted and totaled. This total is then compared to the weight. Four, or perhaps more, methods can be employed to undermine checking procedures. One is to record a false weight. A second is not to weigh, but to claim the weighing has been accomplished, and to dissuade — by threat or implied threat — an independent checker from the accounting department from checking the wrapped coin for comparison with the weight count. A third is romantically to seduce an independent checker, who thus loses independence. Finally, if one can figure out a way to adjust the scales so that the wrapped coin is underweighed to show less value than is actually present — and to be able to hide the difference from the independent checker — the independent checker can be fooled. In this case, all of these methods were alleged, and all needed to be independently documented.

To accomplish this, the scam was broken down into 18 categories: drop procedures, transfer of coin to and from count room, count room procedures, weighing procedures, and so forth. The scam spanned four hotels. For the most part, innocent coin counters, booth cashiers, slot foremen, casino shift bosses, representatives of the casino's accounting department, scale repairmen, and others could be considered observers (even if they were unaware of the significance of their observations) and needed to be interviewed.

Altogether, more than 200 witnesses were interviewed, and some of the interviews lasted as long as five hours. I attended several of these sessions and can verify their thoroughness. All interviews were conducted, under oath, in a small interrogation room at the board offices. The interviews were recorded and later transcribed into 26 books, each about four inches thick.

Each book had to be examined for significant testimony. Employing dictating machines, the auditors would summarize what they thought might be pertinent information, and would list the name of the hotel involved, the subject matter of the testimony, the position of the witnesses in the hotel, the date of the testimony, and the page of the testimony. Some witnesses made similar statements regarding certain aspects of procedures, others offered varying or even contradictory information about the same procedures. Of course, witnesses were testifying to different periods of time, so that deviations did not necessarily indicate contradictory testimony, but rather a shift through time in procedures occurring in the count room or the casino floor.

It was easier to piece together the underlying scheme — the "trick" of underweighing and disposing of the embezzled coin through an auxiliary bank — than to determine precisely who was responsible for the scheme, how much actually was stolen, and who were the ultimate recipients of the stolen receipts (presumably hidden interests).

The process of determining how much was stolen was complicated and time-consuming. One methodology was worked out by the chairman of the University of California's Statistical Department, whom I recruited for the board.

Essentially, it involved estimating what the "hold" should be, based on the reel settings, plus the style of play of the social class of players in each of the casinos. Thus, the two basic variables were probability and play pattern. Actual hold percentages could be checked against those obtained before and after the scam was uncovered. The percentages varied from around 15 percent during the scam period to around 20 percent before and after. The auditors calculated, using the most conservative calculation method, that $5 million had been stolen. They believed that this figure grossly underestimated the actual amount stolen, but wanted to be as conservative as possible in a potential courtroom setting.

The auditors believed that they had enough direct evidence to indict eight or nine persons; specifically, the coin room and slot department managers at each of the hotels, plus the elusive assistant to the treasurer who had escaped to Mexico, plus a corporate executive, who they believed served as a buffer between higher management and the actual perpetrators of the scam. They also felt that enough circumstantial evidence existed to warrant administrative disciplinary action against higher executives and those with an equity interest. Most importantly, the auditors could only speculate about who ultimately received the proceeds of the theft. As is often true for police work aimed at sophisticated criminals — for example, drug importers — law enforcement authorities are able to find evidence to convict minor figures but not higher-ups.

One assumes that some of the loot went into the pockets of the perpetrators, although that is not a certainty, either. The auditors learned from a reliable informant that one of the perpetrators had been himself embezzling from the conspiracy, and was discovered by his co-conspirators. Several days later, four men pulled him out of a Las Vegas bar, took him outside, broke one of his legs, and inflicted assorted other injuries. Clearly, the conspirators were not cast from the same social cloth as the legendary embezzlers who abscond with funds from banks. If organized crime figures did not actually have an interest in this embezzlement, those who did were behaving like characters in a movie about organized crime. It was enough to give the audit chief a nightmare about someone slitting his throat while he was asleep.

4

Ordinarily, the idea of organized crime conveys an image, if not of Mafia families, then at least of the "rackets" — numbers, bookmaking, loansharking, drugs. And we are all familiar with racketeers because we have seen them portrayed in the movies by Edward G. Robinson and Marlon Brando and Al Pacino. The racketeers grew up in New York or Chicago. They are slum kids or the sons of slum kids who have climbed the American success ladder by providing alternate and illegal goods and services to an increasingly large and profitable American market. And when push comes to shove, they are capable of pushing and shoving harder, and of maiming and murdering. Not everybody who engages in questionable and deceptive enterprises in Las Vegas conforms to the stereotype of organized crime. The real-life distinction between organized crime and white collar crime is not so neat as a conceptual one might be.

If organized criminals are educated in the legendary school of hard knocks, white collar criminals are suburbanites, prepared for life and livelihood at Eastern prep schools and Ivy League colleges, where they are taught, presumably, to be gentlemen with moral scruples. A gentleman may be permitted to drive a hard bargain, but he assuredly should not break a leg to enforce it. And were he to trace his ancestry he would discover neither Kunta Kinte, Christopher Columbus, nor an obscure but highly respected Eastern European rabbi.

The white collar criminal's crimes are clean, perhaps even dignified. He, and others like himself — perhaps over martinis at the Yale Club — agree not to engage in what they perceive as cutthroat competition. The Justice Department might define the activity as a conspiracy in violation of the anti-trust laws artificially to raise prices; but the agreement is among gentlemen, and affects an abstraction called the consumer.

In Las Vegas we see the emergence of a new phenomenon, a product of the spectacular post–World War II growth of the so-called "sunbelt," especially of Southern California, but also of Texas, Arizona, New Mexico, Oklahoma, and even of Utah. The growth is haphazard, pell-mell, not uncontrolled, but not planned either. If it is anticipated, it is usually encouraged by culture and government. Several writers have argued that this growth has precipitated a power shift from the Eastern establishment to a newer breed of people with different values and perceptions, wheeler-dealers, promoters who were generating whole new cities with little regard for human and aesthetic consequences.[1] At their most effective — and therefore most dangerous — these promoters manage to combine the business acumen of the corporate Yankee with the bottom-line toughness of the slum kid.

5

As this study was nearing completion, the Audit Division investigated a characteristic "sunbelt promotion" which the Audit Division believed was intended to transfer and hide interests in a medium-sized Las Vegas casino. It is worth describing this promotion more closely to understand further the implications for the control system of trying to eliminate hidden interests in Nevada's pariah industry. Hidden interests are hard to prove. The proof that a third party played so major a role in the financing of a purchase as to make him a principal, is invariably circumstantial. "Board investigators," observed board member Bob Grossman, "are never handed written agreements which evidence the granting of an unlicensed equity interest to third parties."[2]

In 1977, a man whom I shall call "Peter Jones," who owned 20 percent of the stock in the corporation doing business as the "Fiesta" Hotel, sought to acquire the remaining 80 percent. The present holder was in a variety of financial and legal difficulties and wanted to sell. When Jones learned of his partner's interest in selling Jones wanted to buy badly, since the seller was willing to sell at a reasonable price, roughly $21,350,000. Jones's problem was where to obtain the financing to make the purchase, particularly the initial payment of $1¼ million.

Jones approached "Kent Smith," brother of a former high-ranking midwestern office-holder, but a man with a questionable reputation in business, who probably could not have qualified for licensing. Part of Smith's problem was his association with "Clement Wilson," a man who had been arrested for assault with a deadly weapon, and who had been convicted of embezzlement.

The gaming board investigators found that Smith and Wilson were very close. When Smith wanted to locate a "grandaddy shell corporation" he allegedly turned to Wilson to help him find one. A "shell corporation" is one that has already been publicly traded, or was traded prior to the Securities Act of 1933. Thus, the public trading of such a company's shares would at least be initially guaranteed by either its current trading status or by the "grandfathering provision" of the Securities Act. Thus, once such a "shell" is acquired, and a certified financial statement obtained, the stock of the resulting entity can be traded "over the counter," thereby creating a market value for the stock. This facilitates the acquisition, through stock trading, of other companies; and of loans.

The reason such a corporation is called a shell is that it presently lacks significant assets. To rectify this, and to create a respectable balance sheet, Smith approached and made a deal with another friend. The friend owned several high-rise apartment buildings that required variances on permits to be converted to condominiums. These buildings could provide assets for the shell's valuation. The friend was to receive substantial shares of stock of the newly formed corporation — call it ABC. A cooperative and reasonably distinguished CPA was found who would certify the financial statements of ABC, listing the value of the apartment houses at $17,427,000. The valuation was based on three appraisals contingent on the hardly likely assumption that ABC would be able to secure necessary variances, master plan changes, and so forth to convert apartment houses to condominiums. Through this transaction, ABC, a company with essentially no assets, was able to demonstrate a certified balance sheet showing total assets in excess of total liabilities (net worth) of more than $17 million. In the absence of the land deal, the shell corporation's assets would have amounted to $202,143.

Once a corporation possesses a seemingly respectable financial statement, it may well be able to secure a loan from a bank, using as collateral the inflated recorded values. That happened here, but it was only one of several factors arousing the skepticism of the gaming board's auditors. For as they investigated they discovered what they believed was a consistent and apparently logical pattern of conduct and events, involving deception of the gaming authorities, of minority shareholders of public corporations, and of financial institutions. This pattern seemed part of a plan between Jones, Smith, Wilson, and other questionable parties to acquire complete control of the Fiesta and to hide certain of these interests.

For example, the auditors discovered that while Smith was listed as the largest known stockholder of ABC, Wilson's compensation for finding the shell corporation was the right to retain all the "lost shares" he could find. At the time, 44 percent of ABC stock was unknown as to ownership, and Mr. Wilson was able to locate at least 11 percent.

After a while, Jones — the applicant — came to own 146,500 shares of ABC. To minimize the importance of his involvement with the company — with Smith and Wilson — he told the agents he figured the stock was worth only around $1,200. They were able, however, by checking other aspects of his financial background, to find that he had submitted a personal financial statement to a California bank valuing the shares at more than half a million dollars.

The agents also found that ABC had tried in various ways to secure financing for Jones to purchase the Fiesta. They discovered a memorandum planning a public stock offering through ABC to raise $22 million for purchase of the Fiesta. This plan was never carried out. The auditors believed that, given the background of Smith, Wilson, and some of the other major ABC stockholders, the group had feared the investigative potential of the SEC.

The ABC Corporation then engaged the services of a man I shall call "Arturo Dangeleo," a man who had been convicted of violations of securities laws and of fraud, and who was later to cooperate with the gaming authorities by testifying about the whole scheme. Dangeleo lived on the edge of the world of business and financial brokerage, of tax-shelter investments and business loans. Mostly, such brokers bring together lenders and borrowers, and profit from what can be quite substantial "finder's fees." Dangeleo led the group of finance-seekers to an elderly European broker who presumably had access to various sources of Arab oil money. The European broker guaranteed the loan if an initial $40,000 loan fee was advanced.

Financial brokerage is a bewildering world of trust and mistrust. The borrower pays the finder's fee up front because, if he did not, and the name of the lender were revealed, the borrower could presumably go directly to the lender and do the broker out of his fee. But in this international financial version of the old "Murphy game," the broker, having received the money, disappeared with it. The sunbelt promoters had been taken by an elderly European con man.

More important, from the gaming board's viewpoint, the auditors discovered that there had been five contributors to the $40,000 loan fee, including Smith and Wilson, as well as two others, former stockbrokers who had been booted out of their profession by the SEC. That these people would put up the loan fee strongly suggested that they intended to hold a hidden interest in the Fiesta Hotel.

6

The Audit Division was, ironically, most upset by what it found when the ABC group located a legitimate business proposition, the possibility of a controlling interest in a large Wyoming ranch then held by a major California bank as trustee for the estate of its former owner.

The ABC group was aware of how useful a legitimate business would be as a vehicle to obtain future bank financing. The problem was how to bootstrap themselves into a controlling interest in it. The Audit Division's report describes the process — with appropriate name changes.

Smith contacted Jones (the applicant) and proposed that Jones be a principal in the Wyoming purchase. At that time, according to Smith's plans, it was contemplated that a holding company called "Wyoming Ranch Holding Company" would be formed to buy Wyranch Corporation and that such holding company would be owned by Smith, Jones and the Dill brothers. Thomas Dill is an attorney, specializing in land and security acquisitions, and is the brother of Harrison Dill, the chief executive officer and chairman of the board of one of the largest . . . companies in the United States. . . .

Both the Smith and Dill families belong to a sunbelt world of high social standing, legal and financial training, apparent religious probity, and questionable business dealing — at least some of the time. The plan was this: After Wyranch Corporation was acquired, it would advance $3½ million to the holding company to purchase the Fiesta. The Dills did not, however, want to be licensed, evidently because they did not want to be known publicly as men with an interest in a gaming casino. The question was whether their interest was withdrawn.

The way financing was arranged suggested to the auditors that it had not been. Smith, Jones, and the Dills — as Wyoming Ranch Holding Company — initiated negotiations with a New England bank to finance the purchase of a controlling interest in Wyranch. The loan was granted, and was collateralized by the personal guarantees of the four, plus ABC stock valuing the apartment houses at more than $16 million and Jones's share of Fiesta stock, listed as an asset of the holding company. By guaranteeing the stock of a gaming corporation, the auditors felt that Jones had transferred it without the approval of the gaming authorities. That is considered a serious breach of gaming regulations. Furthermore, the auditors looked askance at the valuation of the ABC stock, and were particularly disturbed by what they learned had happened after the holding company got the loan and acquired Wyranch Corporation.

Shortly after the corporation was acquired, three of the five members of the board of directors were replaced by the Dills and their brother-in-law, a dentist. Now in control, this group authorized a loan to Jones of $1¼ million to make his first payment for the Fiesta. The voucher copy of the check contained a typed but marked out notation not visible to the naked eye. A law enforcement agency undertook a laboratory analysis for the Audit Division revealing that the notation was originally typed as follows: "Loan to secure option to purchase 10% interest in the Fiesta Hotel property."

That notation helped to convince the auditors that Smith and Jones were undisclosed interest holders in Wyranch Corporation; and conversely, that Smith and the Dills held undisclosed rights to an interest in the Fiesta Hotel.

The distribution of the loan proceeds was even more incriminatory. Jones kept $750,000 to make his initial payment on the Fiesta, but through a complicated series of transactions involving Smith filtered the remaining $500,000 back to the Dills. As the listed majority shareholders, the Dills were prohibited by California law from borrowing from the corporation without the consent of the minority shareholders. The transaction appeared to be a serious deception and possibly a crime.

Based on the auditors' report, the gaming board felt that Jones could not have obtained the financing to acquire the Fiesta, except for his association with the Dills and Smith and Wilson. When Jones came before them, the chairman of the board read a statement to him that was in effect an indictment of his application to acquire the remaining assets of the Fiesta. "All the logic and evidence," the statement read, "points directly to the conclusion that Peter Jones does not stand alone in this transaction. Even if, contrary to the evidence, Peter Jones does stand alone today, his earlier relationships and involvement with the people discussed today and the means used to effectuate the purpose suggest that Peter Jones would be an unsuitable operator of a major Nevada casino."

Following hearings, the board voted to recommend to the commission that Jones be denied a license. The vote was 2 to 1, Tracy dissenting. Tracy based his vote on the "fact that Mr. Smith is a current licensee, he was under oath. . . . I felt that the testimony of Mr. Smith was much stronger than the testimony we took from the many people who are not licensees who have a lot to gain and nothing to lose."[3]

For Jones to be licensed, the commission would need to vote unanimously to overturn the board (and its auditors). This was the last case for board Chairman Walker; and the commission had a new chairman, a former lieutenant governor, with political ambition. "My candid opinion," he said of the auditors' work, "is that the Board and its investigative arm didn't do a very good job in this instance." The Gaming Control Board's conclusions, he added, "wouldn't hold water in . . . an eighth grade government class, in my opinion."[4] The new chairman felt sorry for "Mr. Smith," the promoter. "I frankly think," he added, "we need more . . . promoters in this country. . . . I personally think our country was made by promoters, people who are willing to take a chance and to make a dollar."[5]

The commission, following its new chairman's lead, voted to license Mr. Jones for a probationary year, a seemingly meaningless gesture since, if there were hidden interests, their prerogatives would scarcely be exercised during such a probationary period.

That was the new chairman's first meeting. During his second, he engineered overturning a 3 to 0 recommendation by the board that yet another "emergency" investor not be permitted to pour $1.5 million into the ailing Parisien Hotel. Recall that state law requires a unanimous vote of the commission to overturn a board licensing recommendation. The chairman ruled that only a simple majority was required in an *emergency* investment situation. (Counting, however, the board members and the dissenting commissioners, the vote was 5 to 3.) The three assenters voted to assure Parisien employees of their paychecks, a move that many regarded as politically expedient for the chairman but disastrous for gaming control. One Las Vegas columnist, a former industry publicist, commented pointedly: "If [the Gaming Control Board's] judgment is no longer valued by the Commissioners, why even keep them in business?"[6] The same question might be asked about the Audit Division.

7

Every two years, when the Nevada legislature convenes, the gaming board appears before the state legislature to offer its budget. Ordinarily, the board and the governor present a unified front before the legislature, as a result of meetings prior to the hearings. The year 1977 was, however, different.

The Audit Division had requested, in addition to its existing 24 agents, an additional 44, nearly tripling the size of the division. Around the agency, the division chief was considered slightly mad. It would be unheard of for a division to double, much less triple, its size.

The governor's budget office was impressed by the division chief's request, but nevertheless viewed it with the skepticism budget offices normally reserve for such requests — as ideals unrealizable in practice. The governor's budget office allotted what it considered a generous and deserved expansion, from 22 positions to 39, nearly doubling the division in size.

The audit chief's presentation had to have been persuasive even to have been allotted 17 new positions. It was. The presentation described the numerous legislative functions required of the division, from audits to fraud examinations, all demanding financial expertise. The report documented a manpower shortage so severe that it forced the division to ignore certain of its functions and to long delay others, sometimes resulting in revenue losses to state and industry.

The audit chief could point to a memorandum where he had warned of the consequences of understaffing, after he had been ordered to complete 50 standard audits before the statute of limitations ran out. In particular, he had described the rumor of problems at the "Flagship" Hotel, and the theft that might be occurring in the meantime. It didn't hurt his credibility that the Audit Division could pridefully point to having eventually uncovered the fraud. Moreover, he also pointed out that lack of manpower caused a late-starting investigation. Had it begun earlier, he contended, the Flagship and associated hotels might have avoided some of the loss — around $2 million in gambling revenues to the hotels and $110,000 in associated tax revenues to the state.

He pointed to other problems the Audit Division has been made aware of in various hotels and casinos, all connected with financial transactions: the actual source of funds for transfers of interest at certain hotels; the operation of present hidden interests by past owners and others; the financial background of counsel advising certain hotels; kickbacks and associated fraud — involving purchasing departments — an area scarcely investigated in the preceding years; and the extent of gaming equipment manufacturer financial influence over Nevada licensees. All of these "problems" suggested three conclusions: (1) how difficult it was to assert control over this financially complex and growing industry; (2) how trained auditors were capable of exerting control, if anyone could; and (3) how auditors pay their own way by recovering lost revenue.

When the legislature considered the governor's budget request, they asked the audit chief to testify, along with board Chairman Walker. Drawing upon his memorandum, the audit chief explained the functions of the Audit Division and emphasized how increased sophistication in audit and special investigations had brought about a substantial increment in revenues to the state. The board chairman backed up this testimony, stressing the gaming industry's growth in size and complexity, and the unique skills of the detective.

He also provided a vivid analysis of understaffing. Stressing the desirability of auditing the roughly 116 locations throughout the state accounting for 97 percent of the revenue once every five years, the board chairman showed that under present staff allocations it was now possible to audit each establishment only once every 73 years!

The legislators were clearly impressed and a bit disturbed. One senator asked for another session with gaming control representatives before coming to a final decision on the budget. In that session, both the audit chief and the board chairman provided greater detail as to the needs of the Audit Division. One senator raised the question of whether the additional 17 auditors recommended by the governor could adequately cover the ground the legislature wanted the Audit Division to be held responsible for. He also indicated that so far as the Finance Committee was concerned, the investigative functions of the Audit Division were more important than the routine audits.

Asked whether he agreed, the audit chief diplomatically replied he thought they were equally important. Actually, he thought special investigations were more significant, in part because he felt the state both exercised more control and derived more revenue from special investigations; and in part because he believed the other divisions were relatively incapable of performing the financial analyses associated with these special investigations. Nevertheless, fearing to appear too openly assertive in claiming investigative hegemony, he affirmed the equality of the importance of the traditional audit function.

The audit chief's appearance impressed both the Senate Finance Committee and the House Ways and Means Committee. The legislature eventually funded 15 additional positions for auditors over the governor's recommended 17 for a total of 32. Thus, the Audit Division was authorized in 1977, just before the appointment of new board and commission chairmen, to nearly triple its size (to 56 positions).

The audit chief was exhilarated. But the new commission chairman, in his first major action, denigrated the same division the legislature had lauded. In a few months, the audit chief, by now thoroughly demoralized, sought other employment.

8

How are we to reconcile the legislature's support of the Audit Division with the new commission chairman's lack of confidence in two of the division's most important investigations? This is not easy, but the sharply divergent visions seem to reflect the ambivalence with which control is regarded in Nevada. The state legislature does take control seriously in two respects: the industry should pay its way through taxes, and auditors are needed to insure payment; and the industry should present a clean image to the financial investment and national law enforcement communities so as to facilitate expansion — and more taxes.

These imperatives suggest support of an aggressive, investigatively oriented Audit Division. At the same time, should the Audit Division become increasingly capable and aggressive, it also becomes threatening to the industry, partly because it may uncover real fraud, and partly because it elicits feelings of discomfort against puritanism, bureaucratic high-handedness, government constraint, and so forth.

A chairman who believes in the social value of "promoters" reflects the other and very lively side of the coin of ambivalence. From this perspective, the real — if unspoken — fact of gaming control is to sanitize the image of the industry. Accordingly, a capable Audit Division understands and accepts, without explicitly being told, that it is to serve as a buffer between Nevada's gaming industry and the rest of the relevant world; and to persuade that world of the gaming industry's integrity by showing a diplomatically correct amount of aggressiveness — enough to keep the boat clean, but not enough to rock it.

The Audit Division I studied was capable, but certainly not diplomatic or tactful, in an industry where it is considered impolite — if not disastrous — to ask too many questions. The gambling culture of Nevada, particularly of Las Vegas, discourages probing into previous experience — where one worked before, for whom, how one obtained money to pay gambling debts, and so forth. But a capable auditor must probe and question hard, and is thus not easily appreciated by those under investigation. An auditor who is too well-liked is not doing his job. It had to be only a matter of time before the imperatives of the gambling culture caught up with the assertiveness of the Audit Division under its sometimes abrasive chief. When he left for a job in New Jersey, the Las Vegas industry was glad to bid him farewell. Some described him as "overzealous" and one casino executive expressed the fond hope that his plane would crash on the way to the East Coast.[7]

VI

England
and America

21

The Political Economy of Casino Gambling

THE PREVIOUS CHAPTERS HAVE HIGHLIGHTED THE LIMITS OF NEVADA'S legal controls over the gambling industry's search for revenue and respectability. These limits are part of a larger and continuing problem. The fundamental dilemma of the legal casino gambling industry is to reconcile expansionist economic imperatives with the reluctance of the wider society to accept the legitimacy of the enterprise.

Nevada has adopted at least two strategies to resolve the dilemma. One is to create a control system limiting entry into the industry and to investigate the activities of those licensed to conduct the business.

The other is to legitimize casino gambling within the state, partly by creating a consensus and belief that the activity is economically beneficial to all, even if its proceeds may actually be quite unevenly distributed; and partly by affirming, in a variety of ways, that casino gambling is a socially acceptable activity.

Yet even Nevada authorities sometimes reveal ambivalence toward casino gambling. For example, in 1975 an applicant asked for a license to place slot machines in a home for the aged located in Las Vegas. *Every* member of the board publicly expressed deep moral indignation at this "exploitation" of the aged. When interviewed later, the board chairman, who used to be welfare commissioner, argued that the elderly are poor, and that poor people can't afford to play slot machines. But, of course, slot machines are accessible throughout the state, to the poor, to the elderly—to anybody but minors. The inconsistency is revealing. Still, casino gambling in Nevada is considered necessary business; necessity is rather easily transformed into propriety.

Perhaps the only substantial group in Las Vegas expressing deeply ambivalent—some would say hypocritical—feelings about gambling is the Mormons, who number approximately 10 to 15 percent of the local population.[1] The Mormon church counsels its members not to gamble and is opposed to further legalization of gambling. Although no formal census has been taken, Mormons are said to form a substantial segment of employees in the gaming industry. Those in good standing with the church are not permitted to engage in any of the actual games, but they are allowed to participate in casino management or management of the hotel and restaurant. "The point is this," one Mormon told me, "not only are the games themselves somewhat enticing, but someone in the church is supposed to be able to provide his brethren with spiritual guidance and comfort; and the casino floor simply isn't a desirable place to engage in serious conversation." So practicing Mormons are to be found in hotel and restaurant management and, when in the casino, in activities away from the games related to the handling of money and credit.

Nevada Mormons seem relatively untroubled by the inconsistency between the church's attitude toward gambling and participation in the industry. Above all, Nevada Mormons seem to be practical. Like everybody else, they understand that without casino gambling many of them would lose their jobs; those who do not participate directly in the industry as well as those who do.

Other churches concur. For example, hearings were held in 1975 by the Commission on the Review of the National Policy Toward Gambling. The only faint opposition to casino gambling was given by a minister, who acknowledged that he would have to close his Las Vegas parish if legal casino gambling were to be abolished.

In short, to resolve "the fiscal crisis of the state," Nevada has opted for a form of partnership—in effect, state capitalism, with respect to the casino gambling industry.

But a state interest of this kind develops a subsidiary dilemma. To the extent that acceptability of the gambling business depends on a perception of it as being legitimate, to what extent can the state interest become so great as to undermine the state's capacity to control? The preceding chapters have already dealt with this question in some detail regarding Nevada. Before concluding, it is worthwhile to take a glance at England in comparison to Nevada. Both legalized casino gambling. The British control apparatus closely resembles Nevada's, and its language and traditions more closely approximate those of Nevada than any other legal casino gambling system in the world. Still, Nevada and other American states and Great Britain differ sharply in their public philosophy toward legal casino gambling and its propriety as a means to resolve the fiscal crisis of the state.[2] In the remainder of this concluding chapter, I shall describe those differences, discuss why they arose, and examine their important consequences.

2

In contrast to the Nevadans, the British officially deplore legal casino gambling. Casino gambling may be legal, but it is seen by the British government as a *social problem* to be repressed as much as possible. Casino gambling is *not* a major source of revenue for the British government, even though gaming tables are taxed and even though the pound has fallen sharply in recent years. The control of gambling is through a gaming board reporting to the Home Office, not to the Treasury, and the success of the gaming board is judged not in the slightest on a rise in the popularity of gaming.

On the contrary, if casino gambling were to disappear entirely from the English scene, the gaming board would be congratulated. As one Home Office official remarked to me in an interview: "We do not want England to become a mecca for gambling. The intent of the 1968 legislation was to legalize gambling in order to meet a demand that already existed so as not to drive gambling underground. We did not think we would necessarily reduce the demand for gambling but the job of the board is to see to it that the demand for gambling is in no way stimulated."³ Thus, although permitted, casino gambling in England is still regarded as a vice.

The British attitude toward gambling derives, at least in part, from the failure of the 1960 Betting and Gaming Act. That act was presumably designed to prevent the exploitation of gaming by commercial interests. Its intent was to allow anyone to gamble, while at the same time prohibiting a commercial interest in casino gambling. Presumably no charges were to be made for gambling, no taxes were to be taken from gambling stakes, and there was to be no edge; every player was to have the same chance of winning as every other player.

Those who drafted the act were not familiar enough with casino gambling to anticipate a variety of loopholes and dodges that could be developed to circumvent the act's intention. For example, although no charge could be made for gambling, almost anybody could gather a group of people, claim to have formed a club, and then charge so-called club fees instead of gambling fees. A number of exclusive proprietary clubs were formed, mostly in the West End of London, where it was feasible to impose substantial charges, up to 20 pounds or more for 30 minutes of play at games like baccarat. Since these were not charges to gamble, but rather to make use of club facilities, the law was easily circumvented.

Another ingenious circumvention came about by introducing games, like roulette, offering a long-term edge or advantage to the bank, and then offering the bank to players who could not afford the considerable short-term risk of accepting it.

Although the House of Lords decided that the practice of offering the bank violated the law in the case of roulette, the judgment came about only after a long series of court actions. The gaming clubs operating under the 1960 act were able to tie up the courts for sufficiently long time-periods so that evasions could be practiced while the courts were deciding whether or not the practice in question was indeed an evasion.

Contrary to the intent of those who proposed the bills, deficiencies of draftsmanship actually allowed commercial interests to introduce into England a wide variety of casino gambling games, at a considerable profit. Clubs sprang up all over the country. At one time it was estimated that there were approximately 1,200 gaming clubs. Since the 1960 act never envisaged that sort of development, the clubs were virtually uncontrolled. However, since technically these were private clubs, the police had no right to enter them except on warrant. Yet, the clubs actually conducted themselves as if they were public gaming houses and advertised freely.

Such profitable enterprises, operating under conditions of governmental immunity, could scarcely fail to attract the attention of organized criminals inside and outside of England. Vincent Teresa, in his book *My Life in the Mafia*, describes his involvement with a major London club, the Colony, during this period:

> When you want to run junkets into the Colony Club, the man you made arrangements through was either [Meyer] Lansky or his right arm, Dino Cellini. They'd give you the clearance and make sure you got a piece of the profits. If you were a mob representative running a junket to the club, they kicked back 15 percent of all the money lost by the people you brought. That could result in some very serious money. . . . The Colony was good for at least three to four million bucks a week in action.[4]

Presumably, organized crime interests were involved also in introducing slot machines into England. When the 1968 bill was moved on February 13, the Home Secretary made a special point of denouncing slot machines. "I do not think that in 1960 there was a clear perception of just how profitable these machines could be," he said. "Machines have been forced on high rentals by protection methods or by ingenious forms of contract designed to secure that the lion's share of the profits go to the dealer. There has been bribery and sometimes downright robbery."[5] As the result of what the government saw as an "ugly situation," it decided that the only choice was between outright suppression of gambling and rigorous control.

Considering that gaming was so widespread, the government felt that suppression would be ineffective and would in the end worsen the situation. "Much of the activity would be driven underground and so into the hands of crooks and racketeers of all kinds who have already battened on to the games. It is only by exposing the activity to the full light of day that we can hope to control it and dislodge the crooks and racketeers."[6] Thus, instead of suppressing and driving underground casino gambling, the government proposed a tightly controlled form of legalization with a different purpose altogether from Nevada and other American places considering legal casino gambling. *Gambling was to be perceived as a social problem, not as a revenue-raising alternative to other forms of taxation.*

3

The British government's attitude toward gambling is European in orientation: it is apparently inconsistent, deploring gambling while at the same time accepting it, but it is based upon social rather than mathematical logic. Europeans are not necessarily less moralistic or opinionated than Americans; but they seem less confident of their ability to stamp out immorality, or presumed immorality, through the criminal law. Legalization is not intended to imply approval.

Another factor distinguishing the European from the American attitude toward gambling is the overt attempt by British and other European governments to regulate gambling according to the social-class positions of potential gamblers. At all levels of society, Europeans seem more class-conscious than Americans. Even more than in America, neighborhood and regional segregation has been fundamental to the structuring of social class and to the development of class consciousness.[7] There is no question, for example, that European governments have traditionally employed concepts of class segregation in forming casino gaming policy and law. Throughout the continent, casino gambling is characteristically restricted to so-called "spas and watering places," thus segregating and presumably protecting the industrial working class from the temptations of casino gambling.

Under the 1968 Gaming Act, London's Mayfair gaming clubs were intended to serve as a functional equivalent to the continental spas and watering places. Casino gaming clubs are not permitted in working-class districts in London. Gaming clubs really are *clubs*, charging membership fees of roughly $10 to $100, fees that would be regarded as substantial enough to be prohibitive to most British workers.

Membership is also "sponsored" — a characteristic of private clubs. The sort of person who would prove acceptable to the members would find no difficulty obtaining a sponsor. And that is just the point. These are exclusive clubs — by definition they are intended to exclude. The law does not prohibit the British worker from the gaming casino. It simply puts it beyond his reach.

The British Gaming Board is all powerful. The attitudes of the British government toward the gambler in general, but particularly the working-class "punter," are rather like those displayed in the past by benign colonial administrations: a combination of paternalism, benevolence, and sharp autocracy. Following Parliament's policy of not stimulating the demand for gambling, and of excluding organized crime elements, the board has restricted severely the number of permitted gaming clubs by a combination of strict licensing procedures and severe zoning restrictions. One ironical result has been to provide British gaming interests with a state-protected monopoly.

Unlike Nevada, where a gaming applicant or group may open a club if they can sustain the burden of showing that they possess requisite and appropriate capital and expertise, the aspiring British gaming entrepreneur must also show the presence of "demand." The concept of "demand" as employed by the British Gaming Board implies already existing social, rather than economic, demand, although that distinction is not always made clear. To an outsider, it seems that the presence of the gaming casinos in London itself stimulates demand, and that perhaps one or two more could profitably open. But, in law and in fact it really doesn't matter. Profitability is not the standard employed by the board, even though the "demand" concept suggests it. The board does not wish to permit new clubs to open because, whether true or not, it wishes to preserve the position that social demand has remained unstimulated since 1968.

Since the board is all powerful, its position is unchallengeable, whether on the issues of the potential for more clubs or on the suitability of an applicant to operate a club (in the unlikely event that one more were to be permitted). Unlike a court's, the board's hearings are totally secret; the board defends its conclusions, or more specifically the reasons for its conclusions, to no one. Given its autonomy and its great power, it is frankly recognized among members and staff that the British Gaming Board under the 1968 act constitutes the most autocratic British institution since the Star Chamber. Serious questions have been raised in this book about the fairness of the procedures employed by the Nevada gaming authorities. Compared to the British board, which operates completely behind closed doors, the Nevada operation appears as a model of democratic openness and due process of law.

4

Autocracy does not preclude benevolence, or at least paternalism. The gambler, it is thought, must be protected from his own impulses. No one is allowed to gamble for the first time in a British gaming club without formally, in writing, declaring his intention to do so 48 hours before game time. After the gambler has joined the club, he may then gamble as he likes. But the act of joining a gambling club is supposed not to be taken trivially. *One should not gamble on impulse*: this is the policy of the act. Since gambling is considered a moral weakness, it should not be encouraged.

In line with the policy of not stimulating demand, the clubs are not allowed to advertise or to offer live entertainment, although, as clubs, they are permitted TV viewing rooms. Nor are they allowed to extend credit. Indeed, not only is credit not permitted, but also the board insists that every check written by a gambler must go through the bank it is written on. So when a gambler writes a check for 1,000 pounds and wins more than that, he cannot recover his check with his winnings. The idea behind the rule is to insure that the check is recoverable as written, that "punters" do not write checks over an amount in their bank account.

Unlike Nevada, gambling debts in England are recoverable in court, but there are no gambling debts as such. There are checks made out to gambling clubs for the purchase of chips, and these checks in England are recoverable. Furthermore, if a gambler makes out a series of such checks through the night, he cannot consolidate four or five checks into one large one.

The point is this: The board wants the banker to know that several checks were written in one night to a gaming club, thus indicating to the banker that the writer has gambled more than his original intention. The purpose of the rule is to deter a "punter" by the potential threat of embarrassment in the banking world from cashing checks in the heat of gambling. Such a disclosure might influence a businessman's credit ranking. The proprietors of the gambling clubs are appalled by these last two requirements, feeling that they constitute little more than inconvenience, but the gaming board insists upon them. It believes in the social value of embarrassing a man who has written several checks in one evening to a gambling club.

There are other forms of such paternalism: not only may English gaming clubs not present live entertainment; in London's Playboy Club, the bunnies who deal the games are required to cover their decolletage with bibs so as not to distract the player's attentions from the game itself. Nor may cocktail waitresses serve alcoholic beverages at the tables, and for the same reason: the player's concentration may be impaired. Indeed, at the blackjack tables there are required sets of instructions explaining to the players the best strategy of the game.

Even the odds are made better, although that is a somewhat complicated process to explain. The simplest example is roulette. Virtually all Nevada clubs employ a double zero, by choice, while in England they are not allowed to do so. The house edge is limited to one zero. Similarly in craps certain bets, known as sucker bets in Nevada, are not allowed. For example, the big six and the big eight, which in Nevada pay even money although the true odds payoff would be six to five, are simply not allowed on the dice layout in England. A knowledgeable Nevada craps player can obtain better odds than in England, but he must know how to bet the "double odds." In general, the policy of the British Gaming Board is to protect the interests of the unsophisticated player.

5

The paternalism of the gaming board is very much influenced by class distinctions. The policy of the board is to suppress casino gambling, particularly for the working class. But a substitute is provided in which approximately 20 percent of the adult population participates. This is the bingo game, played in what used to be large movie theaters in working-class neighborhoods.

To play, one must register 24 hours in advance. Impulsiveness is not permitted here either. There is, however, no fee for joining, although players are required to pay an admission for every round of play. Several of these sessions may be run in a day and the fee for any one session may not exceed 85 pence (around $1.75). To attract customers, the clubs rarely charge more than 50¢ or 75¢ per session depending upon the club and the time of the session. Bingo clubs are clearly intended for working-class consumption.

The clubs are very popular, even more than movies were in the 1930s and '40s. Clubs often draw around 1,000 players per night, and more on the weekends. The atmosphere is friendly between games, tense and expectant as numbers are called. People seem to come to meet their friends, to talk to others. For each session, players purchase sets of bingo cards with the numbers on them, which will last for a session of about two hours. When the games are played all eyes are riveted to the numbered cards. Lack of attention may cost a prize of between $100 and $1,000.

Bingo is an "insurance game." In casino games, the house holds the bank and holds a small edge for each bet, so that over time it must win. In lottery or insurance games, players pool their funds for a prize. Subjectively, the edge doesn't mean all that much, since it is subtracted from the winner. If 1,000 players put up two dollars for an evening of eight games, the prize per game should be $250. It doesn't matter that much to the winner if the cut is 2, 5, 10 or even 20 percent.

The bingo club is the pride of the gaming board. A player need not, indeed cannot, lose more than the cost of an alternative recreational evening, such as a sporting event. It is possible, although unlikely, that a player will win a substantial prize.

Bingo entrepreneurs are permitted to profit only from the admission. From 1,000 players, a typical club will gross about $800 for the evening. From that, the entrepreneurs must pay the rent and upkeep of the club, plus wages for a staff of about five or six persons, plus janitorial service. In addition, the entrepreneurs profit from the sale of food and beverages. For these, players are charged a bit less than they would pay at a pub, a bit more than prices at charity clubs or private clubs run on a nonprofit basis. The gaming board insures that the entrepreneurs do not profit substantially from the bingo games.

The only cut from the betting pool is taken by the taxing authority. Up until 1975 it was 2½ percent and in 1975 it was increased to 5 percent. In an insurance game of this kind — shallow play — the players ultimately receive most of what they've put into the game. Thus, besides social enjoyment, there is an economic rationality to bingo, just as there is to normal insurance.

One of the innovations introduced by the clubs, allowed by the gaming board, is a "linked" game. The "link" is between two clubs in two different neighborhoods and introduces a sort of rivalry between them. It permits an insurance game with approximately 2,000 participants. If each one puts in approximately 50¢, a $1,000 prize is accumulated. While the chances of winning are 2,000 to 1, the chances of a British worker saving $1,000 are most unlikely. Insurance games and lotteries do make a kind of economic sense, provided that the take off the top is within reason. They offer lower-income-bracket players the opportunity to accumulate sizable winnings for a relatively small investment, and of course they also provide a great deal of excitement as well if one wins.

The British Gaming Board policy is thus both benevolent and paternalistic. It would like to suppress gambling for everyone, but especially the industrial working class. It does not try to take gambling away from its proletarians, but offers workable substitutes such as bingo.

For the purposes of this book, I've limited my study of British gaming to casino gambling and bingo, since, at the time of my research, a separate authority regulated betting shops, of which there are many all over England. A recent careful and thoughtful survey of British gaming shows, however, that the majority of bettors stake less than 5 shillings on the average, and stay in the betting shops only for the few minutes necessary to place a single bet.[8] Betting is a working-class phenomenon, with those most prone to frequent gambling being in the upper working class.[9] Gambling appears to be the national pastime and the government has set up a Royal Commission expected to recommend a more centralized form of control over all aspects of gambling. Yet it is inconceivable that any British government could outlaw gambling and remain in power. To deplore is quite acceptable; to outlaw is not.

6

Even so brief and introductory a comparison between the purposes of gaming control in Nevada and England suggests how varied forms of legalization can be, even when they look so similar. For example, neither Nevada nor England ever really considered government-run casinos, even though England has nationalized several industries. Nobody has ever elaborated the reasons, but they are different in England and in Nevada. Since the English see gambling as an evil to be tolerated, but not encouraged, they could scarcely adopt a system of state-owned gambling. The Nevadans do not regard gambling as an evil, but they consider socialism to be one. Moreover, authorities in both systems comprehend how complex casino gambling is, and how difficult it is to control its honesty.

Yet an enormously consequential difference prevails between the English and American models. Superficially, the difference can be summarized by saying that in America the states and localities legalizing casino gambling and other forms of gambling primarily seek to raise revenue, and the government thus becomes dependent on the legalization of gambling for a portion of its annual budget. But in the case of legal casino gambling dependence is compounded. In Atlantic City, for example, casino gambling is intended to renew the economy of a depressed economic area. If casino gambling were made illegal in Nevada, Las Vegas would become a ghost town. Once a locality becomes thoroughly dependent for its economic survival on one industry, the needs of that industry dominate the politics of the community. The overriding political question is no longer whether gambling should be legal, but what sorts of legislative policy — what structure of legalization — will enhance the prosperity of the industry.

It could be argued, with some justification, that casino gambling is in this respect no different from any other recreational industry — fishing or skiing or sunbathing. Resort towns are notoriously subservient to local industrial needs — will the presence of a shark close down the Hamptons on July fourth weekend?

But casino gambling *is* different. In other times and places casino gambling has been considered morally undesirable. It still is, despite legalization, regarded in England as immoral. Once the sort of economic dependence that typifies Las Vegas and Atlantic City sets in, debate is characteristically foreclosed.

I am not here arguing that casino gambling is immoral. I am arguing that economic dependence forecloses social and philosophical discussion of that issue. The community is no longer asked to consider the morality of casino gambling; and rarely bases particular decisions concerning casino gambling policy on moral grounds, but on considerations of economic enhancement.

This is a serious problem for the larger society with respect to casino gambling and other former "vices" as well. If this study has shown anything it has demonstrated that the emergent concern in the area of social deviance is not with the hoary issue of whether vices should be legalized, but with the appropriate purposes and accompanying constraints of legalization models.

When a locality becomes economically dependent upon casino gambling, policies that might otherwise seem prudent and reasonable — e.g., that the activity in question not be widely advertised — become a threat to the industry. If Nevadans had their way, for example, TV stations all over the country would carry advertisements for Las Vegas casinos. Nor will the state of Nevada outlaw credit from the casino gambling industry, even though the granting of credit — as we have seen — invites organized crime into the state, creates continual control problems, and is arguably of questionable morality even if casino gambling is arguably not.

Furthermore, where an industry either dominates or becomes economically significant to politically resourceful populations, it becomes difficult to impose restraints upon it through the political process. There is no doubt, for example, that cigarette smoking is disastrous for the public health of the United States. The American Cancer Society to the contrary notwithstanding, some time will pass — perhaps it will never come — before the Congress will outlaw cigarette advertising, which is of course a very different thing from outlawing cigarette smoking.

7

Recently, the Commission on the Review of the National Policy Toward Gambling analyzed the Nevada system and contrasted its outline with the British one. The basic thrust of the commission's recommendation is twofold: first, that control of legal casino gambling be left to the states, rather than the federal government; and second, that states considering legalization might look to England rather than Nevada as the model.[10]

In theory that sounds quite sensible. In practice it woefully underestimates the force of the economic motives and pressures associated with legal casino gambling where revenue is the reason for legalization. For states other than Nevada or New Jersey, which are considering legal casino gambling, the real question is not whether to adopt the major outlines of the English model, but whether in the American context, local governments can realistically contemplate such a choice.

My conclusion is that the combination of a revenue-producing motive, coupled with the power of already existing economic interests in the casino gambling industry, added to the cultural and legal constraints of American society will insure that if ever casino gambling is adopted by an American state, the Nevada model — with its economic imperatives — will dominate. Let me elaborate.

First, it is simply inconceivable that a movement might prevail in any American state legislature, as it did in the British Parliament, to legalize casino gambling primarily as a means of controlling a social problem. There is a delightful contradiction in American attitudes toward casino gambling and other vices. Americans are reluctant to legalize those activities recognized as vices — in accord with our waning puritanical heritage — but vice is sometimes granted its role in society provided that it pays its way. Apparently, the only heritage in America strong enough to challenge puritanism is capitalism. If an activity makes money, for individuals or for the government, it may be considered to warrant legalization. Social arguments might dictate the same conclusion, but they tend to carry far less weight than economic ones.

If one grants, as experience suggests, that the impetus to legalize casino gambling will be primarily economic, then other economic interests will naturally flow. For example, the British authorities permit only two slot machines per casino. But slot machines provide substantial revenue and will naturally be included in any casino gambling industry holding revenue-production as its primary goal. Indeed, in New Jersey, a major hotel is planned for development by the Bally Manufacturing Corporation (the leading producer of slot machines). Bally will certainly want to promote slot machines in New Jersey.

Moreover, the British authorities did not allow Bally slot machines in the casinos at the time of this study, citing in interviews Bally's early history as evidence of possible present ties to organized crime. One of the company's original principal stockholders was a New Jersey mob figure, Gerardo Catena, whose interest was supposedly bought out in 1965.

According to Sam W. Klein, who in 1975 was Bally's largest single stockholder, Catena's interest in the company had been hidden from him. Then he was told by a Catena partner that "Mr. Catena didn't want to be shown of record before, and now he insists to be on record."

Klein testified before the Gaming Control Board on January 1, 1975:

Well, that alerted me. If he had not said that, I would not have been alerted.

I then started to ask questions because I still didn't know anything, and *I determined that he was a man who was really involved, at least according to the newspapers, with organized crime.* So, on that basis, Mr. O'Donnell, who quite agreed with me, and I said hey, if this guy didn't want to show before, why should we want to show with him now. There must be something radically wrong, and we started negotiating immediately to get him out.

In 1977, the Nevada Gaming Commission forced Klein to sell his stock and pay a substantial fine for having been seen playing golf with Catena.

In England, suspicion alone can be ground for exclusion. Bally was licensed in Nevada, but only barely. The board did not straightforwardly vote to deny Bally a license. Instead, it voted to approve Bally for licensing, subject to certain qualifications, including a major resignation. Since the board voted affirmatively, albeit with conditions, the commission could and did license Bally by a majority vote, rather than the unanimous vote demanded by denial. In short, Bally was licensed in Nevada by what appeared to be the fortunate consequence of a legal technicality. Certainly, serious reservations were expressed by board members regarding the Corporation's leading figures.

In addition to being suspicious of slot machine manufacturing ties to organized crime, the British distinguish between table games and slot machines for fear that the latter will prove essentially attractive to those segments of the population that can least afford to play them. Once again, this is an example of the British system's paternalism, which might not fit well with American values of permitting people to spend their money as they please, or even throw it away.

Still, even the Nevada Gaming Control Board and Commission would not permit slot machines to be put in a home for the aged. Other states might feel that slot machines should not be permitted for the urban poor — and middle class — who will predictably be ripped off, or entertained, at the rate of 20 cents on the dollar. Nevertheless, given the economic imperative to legalize casino gambling, it is unlikely that slot machines would be outlawed by an American state legalizing casino gambling.

Since the British imperative for legalization is social rather than economic, the derivative principle is that demand shall not be stimulated. From this flow at least four major practical consequences: First, the British do not permit junkets. During the era of a falling pound this restriction implies that a considerable number of tourists from other countries, who might be brought into England by gambling casinos, and who would surely leave dollars, marks, francs, dinar, and yen in their wake, are absent because foreigners who wish to gamble in England are required to pay their own way. This makes sense in terms of controlling legal gambling from a social perspective, but it does not make economic sense.

Second, not only are junkets not permitted, neither is the extension of credit. Obviously, the purpose of credit in the gambling industry, as in any other, is to stimulate demand. If legal casino gambling is regarded as in Nevada as no better or worse than any other business, then it makes sense to permit credit to be extended. But if gambling is seen as a social problem, to be permitted but unstimulated, then it is logical for the government to forbid the granting of credit.

Third, when it is considered appropriate to stimulate demand, advertising is encouraged. When policy calls for a reduction, or at least not a stimulation, advertising should be controlled. In Britain, the casinos are not even allowed to print matchbook covers, to say nothing of having large flashing signs to attract the public. But when a state takes an interest in revenue production, it not only protects the industry, but looks with favor on those activities that will draw more customers into sampling its offerings. Thus, under a revenue-production model, the prevailing ethic is capitalism, with both industry and the state seeking ever-increasing profits and industrial expansion. Of course, for these purposes it pays to advertise, to provide lavish entertainment, free drinks, whatever it takes to stimulate demand. Thus, under a Nevada model, the state doesn't simply "legalize" casino gambling — it encourages its growth.

Finally, under the United States Constitution, the capacity of the state both to control entry and to impose discipline is severely limited in contrast to the British system. In some respects, Western democracies are simply not alike, and the control authorities in England enjoy far greater discretion than their Nevada counterparts. I once discussed this issue with a colleague who is a distinguished professor of constitutional law. He pointed out that, constitutional requirements aside, nobody in America would believe in the honesty of a Nevada gaming authority that granted licenses and disciplined in private as the British do. Government officials at every level of our society can scarcely be said to enjoy a presumption of integrity.

It is fair to say, without being strident or indignant about it, that two factors distinguish our society from the English regarding corruption in public office. Given a background of aristocracy, and a commitment to public service, British civil servants are believed to be free from corruption. Public service is not regarded instrumentally — as being a stepping stone to some more rewarding position. Put much too simply, our civil service seems easily to be captured by the spirit of expansionist capitalism, while the British civil service combines the communal ideals of socialism with the service ideals of aristocracy. They are accordingly — and correctly — thought to be more stuffy and self-righteous than ours, but also less corruptible.

Corruption is, after all, a key issue in any discussion of the legalization of casino gambling. In the last chapter, I distinguished analytically among three sorts of corruption relating to casino gambling: the direct corruption of officials by buying them off; the indirect corruption that occurs when an industry dominates an economy; and the cultural, historical, and existential features of the gambling industry that render it peculiarly susceptible to fraudulent activity — the features that have led Nevada and other courts to recognize its attractions to organized crime in various guises.

These three tend to support each other in the casino gambling industry, rendering inseparable the existence of legal casino gambling and a potential for corruption. This is not to deny that in Nevada the legislature continually strives to strengthen the statutory basis for control — as, for example, in 1977 by specifying and extending qualifications for gaming licensees.[11] But during the same session, bowing to industry pressure, and against the inclinations of the control authorities, the legislature permitted Nevada licensees to conduct gaming operations outside Nevada.[12] Nevada's ambivalent attitudes toward control once again were in evidence. The legislature permitted Nevada licensees to be governed by unknown and distant authorities who may turn out to be honest, efficient, knowledgeable, and incorruptible — or who may not.

8

In New Jersey, a similar sort of problem arose almost immediately. Some background is necessary to appreciate its significance. Proponents of the referendum to legalize casino gambling advocated tough controls — tougher than Nevada's — to insure that organized crime would be kept out of New Jersey's casinos. After the referendum passed, state officials were appointed by the governor, the attorney general and the treasurer to set out a policy statement on casino gambling. That statement, published on February 17, 1977, offered three reasons for legalizing casino gambling. The least significant was casino gambling's direct contribution — through taxation of gaming revenues — to the total fiscal needs of New Jersey.

More important was the prospect of general economic stimulation for the state. It was envisioned that as Atlantic City developed, construction, tourist and some supply industries would also be stimulated.

The third and most important incentive was the rehabilitation of a decaying urban resort by stimulating convention, family resort and entertainment industries, meanwhile developing a character markedly different from that of Las Vegas.[13]

If Las Vegas was thought to be a glittering, open, swinging city, Atlantic City would, it was hoped, prove more decorous. A policy group headed by Robert Martinez, later to be appointed director of the Division of Gaming Enforcement, recommended that descriptive advertising be allowed, "but that in no circumstances should such advertisements contain representations of the available odds ('Best slot odds in A.C.!') or such other information" inconsistent with "standards of nondeceptiveness and social graciousness . . . of a family resort."[14]

The influential policy group's vision was elevated and doubtless well intentioned. When, however, on February 15, 1978, a major *New York Times Magazine* article suggested that at least four organized crime groups were moving in to buy up Atlantic City real estate in anticipation of a casino gambling boom, a family resort still seemed possible — but for a "family" of a very different kind from that contemplated by New Jersey authorities only a year earlier.[15]

Nevertheless, the New Jersey Casino Control Act, as initially passed on June 2, 1977, was both stricter and more carefully considered than Nevada's. In line with the idea of developing a model gambling resort, New Jersey's statute limited the number of casinos, their size, the number of rooms, and so forth. The control statute contained stricter conflict-of-interest provisions regarding employment of control agency personnel in the industry; incorporated mild criminal sanctions alongside civil sanctions to insure compliance with regulations; and located the Division of Gaming Enforcement directly in the office of the attorney general.

Still, it was less strict than the policy group's recommendations. Free drinks could be served, if the player asked. More importantly, the policy group recommended against "marker" credit, but the legislature compromised with potential casino operators who were fearful of losing high-roller business. The president of Resorts International warned the legislature that casino gambling would never succeed in Atlantic City without credit. "We must attract and rely on the affluent gambler," remarked Resorts' president I. G. Davis, "who will simply go elsewhere if he can't get credit in Atlantic City."[16]

As in Nevada, the linchpin of the control system was licensing — but New Jersey was slated to do it better and bigger. The Casino Control Act contains forceful language: "Since casino operations are especially sensitive and in need of public control and supervision . . . the regulatory and investigative powers and duties shall be exercised to the fullest extent . . ."[17] Nevada's former audit chief was brought in to head up the special investigations force. Not only were the investigations themselves contemplated to be more penetrating, but more people were to be investigated — those in lower levels of the industry as well as in ancillary businesses supplying goods and services. The promise of strict controls seemed a practical and necessary counterpart to the governor's earnest promise to keep organized crime out of Atlantic City.

It is too early to tell whether that promise can be kept. But it is not too early to report that key aspects of licensing were rather quickly modified. Originally, the policy group had recommended — for various good but perhaps not compelling reasons — that no operating license become effective until *three* casinos qualified. The legislature ignored that recommendation, on the apparent assumption that it might take some time before three applicants were qualified.

In early 1978, it became clear that the major active applicant — Resorts International, a company whose affiliation with gambling in the Bahamas had in the past attracted federal scrutiny — could never be licensed in time for gambling to commence in the summer of 1978. New Jersey authorities were caught on the horns of a major dilemma: how to reconcile the political imperative to bring casino gambling quickly to Atlantic City, with the assurance of a lengthy, detailed investigation of an applicant, an investigation exercising regulatory and investigative powers "to the fullest extent."

Members of the New Jersey attorney general's staff set their minds to solving the problem. They initially proposed that a trustee be appointed to run Resorts International's casino during the summer while the company was being investigated. But such a proposal proved impractical. Could a trustee hire an adequate staff, and what would happen to that staff if the applicant were licensed? Moreover, the proposal was strongly resisted by Resorts International.

Another compromise was reached — allowing temporary gambling licenses for six months, with a ninety-day extension, while the licensees are still under investigation. Under this compromise, which was pushed quickly through the legislature by the governor, and passed on March 17, a trustee would remain in the background while the temporary licensee would be responsible for casino management.[18] Resorts International was permitted to propose the trustee to be approved by state authorities. They named local New Jersey figures — William Marfuggi, former state treasurer; John J. Francis, former supreme court justice; and Leonard Johnson, former head of the New Jersey Manufacturers Association. They did not name a major institution, such as a bank or insurance company, apparently because the major source of financing, the First National Bank of New Jersey, did not require it.[19] Should state investigators find an undisclosed interest by organized crime, or by "undesirables," the trustees would presumably take over. The New Jersey Casino Control Commission enjoys discretionary authority to decide whether that should happen.

Under this compromise, contracts between ancillary businesses and Resorts International were reviewed. Contracts pertaining to nongaming goods and services, such as linen supplies, were temporarily approved. There was a closer scrutiny of contracts with gaming equipment suppliers, and some were held up pending licensing. Still gaming equipment was supplied and used. Every effort was made to permit Resorts International to open its casino in time for Memorial Day weekend.

The opening became a national media event. TV news programs showed people waiting in lines half a mile long for as much as three hours, to enter the casino, which can accommodate 5,500 people. A New Jersey gaming source said that the daily slot drop at Resorts International was nearly five times as large as the largest ever recorded for a single hotel on a single day in Nevada. The *New York Times* published a guide to Atlantic City and its gambling.[20] *U.S. News and World Report* heralded the opening "as a test that will help determine the future not only of this old seaside community but also of more legalized gambling across the U.S."[21] Casino gambling stocks, and the vulnerabilities of the business, were carefully assessed in *Forbes* magazine.[22]

In Nevada, Governor O'Callaghan charged that New Jersey had undermined its promise of control. The Nevada Gaming Control Board's chairman agreed, saying that the temporary licensing formula "destroys" the previously elaborate control structure in New Jersey.[23] Earlier, the Nevada Gaming Policy Board had recommended that licensed casino operators from Nevada should not be blocked from entering New Jersey's industry. The policy board recommendation would immediately affect at least two potential New Jersey applicants, Caesars World and Bally Manufacturing Corporation.

New Jersey Attorney General John J. Degnan, in response, characterized Governor O'Callaghan's remarks as "unjust, uninformed potshots" at New Jersey's casino controls.[24] There was no doubt that public acrimony was escalating between the two legal casino gambling states.

Whatever New Jersey's defense of its temporary licensing, there was no question that the New Jersey authorities looked bad in light of their previously tough stance on the *rationale* for control. The *New York Times* editorialized:

> Such temporary licensing, permitting large investments to be made and investors to become entrenched before they have been adequately screened, is a risky shortcut. It will be difficult enough to keep unsavory elements away from the gaming tables. New Jersey's tough gambling law, which requires thorough investigations of stockholders and key casino employees, was a prudent response to justifiable concern over criminal infiltration.[25]

Either New Jersey had erred in having proposed such strict controls in the first instance, or it has erred in loosening the controls. Surely, it would prove more difficult to dislodge an already ongoing, extremely profitable and thus popular business venture, than to turn down a mere applicant. Political and economic pressures have indeed already shifted the licensing burden and eroded the original conception of superstrict control that had been promised the voters of New Jersey. "In the end," wrote *New York Times* bureau chief Martin Waldron, citing a pattern of small but notable departures from the Casino Act leading to the Memorial Day opening, "New Jersey hurried up and dealt."[26]

9

In conclusion, it seems to me that the spread of legal casino gambling in the United States may contain, to use a worn but potent cliché, the seeds of its own destruction. Should several states legalize casino gambling, three results may be anticipated. First, casino gambling will become a more common activity among larger groups of people, especially working people. Some of these people will gamble improvidently, and the industry will run the risk of creating widespread moral indignation among populations not directly benefiting from its proceeds.

Second, there may be an oversupply of casinos, to the economic detriment of all. A weak industry becomes especially susceptible to infiltration by criminal elements.

Third, the pressure to corrupt legislative, judicial, executive, and administrative authority is especially high and possible in this industry. Corruption can take blatant forms — as in picking up the tab for a public official's offspring's wedding — or it can be quite subtle, and several steps removed, both in payoff and outcome. I have encountered in Nevada some of the most able, honest, and aggressive public administrators one could imagine. The presence of such people also makes clear how easy it is to undermine administrative controls merely by appointing inept, even if honest, officials to key positions.

Should control be undermined, the potential for federal scrutiny rises. Of course, as enough states develop an economic interest in casino gambling, the federal government may be constrained by political influence from asserting itself. Nevertheless, morality and organized crime have traditionally been live and profitable issues for federal politicians. Thus, while legal casino gambling may not be headed for another Kefauver–Kennedy era of severe scrutiny, a future of federal intervention is quite possible, depending on whether scandal develops in connection with the diffusion of legal casino gambling that is virtually assured in the United States. Only the future will tell whether Pandora's box holds butterflies or bees.

Notes

CHAPTER 1

1. William F. Whyte, *Street Corner Society*, 2d ed. (Chicago: University of Chicago Press, 1955).
2. Jerome H. Skolnick, *Justice Without Trial*, 2d ed. (New York: John Wiley, 1975).
3. Georg Simmel, "The Stranger," in Kurt H. Wolff, ed., *The Sociology of Georg Simmel* (Glencoe: Free Press, 1950), p. 404.
4. Herbert L. Packer, *The Limits of the Criminal Sanction* (Stanford: Stanford University Press, 1974), p. 354.
5. James O'Connor, *The Fiscal Crisis of the State* (New York: St. Martin's Press, 1973), p. 3.
6. Joseph Schumpeter, "The Crisis of the Tax State," reprinted in *International Economic Papers*, no. 4 (1954), p. 7.
7. Arthur F. Burns, Statement to the Joint Economic Committee, July 26, 1972, *Federal Reserve Bulletin*, August 1972, p. 699.
8. *Nevada Gaming Abstract*, 1977.
9. Legislative Counsel Bureau Division of Fiscal Analysis, Legislative Appropriations Report 59th Nevada Legislature, Fiscal Years 1977–1978, and 1978–1979.
10. See Edwin M. Schur, *Crimes Without Victims—Deviant Behavior and Public Policy* (Englewood Cliffs, N.J.: Prentice-Hall, 1965). Also see Edwin M. Schur and Hugo Bedau, *Victimless Crimes: Two Sides of a Controversy* (Englewood Cliffs, N.J.: Prentice-Hall, 1974).

CHAPTER 2

1. Lon L. Fuller, *The Morality of Law* (New Haven: Yale University Press, 1964), p. 42.

2. *New York Times*, November 4, 1976, p. 43.

3. See Paul B. Horton and Gerald R. Leslie, *The Sociology of Social Problems* (New York: Appleton-Century-Crofts, 1955). The classic critique of social pathology theory may be found in C. Wright Mills, "The Professional Ideology of Social Pathologists," in Horowitz, ed., *Power, Politics, and People* (New York: Oxford University Press, 1963), pp. 252–552. An elaboration on this theme may be found in Jerome H. Skolnick and Elliott Currie, *Crisis in American Institutions*, 3d ed. (Boston: Little, Brown & Co., 1976).

4. Jeremy Bentham, *Theory of Legislation* (London: Trubner, 1876), pp. 102–103.

5. *Ibid.*, p. 106.

6. Clifford Geertz, *The Interpretation of Cultures* (New York: Basic Books, 1973), p. 434.

7. Tomas Martinez and Marcus Landsberg review Weinstein and Deitch, *The Impact of Legalized Gambling* (New York: Praeger, 1974), in *Society*, vol. 13, no. 1, November/December 1975, pp. 86–87.

8. *Ibid.*, p. 87.

9. Sigmund Freud, "Dostoevsky and Parricide," in Halliday and Fuller, eds., *The Psychology of Gambling* (New York: Harper Colophon, 1974), pp. 157–174.

10. *Ibid.*, p. 170.

11. A description of Dostoevsky's working "under the lash," as he called it, is given in a fascinating introduction by the translator of *The Gambler*, Jessie Coulson, in the 1966 Penguin edition.

12. Freud, in Halliday and Fuller, *op. cit.*, p. 57.

13. Geertz, *op. cit.*, pp. 434–435.

14. Peter Fuller, "Gambling: A Secular 'Religion' for the Obsessional Neurotic," in Halliday and Fuller, *op. cit.*, pp. 1–114.

15. Robert M. Lindner, "The Psychodynamics of Gambling," in Halliday and Fuller, *op. cit.*, pp. 237–238.

16. Fuller, "Gambling," *op. cit.*, pp. 34–43.

17. See Alan Wykes, *Gambling* (London: Aldus Books, 1964).

18. Martinez and Landberg, *op. cit.*, p. 87.

19. Fuller, *op. cit.*, p. 87.

20. B. F. Skinner and C. B. Ferster, *Schedules of Reinforcement* (New York: Appleton-Century-Crofts, 1957).

21. Jay Livingston, "A Culture of Losers," *Psychology Today*, vol. 7, no. 10, March 1974, p. 55.

22. Erving Goffman, *Interaction Ritual* (New York: Anchor Books, 1967), p. 214.

23. William Graham Sumner and A. G. Keller, *Science of Society* (New Haven: Yale University Press, 1927), pp. 737–770.

24. *New York Times*, May 27, 1977, p. 20.

CHAPTER 3

1. Walter Lippmann, *Men of Destiny* (New York: Macmillan, 1928), p. 31.
2. National Commission on Law Observance and Enforcement, *Report on the Enforcement of the Prohibition Laws of the United States*, H.R. Doc. No. 722, 71st Congress, 3d Sess., 1931, p. 21.
3. This passage is quoted in *Narcotics* 172 (J. Williams, ed., 1963).
4. *New York Times*, May 30, 1977.
5. As of 1978, Oregon, California, Alaska, Colorado, Mississippi, Minnesota, Ohio, Maine, Nebraska, North Carolina and South Dakota had enacted marijuana decriminalization bills.
6. *Drug Use in America. Second Report of the National Commission on Marihuana and Drug Abuse* (Washington, D.C.: U.S. Government Printing Office, 1973), pp. 224–225.
7. For a thoughtful discussion see Jennings, "The Victim as Criminal: A Consideration of California's Prostitution Law," 64 *Calif. L. Rev.* 1235 (1976).

CHAPTER 4

1. Numerous books and articles have been written about the ambience of Las Vegas. A serious article, arguing for the architectural interest of the city, was written by Robert Venturi and Denise Scott Brown, "Learning From Las Vegas," and can be found in *Architectural Forum*, vol. 128, no. 2, March 1968. Tom Wolfe captures the feeling of Las Vegas in *The Candy Colored Tangerine-Flake Streamline Baby* (New York: Farrar, Straus and Giroux, 1965). For a druggy yet still relevant vision, see Hunter S. Thompson's *Fear and Loathing in Las Vegas* (New York: Random House, 1971). My own personal favorite is John Gregory Dunne's autobiographical novella, *Vegas: Memoirs of a Dark Season* (New York: Random House, 1974).
2. When auditors make projections about casinos, they will figure conservatively an 85 percent occupancy rate. This I know from the personal experience of projecting the receipts of a major casino with its accountant. In 1977 hotels with casinos with gross gaming revenue between $5 million and $20 million averaged 81.8 percent occupancy. Those in the $20 million-plus category averaged 88.3 percent. (Source: *Nevada Gaming Abstract*, 1975.)
3. Mario Puzo, *Inside Las Vegas* (New York: Grosset & Dunlap, 1977), p. 176.
4. Nevada Revised Statutes 244.345 sets out the criteria for licensing of houses of prostitution. Houses are prohibited in Nevada counties having a population of more than 200,000. This effectively bars houses of prostitution from Reno and Las Vegas. In all other counties, prostitution is allowed by local option. In 1978, most of the small Nevada counties permitted houses of prostitution. Douglas County, which includes the stateline areas around Lake Tahoe, does not, nor does Carson City. Lincoln County voiced

its disapproval in a 1978 referendum. In 1974, according to Richard Symanski, "Prostitution in Nevada," *Annals of the Association of American Geographers*, vol. 64, no. 3, September 1974, there were 33 brothels, employing over 200 prostitutes. Two-thirds of the brothels are in places with populations between 500 and 8,000, and the remaining third in more rural areas. Gabriel Vogliotti's *The Girls of Nevada* (Secaucus, N.J.: The Citadel Press, 1975), offers rich descriptions of Nevada's experience with legalized prostitution, as well as the illegal yet thriving Las Vegas trade in sexual services.

5. Since April 1, 1968, some payoffs to keno and bingo winners have been required to be reported by Nevada gaming casinos. Casinos are not required to file information returns on payoffs to players of slot machines and all other games. All payoffs of $10,000 or more to keno players are subject to reporting requirements. Payoffs of less than that amount will be reported on a sliding scale related to the amount wagered. For example, on a keno ticket of less than 70¢, $600 or more in winnings must be reported. For bingo, all payoffs of $2,400 or more are subject to reporting requirements. A sliding scale similar to the keno schedule exists for determining payoffs reportable from bingo winnings. (Source: IRS Memo to Gaming Industry, Commission, and Accountants, August 1976).

6. Erving Goffman, *Interaction Ritual* (Garden City, N.Y.: Anchor Books, 1967), pp. 202–203.

7. Thurston Clarke's *Dirty Money* (New York: Simon and Schuster, 1975), deals with international and domestic implications of the phenomenon.

8. *New York Times*, June 15, 1975, p. 1.

9. James Henry, "Calling in the Big Bills," *Washington Monthly*, vol. 8, no. 3, May 1976.

CHAPTER 5

1. Regulation 3.010, "Unsuitable locations," reads as follows: "The board may recommend that an application for a state gaming license be denied, and the commission may deny the same, if the board or the commission deems that the place or location for which the license is sought is unsuitable for the conduct of gaming operations. Without limiting the generality of the foregoing, the following places or locations may be deemed unsuitable:

"1. Premises located within the immediate vicinity of churches, hospitals, schools and children's public playgrounds.

"2. Premises located within the immediate vicinity of a military or naval reservation or camp.

"3. Premises located in a place where gaming is contrary to a valid zoning ordinance of any county or city, unless the premises had been used for gaming at a time prior to the effective date of the zoning ordinance.

"4. Premises difficult to police.

"5. Areas where gaming operations would not be conducive to good relations with neighboring states."

2. There are several good books describing the games: Allan N. Wilson, *The Casino Gambler's Guide* (New York: Harper & Row, 1970); Edward O. Thorp, *Beat the Dealer* (New York: Vintage Books, 1966); Bill Friedman, *Casino Games* (New York: Golden Press, 1973); John Scarne, *Scarne on Cards* (New York: New American Library, 1973). The Gambler's Book Club in Las Vegas publishes a number of books on gambling. I have learned about gambling from many of these books as well as from persons in the gaming industry.

3. Jonathan H. Green, *Gambling Exposed* (Montclair, N.J.: Patterson Smith, 1973), p. 162.

4. John Philip Quinn, *Gambling and Gambling Devices* (Montclair, N.J.: Patterson Smith, 1969).

5. Bill Friedman, *Casino Games* (New York: Golden Press, 1973), p. 140.

6. Thorp, *op. cit.*, p. 106.

7. *Ibid.*, p. 6.

8. I learned this from an interview with a Berkeley graduate student whose friend was functioning as a member of a count team. This strategy was reported in more detail in Ken Uston's *The Big Player* (New York: Holt, Rinehart, and Winston, 1977).

9. Thomas Thompson, "Winning (Habitually) in Vegas," The *New York Times Magazine*, June 27, 1976, p. 8.

10. On March 21, 1978, U.S. District Court Judge Roger Foley dismissed a suit brought against the Flamingo Hilton by Kenneth Uston (*Valley Times*, March 22, 1978).

11. Allan N. Wilson, *The Casino Gambler's Guide* (New York: Harper & Row, 1970), p. 123.

12. For 1977, the gross slot machine revenue represents an increase of 31.9 percent over 1976. (Source: Nevada State Gaming Control Board). In the $2 million to $5 million gross gaming revenue range, 48 percent of the casinos' revenue is from slots and other devices. In the $5 to $20 million range, that figure drops to 40 percent, and drops even further to 25 percent for those hotel-casinos whose gross gaming revenue exceeds $20 million annually. (Source: *Nevada Gaming Abstract*, 1977).

CHAPTER 6

1. Alan Wykes, *Gambling* (London: Aldus Books, 1964), pp. 282–287.

2. The Nevada Gaming Commission has issued a set of instructions under the general rubric of Regulation 6, the Accounting Regulation. In addition, each casino must present to the Audit Division of the Gaming Control Board an internal control program that deals with most of the measures to be discussed in this chapter. I have not attempted to footnote subsections of Regulation 6, since this book is not intended as a guide to running a gaming casino. Instead, it is meant to be an analysis of the dilemmas involved in casino management. For a comprehensive and thoughtful textbook from which I have learned a great deal about the business side of the casino, see Bill Friedman, *Casino Management* (Secaucus, N.J.: Lyle Stuart, 1974).

3. Franklin Navarro, "Collection of Gaming Debts," Seminar, Flamingo Hotel, October 11, 1972 (unpublished).

CHAPTER 7

1. Nevada State Gaming Control Board, Transcript of Proceedings, January 15, 1975.
2. George V. Higgins has built a novel around this theme: *The Digger's Game* (New York: Popular Library, 1973).
3. Testimony before the Nevada State Senate Judiciary Committee on SB 399, May 10, 1975.

CHAPTER 8

1. Letter to Joseph F. McDonald, July 3, 1951. Courtesy of the McCarran Project, Holy Names College, Oakland, California.
2. Howard Becker, a leading theorist of the labeling perspective, explains its tenets in his classic *Outsiders* (Glencoe: The Free Press, 1963), p. 9:

> Social groups create deviance by making the rules whose information constitutes deviance, and by applying those rules to particular people and labeling them as outsiders. From this point of view, deviance is not a quality of the act the person commits, but rather a consequence of the application by others of rules and sanctions to an "offender." The deviant is one to whom that label has successfully been applied; deviant behavior is behavior that people so label.

In *The Other Side* (Glencoe, Illinois: The Free Press, 1964), Becker presents a few crucial questions for research and theory building in the field of deviance: Who applies the label of deviant to whom? What consequences does the application of a label have for the person labeled? Under what circumstances is the label of deviant successfully applied? Other noteworthy theorists utilizing this perspective are David Matza, *Becoming Deviant* (Englewood Cliffs: Prentice-Hall, 1969), and Edwin Lemert, *Human Deviance, Social Problems, and Social Control* (Englewood Cliffs: Prentice-Hall, 1967).
3. *New York Times*, November 7, 1976, p. E4.
4. Cornell Law School Gambling Project, *The Development of the Law of Gambling, 1776–1976*, draft, p. 403.
5. *Ibid.*, p. 404.
6. Mark Twain, *Roughing It* (New York: New American Library, 1962), pp. 146–147.
7. Cornell Project, *op. cit.*, p. 405.

8. Russell R. Elliott, *History of Nevada* (Lincoln: University of Nebraska Press, 1973), p. 72.

9. *Ibid.*, pp. *xi*, 69–89.

10. Nevada is currently the fourth-smallest state in the Union, only Vermont, Wyoming and Alaska being less populous (1970 census).

11. Cornell Project, *op. cit.*, pp. 415–416.

12. Nevada Gaming Commission, "Legalized Gambling in Nevada," 2d ed., 1970, p. 7.

13. *Ibid.*, p. 9.

14. Elliott, *op. cit.*, pp. 170–209.

15. Cornell Project, *op. cit.*, pp. 415–416.

16. Elliott, *op. cit.*, pp. 210–232, 396.

17. Cornell Project, *op. cit.*, p. 423.

18. *Ibid.*, pp. 426–427.

19. *Ibid.*, p. 427.

20. Nevada Gaming Commission, *op. cit.*, p. 9.

21. *Nevada State Journal*, January 18, 1931.

22. *San Francisco Chronicle*, December 9, 1976.

23. Nevada State Gaming Control Board, "Gaming Nevada Style" (1975), p. 3.

24. Cornell Project, *op. cit.*, p. 435.

25. Elliott, *op. cit.*, p. 283.

26. *Ibid.*, pp. 282–283.

27. Keith Monroe, "The New Gambling King and the Social Scientists," *Harper's*, vol. 224, no. 1340, January 1962, p. 35.

28. Elliott, *op. cit.*, pp. 275–277.

29. *Ibid.*, pp. 307–324.

30. Reuben A. Zubrow, *et al.*, *Financing State and Local Governments in Nevada* (Carson City, 1960); Nevada State Gaming Control Board, *op. cit.*, p. 4.

31. Elliott, *op. cit.*, p. 316.

32. David W. Toll, *The Compleat Nevada Traveler* (Reno: University of Nevada Press, 1976), p. 226.

33. *Ibid.*, pp. 227–228.

34. *Ibid.*

35. Martin A. Gosch and Richard Hammer, *The Last Testament of Lucky Luciano* (Boston: Little, Brown and Co., 1974), p. 316.

36. Nevada Gaming Commission, *op. cit.*, p. 6.

37. *Ibid.*

38. Nevada State Gaming Control Board, *Gaming Abstract*, 1977.

39. Robbins Cahill, *Recollections of Work in State Politics, Government, Taxation, Gaming Control, Clark County Administration, and the Nevada Resort Association*. University of Nevada Oral History Project, 1976, pp. 271–320.

40. *Ibid.*, p. 289.

41. *Ibid.*, p. 290.

42. *Las Vegas Sun*, March 15, 1951.

43. Cahill, *op. cit.*, p. 588.

44. Mary Ellen Glass, "Nevada in the Fifties: A Glance at State Politics and Economics," *Nevada Historical Society Quarterly*, vol. 19, no. 2 (Summer 1976), p. 132.

45. Legislative Counsel Bureau Division of Fiscal Analysis, Legislative Appropriations Report, 59th Nevada Legislature, Fiscal Years 1977–1978, and 1978–1979; State of Nevada, *The Executive Budget*, 1969–1970.

46. Las Vegas Convention and Visitors Authority, "Marketing Bulletin: 1976 Summary."

47. State of California, 1977–1978 Governor's Budget.

48. Estes Kefauver, *Crime in America* (Garden City: Doubleday, 1951), p. 237.

49. *Ibid.*, pp. 229–237.

50. *Ibid.*, p. 233.

CHAPTER 9

1. 73 Nev. 115 (1957).

2. 365 F.2d 105 (1966).

3. Edward A. Olsen, "The Black Book Episode — An Exercise in Muscle," in Eleanore Bushnell, ed., *Sagebrush and Neon* (Reno: University of Nevada Press, 1973), p. 8.

4. *Ibid.*, p. 12.

5. *Ibid.*, p. 13.

6. *Marshall v. Sawyer*, 301 F.2d 652, 653 (1962).

7. Robert Kennedy, *The Enemy Within* (New York: Harper & Row, 1960), p. 265.

8. Nevada Gaming Commission, "Skim Report," September 1, 1966, p. 1.

9. Gabriel Vogliotti, *The Girls of Nevada* (Secaucus, N.J.: Citadel Press, 1975), p. 16.

10. Victor Navasky, *Kennedy Justice* (New York: Atheneum, 1971), pp. 49–50.

11. *Ibid.*, p. 54.

12. Vogliotti, *op. cit.*, p. 77.

13. Interview with Edward Olsen, March 1976.

14. Nevada Gaming Commission, *op. cit.*, p. 3.

15. Vogliotti, *op. cit.*, pp. 17–18.

16. Nevada Gaming Commission, *op. cit.*, p. 3.

17. Interview with Edward Olsen, March 1976.

18. Nevada Gaming Commission, *op. cit.*, p. 3.

19. *Alderman v. U.S.*, 89 S. Court 961 (1969).

20. Alan Barth, "Lawless Lawmen," *The New Republic*, vol. 155, no. 4–5, July 30, 1966, p. 21.

21. Edward F. Sherman, "Nevada: The End of the Casino Era," *Atlantic*, vol. 218, no. 4, October 1966, p. 116.

22. Vogliotti, *op. cit.*, p. 203.

23. Drew Pearson, "Sawyer Lauded for Standing Up to FBI," *Nevada State Journal*, September 5, 1966.

24. "Charges of Tax Fraud, Mobster Ties Leveled at Casinos in Nevada," *Wall Street Journal*, August 24, 1966.

25. Interviews conducted June 1977.

26. *Las Vegas Review Journal,* January 16, 1973; *Miami Herald,* January 17, 1973.

27. Interviews conducted with former Department of Justice officials, who also affirmed that Sandy Smith's articles were correct in their details. See note 28 below.

28. Sandy Smith, "Mobsters in the Marketplace: Money Muscle, Murder," *Life,* vol. 63, no. 10, September 8, 1967, p. 98.

29. *U.S. v. Meyer Lansky, Samuel Cohen, Morris Lansburgh, Jerry W. Gordon, Samuel Ziegman, Steve Delmont, and Harry Goldberg,* U.S. District Court, Nevada, August 21, 1974. Two Nevada newspapers discuss the Judge's ruling. The *Las Vegas Review Journal,* August 6, 1974, concentrates on the doctor's testimony; the *Nevada State Journal,* August 23, 1974, on the Judge's rationale.

30. *Miami Herald,* March 27, 1977.

31. "Nevada Denies Gangsters Get Casino Money," *Reno Evening Gazette,* September 2, 1966.

32. *Ibid.*

33. "A Silent War: Is It Now Over?" *Las Vegas Sun,* September 2, 1966.

34. *Ibid.*

35. Hank Greenspun, "Where I Stand," *Las Vegas Sun,* September 17, 1966.

36. "Baring: Kennedy Behind Skim Stir," *Nevada State Journal,* August 28, 1966.

37. "Laxalt Fears for Future of Gambling," *Reno Evening Gazette,* September 26, 1966.

CHAPTER 10

1. *Nevada Report,* vol. 1, no. 1, July 15, 1969, p. 2.

2. Hughes's death in 1976 sparked a renewal of interest in his life and business dealings. He was, of course, the subject of *Time* and *Newsweek* cover stories that week. James Phelan's *Howard Hughes: The Hidden Years* (New York: Random House, 1976), is an informed portrayal of Hughes's later years, based upon the reports of two Hughes attendants, and the expertise of veteran reporter Phelan on Hughes. Elaine Davenport and Paul Eddy have written a comprehensive book about Hughes's business dealings, *The Hughes Papers* (New York: Ballantine Books, 1976), and based it upon testimony and depositions taken in the various court proceedings regarding Hughes and his holdings. A couple of more dated works are also useful: John Keats, *Howard Hughes* (New York: Random House, 1972), and Omar Garrison, *Howard Hughes in Las Vegas* (New York: Lyle Stuart, Inc., 1970).

3. Phelan, *op. cit.,* p. 56.

4. Davenport and Eddy, *op. cit.,* p. 60.

5. *Ibid.*

6. Figures of the privately owned casinos are not for public consumption. This estimate is based upon some newspaper accounts, and on interviews with present and former gaming control authorities.

7. Phelan, *op. cit.*, p. 78.
8. *Ibid.*, p. 75.
9. *Ibid.*, p. 118.
10. Davenport and Eddy, *op. cit.*, p. 241.
11. Phelan, *op. cit.*, pp. 126–127.
12. Interview with the Gaming Control Board chairman, August 1976.
13. Phelan, *op. cit.*, p. 174.
14. Davenport and Eddy, *op. cit.*, p. 155.
15. Samuel W. Belford II and James J. Noel, "Regulation 16, Publicly Traded Corporations: Comments," internal memorandum, Nevada State Gaming Control Board, no date.
16. *Valley Times*, December 29, 1976.
17. Vogliotti, *op. cit.*, p. 4.
18. Interview with Grant Sawyer, August 1976.
19. Hilton Hotels Corporation, Form 10–K, December 31, 1975, p. 1.

CHAPTER 11

1. James M. Landis, *The Administrative Process* (New Haven: Yale University Press, 1938), p. 15.
2. Richard Stewart, "The Reformation of American Administrative Law," 88 *Harv. L. Rev.* 1670 (1975).
3. This is the total number budgeted for 1977–1978. The Audit Division was allocated 67 positions, Investigations 32, and Enforcement 30. The remainder are administrative personnel. The Gaming Control Board general fund allocation is $3,996,204 for 1977–1978, and the Investigative Fund allocation is $1 million for the same time period. (Source: Legislative Counsel Bureau, Division of Fiscal Analysis.)
4. Nevada Revised Statutes 463.022, 463.023, 463.024, 463.025, 463.026.
5. Nevada Revised Statutes 463.040.
6. *Ibid.*
7. Kenneth Culp Davis, *Administrative Law Text*, 3d ed. (St. Paul: West Publishing Co., 1972), p. 143.
8. Nevada Revised Statutes 463.090.
9. Nevada Revised Statutes 463.637.
10. Nevada Revised Statutes 463.635.
11. Regulation 5.2, now Nevada Revised Statutes 463.1594.
12. Nevada State Gaming Control Board, Transcript of Hearing, September 1976.
13. Chapter 571 of the 1977 Nevada statutes.
14. Regulation 16.400.
15. *Valley Times*, March 24, 1978.
16. Leo Tolstoy, *War and Peace* (Chicago: Encyclopedia Britannica, Inc., 1952), p. 471.
17. *Las Vegas Today*, June 25, 1975, p. 9.
18. Formal Opinion 342, 62 *A.B.A.J.* 517 (1975).

19. Gaming Policy Committee Transcript, May 26, 1972.
20. Nevada Revised Statutes 463.021.
21. Gaming Policy Committee, *op. cit.*, p. 79.
22. *Ibid.*, p. 80.
23. Title 18, §284.
24. *New York Times*, August 1, 1976.
25. Davis, *op. cit.*, p. 6.
26. *Ibid.*
27. Gabriel Kolko, *Railroads and Regulation, 1877–1916* (Princeton: Princeton University Press, 1965), p. 231.

CHAPTER 12

1. Max Weber, "The Protestant Sects and the Spirit of Capitalism," in H. H. Gerth and C. Wright Mills, eds., *From Max Weber* (New York: Oxford University Press, 1958), pp. 303, 319.
2. Fowler V. Harper and Jerome H. Skolnick, *Problems of the Family*, 2d ed. (Indianapolis: Bobbs-Merrill, 1962), pp. 96–98.
3. Joel Feinberg, *Doing and Deserving* (Princeton: Princeton University Press, 1970), p. 109. For an informed historical discussion of the topics of occupational licensing, see Friedman, "Freedom of Contract and Occupational Licensing 1890–1910: A Legal and Social Study," 53 *Calif. L. Rev.* 487–534 (1965).
4. Nevada Revised Statutes 463–170.
5. Milton M. Carrow, *The Licensing Power in New York City* (South Hackensack, N.J.: Fred B. Rothman, 1968), p. 18.
6. *Ibid.*, pp. 19–20.
7. *Marshall v. Sawyer*, 301 F.2d 639 (1962).
8. Nevada Revised Statutes 463.210.
9. Regulation 1.050.
10. *Nevada Tax Commission v. Hicks*, 73 Nev. 115 (1957).
11. The literature on organized crime is enormously variable in quality and accuracy. Nevertheless, certain basic facts are agreed upon by all students, e.g., that Lucky Luciano, Meyer Lansky, and Frank Costello were all involved in bootlegging, illegal gambling, and the corruption of public officials. The debates are usually over the structure of organized crime. Donald Cressey, in *Theft of the Nation* (New York: Harper & Row, 1969), concludes that a nationwide alliance of 24 tightly knit criminal families exists in the United States, and that these families are linked together by understandings, arguments, treaties, and obedience to a commission comprised of leaders of the most powerful families. He describes criminal syndicates in the language of formal organization theory: they are deliberately designed and constructed to achieve specific goals. Cressey's work is the most articulate of these adopting a law enforcement perspective. Other works supporting this perspective are Rufus King, *Gambling and Organized Crime* (Washington: Public Affairs Press, 1969); Ralph Salerno, *The Crime Confederation* (New York: Double-

day, 1969); Burton B. Turkus and Sid Feder, *Murder, Inc.* (London: Victor Golanez, 1953). Francis Ianni, drawing upon his participant observation of a crime "family," contends in *A Family Business* (New York: Russell Sage Foundation, 1972) that secret criminal organizations are traditional social systems, organized by action and by cultural values which bear little resemblance to major corporate structures. However, the values attributed by all writers include acceptance of force and violence for business gain. Essentially, Ianni's social anthropology does not dispute the value system suggested by Puzo's *The Godfather*. Nor do other informed scholarly works such as: William Howard Moore, *The Kefauver Committee and the Politics of Crime, 1950-1952* (Columbia: University of Missouri Press, 1974); Joseph L. Albini, *The American Mafia* (New York: Appleton-Century-Crofts, 1971); and Dwight Smith, *The Mafia Mystique* (New York: Basic Books, 1975).

CHAPTER 13

1. *FCC v. Pottsville Broadcasting Co.*, 309 U.S. 134, 143 (1940).
2. Henry Friendly, "Some Kind of Hearing," 123 *U. Penn. L. Rev.* 1267, 1269 (1975).
3. Nevada Revised Statutes 241.
4. Nevada Revised Statutes 463.110.
5. "Nevada Open Meeting Law Manual," Office of the Attorney General, Carson City, Nevada, September 1974.
6. *Sacramento Newspaper Guild v. Sacramento County Board of Supervisors*, 69 Cal. Rptr. 480 (1968).

CHAPTER 14

1. *Valley Times*, December 28, 1976.
2. Erving Goffman, *Strategic Interaction* (Philadelphia: University of Pennsylvania Press, 1969), p. 83.
3. *Wall Street Journal*, December 27, 1976.
4. Transcript of Proceedings Before the State Gaming Control Board, Hearing on Argent Corporation, July 17, 1974, p. 4.
5. *Ibid.*, p. 13.
6. *Newsweek*, November 24, 1975, p. 91.
7. *O'Callaghan v. Eighth J.D. Ct., In & For Cty. of Clark*, 505 P.2d 1215 (1973).
8. Transcript of Proceedings, January 1976 Meeting of the Nevada State Gaming Control Board, Hearing on Argent Corporation and Frank L. Rosenthal, p. 247.
9. *Time*, March 14, 1977, p. 21.

10. Transcript of Proceedings, January 1976 Meeting of the Nevada State Gaming Control Board, Hearing on Argent Corporation and Frank L. Rosenthal, p. 256.

11. *San Francisco Chronicle*, March 15, 1977, p. 1.

12. Transcript of Proceedings, January 1976 Meeting of the Nevada State Gaming Control Board, Hearing on Argent Corporation and Frank L. Rosenthal, pp. 180–186.

13. *Rosenthal v. Nevada*, Supreme Court, State of Nevada, Points and Authorities in Opposition to the Petition for Judicial Review, p. 46.

14. *Nevada v. Rosenthal*, Supreme Court, State of Nevada, Appellants' Reply Brief, Addendum Item 1, pp. 2–3.

15. Argent Corporation, S.E.C. Form 10–K, August 31, 1976, p. 61.

16. *Rosenthal v. Nevada*, 8th Judicial District Court, State of Nevada, Dec. 2, 1976, p. 3.

17. *Los Angeles Times*, April 14, 1977, pp. 3, 26.

18. *Nevada v. Rosenthal*, Supreme Court, State of Nevada, Brief of MGM Grand Hotel, Inc., as *amicus curiae*, in support of reversal, pp. 2–3.

CHAPTER 15

1. *Board of Regents v. Roth*, 408 U.S. 564 (1972); *Bishop v. Wood*, 426 U.S. 341 (1976).

2. William Van Alstyne, "The Demise of the Right-Privilege Distinction in Constitutional Law," 81 *Harv. L. Rev.* 1463–1464 (1968).

3. *Bishop v. Wood*, 426 U.S. 341, 349–350.

4. *Ibid.*, at 354.

5. *Board of Regents v. Roth*, 408 U.S. 591 (1972).

6. In *Mathews v. Eldridge*, 424 U.S. 319, 334–335 (1976), the U.S. Supreme Court eventually was to introduce something like a general formula for deciding what process is due. In that case, the Court identified three factors to be considered and balanced: (1) the private interest; (2) the risk of erroneous deprivation of such interest as against the protections provided by adding or substituting procedural safeguards; (3) "the government's interest, *including the function involved*," plus the "fiscal and administrative" burdens the government would have to bear by substituting or adding procedural requirements.

A broad span of cases decided in the 1970s — after the "due process revolution" — suggests that a more conservative Court is willing to entertain the idea that a whole range of governmental interests can justify withholding requested due process procedures.

A 1975 note in the *Harvard Law Review* (88: 1515n) cites the following governmental interests.

These include maintaining the discipline and efficiency of government employees, *Arnett v. Kennedy*, 416 U.S. 134, 168 (1974) (Powell, J., concurring); maintaining order in prisons, *Wolff v. McDonnell*, 418 U.S. 539, 561–563, 568 (1974); protecting society from antisocial acts which might be committed by parolees, *Morrissey v. Brewer,* 408 U.S. 471, 483 (1972); preserving the rehabilitative climate in probation revocation hearings, *Gagnon v. Scarpelli,* 411 U.S. 778, 787–788 (1973); protection of the public fisc against unwarranted expenditures, *Goldberg v. Kelly,* 397 U.S. 254, 265 (1970); protecting the security interest held by creditors in goods sold on credit, *Mitchell v. W.T. Grant Co.,* 416 U.S. 600, 604–610 (1974); *Fuentes v. Shevin,* 407 U.S. 67 (1972); preventing frivolous litigation, *Boddie v. Connecticut,* 401 U.S. 371, 381 (1971); and preserving discipline and order in public high schools, *Goss v. Lopez,* 95 S.Ct. 729, 740–741 (1975).

For an exceptionally clear discussion of due process requirements see Laurence H. Tribe, *American Constitutional Law* (Mineola, N.Y.: Foundation Press, 1978), pp. 532–543. For a learned critique of the Supreme Court's balancing approach see Jerry L. Mashow, "The Supreme Court's Due Process Calculus for Administrative Adjudication in *Mathews v. Eldridge*: Three Factors in Search of a Theory of Value," 44 *U. Chi. L. Rev.* (28) 1976.

7. Kenneth Culp Davis, *Administrative Law Text,* 3d ed. (St. Paul: West Publishing Co., 1972), Chapter 13, "Separation of Functions."

8. Such "sunshine" laws do impose some constraints, but these are so easily evaded that perhaps they are not worth the trouble.

9. "Nevada Open Meeting Law Manual," Office of the Attorney General, Carson City, Nevada, September 1974.

10. Regulation 3.090.

11. *Nevada v. Rosenthal,* Supreme Court, State of Nevada, Respondents Answering Brief, p. 20.

12. *Nevada Tax Commission v. Hicks,* 73 Nev. 115 (1957), and *Marshall v. Sawyer,* 301 F.2d 639 (1962).

13. 46 U.S.L.W. 3187.

14. Davis, *op. cit.,* pp. 254–255. There is very little law on this subject. Davis writes (at p. 254): "The courts have strangely refrained from their usual leadership in working out minimal standards of fairness; their principal role has been to interpret and apply the legislation."

15. *Rachid v. State,* 8th Judicial District Court, case no. A145535.

16. Nevada Revised Statutes 463.337.

CHAPTER 16

1. George L. Kelling *et al., The Kansas City Preventive Patrol Experiment* (New York: Police Foundation, 1974).

2. Jerome H. Skolnick, "Scientific Theory and Scientific Evidence: An Analysis of Lie Detection," 70 *Yale L. J.* 696–697 (1961). This article discusses and approximately footnotes the history of lie detection.

3. R. D. Hare, "Autonomic Activity and Conditioning in Psychopaths," in B. Maher, ed., *Contemporary Abnormal Psychology* (Middlesex, England: Penguin Books, 1973), p. 225.

CHAPTER 17

1. John Rawls, *A Theory of Justice* (Cambridge: Harvard University Press, 1971), p. 235.

2. Joseph Wambaugh, *The Choirboys* (New York: Dell, 1975), p. 63.

3. Lee J. Seidler, *et al.*, *The Equity Funding Papers: The Anatomy of a Fraud* (Santa Barbara: Wiley, 1977), p. 10.

CHAPTER 18

1. Sidney Davidson, *et al.*, *Fundamentals of Accounting*, 5th ed. (Hinsdale, Illinois: The Dryden Press, 1975), p. 8.

2. "Why Everybody's Jumping on the Accountants These Days," *Forbes*, March 15, 1977, pp. 37–43.

3. Kenneth I. Solomon and Hyman Muller, "Illegal Payments: Where the Auditor Stands," *The Journal of Accounting*, January 1977, p. 52.

4. *Forbes, op. cit.*, p. 43.

5. Egon Bittner, *The Functions of the Police in Modern Society* (National Institute of Mental Health, 1970), pp. 36–47.

6. Jonathan Rubenstein, *City Police* (New York: Farrar, Straus & Giroux, 1973), pp. 267–277.

CHAPTER 19

1. Linda Snyder, "Gambling Stocks Are Riding a Winning Streak," *Fortune*, vol. XCVI, no. 3, September 1977, p. 65.

2. From Gaming Control Board intelligence files.

3. Based on the Teamsters Central States Pension Fund, form 5500 filed with the U.S. Department of Labor, February 3, 1978.

4. See Ralph C. James and Estelle Dinerstein James, *Hoffa and the Teamsters* (Princeton: D. Van Nostrand, 1965), pp. 213–260, for a more complete discussion of the Teamsters Central States Pension Fund's investment policy.

5. *U.S. News and World Report*, July 12, 1976, p. 74.

6. James and James, *op. cit.*, p. 235.

7. Walter Sheridan, who was Robert Kennedy's assistant with both the McClellan Committee and the Department of Justice, carefully documents Hoffa's legal problems in his book, *The Fall and Rise of Jimmy Hoffa* (New York: Saturday Review Press, 1972).

8. Lester Velie, *Desperate Bargain: Why Jimmy Hoffa Had to Die* (New York: Reader's Digest Press, 1977).

9. James R. Hoffa, *Hoffa: The Real Story* (New York: Stein and Day, 1975), p. 15.

10. Jim Drinkhall, "Central States Pension Fund — Bankroll for the Mafia," *Overture*, July 1972, p. 48.

11. *Newsweek*, November 24, 1975, p. 89.

12. *Ibid.*

13. *Newsweek, op. cit.*, p. 91.

14. *Chicago Tribune*, August 1, 1976, p. 22.

15. *Los Angeles Times*, December 1, 1976.

16. *New York Times*, June 28, 1976.

17. The Teamsters Central States, Southeast and Southwest Areas Pension Fund reported for 1976 (its last reporting period) that it provided coverage for 415,555 union members as well as for 69,295 retirees and disabled members. The maximum contributions to the fund were $322 million in 1976; benefits paid averaged $19 million a month. (Source: Teamsters Central States Pension Fund, Form 5500, for the year ending December 31, 1976.)

18. *New York Times*, October 28, 1976.

19. *U.S. News and World Report, op. cit.*

20. *Ibid.*

21. Jim Drinkhall, "Teamsters Central States Fund Trustees Are Repudiating 1977 Accord with U.S.," *Wall Street Journal*, May 23, 1978.

CHAPTER 20

1. See Kirkpatrick Sale, *Power Shift* (New York: Random House, 1975), and Carl Oglesby, *The Yankee and Cowboy War* (New York: Berkley Publishing, 1977).

2. Nevada Gaming Commission, Transcript of Proceedings, July 21, 1977, p. 3.

3. *Ibid.*, p. 8.

4. *Ibid.*, p. 94.

5. *Ibid.*, pp. 92–93.

6. *Valley Times*, September 19, 1977.

7. *Las Vegas Today*, October 18, 1977, p. 16.

CHAPTER 21

1. Church membership figures for Nevada as a whole are not available. Russell Elliott, *History of Nevada* (Lincoln: University of Nebraska Press, 1973), p. 374. My figure is based upon 1970 census data showing 160,000 adults in the Las Vegas Standard Metropolitan Statistical Area, and estimates by the Church of Jesus Christ of Latter Day Saints of 600 adults in each of the 50 wards the church has in the area.

2. See Daniel Bell, "The Public Household: On 'Fiscal Sociology' and the Liberal Society," in *The Cultural Contradictions of Capitalism* (New York: Basic Books, 1976), pp. 220–282. Bell argues, at p. 231, that all in-

dustrial or industrializing societies, including those that call themselves social-ist, experience the dilemma of resolving problems of capital accumulation with legitimation.

3. The information on British gaming derives from field-research inter-views conducted during October 1975 with officials of the Home Office and the Gaming Board for Great Britain, and various operatives of gaming clubs. The failure of the 1960 act is also spelled out in the debates on the 1968 gaming bill, February 13, 1968, in the House of Commons; June 20, 1968, in the House of Lords.

4. Vincent Teresa, with Thomas C. Renner, *My Life in the Mafia* (Fawcett Crest, 1973), pp. 219–220.

5. *Hansards*, 31, February 1968, p. 1168.

6. *Ibid.*, p. 1169.

7. Anthony Giddens, *The Class Structure of the Advanced Societies* (London: Hutchinson University Library, 1973), pp. 19–20.

8. D. M. Downes, *et al.*, *Gambling, Work, and Leisure* (London: Rout-ledge & Kegan Paul, 1976), p. 126.

9. *Ibid.*, p. 90.

10. Commission on the Review of the National Policy Toward Gambling, *Gambling in America* (Washington: U.S. Government Printing Office, 1976), pp. 100–101.

11. Chapter 355, Statutes of Nevada, 1977.

12. Chapter 569, Statutes of Nevada, 1977.

13. Staff Policy Group on Casino Gambling, "Second Interim Report," February 17, 1977, pp. 4–5.

14. *Ibid.*, p. 30. In addition, the Casino Control Act (P.L. 1977, c. 110, Article 4, Section 70) provides that regulations governing advertisement must require the words, "Bet with your head, not over it," to appear in all bill-boards, signs, and other on-sight advertising of a casino operation.

15. Howard Blum and Jeff Gerth, "The Mob Gambles on Atlantic City," *The New York Times Magazine*, February 5, 1978, p. 16. See also Michael Dorman, "The Mob Wades Ashore in Atlantic City," *New York*, January 30, 1978.

16. *New York Times*, April 16, 1977.

17. Casino Control Act (P.L. 1977, c. 110, Article 1, Section 9).

18. P.L. 1978, c. 7.

19. Based on interviews with New Jersey authorities. In general, my in-formation about New Jersey gambling derives from three sources: continuing conversations with New Jersey authorities prior to and following a visit in January 1978; newspaper and magazine accounts, as indicated; and other persons in and around New Jersey who are informed observers of the scene.

20. *New York Times*, May 26, 1978.

21. "Gambling Spree Across the Nation," *U.S. News and World Report*, May 29, 1978, p. 35.

22. Paul W. Sturm, "Casinos — Corporate Style," *Forbes*, June 12, 1978, pp. 29–31.

23. *The Valley Times*, April 12, 1978.

24. *The Valley Times*, April 26, 1978.

25. *New York Times*, March 16, 1978.

26. *New York Times*, June 4, 1978.